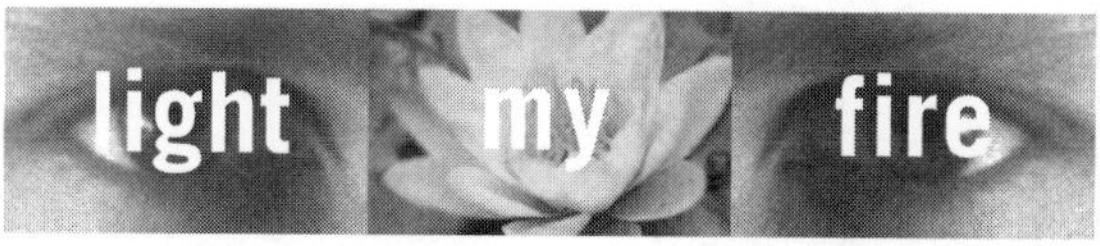
light my fire

ray manzarek

my life with the doors

g. p. putnam's sons

new york

G. P. Putnam's Sons
Publishers Since 1838
a member of
Penguin Putnam Inc.
200 Madison Avenue
New York, NY 10016

Library of Congress Cataloging-in-Publication Data

Manzarek, Ray.
Light my fire : my life with the Doors / by Ray Manzarek.
p.   cm.
ISBN 0-399-14399-8 (acid-free paper)
1. Doors (Musical group).   2. Manzarek, Ray.   Rock
musicians—United States—Biography.   I. Title.
ML421.D66M36   1998   98-6303 CIP MN

Printed in the United States of America

1   3   5   7   9   10   8   6   4   2

This book is printed on acid-free paper. ∞

Book design by JUDITH STAGNITTO ABBATE

Interior photo of lotus flower by JONELLE WEAVER

To Fiona Matthews, Maureen and Eric Lasher, Nanscy Neiman-Legette, Eric Degans, Harvey Kubernick, Rick Schmidlin, Danny Sugarman, Rick Valentine, Michael McClure, and Todd Gray. Your help and support were invaluable.

To Dorothy, my Love

contents

Take the highway to the end of the night.
Take a journey to the bright midnight

Jim Morrison

In some way he had won a great victory, broken through
into a world where he could finally live. His life had been a long,
tense drama of resistance and of pressure against constraint.
But now, in that moment, he had broken down the
resistance and emerged loose and free in the night.

D. H. Lawrence

light my fire

the death of jim morrison

We don't know what happened to Jim Morrison in Paris. To be honest, I don't think we're ever going to know. Rumors, innuendoes, self-serving lies, psychic projections to justify inner needs and maladies, and just plain goofiness cloud the truth. There are simply too many conflicting theories. He went to a movie (like Oswald). No, he didn't go to the cinema, he went to a bar called the Rock & Roll Circus. Evidently a sleazy French noir place not unlike Van Gogh's *Night Café*... "It was the kind of place where a man could go mad, or commit a crime."

We could plan a murder, or start a religion.

He didn't go to the Rock & Roll Circus—he was home with Pam. No, he was brought home by three French gentlemen of the evening. Comatose. He had done heroin. (To my knowledge, Jim had never tried heroin. Certainly not in the States. However, Pam had. And liked it. But then most people who try it like it . . . wouldn't you?) No, he was drunk. They put him to bed. No, he hadn't gone out at all, he was ill. He had seen a doctor the day before. A bad cough. Pam was going to cook dinner for the two of them. No, they were going out to dinner and then nightclubbing for the rest of the evening. No, he went to bed early and then woke up at about midnight, not feeling well, needing a bath to warm himself—everyone agrees on the watery aspect. The liquid. The waters of the unconscious. The womb. An immersion. A baptism. A cleansing. The sublime rest in the waters of the mother. Pam wasn't even there. She had gone out to see the Count. He was always referred to simply as "the Count." He was an aristocrat. Pam liked that; hobnobbing with royalty. His name was impossible to pronounce. We couldn't speak any French. We were Americans. We knew about the art, the music, the poetry, and the films but we couldn't speak the language. What the Count's name was, I don't know to this day. I do know he was Jim's rival for Cinnamon Pam. But he's dead, too. Heroin got him.

No, Pam was in bed with Jim. She wouldn't have left him if he wasn't feeling well. No, he was in the bath. He called out his last words to her from the tub. She heard him through the door. (I saw her a year later at a seaside restaurant in Marin, across the bridge from San Francisco. She was completely distraught. Shattered. I could only hold her in my arms and try to comfort her. It was impossible to ask the necessary question: "What happened to him?" She was in tears. She could only tell me how much she loved him. How she needed him. How much she missed him and how lesser the world was without him. But then she said, "Do you know what his last words were?" I thought, "More light" or perhaps "Eureka." Or best of all . . . "One."

I said, "No, Pam, what did he say?"

She looked at me, tears on her cheek, frail, broken. . . . " 'Pam, are you still there?' " she said. And then she repeated it. Softly, in her little girl's voice, as if to herself . . . " 'Pam, are you still there?' "

"That's beautiful," I said, trying to comfort this lost little girl. "His last thoughts were of you." And she began to cry again.)

And evidently she fell back asleep, probably content and happy. She had her man with her. She was in Paris. She was young and beautiful. He was a famous artist and he was going to write again. And she would be his muse. But she awoke with a start. An hour or two later. Alone, Jim wasn't with her . . . in fear, she rushed to the bathroom.

Now run to the mirror in the bathroom. Look!

And her worst fears were realized. He was dead . . . and her mind began to unhinge. An overload. Emotions beyond control. Words flooding her psyche. "Alone! Never again! Empty! Hold me! My fault! He won't ever hold me ever again! My fault! I'm lost! Afraid! Oh, God, why?! Why?! Jim!"

In her panic, she called the Count. (Who else could she turn to?) And he came to their apartment in the Marais. But he came with, and this is odd, Marianne Faithfull. (Pam's rival?) No, he didn't come with her. Marianne Faithfull says she was never there. Then who was there? Was the Count even there? No, she didn't call the Count. She called Alain Ronay, a UCLA buddy, and Agnes Varda, a filmmaker friend. They took care of everything. Called the police. The *flics* arrived at nine A.M. No, they came at five A.M. Who knows?

Later, reports said that Jim had a smile on his face. I love that part. Whatever happened to him, he went out grinning.

Death, old friend.

Don't they say death is sweet? Well, he deserved a sweet exit. Because of all the pressures, the pain, the trials, the dark nights of the soul that too-young man went through, he deserved to "leap upward, into the loam" with a satyr's leer covering his now smooth and substantial jowls.

No. He's not dead at all. He staged his own death. Hadn't Agnes Varda been researching the story of a French accountant who staged his own death and disappeared in the Marquesas during the twenties? With a hundred fifty pounds of bricks in a coffin and a phony death certificate—add a paid-off Algerian doctor, with perhaps $5,000; a nice piece of change in 1971 money. The complicity of a friend or two—French friends, perhaps filmmakers themselves, to make the necessary arrangements. Well, anything is possible in Paris!

So what is the story? Will we ever know the truth? Do we *want* to know the truth? Do we *need* to know the truth? And why? I mean, what difference does it make how he died, as long as it wasn't murder? It really doesn't matter how an artist exits the planet. It's the ART . . . that matters. It's *only* the art that matters. It's what we *do*, for cri-sake. Jim was an artist. He wants you to listen to the words. To take the words into your depths. Into those deep places. Those secret places. Those parts of your internal makeup where the vulnerable child lives. The terrified one. The frightened one. The soft one. The sweet and delicate and gentle one. We're all in the same boat. We all have the same internal makeup. And we're all frightened.

But art is our salvation. *We* become the creators. *We* are the inventors. And the joy, and the escape, and the great leap out of ourselves—out of the closed circle we constantly occupy—out of the shell and armor of our ego, outward into a "cleaner, purer realm," as Jim once said . . . *that* is our proper destination. To become enlightened creators. Knowing the oneness of all things. The divine and eternal one. ("Tat tvam asi." "You are that," as they say in India.) And then daring to snatch duality out of that oneness. Making the choice to create. Making the choice to exist. We are all the creator. And this existence is *our* creation. It belongs to *us* and *we* are responsible for the whole damned thing!

That's art. For me, that's what making music is all about. Plucking the notes out of the void. And for Jim it was about plucking the words out of the ether. Then placing them in an imaginative juxtaposition. Images. Deep and penetrating. Confessional. Sometimes mundane, often profound. Never without meaning. Instead, usually a multilayered meaning. I used to love to listen to his words. What depth and what phrase turning. A word man, indeed.

O great creator of being, grant us one more hour
to perform our art and perfect our lives.

I wanted that on his tombstone.

Coda queen, be my bride.
Rage in darkness by my side.
Seize the summer in your pride.
Let's ride!

That was for Pam.

Wild child, natural child.
Not your mother's or your father's child;
you're our child, screaming wild.

That was for Danny.

Well, she's fashionably lean,
And she's fashionably late.
She'll never rank a scene,
She'll never break a date.
But she's no drag,
Just watch the way she walks.
She's a twentieth-century fox.

That was for Dorothy.

Persian night, babe.
See the light, babe.
Jesus!
Save us!

That was for him.

I love the friends I have gathered together on this thin
raft. We have constructed pyramids in honor of our escaping.

That was for John and Robby.

Lost in a Roman wilderness of pain.
And all the children are insane,
Waiting for the summer rain.

That was for all of us.

His words. Always a place of magic. A refuge from the howling madness of the night. I knew we were human and strong and good and divine when I read his words. I knew we could all face the terror. His words proved the potency of creation. Of our willing the art of creation. Of our ability to rise upward, out of the mud, into that great golden orb of energy that warms and protects us. That sun.

That molten disc. That manifestation of our original act of creation when we willed existence into existence. That energy. Divine and human. Ours. All of ours. And Jim's words. For us. All of us.

In that year we had an intense visitation of energy.

That year lasted from the summer of 1965 to July 3, 1971.

※

The last time I saw Jim Morrison was in the recording studio in the spring of 1971—8512 Santa Monica Boulevard, corner of La Cienega and Santa Monica. We had turned the Doors office/work-shop into a studio for the *L.A. Woman* sessions. We knew the sound of the room. We felt comfortable there. The vibrations were well tuned through years of rehearsal, laughter, drinking, philosophizing, and pot smoking. This was home for us. And this time *we* were going to be the producers.

Paul Rothchild had bailed on the project. He used a great ploy to get us motivated. Paul was a real gambler. "I'm bored," he said. "If this is the best you can do, I quit. You guys can just do it yourselves." And he walked out of a very dull rehearsal. Yikes! Do it ourselves? Well . . . why not! Hell, we can do it. We're capable. Bruce Botnick as co-producer. Of course he's a virgin, too. But he knows our sound. He knows what we want. He's been our engineer since the first album. He helped create our sound and now he's our co-producer.

So we made the existential leap together—John, Robby, Jim, Ray, and Bruce Botnick. And as is usually the case with anyone's act of courage . . . we landed on our feet. A critically and aesthetically successful undertaking. The energy was with us.

Bruce wheeled an eight-track recorder across La Cienega Boulevard from Elektra's studio just down the street and around the corner. Also mics, cables, baffles, amplification . . . the works. And a big old tube board from Sunset Sound, where we cut our eyeteeth on the first two Doors' albums; *The Doors* and *Strange Days*. No one used a tube board anymore. They were obsolete but, man, they were warm. What a rich, full sound. And this one looked like something left over from a Gene Krupa big band date, or the control panel from one of Flash Gordon's sparkle craft. Big, black Bakelite knobs. No slide pots, but rotary knobs. A man could get his hands on those knobs. They had a heft to them that felt satisfying and good. Like you were in a continuum of past artists; advancing the art of recording but maintaining a sense of tradition, of continuity. And it was all black and silver with illuminated meters that we constantly bounced into the red zone. Pushing that sweet-sounding board to its limits. And it never let us down.

We placed the instruments downstairs, put up baffles for a bit of isolation, set the mics in front of the amps, put a vocal mic in Jim's isolation booth—the downstairs bathroom—ran cables out the back door and up the back staircase, put the board and the eight-track upstairs in the office, plugged in the cables, and voilà! A recording studio in the Doors' workshop. We were home and ready to go!

Are you a lucky little lady in the city of light . . .
Or just another lost angel . . .
City of night.
City of night.
City of night.
City of night!!

And we rocked that little room. Wrestled those songs into shape. Did a Jacob on the angel of creativity, and caught the muse. Everything was going great and the finish line was in sight. Jim had completed his vocals. All that was left for him to do was to put the whisper vocal on the song "Riders on the Storm"—right after the last verse:

Riders on the storm
Riders on the storm
Into this house we're born
Into this world we're thrown
Like a dog without a bone
An actor out on loan
Riders on the storm

Then Jim would come in with a haunted, spooky whisper voice behind his singing:

And it was very eerie. I should have known then that it was a portent. We finished the take and he came up to the office/control room. Everyone thought it was a great vocal. He was very pleased with the effort.

"I like the effect," he said. "Good idea, Ray."

And then Robby spoke up. "Ya know, that song feels like I'm out on the desert. I see thunderclouds, big ones, off in the distance. Why don't we add the sound of thunder and maybe some rain? Put the listener out there, too."

Botnick said, "I've got access to lots of sound effects. Let me see what I can find."

Jim was just standing there, humming the melody line to himself . . . and smiling. The Doors were together, in the studio, making music. It felt right. We were into it and the art was good. It was working. We all knew it and smiled to ourselves. Just like Jim was smiling.

And then he dropped the napalm.

"I'm going to Paris," he said.

Silence. Psychic wheels began spinning. Doubts, omens, fears entered the room. A dark green thing attached itself to the base of my spine. Bruce and Robby stood frozen for a beat. John coughed nervously, unable to bear the tension.

"We're close to being finished here," he continued. "Most of the mixes are done. Everything sounds great. Why don't *you* guys go ahead and finish it up. I'm leaving for Paris in two days. Pam's already there, she's got a little apartment . . . got it all set up. I'm going to join her over there."

And that was it. A simple little statement innocently tossed out, and the fate of the band was decided in an instant. But we didn't know it. No one did. Not right then. Not in the midst of all that creativity. All the brotherhood. All that art. All I knew was that the green thing put a tentacle into my stomach and tightened it a bit. This was not right.

Something's wrong, something's not quite right.

Jim would always be around for the final mixes. That's when all the creativity and hard work would finally come together. When we would fine-tune all the variables. The volume levels, the EQ settings, the placement of the instruments in the sonic spectrum, the signal-processing devices, even the edits—everything had to be finessed and cajoled down to the two-track final mix. The mix that went on the record. The mix that everyone was going to hear at home. Our baby.

This was the delivery of the baby. After months of gestation. From initial inspiration, to rehearsal, to seducing the muse of each piece, to capturing its essence, to finally being ready to put it all down on tape, to all-night recording sessions, trying to get the muse to come back and make love to us one more time while the tape machine was running (oh, she is fickle, and demanding of surrender; and can never be fooled or tricked into appearing), to vocal takes, to overdubs of tack pianos and bottleneck guitars.

And Jim was going to leave before he heard the final, finished album—before he knew what form all those weeks and months of work would take at the end of it all?

I should have known.

Something was wrong, I didn't know what, but it didn't sit right. Still, I tried to be encouraging. Mostly because deep down, I thought this trip was a good idea.

"Paris, huh?" I said. "Now, that's interesting, man. That would be a good place to get away for a while."

"Yeah, I think so, too," he said.

"How long, uhh . . . how long you gonna be there?"

"You know, Ray, I don't know," Jim said, a look in his eyes like the thousand-yard stare. Faraway. Not really there, and yet seeing everything. Especially the tragedy, the fragility of life.

All my life's a torn curtain.
All my mind come tumbling down.

"I don't have any plans yet," he said. "I just need a break. Some time to myself. A couple of months, six months. Maybe a year. Who knows, man? I don't."

"It'll give you a chance to work on those notes from Miami," I encouraged. "I want to read that book." It was to be called *Observations on America, While on Trial for Obscenity.*

He smiled. "I'm gonna rake 'em over the coals. This time it's my turn."

"A new de Tocqueville," I said. "We need one for the twentieth century."

He just smiled that sheepish little-boy grin of his and waved his hand at me. "Oh, man."

"Hey, you can do it. Who better?"

※

In a way, his leaving made a strange kind of sense. After we delivered *L.A. Woman,* our sixth studio album in four years, plus *Absolutely Live,* that made seven albums. The number of steps to heaven. The number of the chakras—yogic energy centers that run up the spine from the coccyx to the top of the brain. The number of albums we owed Elektra Records on our renegotiated deal. After delivery, we'd be finished with our Elektra contract. We were free and clear. We could resign, sign with Atlantic Records (Ahmet Ertegun, the president, was courting us), not sign with anybody, break up the band, stay together, make films, write books, paint, dance, whatever. We were free to do whatever we wanted. Or to do nothing. Take a long break and think about man, God, and existence.

To be honest, I hoped Jim would use the break to get away from his drinking buddies; get away from the hangers-on who were always attaching themselves to him and taking him to the too many bars, dives, gin mills, and wherevers. The sycophants. The leeches, as John and Robby and I called them. His "friends," as they became called in later years. And the evening was always on Jim's nickel, of course. Jim always paid. One way or the other. He would wine and dine those ne'er-do-well friends of his, and meanwhile they were just sucking up his energy, keeping him from being a poet.

With them, he'd sit in a bar and talk all his energy away. Booze does that to you. So do guys that laugh too loud at your jokes. Elvis had them. The Memphis Mafia. Jim had them, too. We called his the Santa Monica Mafia.

They'd laugh and joke and cut up and carry on, and he wouldn't be writing. He wouldn't be creating. He should have been spinning out great passages of new verse, instead of talking it out and staggering home to Pam way past the midnight hour. How many great lyrics got lost in that senseless flood of drunken activity? How many great poems fell victim to those bad habits, wasted on besotted, uncaring ears that were just humoring him until they could divine how to weasel the next drink out of him, or the next high?

They were a real sore spot with Pam Courson, Jim's live-in lady and soul mate. Pam was always angry because Jim was running around and getting drunk with his friends. With them, he might disappear for days on end, only to pop back into her life as if nothing had happened. I guess you could say, euphemistically, they had a "stormy" relationship. However, volatile to the point of self-immolation would be more to the truth.

. . . and our love becomes a funeral pyre.

So to make things up to her, on her suggestion, he was going to take her to Paris.

Hell, it seemed like a good idea; at least at the time. Paris was the City of Light—and he could certainly use an infusion of luminosity into that shadow world of his—the city of artists. He could be the next generation of the bohemian ideal, an American in Paris. Our literary heroes had gone there. Why not Jim, too? Ernest Hemingway, F. Scott Fitzgerald, Henry Miller, Jim Morrison, I liked the ring of that. Good company.

And the *inspiration* of that glorious city. I wanted him to go to Paris and *write* again. Forget about being a rock star. It was time for Jim Morrison to be an artist again. Just like in the beginning. Just like in the summer of '65, when we were young and idealistic, charged with energy and ready to change the world. I wanted that guy back. The sensitive, caring, funny human being I sat down with on the sands of Venice Beach, six years before; the guy I put the Doors together with. That was the guy I thought was one of the best poets I had ever read. (Legendary beat poet Michael McClure has referred to Jim as "the best poet of his generation.") That guy was an artist, and that guy was my bud.

"Okay, I'll see you, brother," Jim said, that occasional lapse into a sorta-southern accent—an endearing legacy of his Florida childhood—coloring his words. A lapse that occurred only under moments of stress or silly joy. Or sometimes, now occurring more frequently, when a bottle of Wild Turkey would take possession of Jim Morrison and turn him into a person I did not know. So off he went. Left the session, just like that. John and Robby and I just looked at each other, dumbfounded. All we could do was shrug our shoulders.

"I think it's a good idea," said Robby.

"Me too," I agreed. "Paris and writers, it's a natural."

"Maybe he'll get the muse back," Robby said hopefully.

"But what if he doesn't stop drinking? He'll never write anything good again," John the worry-wart piped in.

"Don't worry, John," I said, trying to allay his fears. "The poet's in there, he'll come out in Paris."

"Yeah," he half snarled, "what about Jimbo?"

We stopped for a beat. Silence. An entity of fear passed over us. John broke the silence by once again doing his usual nervous cough. We tried to go back to work. It was impossible. The finishing of *L.A. Woman*, without Jim, would have to wait for another day. We didn't know it then, but that would be the last time we ever saw Jim Morrison, dead or alive.

Two months later, we hadn't heard anything from Jim. *L.A. Woman* had turned into our comeback album. Critics loved it. "The Doors are back!" "A unique blend of power and precision." "Raw and real." "Morrison's lyrics are eloquent and revealing." The first single, "Love Her Madly"—a chugging, tuneful tribute to a fight Robby Krieger once had with a girlfriend—was a hit. Our radio song. The intellectual long cuts (or epics, as we called them)—a necessary component of any Doors' album—were represented by "Riders on the Storm" and the title cut. "Been Down So Long" and "Maggie M'Gill" covered our blues roots. Everything was jake with one exception . . . Jim wasn't around.

We were getting itchy to play so we went back into rehearsal, working on new tunes. Doing what we did, making music together. Robby had some new compositions and both John and I were turning our hand to actual songwriting. Rehearsals were going well, interviews were being requested to talk about *L.A. Woman*, the record company was very happy with the new album, offers for tours were pouring in, and no one knew that Jim Morrison had gone to Paris for some very necessary R and R. We didn't exactly keep it a secret, but neither did we volunteer the information to anyone outside of the immediate Doors family. Consequently, everything was progressing and yet everything was on hold.

John finally said, impatiently, "I'm gonna call him." I said, "Why? Let him alone for a while. He doesn't want anybody bugging him. He'll call when he's ready." John paced the rehearsal room, unable to control his anxiety. "I just gotta know," he said. "I can't wait any longer." And so he called him.

The next day John reported in. Everything was okay. Jim was feeling good, having a good time. He had shaved his beard, he was excited about the critical acclaim for the record and, best of all, he was looking forward to playing again.

"As soon as I get back we gotta go on the road," he told John. "I want to play those songs live. We never got a real chance to do that."

"Exactly," John enthused. "And you know what, we could even take a bass player out with us. Maybe a rhythm guitar, too. Like the album. Ray and Robby and I have been talking about it."

"Let's take the bass player who played on the record," Jim said, catching John's excitement. "What's his name?"

"Jerry . . . Jerry Scheff," said John over the transcontinental connection. "And we'll take the other guy, too, Marc something or other."

"Well, shiiiit, John, let's just book a little tour. What d'ya say?"

"When?"

"When I get back."

"When's that?"

"I don't know . . . I'm having a pretty good time," Jim answered. "I'll be here a while yet."

"Well, okay," said John. "I'll tell the guys."

"Good, give 'em my love," answered Jim. "And one more thing, John." Jim paused. "Try to stay cool, will ya?"

CLICK.

That was the last time anyone heard from Jim. That was early June. A month later, on July 3, 1971, Jim Morrison died under what can only be called "mysterious circumstances."

⁂

I got a phone call from this guy who was, ostensibly, our manager. Actually, he was our roadie and we promoted him to phone answerer, but, wouldn't you know it, it went to his head. He became arrogant. Lording it over concert promoters and writers requesting interviews. But what the hell, he was trustworthy. Bill "South Bay" Siddons.

"Ray, I got some bad news. I just got a phone call from Paris. Jim's dead."

Bullshit, I thought, because at the end of the sixties and the beginning of the seventies a wave of paranoia had swept over the youth of America. Death and the rumor of death had descended upon us, entered our conscious mind, and filtered down into our subconscious, where they lodged like a bad cancer.

In those dark years, everybody was dead . . . one way or another. Janis Joplin was dead, Jimi Hendrix was dead. Paul McCartney was dead because he was walking across the Beatles' *Abbey Road* album cover without shoes—the way they bury a corpse in Italy. He was barefoot, in a suit, and out of step with the other three lads, so he had to be dead—or so the rumor went. The Kennedys were dead. Martin Luther King was dead. People were starting to get death obsessed. And these were our heroes. This planet was also rapidly filling up with the ghosts of dead young soldiers—American and Vietnamese and Vietnamese women and children. The whole thing was getting a little too weird for the conscious mind to handle, and rumors were sprouting like milkweed.

We were at a party, rock and roll in Hollywood. Lots of people. Lots of pot and cheap wine. Real boho style. Jim was supposed to be there but he was late, as usual. All of a sudden, somebody runs in and says . . .

"Oh, my God! Oh, God! Jim Morrison's just been killed in an automobile accident!"

Of course Jim was driving the "Blue Lady," his Shelby GT 500. A terrible and mean machine; so it was actually possible. Nobody knew what to do. We all just kind of blathered and moved our feet in nervous, panicky little steps. "How? Where? What should we do? Somebody call an ambulance. Send it where? It'll come here. We don't need it here, we need it at the scene of the accident. Where's that? Ask that guy. Where is he? Who is he?" And no one knew who the guy was. Or was it actually a girl? No one could say for sure. A wave of anxiety and its evil twin, impotence, swept through our lower three chakras. We had entered the darkness and it was a fearful place.

So what the hell happens next? Within five minutes, in walks Jim Morrison. Alive and ready to party! We say, "Jesus Christ, Jim, we heard you were dead." He looks at us, quizzically, and then he comes up with the great Mark Twain line: "No, man, the rumors of my death have been greatly exaggerated." Everyone sighs a great relief, we laugh at our gullibility, and the party continues . . . long into the Hollywood night.

So when Siddons told me our singer was dead again, I didn't believe him. And it wasn't because I didn't want to think my good friend had died. I could only think, at that moment, of Jim standing in the middle of that party, a lazy smile spreading across his darkly handsome face as he enjoyed the absurdity of being pronounced dead while you're still around to enjoy life. I thought about how ridiculous it all seemed that night and decided to dismiss the whole thing—treat it like a thousand other half-cocked legends I'd heard before. It was just more of that paranoid death miasma spreading its bile. And I sure as hell wasn't going to Paris to check out some silly rumor.

"I don't believe it, Bill. And I'm certainly not going to Paris. Remember that party?"

"I think it's serious this time, Ray," Bill said.

I thought for a moment, noting the sense of panic in Siddons's voice.

"I'll tell you what," I said. "There's a noon flight to Paris, right? Book a ticket, first class, and get over there."

"I've already done that, Ray. I just need your okay."

"Well, you got it, man. Now go."

"I'll call you," he said, "from there."

"And, Bill," I cautioned, "just make sure, will ya? This time make sure." And I hung up the phone.

Three days later, he did call.

"We just buried Jim Morrison," the voice on the line said.

"Who is this?" I angrily shouted into the phone.

"It's Bill, Bill Siddons," the voice meekly responded.

"Bill! What the fuck do you mean, 'buried'? You're telling me this isn't some silly paranoid fantasy? You're telling me he's really dead?"

"It's true this time, Ray."

"How could that be? What . . . what happened? I mean, was he hit by a car, or was he in an accident? Or did a fucking building fall on him? . . ." I was pissed.

"We don't know."

". . . or was he murdered, for cri-sake? Did somebody shoot him, or stab him to death?"

"I don't know, Ray."

"Asshole, what do you mean, 'I don't know'?"

"It was none of those things. He just . . . died."

"Jesus Christ." I tried to let that sink in. It didn't compute. "What?! Where?"

"In his apartment. In the bathtub."

"Did somebody try to drown him or something?"

"No," Bill said. "The doctor's certificate says something like, 'his heart stopped.' It's all in French, and I can't read it."

"Oh, man. Well, how did he look?"

"I don't know, Ray."

"If you say that one more time, I'm gonna strangle you. I'm asking you how he looked. Don't tell me 'I don't know.' " And then he drops another bomb on me.

"I don't know. I never saw his *body*."

"How could you not see his body?" I wanted to bang the telephone on the kitchen counter, where Dorothy and I were having breakfast. Or bang it on Siddons's head. Talk about sending a child to do a man's job.

"It was a sealed coffin."

"You're telling me you never saw Jim's body?! Why didn't you open the coffin?" I was livid.

His voice got quavery. "I couldn't."

"Why didn't you *demand* to see it? Why didn't you say, 'Let me see Jim Morrison. I'm the manager and I *have* to see his body!' Why didn't you do that?" And then the absurdity . . .

"I was afraid," he said.

"So you buried a *coffin?*"

"That's right, Ray. We buried him this morning."

"How do you even know he was *in* the coffin?" I raged at him. "How do you know it wasn't one hundred fifty pounds of fucking *sand?*"

"Well, uhh, Pam was all broke up, crying and everything. And, uhh, I mean . . . he was in there. I know."

"Oh, Jesus." The air was being sucked out of my body. The whole confused story was beginning to take its place.

"Bill, I told you to make sure. And you don't know squat." I paused, gulping for air and grabbing for some reality. "Where . . . where did you bury him?"

"In Paris. Something called Père Lachaise cemetery. I don't really know how to pronounce it, Ray."

"No shit, Bill."

"It's really nice," he said, trying to make amends. "A lot of famous artists are buried there. Chopin and, uhh, Sarah Bernhardt and Oscar Wilde, and . . . uhh . . ." I could hear the gears grinding. "I don't know who else, but lots of others."

"That's great, Bill. But is *Jim* buried there?"

"I just told you. Yeah, we just buried him."

"You buried a sealed coffin, man. We'll never know the *real* truth now. It's all gonna be rumors and stories from here on out."

"What do you mean, Ray?"

"Never mind, Bill. You'll understand someday. Come home now."

I just hung up the phone. There was nothing else to say. I later found out that Agnes Varda, Alain Ronay, Pam, and Siddons were the only ones there. Just four people on a beautiful Paris morning. And he was gone. Went to Paris for a vacation. For a little R and R. And he died. Simple as that. And confused as that.

Some public announcements were made. The press was notified. Elektra Records was notified. Our attorney was notified. And then the rumors began to fly. I won't even dignify those innuendoes by discussing them. But if you're reading this book . . . you've probably heard a few. Suicide, murder, CIA plot, he's alive in Africa, Australian outback, he's become a Tibetan monk. That sort of thing. The late-twentieth-century penchant for embellishment. The pathetic need for secret plots. Conspiracies everywhere. We have descended into the depths of paranoia. We're consumed by fear and mistrust. We have no faith in the energy. The energy that *is* us and supports all life. We've lost understanding of the cycles of life. We don't even believe in cycles. It's all a straight line to us. It's all progress. We must progress from one point to another. We must be going toward a goal. If the Judeo-Christian-Islamic man is not progressing, he will go mad. If life is circular, he will go mad. If he does not advance, he will go mad.

And we are, indeed, going mad.

We met at the Doors' office later that afternoon. We were completely distraught. All of us: John, Robby and I, Kathy Lisciandro (our secretary), Leon Barnard (our publicist), Vince Treanor (our equipment designer and road manager), and little Danny Sugerman (office boy and Doors' manager-to-be). We were shattered, destroyed. We had been waiting for Jim to come back, going about our business, working on new tunes, woodshedding in our rehearsal space. We were looking forward to playing again, another album (the new tunes were great), gigs, fun times, another great experience. All of a sudden, not only is Jim not coming back, he's *dead*.

We'll never make art again. We'll never make love on stage again. Jim and I will never do our Dionysus-and-Apollo dichotomy thing again. The four of us will never enter that zone again, that holy place, that transcendent place . . . making Doors music . . . again. It was over and we would all be something slightly less. We would always have a piece of us missing. For the rest of our lives.

the south side of chicago

I didn't even know that piece was going to be missing back on the corner of 34th and Bell Avenue in Chicago, Illinois, the city of my birth—on February 12, 1939—and the corner of my home and my grammar school. All I knew was that I was alive and the adventure began at that intersection. My *axis mundi.*

My time of arrival on this planet was 3:30 A.M., smack dab in the middle of the hour of the wolf, and on Abraham Lincoln's birthday to boot. He, too, is an Aquarian, and our card is the King of Diamonds. I was born in the year of the Rabbit, the lucky sign in the Oriental zodiac . . . and I've certainly had no complaints that way. My moon sign is in Sagittarius, as is Jim's rising sign.

I went to a little grammar school called Everett School. I did eight years there. We lived right across the street, 3358 South Bell Avenue. Very convenient. I came home for lunch every day. Can you imagine? So did my two younger brothers, Rich and Jim. What a life, huh? Mom fixes you lunch at home! My father, Ray Sr., worked at International Harvester's McCormick Works as a tool-and-die man. A good UAW union man. My mother, Helen, took care of her four males. They both did a great job. Wonderful parents. Very supportive . . . most of the time.

My ethnic lineage is Polish. Manzarek (original spelling Manczarek) is a Polish name. I'm third-generation. My grandparents came over during the great immigration to America from eastern and southern Europe in the 1890s.

They worked incredibly hard. And our parents worked hard and wanted their children to go to school. To better themselves. To get an education. And that's what we did. We went to college. "You kids are gonna go to university and have a better life than we had." "Well, okay, Mom and Dad, we can do that." Unfortunately, we went off to UCLA and became artists. I don't think that's what they had in mind. We were supposed to be professional people. I was supposed to be an attorney. Dorothy Fujikawa—my wife-to-be— was supposed to study medicine. Jim Morrison was supposed to be a diplomat. If he wasn't going to go to the U.S. Naval Academy at Annapolis (as his father had), he was to enter the diplomatic service. Jim Morrison at a military academy? Can you picture it? Impossible. So instead of realizing our parents' dreams, much to their chagrin we created our own dreams. We became artists! And even worse . . . we became intoxicants. We ingested psychedelic substances, smoked the herb, and broke on through to the other side. The veil—the web of maya, as the Hindus call it—fell away from our eyes as we opened the doors of perception. I don't think that's exactly what Mom and Dad had in mind for us. "You kids have to stop smoking those marijuanas," my father once said to me. "But, Dad," I replied, "I'm happier now than I've ever been in my entire life." What could he say to that? "And you really ought to stop living with that Chinese girl . . . you know the twain don't meet." I almost laughed. "No, Dad," I said, suppressing a smirk, "she's Japanese and, besides, I love her." What could he say to *that?* He left our apartment on Fraser, having said what he felt he *had* to say, going on the public record. He was just being a concerned father. Just making a stand for his acquired principles, for his version of how things ought to be. And I couldn't fault him for that. I loved my father. He died in 1986. He thought the Doors were the greatest and he grew to love Dorothy and was a complete fool for his grandson, our little boy, Pablo. He was especially fond of my recording of Carl Orff's *Carmina Burana*. Renegade monks and wild Latin chants struck a very responsive chord in him. He had become a renegade Catholic in his later years . . . after he moved with the entire family to California. The light and the freedom finally zapped *him*, too. He wanted the piece "The Roasted Swan" played at his funeral. What a kook.

Chicago was a well-thought-out, well-laid-out city, and the Manzarek family took advantage of it all. My father took us everywhere. To the parks, the summer beaches on Lake Michigan, the museums—both Natural History and Science and Industry, the great downtown "Loop" and the first-run theaters, such as the Chicago and the Oriental, the forest preserves ringing the city to the west for camping and meat grilling and picnicking and nature walks, Soldier's Field for stock car races and football games, Riverview Amusement Park for roller-coaster rides, the International Amphitheater for rodeos and sports and the yearly new-car automobile show, and . . . everything! We did it all and my father was the leader of the pack. He was wonderful. However, he was also a tough guy who would kick your butt if your butt needed it. But mainly he was wonderful and supportive and strong and manly and protective.

Of course, he had no idea *what* in the hell I was up to. But when I sat down at the piano and played some boogie-woogie or a cute little Bach two-part invention, he loved it. He was my slave. I was his firstborn son and he was proud of his issue. He was an extremely supportive man . . . as long as I stayed in school and got good grades.

My mother, of course, was the queen of the castle. Her maiden name was Helen Kolenda (she likes to say it means "Christmas carol" in Polish). She has a great singing voice. A very pure tone. She loves music and she loves the Doors. She fell in love with Jim Morrison and thought he was her fourth son. She would have loved to have nurtured him, too, just as she nurtured her first three boys. With her great heart and her wonderful home cooking. With her big golden brown oven-roasted tom turkeys, all moist and succulent with crispy, crackling skin. With her delicious roasted leg of lamb redolent of garlic and homemade steaming pots of vegetable beef soup and ears of Illini Chief sweet corn and sliced beefsteak tomatoes from the farms and fields of the midwestern breadbasket. And homemade poppy seed egg bread, hot and golden and slathered with fresh local butter. And her lemon meringue pie, all sweet and tart and standing almost a foot high with peaks and swirls of pale gold-and-white meringue. And her apple slices in large loaf pans, drizzled with creamy white frosting on the outside and filled with cinnamon brown-sugared apples on the inside. Delicious.

What a well-fed childhood I had. And wasn't it a sybaritic indulgence to come home for lunch during the school week. No crappy cafeteria food. No brown-bagging it. A nice little hot lunch, prepared by your own mother. Nothing fancy, just the regular all-American 1950s lunch of, for instance, Campbell's tomato soup, a grilled-cheese sandwich, some carrot or celery sticks, and a glass of milk. We'd wolf it down and boom, off we'd go. Run back across the street into the school playground, fool around for fifteen, twenty minutes and back to class. What a secure routine.

My two brothers and I did a lot of running around in Chicago. Lots of sports. Lots of goofing around. The city was made for outdoor activities. It was laid out in a grid, smack up against Lake Michigan, with a public playground or a city park every four blocks or so, sprinkled over the *entire* city. Kids and teenagers running off their excess energy all over the place. Down the street from my home, three blocks away on 34th and Hoyne, was the eponymous Hoyne Playground, our local maniac yard. It had a baseball diamond—complete with lights for night games for the big guys—an outdoor basketball court, where I shot my brains out, a single tennis court and swings and teeter-totters and a sandpit for the little kids. A small brick building contained the office and supply room—they would actually pass out sports equipment for the kids to use, balls and bats and jump ropes and such—and the desk of old Ralph, the chief of the playground. He had worked in the Chicago Playground District for forty years and this was his last assignment. He was a sweet old man, he loved kids, and he kept Hoyne all shipshape. Me and a bunch of the local guys won the boys' city softball championship for him. We had a great team.

I played first base and batted third in the lineup. We were all thirteen and fourteen years old. Bunch of fifties Chicago kids and we could hit, catch, and run like the wind. And it was old Ralph's first championship in all his years. He almost broke down and cried with delight after the final out.

My father liked to call us the Hoyne Giants; he always said it jokingly with a pseudo-Chinese inflection. Wise guy. That fall we also won the City Touch-Football championship. Same bunch of playground rats blocking, passing, and running our young teen asses off.

But basketball was my main sport. In Chicago, in the wintertime, you had one of two choices for your organized-sports activities: hockey or basketball. Hockey?! Forget it, man, I was not going to play hockey. It's freezing outside. It's as cold as Dante's ninth circle. Who wants to be outside in the ice and snow? Skating around in the frozen white, hitting a hockey puck. The damned skates bother your ankles. Your ankles are always going one way or the other, in or out, knock-kneed or bowlegged. And somebody is going to hit you in the shins for sure with that big, hard hockey stick. It's practically a lethal weapon, for cri-sake. And the puck is way too hard. It's like a rubber bullet shot off the end of that lethal weapon. And you're in the line of fire and it's fucking freezing on top of it. But in contrast, there's the basketball court . . . and it's inside . . . and it's hot. You take your clothes off, it's like being in Hawaii. You're wearing little shorts and a tank top. And it's eighty degrees. Ahh . . . paradise.

I was fourteen years old, six feet tall, and I was good. I played a lot of b-ball with my good friend Joe Nies and we were the main cogs on the McKinley Park City Championship basketball team of the next winter. I was the center and he was the point guard. I was the same height then that I am now. I was the big guy. Six feet tall, 145 pounds, a "force" in the middle. I had a jump shot, a hook shot, a decent spin step; I could rebound, play face-to-face defense. I could do it all. And Joe Nies was a great ball handler and passer. And we won the boys-fourteen-years-old-and-under Chicago Park District city championship. I was very proud of our team. A good bunch of guys.

I didn't realize it in the ebullience of our victory, but that was the high point of my basketball career. The next year I was six feet tall and 145 pounds, and the guys who were guards are now playing forward. They've grown and I haven't. By the time I'm sixteen years old, the guys who were playing guard are now six feet five and I'm still six feet tall and 145 pounds. Everybody just got taller and taller . . . except me. I went from being the big guy at fourteen to a forward at fifteen, and by the time I was sixteen, they said, "Ray, play guard." I said, "I don't play guard. I don't handle the ball, I'm not a dribbler. I crash the boards. I wheel and deal in the paint. I'm a rebounder. I muscle for position. I'm an inside shooter." And they said, "No, you're not tall enough to be a rebounder anymore, Ray. You have to play guard now." And that was it, the end of my basketball jones. I was sixteen and I hadn't grown. So I said, "Well, I guess it's going to be music after this."

⚜

My long march into the "floating world" of music began with the first step of . . . piano lessons! My mother and father had bought a huge upright piano. A carved-wood upright. Of a style I can only describe as country German. Turned legs, a carved flower here and there, a deep brown color, and all of it massive. They had it deposited in the basement rumpus room, had a half dozen piano movers wrestle it in, and said, "Raymond, you are going to learn how to play the piano." I was seven or eight years old. I pounded on the keys, went slightly goofy, made a ruckus, and thought, Why not? This could be fun. Thank God my mom and dad were hip and didn't bring home an accordion. Lots of kids in Chicago had to learn to play the accordion. In the post–World War II Midwest, the accordion was a very popular instrument. Large masses of children played "Lady of Spain" together on stages all over the city. It was not a pretty sight. Chicago, Milwaukee, and the entire state of Pennsylvania were the accordion capitals of America. But my parents were too hip for that. My father played the guitar and a mean ukulele. All the young cats in their raccoon coats in the roaring twenties and the Depression thirties played the ukulele and sang of moon, spoon, and June to their little kittens. And my father sang to my mother. And she sang right back to him, only better. She had the great voice in the family. And together they would harmonize and sing songs of love in a little Spanish town and jump tunes about coming to get you in a taxi, honey. They told me many years later about their record collection of 78s that melted in a fire just before I was born. Blues records. Bessie Smith and other singers and musical groups they couldn't remember. And all black. South Side of Chicago music. My mother told me the two of them would go record hunting together.

"We used to go to Maxwell Street and we'd go into these little record stores," she said. "But they weren't even stores. People lived in them and sold records, too. And people were poor in those days. They would have a rug hanging in the doorway to keep the cold out and you'd go in behind the rug and they would have records for sale. You could hear the music from the street as you'd walk by and just went in, under the rug. They would have the greatest music playing. I tell you, Raymond, those black people . . . they've got it!"

"Yeah, Mom, I agree." I laughed. "Those black people, they've got it." Man, would I love to have that record collection today.

So it was to be piano lessons. The fateful day arrived one Saturday morning—ten o'clock sharp. My father and I walked to 35th and Archer Avenue, a small commercial area, entered a two-story building, climbed a flight of stairs, and entered the studio of "the little professor," as my father, always the wise guy, would call him. I'll never forget that morning. It's seared in the synapses. The studio was darkened, I don't know why, and it was vaguely eerie. It was Saturday *morning*, free-from-school day, and his room was *dark*. Open the shades, for cri-sake, my brain shouted to itself. More light. And the smell was musty, as it should be for an old man who left Europe in the pre–World War II days. The man greeted me and I instinctively drew back. He was a strange, wizened creature. Today I know who he was, he was Shygoltz from the film *Pandora's Box*. (He was Louise Brooks's first patron. Her character was Lulu and the gnomelike Shygoltz was her first lover.) I wanted to get the hell out of there, fast! It was Saturday morning. Kids' shows were on the radio. Just like cartoons on TV today. We were on the cusp of the radio-to-TV changeover and everyone I knew loved those Saturday-morning shows. *The Lone Ranger* and the great *Captain Midnight*—you *had* to have a decoder ring; two General Mills cereal box tops and a quarter got you a little plastic piece-of-junk ring that you loved, and it worked maybe a half dozen times and then it broke, but you wore it anyway because it was cool and you were part of Captain Midnight's Billy Batson Boy Rangers Club—and Smiling Ed McConnel's Gang with Froggy the Gremlin. "Pluck your magic twanger, Froggy . . . boinnggg!" And I loved that stuff and there I was, stuck with Shygoltz and no Lulu to dance for us. Shit!

As if being there weren't bad enough, now he began the terrible mental torture. He opened a red music book. It contained pieces of music. Very simple little pieces of music.

He said, in a *mittel European* accent, "Okay, Raymont . . . zis is musick. And zis is how it is written."

And I looked at it and I thought, This is some kind of message from outer space. Surely it was something from Ming the Merciless. It was indecipherable. If only I had my Captain Midnight decoder ring, I thought. The page was filled with lines and dots. Horizontal lines with dots scattered randomly about. Vertical lines divided the dots into groupings of no discernible pattern. The dots had little tails sticking up in the air. Some of the tails had a little flag on the end of them. Some had a double flag. At the beginning of the left-hand side of the page, the lines had a bizarre symbol: a baroque curlicue covering all five of the lines. What an arcane language!

"What do these lines and dots mean, sir?" I asked the little professor. "I don't understand any of this."

He chuckled. "It's all quite isey, son. See zis note?"

Ah-hah, the dots with tails were called notes. He pointed to a dot at the bottom of the five lines that had a small line cutting through it.

"Zis is mittle C. Zis corresponds to mittle C on za piano." And he played a C note. Now, I'm looking at eighty-eight keys in front of me. They're all black and white. They're all exactly the same. And Shygoltz, for cri-sake, can distinguish one key from another. How? My brain started turning into Wheatena. They all look exactly the same, it screamed as it became hot cereal mush. All the white keys and all the black keys. There are some low ones over here to the left and some high ones over here to the right . . . but they're exactly the same! This is totally insane! How can anyone understand any of this?! It was beyond me how anyone could possibly comprehend where *anything* was on that keyboard.

He repeated, "Zis is mittle C," and plunked on the note. "You try it, Raymont." And he took my hand as I extended my index finger and moved my hand up and down and I plunked the note a few times.

I thought, Don't hold my hand! I'm not a baby. I can plunk the note without your help, thank you. I was pissed. Why did my father bring me to this house of pain?

"Very goot, Raymond. Now I play za whole piece for you."

I wanted to stop him right there. Don't go any further! I can't do this, I thought. I will never, in a million years, be able to decipher this encoded message from Ming. Stop!! But on he went, and the piece he played was (go to your piano now, dear reader) C-D-E, E-D-C, D-E-C. That was it.

"Step-ping up, step-ping down, then a skip." And it had a rhythm to it. And a logic and a symmetry. It was clean and precise and symmetrical. He played it again.

"Step-ping up, step-ping down, then a skip."

And a lightbulb turned on in my brain. The Wheatena was gone. I was Raymond Daniel Manzarek Jr. again. IQ of 135. I can do this. Yes! This is not beyond me, my brain cartwheeled in its pan.

"You try it," Shygoltz said.

And I did . . . index finger on each note. I did it once, and then I sang the words as I played it, "Step-ping up, step-ping down, then a skip."

And the little professor grinned. "Very goot, Raymont."

And my father clapped his hands together—my first applause—and beamed at his little boy. And I was on my way. The little musician.

And we're on our way and we can't turn back.

And that was the beginning of many long years of practice. A half hour after school and a half hour after dinner. The half hour after dinner was easy because my mother shrewdly gave me the choice of practicing the piano or helping her with the dishes. Naturally, I opted for the former. And she loved it. She would do the dishes and hum along as her boy would play the piano in the next room, her husband would read the paper, and Rich and Jim would scurry around on the floor. This was her family. And she was a happy woman.

The after-school practicing, however, was purgatory. My mother and I fought every other day. Half hour after school? No way, Jack. Not this pent-up-energy boy. I needed to blow off steam. I had a rocket in my pocket and I wanted to move! And we lived right across the street from the school and the two school yards. The fun yards. I could hear the kids playing. I could hear that high-pitched yelling and squealing that trips the wild-child switch in a kid's brain and sends his nervous system into the hyper zone. I could look out the window and see goofy stuff going on in the yards and, ohh, I wanted to be there.

"I don't want to practice today, Mom," I'd whine. "I wanna go and play."

My mother would try to maintain a calm demeanor. "You can play after you've practiced."

"But it's too long . . . I don't feel like it," I countered.

"It's only a half hour, Raymond," she said in that soothing way of hers that could be so infuriating to a young maniac.

Maybe I can bargain with her, I thought. My evil and conniving mind would stoop to any lie. "I'll make it up after supper. I'll practice a whole hour then," I blurted out.

"Raymond . . ." I hated it when she called me Raymond like that. "You can't fool me. I'm your mother. I know you won't do an hour after supper. You'll just make up another fanciful excuse." She was right, of course. And then she would get logical on me. . . . "You're wasting time as we're arguing. You could be out there before you know it if you start right now."

Her logic was unassailable. My last resort was rage. "I *hate* the piano," I shouted. "I don't want to practice ever again . . . I hate it!" What an act, bet she doesn't have a comeback for that one, I thought.

But she did. And it was apocalyptic, complete with a catch in the throat and a faux tear. "Well, then . . . let's just throw the piano out of the house. Let's just throw it in the alley. . . ." A faux sob. "I don't care anymore. You don't ever have to play again." And for emphasis . . . "Ever!"

Whoa, Mom. Hold your horses. Never again? I didn't mean I hate it *that* much! My brain reeled at her full frontal assault. Adults can always push it further than kids want to go. They have the psychic strength to beat a kid down. They always win. When they try it on each other, however, it's called war. Or murder.

"Okay, okay. I'll practice now," I gave in.

But she wouldn't accept her victory that readily.

"No. Don't practice . . . we'll just get rid of the piano. In the alley."

I didn't want to get rid of the piano. Hell, I *liked* playing the piano. I was good at it. She knew I liked it, and that's why she pushed that particular button. Adults can be so clever sometimes. I was beaten.

"Ma, I'll practice." And I headed for the basement rumpus room and began my Czerny finger exercises, as those high-pitched screams and giggles continued off in the distance. Torture!

This went on for the next two years until I changed piano teachers. Shygoltz was gone and I was now in the hands of a young teacher, Bruno Michelotti. A dance band leader and a real cool cat. He taught me virtually everything I know about music. Put a sheet of music in front of me called "Rag Mop," a hit of the day. Kind of a jump tune in a I-IV-V blues structure. Showed me stride piano with the left hand. Key of C—low C with the little finger on beat one, C triad an octave up on beat two, low G below C on beat three, C triad again on beat four. That was the tricky part, the long jump from low G to the C triad. But once mastered, stride piano became fun. Pumping an oompah beat in the left hand, with "Rag Mop" melody on top with the right hand, I thought, Hey! This is not bad. This is kind of cool. This has a little beat to it. A little jump thing. A little groove to it. And I played that stride stuff . . . without ever again having a fight with my mother.

I played stride until my second epiphany a year later: boogie-woogie! That's what really hooked me. And to tell you the truth, I am its slave to this very day. That rolling snake beat in the left hand. That repetitive mantra of hip-swaying sex rhythm. Over and over and over. Never changing. Never *needing* to change. Why? How could you get bored with it? It was the rhythm of the act of love. The rhythm of creation. The sway of a woman's hips. The thrust of a man's haunches. Hard backbeat on two and four. Implied seduction. Unstated but always understood penetration. And right-hand filigrees? My Lord, what a delicious Bach-like dance of fingers. Clean and precise. Joyous and spontaneous. With just a hint of sadness.

I heard a recording of the *Giants of Boogie Woogie*—Albert Ammons, Meade Lux Lewis (I love the Lux in the middle. The dictionary defines *lux* as being the "international unit of illumination."), and Pine Top Smith. And they were burning. Tearing up the ivories, melting the black and whites. And I was transfixed. Frozen in time for a beat and then released to bop.

I gotta learn to do that, I said to myself. Stride piano couldn't compare to boogie-woogie. Stride was white man's piano. A little stiff but well meaning in its attempt to groove. But, man, you hear a black guy playing boogie piano and it's all over. You've just got to do it. And I sat at our country German upright and worked on my left hand, over and over, trying to get that beat, trying to make that snake crawl out of my fingers. Trying to hypnotize myself with the mantralike repetitive rhythm. And I did it. I got the hang of it. I could do it! And my parents, those blues record collectors, loved it. My mother smiled and my father tapped his foot as he relaxed in his chair with his *Chicago Sun-Times*. I once heard him say to my mom, "That boy's getting good, Helen." And as John Lee Hooker said, "I felt so good. I boogied in the house!" And you know what? . . . My left hand eventually became the bass player for the Doors. That boogie-woogie technique and "lefty" and his Fender Rhodes keyboard bass combined to create the hypnotic drone sound of the Doors. All that practice gave my left hand the dexterity to become the foundation upon which the Doors' Bauhaus-like structure was built. The clean and efficient Mies van der Rohe bass lines were a natural evolution from that twelve-year-old Chicago boy's explorations and repetitions of barrelhouse boogie-woogie. You know the old joke: Tourist in New York asks a police officer, "Officer, how do you get to Carnegie Hall?" New York cop says, "Practice, practice, practice."

That took care of my left hand; now it was time to enter into the mystic. Into the blues!

It's the middle of summer. It's Chicago. And it's hot and humid and steamy. It's Tennessee Williams country, North. It's the long, hot summer. It's the sweat basket of America. As soon as you become active the sweat begins to drip off your body. But so what? You're thirteen years old, you're looking for something to come around the corner and just blow you away. To take you to a new psychic space. And for me it came in the form of the blues.

I was at Hoyne Playground, playing ball. And as you know, if you play baseball, the whole point of the game is to get up to bat. You want to hit! That's it. You only tolerate being a fielder because those are the rules of the game. You give the other team a chance to bat and you have to go out in the field and catch the ball. But who cares? It's boring. You just want to hit the ball. You want to be up to bat, all tight and coiled with your Louisville Slugger cocked and armed and ready to explode from its perch on your shoulders. You want to put your whole damned *body* into it. Like a woman. And the pitcher floats that softball up to you—slow-pitch softball in Chicago—and it's like a dream cloud and you just explode on it. Blast that sucker. Swing for all you're worth with all your power. And I was worth some pretty good power. I was pumping iron at home. I was working out, getting strong. I was up to about 135 pounds. I was thirteen years old and I was packing a touch of teen muscle. Semen and muscle, what a dangerous combination. I'd take out all my aggressions on the ball. "Just let me hit that ball, god-damn it! Just let me hit!"

It was our turn to bat. I was the second batter of the inning. First guy up gets a double. Oh, boy, man on second. It's always great to bat with men on base. You could hit the shit out of the ball *and* drive in a run. That, my friends, is the whole point of baseball. So I'm coming up to the plate, swinging my war club, and I'm just about to step into the batter's box when I hear, off to the right-hand side of the diamond, from a radio in the stands . . . a mournful sound. A sound unlike anything I had ever heard before. A dark blue wail. It was electric and emanating from a deep blue cavern. The mournful wail of a harmonica. And behind it was a backbeat on two and four. Hard and dark. And I heard an electric guitar playing some kind of a snaky I don't know what. I had never heard a guitar played like that. It definitely wasn't Les Paul and Mary Ford's "How High the Moon." It was as if the neck of the guitar had become reptilian and the frets had become its ribs. And, riding over it all, a man's voice. Full and deep and throaty. Full of an anguish and a passion and a *knowledge* that I'd never heard before. That I'd never realized even *existed* before. I heard that music and I just stopped and listened. I was about to step into the batter's box but I came to a dead stop. Staring in the direction of the music. And time stopped with me.

The guy behind me, the next batter, said, "Hey, Ray, get in there . . . get in there and hit, it's your turn. We got a man on second. C'mon, get in there. What'a ya waiting for?"

And I turned around, handed him my weapon, and said, "Here, man, you go ahead and hit. I gotta see what this is over here." And off I went, sacrificing the game's raison d'être, my precious turn at bat, to hear this music . . . this dark, mournful, unknown music.

I got to the source and still didn't know what this music was. I picked up the radio and saw where the dial was set. Far right-hand side of the dial, ethnic side of the dial. German, Polish, Italian, Greek, Lithuanian . . . and Negro. I looked at the guy who owned the radio and said, "This is great music." He was a hoodlum type in Levi's and engineer boots. Regulation uniform . . . even in the summer. What a Neanderthal.

"Yeah," he said. "These are some real cool cats."

"Who are they?" I asked.

"Fuck if I know," he grunted.

Well, my friends, I know now what it was. It was the *blues*. It was the South Side of Chicago. It was the music of descendants of Africa. It was black, and it was the blues. A unique creation on this planet. A musical art form unlike anything else that has ever existed.

I don't know to this day who the artist was that was singing to me on that hot summer afternoon. But he changed my life. He opened the door to the sadness of life. The pain and suffering of a love lost. The *tragique*. The French know it: *triste*. It could have been Muddy Waters, it could have been John Lee Hooker, it could have been Magic Sam, Sonny Boy Williamson, Howlin' Wolf. It could have been any one of a hundred guys. But when I heard that music I thought, Oh, my God! This is the most amazing music I've ever heard. It's got a snakiness. It's got a rhythm. It's got a fury . . . and a passion . . . and a *compassion*. The singer's voice was so full of wisdom, and so full of pain. Both existing at the same moment in time. It was mournful and deep and heavy. You know what it was like? It was like Russian classical music. Like Tchaikovsky and Prokofiev and Stravinsky. Also like Bartok and Smetana. Like a Chopin Polonaise. It was like Slavic music. Heavy and deep and mournful. Put that with a two-and-four backbeat and a I-IV-V, twelve-bar blues progression, and the Chicago boy enters heaven. The *blues!* That was it. Changed my whole life. Why . . . I even gave up my turn at bat . . . for the blues.

✺

In those formative years I was actually able to *see* the blues performed live. Not at a nightclub; that wouldn't come until I was older—but instead at the legendary Maxwell Street market, where my parents, when they were dating, bought their records. An outdoor market. A very big outdoor market in the quote-unquote "ghetto." Every weekend stalls lined the streets for blocks in every direction, selling a myriad of things. Junk and desirables of every description. Hair tonic to hubcaps. Tools to tires. Ladies' clothes to nylon hose. Kitchenware to shoe repair (while you wait). Gewgaws, knickknacks, gimcracks, and junk. Old bottles of a cobalt blue not used in bottle making since the discovery of its dangerous properties, but what a beautiful deep blue color. Old lamps, old pots and pans, old car parts, old clothes, old family photographs, old books, old drapes, old furniture, old records (not hip ones), old newspapers, old everything and anything. All spread out on makeshift tables of two sawhorses and a piece of plywood, or on a blanket on the street, or just held in the offerer's hands—sadly and entreatingly. And musicians on the corners. Street musicians begging a little spare change and playing gospel music and some, not many, playing the blues. That Maxwell Street market was filled with people and life and jive and experiences of an ilk this young boy had never seen before. It was like market day in the Middle Ages. Or a street fair in Islamabad. I was in a Persian bazaar. I was in a place of magic. And I was safe and secure. I was with my father. And his strong hand held mine securely as we walked into the magic.

My mother and father had grown up in that area of Chicago, the Bridgeport area. They had gone to school, dated, courted, and were married on the fringes of that ghetto and had many friends who now ran the regular businesses that lined the streets of Halsted and 14th. Clothing, shoes, wholesale cosmetics and barber supplies, hardware stores and delicatessens. My father knew a lot of guys down there. And sometimes he'd take me into one of the wholesale outlets and we'd buy, for instance, a barbershop-sized bottle of Vitalis. Had to, cowlicks everywhere. After you washed your hair you had to put something on it to hold down those insane energy swirls that would send your midwestern golden corn-boy locks careening off in a hundred different directions. And with three boys and one adult male, well . . . we poured a lot of Vitalis on our heads.

Sometimes we would go in and buy a pair of shoes from some of the guys he knew. Sid's Shoes. And he would introduce me: "Sid, this is my son."

"Hey, Ray!" Sid had to acknowledge my father first. Certain rules of masculine protocol had to be followed before a young pup could be recognized. "Haven't seen you in a long time. How's the wife, how's the kids?"

"Helen's fine. This is my oldest boy, Ray Jr."

"Good-lookin' boy, Ray," said Sid.

"Raymond, say hello to Mr. Bernstein," my father ordered.

"Hello, Mr. Bernstein. How are *you*, sir?" I had my polite hat squarely on my head.

Sid pumped my hand in a big bear handshake. "Well, I'm fine, Ray Jr. Thanks for asking." He pumped a few more times, grinned, and finally released me. What a bear of a man. Big and tough, like all the kids of the immigrants who survived the trauma of the 1890s diaspora.

"You know, Ray," he said to my father, "when that kid is ready to get a nice suit for graduation"—he turned to me—"what grade you in, kid?"

"Going on eighth grade, sir."

"You bring him down here and I'll fix him up with something sharp. We'll take him next door to my brother's shop. He's got all the latest goods." The brothers Bernstein were very fashion conscious. Very au courant—but strictly in a street-smart way. And ten months later I did it. For graduation from Everett School, my father bought me—from the Bernstein brothers—one of the sharpest suits I've ever worn in my life. It was a one-button roll in a deep and cool blue color. Not a business blue but a sort of crazed and electric blue. Very cool.

And I wore it with a pink "Mr. B" collared shirt. A wide-sweeping wing collar, all soft and pliable for the rolling under of the collar points. It looked as though the wings of a Pan Am Clipper or a TWA four-engine cross-continental flyer were attached to my neck. It was all the rage. It was simply "too cool." And, dig this, I wore that shirt with a *lime green* tie! To my grammar school graduation. Oww! Look out . . . the kid was sharp! Looked like Bo Diddley or something, with a whole jelly-roll kind of thing going on.

After we left Mr. Bernstein—Sid's Shoes—it was time for lunch, and my father introduced me to the delights of a delicatessen. It was the first time I had ever experienced a corned-beef sandwich. We walked into one of the delis down on Halsted Street and the divine smells hit my nose. I inhaled deeply and I thought, I am in meat heaven. The garlic and the spices from the steam tables . . . ambrosia.

Huge mounds of corned beef and pastrami and rye bread. All sliced and ready to go. Mountains of sautéed onions and Chicago hot dogs. On a grill, dozens of them with crisped skin, sizzling away. Just waiting to become one of those famous Chicago red-hots.

"You wanna red-hot?! Hey, kid, want a red-hot? Ray, you want a corn beef?" The jowly man behind the counter greeted my father. Another old friend from his youth, Marty Glickman.

"A pastrami on rye, Marty. Easy on the mustard," he called back. "Hot dog for you, Ray?" he asked me.

I nodded, salivating like a hound dog.

"Red-hot for Ray Jr., Marty." He thought for a beat, touched his stomach, and said, "Make it a corned beef, instead. My stomach's acting up again." (And now mine does, too.)

"You want mustard then, Ray?"

"Easy, Marty. You got a heavy hand, my friend."

Marty laughed and his jowls bobbled. Years of corned beef had disappeared into that maw of his, and it showed. He plopped down a couple of plates, piled on the grilled onions, and set a foot-high over-stuffed sandwich on one and what looked to be at least a two-foot-long red hot dog in a poppy-seed bun on the other. Wow!

I wolfed that dog. My father *inhaled* his corned beef. And we were stuffed and contented. I sat back . . . and burped. Man, what an experience. It was a nose experience. An olfactory experience like my aural experience of hearing the blues at Hoyne Playground. Another new world had opened itself to me. And I was ready!

We walked out of the deli happy males, and off into the swarm of the Turkish bazaar. Down Maxwell Street. On our way to the blues.

Because on the next corner . . . there it was. A guy with an electric guitar and a small amp—a cord running into someone's house to power it—and another guy on snare drum. And they were laying down the funk. Laying down a tinny, amp-distorted, primitive electric blues. And they were in a trance. Off in another place. The guitar player's eyes were closed and he sang into a small microphone. Songs of love lost and love found. Songs of bondage and songs of redemption. Songs filled with the tragedy and fragility of life on planet earth. His voice was a reedy tenor that cut through the air like a switchblade. The drummer's eyes had sort of rolled back in their sockets and only the whites were showing beneath half-closed lids. I thought at first he was a blind man, but he was just tranced out. And he was laying down a very insistent rhythm that locked into a pattern and never varied. The same little shuffle over and over; probably the very thing responsible for their trance state.

And I, too, was transfixed. This was what I had heard on the radio. But live! Dudes were actually doing it live, in the street. In the flesh. And the flesh was made funky. And, Lord, it was good. I thought, This is unreal. This is absolutely unreal.

I thought to myself, White people are not capable of this. There is a soul here, there is a grace, there is a dignity, there is a passion, and there is another place that you can go to that white people just can't. Not in the early 1950s. It was unheard of. It was an unattainable state of consciousness that was simply not allowed. It was labeled "Whites need not apply." Thank God, what has happened since is that rock and roll has opened up that area of passion to white people. We are all able to share in the power of the rhythm through the genius of blues masters like Muddy Waters and Howlin' Wolf and John Lee Hooker and Jimmy Reed and Little Walter. They unlocked the door for us and then the rockers ripped it off its hinges. Chuck Berry and Little Richard exploded! They were the twin inventors, the Castor and Pollux, of the empire of rock and roll.

Hail, hail, rock and roll
deliver me from the days of old
Long live rock and roll.
—Chuck Berry

Tutti frutti, aw-rooti!
—Little Richard

After graduation from Everett, a public elementary school, I entered St. Rita High School. A private parochial school . . . and all boys. The Catholic high schools were sexually divided. All girls, all boys. And it was very depressing. Guys. Nothing but pubescent guys. Two thousand guys at St. Rita. All sweaty, funky, horny, full of anger, full of semen, and ready for something. What, nobody knew . . . but ready anyway. Except, what are you going to do, take it out on each other? There's no reason to. It's just a bunch of guys. There were hardly any fights or any trouble at St. Rita. A couple of guys would shove each other once in a while. So what? It would never escalate beyond that because there were no girls. There were no girls around to show off for. It was just a bunch of guys. Two thousand guys. Man, it was depressing.

The classes were very rigorous, however. The teachers were excellent. Dominican priests in long brown monk's cassocks. Complete with hood and braided rope belt around the waist. It was a good look. Very scholarly, very medieval. God bless those men, they had devoted their lives to the teaching of young goof-offs. Young sperm bags with nary a thought in their heads except their dicks. High IQs, though. And the priests were actually able to get through to us. They all had a different style for accomplishing the impossible. Father Crawford would punch out your lights if necessary. He was the vice-principal and boxing team coach. Teachers could hit students in those days—in Catholic schools only, not in public schools. Although it rarely happened at St. Rita, the threat was always there, and by God it kept the maniacs in line, tethered on a short leash of fear. Father Foley, on the other hand, would make you laugh. He was the Latin teacher, and the dryness of that dead language required an antidote of levity and wit. He was brilliant. Father O'Malley's approach was to smother everyone with love, attention, and mothering. He would always commiserate with your problems. You could talk to him about anything and he was on your side.

Anything but sex, of course. The subject was taboo. They were priests and they were celibate. I always wondered how it was possible for them. It seemed so unnatural and yet they were good men. Plugged in and modern. Intelligent. Worthy of emulation. Every boy in that school had entertained the thought of joining the priesthood. All Catholic boys do. So had I. But the idea of never being able to dip your wick . . . well, impossible. And no pud pulling, either. Masturbation, my friends, is a mortal sin; and that means you will burn in hell forever and ever in the hellfires of eternal damnation. Not going to Mass on Sunday . . . you will go to hell and burn forever in the hellfires of eternal damnation. Knowingly eat meat on Friday? Hellfire of eternal damnation. Sex before marriage? Eternal damnation. Abortion? Most definitely hellfire! Use a condom . . . more hellfire. What a lot of burning and pain and suffering . . . and for all eternity. Lord, have mercy.

Eventually, I had to turn to the words of the heart master himself, Jesus the Christ. And in contrast to the official Catholic party line, they felt awfully good. They were: love, love, love. Love everything. Love everything and everyone! Love the whole, good earth and love thy neighbor as thyself. Love it all, my friends. It makes eminent sense. It feels real good. And we can *all* be the Buddha!

⁂

What got me through four years of high school was the radio in Chicago. Rhythm-and-blues stations. Al Benson and Big Bill Hill. DJs of soul and grit. The real stuff. On the radio and snaking. Al Benson all afternoon and early evening. Big Bill Hill from nine o'clock till well beyond midnight.

I'd come home after school, turn on the radio, and there they were. My heroes. The men. The giants. And it was all taken for granted by Al Benson.

"Here's a new single we just got in by Muddy Waters. Let's give it a spin. It's called 'Hoochie Coochie Man.' "

And he would play it. And it was incredible. The most soulful harp I've ever heard. The tightest groove. The most dangerous singing. And the most evil implications, simply by the nature of the song's existence and Muddy's performance of Willie Dixon's classic. . . .

> *I got a black cat bone*
> *I got a mojo, too*
> *I got a John the Conqueror root*
> *I'm gonna mess with you (Lord, have mercy)*
> *I'm gonna make you girls*
> *Lead me by the hand*
> *Then the world will know*
> *That's a hoochie coochie man.*

And the whole band hit the chord change! Little Walter, Otis Spann, and the boys, rocking. And the top of my head rose up. Kundalini uncoiled and set shivers up my spine. The band wailed. Muddy told you that he, indeed, was that hoochie coochie man . . . and I was gone again. What a fucking piece of music! Today it's a classic . . . then it was merely the latest single by Muddy Waters on

Chess Records. It came out of the void, unknown. And it was thrilling. It was part of a great wave of inspiration that swept over the blues men of South Side Chicago.

The radio was on fire with "hit singles," except they weren't pop songs. They were blues classics! And they were brand new. Fresh out of the recording studio, hot-pressed onto vinyl, rushed over to the radio station, blasted onto the airwaves, and roaring out of radio speakers into my fevered brain. Dionysus had entered me . . . through the ears!

And it was nonstop. "Here's a new record by Howlin' Wolf." And out came "Smokestack Lightnin'." It killed me. The repetitive riff of that great classic. No chord changes! One chord over and over. Hammering at your rhythm center. Over and over. Funky, dark, gritty, evil. Over and over. The same chord. The same riff. Again and again and again. Trance state . . . here I come. My radio was hypnotizing me. The Howlin' Wolf had me in his control. And his words . . .

Smokestack lightning, shining just like gold.
—Howlin' Wolf

And he would howl and cry like a lost wolf. Crying for his lost love. Alone and afraid, vulnerable and yet powerful. A man. A real mensch. What a voice.

And what on earth do those words mean? What is smokestack lightning and why is it shining just like gold? I still don't know. And I love it. So fucking mysterious. A man wailing like a wolf and the musical riff repeating over and over. Dark and nasty bends in the blue notes. The same chords, the same notes. Over and over and over, burning a hypnotic hole into your mind, consuming your consciousness. A mantra. A black American mantra. My later studies of yogic mantra meditation opened the door to India and the inner energy of the human form. Howlin' Wolf opened the door to Dionysus . . . and he leapt in through my ears.

"Here's a new one by my good friend Bo Diddley," Al Benson would say to me. "Who Do You Love?" And we were off again. This time riding that Bo Diddley beat. That African tribal drumbeat over which Bo so coolly floated his dark and dangerous words:

Tell me, hoodoo you love?
—Bo Diddley

Dig it. Hoodoo you love. The juju and the voodoo and the gris-gris and the hoodoo were all walking around in my room, after school . . . and in my brain!

And then John Lee Hooker would jump out of my radio—after a commercial for Dixie Peach Hair Pomade—and he would be singing his latest hit, "Boogie Chillun." And then Jimmy Reed would sing, "You got me runnin', you got me hidin'." Magic Sam . . . "I'm a king bee." It's all on my radio. It's all new. The classics are brand new and swimming in my head. All of this inspiration is on my radio and I'm fifteen, sixteen years old. I'm a sophomore at St. Rita High School with two thousand guys. Nothing is going on. I've never been laid. I don't know if I'd even kissed a girl. How do you meet a girl? How do you talk to a girl? But on the radio it was just smoking. It was pure sex, pure energy, pure power, and pure passion. And I loved it! My friends, the radio saved my life. It saved my soul.

Then . . . Elvis Presley on TV! A summer replacement show for the *Jackie Gleason Hour.* We always watched Jackie Gleason, a family ritual. Sid Caesar, too. And anything with Laurel and Hardy. *The Twilight Zone.* Boxing for my father and baseball, basketball, and football for me. That was the Manzarek family viewing regimen. Throw in some *Playhouse 90* and other TV dramas—great dramas in the fifties—and that's what we watched on the tube.

The summer replacement was on. My parents were watching, ritualistically, the *Tommy and Jimmy Dorsey Show*, the band for Jackie Gleason. And one of the guest artists that week was none other than Elvis Presley. On national TV! I was in another room, reading or pud pulling or doing something teenage. I wasn't going to watch a corny old big band on television, I was a blues boy . . . and my mother calls me. "Raymond! Raymond, come in here! You better see this guy. He's a real cool cat. You like this kind of stuff." And I hear from the TV, "Well, it's one for the money, two for the show, three to get ready, now go cat go!" I leap out of my chair, run into the living room, look at the TV and there's Elvis Presley doing "Blue Suede Shoes." What a killer! He just blew me away. Finally, a white guy

doing it. Doing the blues. I'd been listening to all the black guys
doing it. I wanted to be like them. I'm trying to imitate a black guy;
doing Muddy and Jimmy Reed on the piano, John Lee Hooker and
Howlin' Wolf to the best of my abilities—my limited abilities—and
here's a white guy doing the bop on TV. He was dressed in a cream-
colored suit, a dark shirt, and a cream-colored tie. Looked like he
was wearing blue suede shoes, too. He had Scottie Moore on guitar,
he had Bill Black on bass, and D. J. Fontana on drums. And they
were kicking it! They were rocking the boob tube. Elvis was singing
in that lush, deep voice of his and wiggling his pelvis in a most
Dionysian fashion. They had it! My eyeballs fell out of my head.
Wow! "I told you you'd like it," my mother said, grinning smugly,
when the song ended. "Yes, ma'am!" And then he did another. And it
was cool and rocking, too. What was so cool about it was that it was
a country kind of thing. It wasn't the big-city Chicago sound with
the mournful wailing that I was used to. It was a little . . . lighter. It
was white. Acoustic guitar on Elvis, stand-up bass, electric country
blues guitar, and drums. It was rockabilly. The soul of the black man
had entered into the white man. The honky could now understand
and *respect* the Negro. The promised land was in sight. And the
floodgates just exploded with rock and roll!

After Elvis was on TV, the radio went rock crazy. Little
Richard was on the radio doing "Tutti Frutti." Jerry Lee Lewis
doing "Good Rockin' Tonight." Chuck Berry singing, "Roll Over
Beethoven and tell Tchaikovsky the news!" Fats Domino, "I'm
Walkin'." Bill Haley and the Comets, "Rock Around the Clock."
Gene Vincent and the Blue Caps singing, "Be-bop-a-lula, she's my
baby." It was rock and roll madness. It was the first wave of rock
and the first time white America had heard anything like it. It was
wild and dark and dangerous. Every white kid in America went totally bonkers, totally insane, and just went absolutely fuck-crazy!
And the parents knew. . . . "This is the end. This is the end of Western civilization as we now know it. Our teenage daughters are completely gone. And they're listening to this wild, insane, crazed music.
This sexually explicit music." And the boys, who were sex mad to
begin with anyway, now had this thrusting, gyrating pelvic movement of Elvis Presley to try on the daughters of America. We went
mad!

I rocked my piano for all it was worth. I added all the great rockers to my blues men and I sang my lungs out to all the hits of the day, pounding that left hand while doing a glissando and then triplets with my right. I had long since moved out of the rumpus room, away from the country German Golem, and upstairs to the living room and a refined and tasteful spinet piano. And I smashed on that sucker. Altered the whole purpose of piano lessons. I was supposed to play Bach . . . and I did . . . but I loved to rock. Hell, my mom and dad loved it, too. As long as I got good grades and continued my classical music studies I could play anything my mad teen mind desired. And my fevered brain desired rock and roll and the blues.

⁂

When I was a bit older—in 1958—I actually saw Muddy Waters perform live at Pepper's Lounge on 43rd and Vincennes. The Hoochie Coochie Man himself. On the weekend. For his people. Pepper's was a cool and funky nightclub situated in the breadbasket of the South Side of Chicago. Neon sign, blood red, in the front window proclaiming PEPPER'S LOUNGE, daring you to enter. Wooden tables and chairs left over from another era—probably a speakeasy in the thirties—bar with neon under the bottles to give it that film noir glow and a bandstand no more than two feet off the floor on the opposite end. And on this weekend night of my baptism into paganism, the place was packed. Maybe 350 people . . . and three of them white . . . me and my two friends from school, Dick Ellman and Frank Mazzoni. Three white boys looking for the truth. And we found it in that neon juke joint.

That night, Muddy was playing for *his* people, *his* audience, the working men of Chicago. Men employed, like my father, in industrial automobile, aircraft, and agricultural manufacturing. Workers in the factories of the city of broad shoulders. Union men. Men with good-paying jobs. Men who gave an honest day's work for an honest day's wage. And now it was the weekend. They had money in their pockets. And they had come to see the great Muddy Waters, and they were ready for anything.

I'm drinkin' T.N.T. I'm smokin' dynamite
I hope some screwball starts a fight.

'Cause I'm ready, ready as anybody can be.
I'm ready for you, I hope you're ready for me.
— Willie Dixon

They were dressed to the nines. In a blues club. The men were wearing suits and ties. The women were coiffed, perfumed, and well appointed. Everyone looked good. It was a big deal, it was a night out on the town. The men of the South Side of Chicago were taking their wives or girlfriends to Pepper's Lounge for an evening of entertainment. For drinks and a show. Except in this case the showman was a shaman.

And Muddy was in great form that night. He had entered the alternate space occupied by mystics, artists, and the insane. He was on fire. He was the very definition of the term *blues man.* I saw one of the most incredible performances of my life. Muddy was absolutely spellbinding. Captivating. And he was home. He wasn't playing for a white college crowd. He wasn't playing at the Newport Jazz Festival for an audience of quasi-appreciative dilettantes. Hell no. Dionysus was in his temple and his devotees were in attendance. And he rocked us!

I want you to rock me
Rock me all night long.
I want you to rock me, baby
Like my back ain't got no bone.
—Muddy Waters

The band was deep in the pocket. Steady and insistent. Drums, bass, guitar, piano, and harmonica. A Chicago blues band. James Cotton was on harp—unfortunately, Little Walter had already gone off planet—and the great Otis Spann was on piano. Spann was the man. He and Johnny Johnson with Chuck Berry taught me how to play blues/rock piano. They were the masters of the craft. Listening to them gave me the way into the labyrinth. And the way was in the silence. The space. Here's what you do: You leave space for the guitar player to make *his* statement; maybe you comp a little behind him, play a simple little repetitive pattern as a foundation for him to float over. Allow him to make his musical statement . . . and then you answer him. You follow the same procedure with the singer. But when it comes time to do your own solo then *you* become the lead. The psychic energy is all yours. When I solo, *I* am the lord and master. I control the destiny of the song. All must obey me. I have a paroxysm, I go manic . . . and then I acquiesce. I harmonize again with the energy of the group. The collective energy. I become a cog in the gear, again.

And the secret is to listen. Listen to the other guy, give him his space, complement what he's saying with a few little punctuations, and then answer his statement with your own statement of wit and profundity. And . . . "practice, practice, practice!"

So seeing Otis Spann live was just the greatest. Being at that club and watching Otis and Muddy do it live . . . well, I'm adjective-less. They had entered the space beyond words. The space of energy and vibrations. The abode of the elementals. The essence. And they took us all with them. As the evening progressed and the blues continued to work its magic, the well-dressed men in their suits and ties, and their ladies all coiffed and bejeweled, began to become undone. The top button began to be unbuttoned, the tie was pulled down a little to allow space for the expansion and contraction of neck muscles not accustomed to confinement. M'ladies hair began to tumble from its fifties perch. A ringlet of hair falling loose and down onto the forehead. A now-moist forehead glistening with little beads of perspiration. A drop of sweat falling from the tip of a gentleman's nose. The heat was on the increase . . . and another round of drinks was served. People started to loosen up. The atmosphere started to darken and intensify. Restraint was tossed aside. Inhibitions forgotten. And the audience began talking to Muddy as he was singing on-stage. They were telling him, "Go, Muddy! Get it, man! All right, all night!" And in response he would do a little gesture, one of those little hip wiggles of his, or he would ever so quickly brush his hand across his crotch or, as the evening lengthened, quickly grab and squeeze the Morganfield family jewels. And a woman or two would shriek. A cry of delight. Of anticipation. I turned to look and ladies were giggling, their men moving with undulating grace behind now heavily lidded eyes. Pepper's Lounge had become electric. Man, what an evening. The passion and the raw power that had been unleashed were overwhelming to this white boy.

I realized then that I had entered into a different realm, a

Dionysian realm in which the forces of fecundity now prevailed. Europeans—Western civilization—would call it the darkness; but it wasn't darkness as a negative, it was the darkness of fecundity. It was the darkness of creation. The darkness of passion. It was where sex comes from. It was the regenerative powers of the earth. All of nature, all living things, everything regenerates itself from these dark forces. The Dionysian forces. In 1958 Chicago I had no idea what it was called, but I knew I was experiencing something I had never experienced before. And it was not European. It was not proper. It was not correct. But it was so full of passion and exhilaration that it was undeniably the way to live your life.

People were undulating and gyrating at their tables, at the bar, in the aisles, everywhere at Pepper's that evening. No dance floor. Tables had taken up that space. Muddy Waters was playing and the house was packed beyond legal limits. And rocking beyond Judeo-Christian limits. We were right up close, Dick, Frank, and I. And everyone was getting it on. Drinking, laughing, talking, wiggling; all husky and deep in the throat. You could hear the tone of people's voices settle down into a deeper register as the night uncoiled itself. Perhaps the alcohol had begun to take hold, but I think it was the Dionysian revelry, the passion, the spell Muddy was casting that was really responsible. Muddy Waters was casting a spell like a shaman. That's what was going on that evening. It was a shamanic ritual, and had we stayed till closing hour at four in the morning— we left at two A.M., and it was about as much as three novice white pups could possibly absorb—God knows what we would have been capable of. Why, we could have healed the sick. We could have raised the dead. We could have made the little girls talk out of their heads. If you were ready, ready as anybody can be. And . . . if you had your mojo working! And that night, *everyone* did. Lord, have mercy!

※

After I graduated from St. Rita High School and left behind, forever, those two thousand guys, I went off to De Paul University. Very good Chicago-area college, *and* co-ed. Yes, finally. Girls! In class with you, in the hallways, in the locker next to yours. There to be spoken to, laughed with, drooled over, and asked out on dates. Girls! How sweet and fine they are. I went crazy.

And because of that craziness I never really learned anything in class. My fours years at De Paul were, in hindsight, only for the purpose of extracurricular activities. To wit . . . girls and art. I was an economics major in the College of Commerce and that, along with the music school, the law school, and the graduate school of business administration, was located smack dab in the middle of the Chicago Loop. The heart of the action. Downtown central. The Art Institute was two blocks away. Orchestra Hall, the home of the Chicago Symphony, with Fritz Reiner at the helm, was down the street and around the corner. The World Cinema, a foreign-film art house, was right next to Orchestra Hall. Lake Michigan was three blocks away, due east. The Field Museum of Natural History—an amazing collection of dinosaur bones, American Indian, Egyptian, and Chinese art and artifacts—was within walking distance, as were the Shedd Aquarium and the Hayden Planetarium. The great Chicago Public Library was directly across Michigan Avenue, opposite the Art Institute. Hofbraus and beer *stubes* from the turn of the century dotted the downtown for your whistle-whetting pleasure, offering roast beef sandwiches on rye with German mustard for your consumption at great and long wooden stand-up bars, not unlike my first country German piano. Architectural landmarks by Louis Sullivan dotted the downtown Loop: the Marshall Field department store, the jewel box–like Auditorium Theater. (Within a decade, the Doors would actually perform at the Auditorium Theater. Being on that stage, looking out at the tiers of seats, was like being on the inside of a Tiffany lamp . . . a golden Tiffany wall sconce. Perhaps the most beautiful venue I've ever performed in.) And the streets themselves were in a constant state of bustle with businessmen, secretaries, shoppers, tourists, and skid-row bums. What a delicious stew, and what a setting in which to place a college.

So I dated girls and immersed myself in the arts. I saw the great and enormous Picasso exhibit of the late fifties. A touring show that Dorothy also saw when it came to Los Angeles. Destiny, huh? I saw, "live and in person," *Les Demoiselles d' Avignon!* I saw *The Three Musicians*. I had a small print of it on my wall at home. A cubist rendering of my two brothers, Rich and Jim, and my rock and roll trio—complete with family dog silhouetted on the right. When I saw it in person it was mind-boggling. The colors were so vibrant, the size was so overwhelming, the lighting was so dramatic that I almost fell to my knees. A genuflection and a sign of the cross in the Catholic manner seemed the only proper response to . . . well . . . God on canvas. This was not a reproduction. Picasso, the master himself, had actually put brush to oils and oils to canvas. *This* canvas! This very canvas that I was standing in front of, bleeding. And he had done it in 1921 and it was here! The real thing. Ahh . . . art.

I went to the World Cinema to see "foreign films." I saw Truffaut's *The 400 Blows*. Ingmar Bergman's *Wild Strawberries* and *The Seventh Seal*. Marcel Camus's *Black Orpheus* — my favorite. Michelangelo Antonioni's *L'Avventura*, a very adult flick of ennui and alienation. Emotions that I did not understand back then and I'm not sure I understand today. And I saw Orson Welles's *Citizen Kane*. A magnificent work of art. I've seen it fifteen to twenty times since that first viewing at the World Cinema. And does it stand the test of time? Does it stand up to repeated viewings? Do I *want* to see it again? Affirmative! Those are the questions to which a cinematic piece of art must answer a resounding "Yes." If it doesn't . . . it ain't art. Akira Kurosawa's *Rashomon* and *The Seven Samurai* get a resounding yes! I love him. And *Ran* was made when he was in his seventies. Perhaps his greatest work of art . . . at seventy-five! What a strength of will. And Bergman, in his late sixties, making the equally brilliant *Fanny and Alexander.* Pray that we can *all* be consumed with such an artistic fervor, such passion, at those ages.

The films I saw at that little theater next to Orchestra Hall were mind-boggling. I didn't know that sort of film could be made, could be *allowed* to be made. I wasn't much of a movie buff back in the fifties. Hollywood product. Who cares? James Dean, yes. Anything else, forget it. But the World Cinema opened my eyes to the possibility of *art* in the cinema.

☀

I did a lot of dating at De Paul University. Lots of good-looking women. A real melting pot of Irish, Italian, Polish, German, WASP, and Jewish chicks. Hot times and hot dates. Great and frustrating necking. It was the fifties, so girls were always trying to save themselves for their husbands. Man, drive you crazy with heat. You'd neck in the car. Clinches and gropings and tongues in mouths; arms and legs and tastes of lipstick and saliva and steam on the windows from the joint body hots. I was hard as a rock, she must have been lush with lubrication, we were "ready as anybody can be," ready for consummation, ready to bang the gong . . . and "No, no, no. Let's not go that far, Ray."

I was crazed. She couldn't pull back now!

"We have to, Barbara," I begged. "I can't wait any longer."

"No, Ray. I'm saving myself."

"For what?"

"I don't know. It's just not right." She gets religious on me.

"It *is* right . . . it's beautiful," I schemed. "We should make love . . . now. Here." I hesitated from saying please.

"I can't, Ray. It's a sin." Damn Catholic girls.

"It's not a sin, I promise."

"You can't promise that . . . only God can."

My hand is on her breast. It's full and hard and youthful. Steam is rising from the top of my head. She is beautiful . . . I think. I lust after her. I *want* this woman.

"Barbara, this is all a sin. Everything we've done tonight." I try logic. "Why not just complete it?"

"I won't do it, Ray. I won't . . . I won't."

I grab her and kiss her full on the mouth. Her tongue darts against mine like a snake. We suck on each other's tongues. I press against her, her leg is against my dick. Little Ray is pure throbbing gristle. He's crazed, beside himself. I have no control over him. He rules me. He wants to explode. I begin to undulate against her leg. I'm gone. I can't take it any longer. I've got to come! So . . . BAM! I ejaculate in my pants. Blessed relief. Shivers of ecstasy. I squeeze her against me. Warm time. God, that feels good! But now it's in my pants and no longer in my body. Uggh, what a mess.

I check my watch as the warm semen spreads around in my shorts. "I think it's time to go, Barb. I don't want your parents to be mad at me."

"Ohh, Ray, let's not go yet." She's steaming, too. She doesn't want to come down from her estrous high. I don't want her to, either. But the warm semen will rapidly cool and get real sticky . . . and, besides, I'm done. And she's not going to let me touch her lamb pit, anyway.

"No, Barb. I think it's better we go now." I start the car and off we go. Out of Marquette Park. To her home. I kiss her good night. I can't walk her to the door. I've got a huge stain of cold semen on my pants. How embarrassing.

"I'll see you in school, Ray." And it's over. And that, my friends, was sex in the fifties. Bummer!

Until my first love, that is. We met in my sophomore year. She was beautiful. She wore black leotards. She was blond and she was hip. One of my friends said to me, "Got yourself a beatnik chick, ehh, Ray?" We started fucking right away. Did it on my own bed in my own house. I brought her home—my family was away—we got naked, and I entered a woman for the first time in my life. Yes! It was everything it was supposed to be. I exploded into a condom and we were safe and sated. And then I discovered her flesh. The lust subsided and the poetry began. And being naked, on top of a woman, in some kind of late-adolescent love was almost divine. The softness of female flesh, with its pliability, its resilient firmness; with its eye-dazzling silky down, its intoxicating perfumed headiness . . . well . . . I'm in love. It's the best thing on earth. It's the consummation, the purpose, the *reason* for flesh. Hell, otherwise we might as well be made of wood.

We lasted three years. I went to California, she went to Europe.

※

My sexual knowledge was well taken care of. After all, how difficult is it? My artistic knowledge, however, still had a *long* way to go.

> *I'm sittin' here wondering*
> *if a match box'll hold my clothes.*
> *I ain't got no matches but I sure*
> *got a long way to go.*
> *—Carl Perkins*

Orchestra Hall was the scene of my next epiphany. Courtesy of Fritz Reiner and the Chicago Symphony. I would go on Wednesday afternoons, the matinee, and student tickets were two bucks. It didn't matter what they were playing, it was Fritz Reiner and it was going to be huge. Of course, the seats were the worst in the house, but so what? It was Orchestra Hall and it was only two bucks.

I paid my deuce and began the climb to the top. A great and magnificent auditorium spread itself out in front of me as I pushed open the doors on level six. I took a seat, head nearly against the ceiling, but it was just fine. An ornate and baroque ceiling, carved and filigreed, and a great sight line. It was like the first dip on a roller-coaster ride. A very steep angle. Had we been on a thrill ride, this would have been one of the scariest rides of all, looking virtually straight down. I felt a slight touch of vertigo. But there they were, the orchestra, tuning up. And the sound was glorious. The tuning cacophony. Always filled with possibilities. The sound of the void, out of which order will be plucked.

I didn't even get a program that day. I just wanted to sit there and let the water wash over me, let that sound come up from the orchestra, hit the ceiling, move across the ceiling to the top balcony and just wash over my head and chest and dip right behind me. I would always sit in the last row so that I could be up against the wall and have the music swirl around the auditorium and come right in over my head, around and down through my feet and back out through the balcony. A very sensual experience and the best way to listen to classical music.

Fritz Reiner took the stage. A hush fell over everything. And the music began. Soft and lush, wave after wave, building and building to one climax after another. It was oceanic, it was like the sea. Talk about waves of water washing over me. I was being inundated, drowning in a modernist lushness. It was glorious and I had no idea what it was. And it continued and continued; I never wanted it to end. It was so redolent of the sea that I was transported to the middle of the Atlantic Ocean. I was engulfed with water. And I thought, What is this music? Who is this genius composer? Who is this man?

It finally concluded and I was spellbound. I rushed to the usher for a program, rifled through the pages to the day's performance, and there it was . . . Claude Debussy, *La Mer*. My first time for live Debussy and my first time for *La Mer*. I became a fanatic. A Debussy fanatic. And then I heard him in Bill Evans's music. My favorite piano player and *he* was doing Debussy in jazz! Fantastic. That lushness. That early-twentieth-century French romanticism, that sheer beauty . . . in jazz? Well . . . I had to try that, too! I spent a lot of time working on those inner voicings, those tone clusters. And one of these days I may just get good at it. "Practice, practice, practice."

Some great theater was happening in the fifties. Broadway touring companies of the hottest plays and musicals came through Chicago on a regular basis, and student tickets were $2.50 for Wednesday matinees; the theaters were within walking distance of De Paul. I tried to see as many as I could. I saw Tennessee Williams's *Suddenly Last Summer* with Diana Barrymore in the role Elizabeth Taylor played in the film version, which also starred Katharine Hepburn and Montgomery Clift. You really ought to see it. It's on videotape. But on stage, wow! When Diana Barrymore screams out at the end, "They had devoured him!" it was like a bloodcurdling shriek of pain from the hell mouth of a soul in terrible anguish. It froze everybody in the audience. The power of her performance. The agony of those lines. "They had devoured him." Overwhelming.

Next season it was Rip Torn and Geraldine Page in *Sweet Bird of Youth*. What a play. What great writing. What a performance! Tennessee Williams's *Sweet Bird of Youth* with Rip Torn as Chance Wayne and the incomparable Geraldine Page as the incomparable Princess Kosmonopolis. It doesn't get much better than that . . . and for $2.50. I loved it. Theater in the fifties was inspiring. I wanted to do that, too. I wanted to be in — or write — or direct plays like that. I wanted to be a part of that energy. I wanted some meaning in my life. I wanted that passion that I saw on the stage. I wanted in!

And then it was *West Side Story*, with Chita Rivera and Larry Kert from the original Broadway cast. I didn't know *what* to expect. Romeo and Juliet as gang kids in New York? Could work. Leonard Bernstein/Stephen Sondheim music . . . well, that had to be good. Shit, it was brilliant. The music was inspired. Great Aaron Copland–like motifs. Great rhythms. Ballads of love and loss that still swirl through the jukebox of my brain. Hot, smoking, incendiary Jerome Robbins dancing! And tragic love . . . and death. What more could a young college man ask for? It's the best musical theater I've ever seen. The culmination of American music, dance, and theater. It's the high watermark of what a Broadway musical can be. And I wanted to do that, too. I wanted all of it. I was greedy and lustful and deeply desirous of that kind of passion. I wanted that kind of commitment . . . to art.

And so did Jim Morrison. He had, in one way or another, seen, heard, and experienced the same artistic things that I had. All these little epiphanies are part of the soul of the Doors. These little moments of light and clarity and inspiration are what brought us together and what we tried to infuse into our music. Jim, too, was a devotee of Tennessee Williams. He loved his body of work, and knew it well. Even fancied himself as a bit of a Chance Wayne. At his college in Florida they had staged *Cat on a Hot Tin Roof*, and Jim was the set designer. Whether he acted in the play or not, I don't know. But what he did with the set was inspired. He had a slide of a cancer cell—Big Daddy is dying of cancer in the play—projected on the back wall of the stage. And Jim had that cell enlarging ever so slowly, enlarging through the entire course of the play. Until at the end of the play, when it is found out that Big Daddy has *not* kicked the cancer and is in fact *dying* of the disease, Jim had the cancer cell filling the entire back wall of the stage, pulsating, eating . . . devouring everything. "They had devoured him!"

Jim was into the same things that I was into. He went to the film school at UCLA because he had seen the same films I had seen. He'd seen *Black Orpheus* and *The Seventh Seal*. He'd seen Death and the Knight—Max Von Sydow—play chess. Gambling for the Knight's very life. The life of Antonius Block. Jim loved Bergman. The bleak and haunted landscapes of the great Swedish master. Both exterior and interior. The existentialism. Everything seen through a glass, darkly. But also the never-ending courage of his puppets. His characters' courage to face life. To dare to live it. To be alive, and to live through the terror . . . that we are alone. Jim had seen *Rashomon* and *The 400 Blows* and all the other first crashings of the Nouvelle Vague and he was in love. In love with the possibility that *he* could be an artist. In love with the idea of freedom! Freedom of expression, freedom of thought. The freedom to *be*. And when it came time to decide what to do with his life . . . when he arrived at the crossroads, at that existential moment . . . he chose UCLA. The Film School. Just as I did.

You got to meet me at the crossroads.
Meet me at the edge of town.
Outskirts of the city.
You better come alone . . .

He was drawn to the cinema, just as I was. For both of us it combined all the arts. It combined theater, photography, music, acting, writing . . . everything. And there were no experts! There were geniuses, but no experts. Jim said to me . . . , "The thing about cinema is there are no experts. Anyone can know the body of work. The entire history of film is only about sixty years old. Anyone can know its complete history. Anyone can be an expert. I love that about the cinema." And he was right. All you had to do was study, and the entire history of world cinema could easily be digested. *We* could be experts . . . and artists . . . and free men.

These are the things that put me into the Department of Cinematography at UCLA, and these are the same things that called Jim Morrison out of the Florida swamps to the setting sun of the Western dream and UCLA. And our task became, how to incorporate our artistic backgrounds into the Doors. How do we bring all of this good stuff into the Doors? How do we bring the drama, how do we bring the depth of emotion, how do we bring the pathos, the joy, the sorrow, the terror into rock and roll music? How do we bring the terror, indeed. *That's* what the Doors are all about.

chapter three

destiny and the ucla film school

I first met Jim Morrison at the UCLA Film School. The University of California at Los Angeles. We had enrolled in the Department of Cinematography, seeking a study of the *art* of the cinema. Jim and I, both being apprentice "artistes," had heard the seductive, siren call of the muses and found it irresistible. And it came from the West. From California! Mythic land of surf, palm trees, chicks, beatniks, hot rods, and freedom!

The West is the best.
Get here, we'll do the rest.

Jim and I met through our mutual friend John DeBella. A big weight lifter/poet from New York, DeBella was intelligent, obtuse, and sometimes clownish. Somebody once called him the intellectual Huntz Hall. Never learning to drive a car only added to that image.

John was my cameraman on my student movie *Evergreen*. He was also Jim's cameraman on Jim's student movie. It had no title and has long since disappeared. The student movies were our term papers. You completed one for the end of the semester, at which time the students—and I mean *all* the students—assembled in bungalow 3K7 for a weeklong session of disembowelment and psychological mutilation. At five marathon screenings, we viewed one another's films and critiqued them. The teachers sat in the last row of the small theater and watched their charges devour one another. You see, each director had to stand in front of the assembled smart-ass, wise-guy intellectuals (the students) and receive his or her fair share of verbal abuse. Or, as it was called, constructive criticism. Man, it could be brutal. I saw sensitive young artists reduced to tears. And Jim's film was pretty much raked over the coals.

I remember his film, and the thing about his misunderstood 170 project was that, basically . . . it was poetry. It was cinematic poetry. It was a juxtaposition of images that really didn't have any relationship to one another in a linear, narrative form. But after five minutes went by, it became a collective "whole." It became a poetic piece. I thought it was excellent! It was nonlinear; it was purely experimental. And it was fun. One shot had Jim doing a great hit off a huge bomber. You know, a spliff, a doob, a blunt, a joint. Jim takes this monster hit, eyes and cheeks bulge out, and he cuts to an atomic bomb explosion. Ka-*blam!* Associative editing. Sergei Eisenstein did it first. Jim was in the tradition.

Another sequence, a bunch of guys (the crew) having a little party. College guys goofing, drinking beer. They were throwing darts at a *Playboy* centerfold hung on the wall. The *Playboy* pinup was hung upside down. It was lit from the side, and as the darts were going in there was a strange ninety-degree angle of shadow, light, and actuality. Completely disorienting and most effective. The sound track had American Indian peyote chanting and musique concrète.

In the Oliver Stone movie *The Doors*, Oliver tried to re-create Jim's film based on what I told him and what I'm now telling you. Of course, he went completely over the top. A grotesque exaggeration. And how he turned Jim into a disciple of Adolf Hitler, well . . . perhaps someone ought to look into Mr. Stone's psyche; into what I perceive to be his latent anti-Semitism, and not-so-latent fascist tendencies. I like to think that little student movie is as revealing of

Oliver's real problems as anything he's ever done. It's all there in capsule form. A wonderful reduction of psychotic leanings.

And what a misreading of Friedrich Nietzsche. Typical Leopold and Loeb–type of misinterpretation. If you don't understand the concept of the *Übermensch,* Oliver, don't quote Nietzsche. Don't do what the Nazis did. Don't interpret the warrior's freedom from the lowered state of consciousness of the first three chakras. That only begets a Hell's Angels type of man. It uses the will to power as a justification to be the bringer of death instead of a bringer of joy and creativity. The lowered consciousness shouldn't approach Nietzsche. He's too dangerous. Nietzsche would have you leave all your preconceptions, all your childish beliefs, all your fears, and step into the light of freedom and divine responsibility. He would have you become a creator, if you dared. A creator who was responsible for the continuation of this existence. A lover of life. A dancer. A proud, bold, laughing man who delights in all the nuances and dangers of this all-too-brief life of ours. Not a naysayer or an extinguisher of life, but one who embraces it all and says, *"Again!"* And if you don't understand that, don't get too close to the fire. It's highly volatile. This heat is definitely more than you should approach, Mr. Oliver Stone.

And, for God's sake, don't put your fascist, Hell's Angels interpretation onto Jim Morrison's student film. There wasn't any *"Sieg heil,"* Aryan-nation business in it. That's in your head.

Here's what happened, and here's what I told Stone.

Big John DeBella had a girlfriend named Elke. Big, blond German girl. (They were a good fit; their kids would have been giants.) They're shooting film at Jim's apartment over on Goshen in West L.A. John's got the camera trained on the TV set. One of those too-fat, too-large all-American TV sets that people used to have in the old days. A real piece of furniture. Blond wood. Fits all decors. And Elke was on top of the TV set (you could actually stand on those monsters) wearing a bra, panties, maybe a little filmy sliptop for discretion, and black stockings. Long stockings with a garter belt. Very sexy, with high heels on top of this big piece of furniture. And she's doing a very Germanic bump 'n' grind! Jim shouted over the rock and roll music that was playing, "Turn the TV on, turn the TV on!" DeBella reaches over, turns on the TV, does two dial flips, and what should come on the screen? Scenes from World War II,

Hitler, stormtroopers, and Nazis marching through Berlin, or Prague, or the Sudetenland. And Jim says, "Leave it! Leave it! It's perfect." So he's got this German girl, in a black négligée, on top of the TV set, doing a nauch girl routine. He's got Nazis on the screen and American rock and roll music is blasting. It's great!

Somehow or other, Oliver Stone perverted this into the bizarre, strangely anti-Semitic tract that he put into *his* version of Jim's film. And then it goes up on the big screen as the truth, as reality. And people see the movie and think, That Jim Morrison was one sick dude. But it ain't Jim, you dig? It was the Stone. My friend's student movie was a much lighter, much friendlier, much funnier kind of thing. You see, we were all heads at the time. That's the whole point of it. The whole point of the UCLA Film School in those days—the sixties—is that we were all heads. Everyone was high. Everyone was giggling and laughing and just having the grandest time. That's what that intoxicant does to you. The good green herb that grows on God's good green planet is a mild intoxicant. Slightly psychedelic and far less deleterious than alcohol. And it's only for adults. Children aren't allowed to smoke pot or drink alcohol in my universe. But for grown-ups . . . it's a delightful thing that takes you into another state of being. That puts you into a very silly, funny state. And at times a very perceptive state. I suppose that's why it's illegal. It enables you to actually see through the bullshit. You begin to see the lies and the motives for the lies. And the powers that be can't have *that*. They can't have the populace pinning them. They can't have the people saying, "Ah-hah, I see what you're up to!" Because if we could see behind the curtain we'd all rise up and tell them, "Stop it!" That's what they're afraid of. "Stop cutting down the forests! What's going to make the oxygen if you cut down the trees?" "Stop using artificial fertilizers and deadly pesticides! How can we eat the food if the soil is depleted and the fruits and vegetables are covered with poison?" "Stop the burning of fossil fuel! How can we breathe the filthy, hydro-carboned air?" "Stop the exploitation of the working man; the common man. Give him a decent wage and working conditions! Or else how can he support his family? How can he live?" "Stop ruining the children's minds in your terrible schools! Teach them love and respect! Nurture them! Or else how can we have responsible adults? How can we have a contented citizenry without education?" And most important . . . "Stop war! Stop the killing!

Love thy neighbor as thyself and do unto others as you would have others do unto you."

It's all so simple, isn't it? It's what the sixties were all about. It's why we were in the streets, protesting, fighting the Establishment. Trying to get them to just STOP! We were trying to remake the world in a more decent fashion. To love the world and all its tender, fragile lives. Plants, animals, fishes, birds, people. All living together in harmony, a symbiosis. All dependent on all. Perhaps someday we can return to those goals and actually accomplish the transformation that was dreamed of in the sixties.

> *Let's reinvent the gods.*
> *All the myths of the ages.*
> *Celebrate symbols from deep, elder forests.*

So marijuana is illegal and alcohol is not. Shit-faced drunk versus pothead hippie. Mean, drunken, wife-beating, car-wrecking, child-abusing, fighting, swearing, brawling, puking alcoholic is allowed to buy his booze at the corner liquor store. But flower-child hippie can be thrown in jail for a joint. It doesn't make any sense today and it didn't make sense back in the sixties. Especially for us Venice Beach dwellers, who were usually walking around in a very silly, funny state. And Jim Morrison's student movie was a very silly, funny, very poetic film following the aesthetic lines of Jonas Mekas's *Film Culture* out of New York City. And in the manner of Stan Brakhage and his famous *Dog StarMan.*

Now, I also had made a couple of films while I was a student at UCLA. Starring my girlfriend at the time, Dorothy Fujikawa (who has long since become my wife; we're still happily married and still together and it's been a wonderful relationship). She was an art student. We became lovers and she became my leading lady. She had a vulnerable intensity that the camera just adored. A great look and a great way of delivering a line. She had a quality in her voice that gave the lines I had written for her a truth and life of their own; far deeper than what I had originally conceived. I heard the words being spoken in my mind's ear . . . but she brought them to *life.* And her eyes. She could look into you and through you. No games, no lies. She was in her moment of time. In the suchness, as Zen master and author D. T. Suzuki would say. And she was cute as hell.

The best of all the student films were screened twice a year for the public at what was called the "Royce Hall Screenings." The faculty would select a dozen or so films to be composite-printed and projected up onto the big screen of Royce Hall. Dignitaries were invited. Critics were invited. And the carved, Spanish-style doors were flung open to the public as if to say, "See, we're not insane here. We can do good work." And, oh, how the faculty would strut. Because Royce Hall was *the* prestigious auditorium on the entire west side of Los Angeles. Symphonies were performed there, great jazz artists and intense folksingers of the time performed there. I saw the Modern Jazz Quartet play there. The great Odetta sang there. The Los Angeles Philharmonic Orchestra performed there. I walked in one afternoon on a rehearsal of Stravinsky's *Rite of Spring* and it was absolutely overwhelming, standing at the foot of the stage—Zubin Mehta was the conductor—and I'm watching the L.A. Philharmonic power their way through the *Rite of Spring* . . . in Royce Hall. Thrilling.

Well, lo and behold, a few months later a Ray Manzarek student film, *Induction* (and the year before that *Evergreen*), was to be shown at the Royce Hall Screening. It was certainly an honor for me. I was very pleased with those films. They worked. And I was very proud of my cameramen, John DeBella and Christopher (Kit) Gray, and my actors, Dorothy Fujikawa, Hank Olguin, and Kathy Zeller.

Jim's movie, unfortunately, didn't make it into Royce Hall. He was panned by the teachers and panned by many of the students. What a bunch of dolts! They just didn't get it. However, they did appear to take great delight in raking Jim over the coals. Jim always rubbed a lot of them the wrong way—those people were called squares—hell, he's still doing that. And they're still squares.

"Nonlinear, Mr. Morrison." "Doesn't make any sense." "You've violated basic rules of screen direction on the shot with the darts, Morrison." "Male chauvinist! Why's the girl in her underwear?" "What are you, a stoner or something?" "Fascist!" "This isn't the way we make movies in America, Morrison. This is like a Communist would think."

So his film didn't make it into the screenings . . . nor did it make it through the projector. He had trouble making splices. Jim's forte was not splicing two pieces of film together with the tiny little tape and the tiny little 16mm splicer you had to use. But it *was* an extremely poetic movie.

It doesn't exist anymore. It was tossed out with three hundred or so other student movies at the end of the semester. The only films that were saved were the ones that had the negative cut and a composite made for the big show in Royce. The other films were like term papers—seen once and tossed. Just too many to save. So Jim's is gone. Into the dumpster and into the ether.

The two films that I directed, however, still exist. They are on the Doors' laser disc special edition called *The Doors Collection* on Universal Home Video. We can look back and see what the UCLA Film School was like in 1963, '64, and '65. The early days. The golden years of the film department. In *Evergreen* you can see the actual Venice Beach apartment we lived in. Ray, Dorothy, and Jim (after we started the band he moved in with us). And you can, today, see me and Jim together on the screen before the Doors were even conceived of. A party is taking place in *Induction* and Jim and I exchange a conspiratorial moment together. It's brief, but there we are, young pups together.

There was a lot of controversy about *Evergreen*, my student directorial debut. A scene in the shower had to be cut before it would be allowed to be screened for the public. It was an innocent scene. It was just two young people fucking in the shower. Or so it appeared. "Hell, what's wrong with that?" I asked the faculty. "Well, Ray," came the stentorian reply, "we just can't have that sort of thing in the Royce Hall Screenings." Another rumbling voice said, "You've just gone too far, young man. We simply can't allow it. Not in front of the public." A third voice: "Ray, we love the film, just cut the shower scene, that's all."

Here's the scene. Dorothy's in the shower with Hank Olguin, who billed himself as Henry Crismonde at the time. (The first time the Doors played together was at Hank's house; a legendary pink house on the alley behind the Greyhound bus terminal in Santa Monica. Hank was the only guy I knew who had a piano.) They're in the shower making love. The two of them aren't naked. Dorothy's wearing underwear and Hank's wearing underwear and I'm shooting up high, around their chests, so it looks very sensual but nothing is really going on. The water's streaming down and it's a hot, steamy, sensual kind of scene. And then . . . Dorothy's leg comes up around Hank's waist!

"Okay, now make it look like . . . all we need is one leg, honey . . . bring one leg up around Hank's waist. The outside leg. That's it. Good. John, roll camera. OK, Dorothy, one more time. Action!" I yelled.

They're supposed to be naked, you don't want to see anybody's underwear, right? So I was a little bit below the thigh line of the underwear, about mid-leg, angled down. Dorothy brings her leg up and it looks like . . . well, it looks like they're doing it in the shower, folks. I mean, it looks like she's brought both legs up and she's on top of his tool and they're doing the dog right there in the shower. It's a great shot. Then I cut to the most controversial shot of all; the shower head, streaming and steaming and shooting out water. Very symbolic in a very naive student way, basic bottom-line Freud. But nevertheless a very effective shot. And the faculty freaked.

"That's symbolic of a male orgasm, and you cannot have that in a student movie. We simply can't allow it." (It was a surprisingly repressive time, those psychedelic sixties. It was a battle between the pro–status quo Establishment types and the wild, tribal freedom-loving young people. The Establishment called the sixties the "swinging sixties," but we knew the decade was really "psychedelic." And therein lies the difference. The status quo moves into the future backward. Always looking at the past. That's why they used the term *swinging*. An archaic concept, it connotated a Rat Pack/gangster/Las Vegas aesthetic. They all wanted to be in Frank Sinatra's rat pack, "swinging" with the "Chairman of the Board" and have a lot of "broads" hanging on them. It was a lounge lizard mentality and it ruled the day—Christ, perhaps it still does! The adventurer, however, moves into the future facing the unknown. Daring to look into the emptiness and *create* the new world. In love with life, immersed in the energy and trusting in the divine will that guides the destiny of this planet. In other words, trusting in ourselves. Because destiny is ours to control . . . if we have the courage. Back then we did, and they hated us for it.

"So if you don't cut, Mr. Manzarek, your film will not be shown in Royce Hall." And there it was. Censorship. For the first time in my life I was being censored. It didn't feel good. It felt very leaden and repressive. It felt like they were trying to take away some of my energy and enthusiasm. To bring me down to a lower level of consciousness. To place the yoke on my shoulders. The yoke of decent, wholesome, traditional values. Well, my acid-infused eyes had seen through all *their* lies. I had seen the swinger hiding behind the minister's cloth, the alcoholic behind the senator's three-piece suit, the lust for death behind the general's stars, and I was going to fight the bastards. Any way I could. And here was my line in the sand. Of course, here also was my opportunity to have my film shown in the prestigious Royce Hall Screenings. And I wanted that. Wouldn't you?

I looked the three-member faculty panel dead in the eye, took a deep breath, put on my most obsequious smile, and said, "Okay, I can make some cuts." And that was it. I was in Royce Hall. Now the question became how to reap the ego rewards while still maintaining any sense of integrity. In other words, how to get *Evergreen* up on the big screen and still stick it to them.

So I made two cuts—can't be a total liar—one in and one out. The shower head! Who cares? It's better with it in but it doesn't change anything if it's out. Dorothy's leg going up around Hank's waist. Now that's the shot I would not lose. That's *the* shot of the scene. I punctuated it with the opening of the Jazz Crusaders' "Young Rabbits." A great POW! And a gliss down by Wilton Felder, Wayne Henderson, and Joe Sample coinciding with the leg lift. The drums and bass kick in at a furious pace and I cut to Hank running through a pedestrian tunnel under Santa Monica Boulevard. Very symbolic. Very student, but very effective. Hell, it got a rise out of the faculty.

I made the cut and delivered the final composite print to Gary Essert (he ran the technical side of the screenings; he was cool, a student, and he could care less about a leg and a shower head and young rabbits) just one day before the first showing. The next night it went up on that big, sparkling, light-reflecting screen. The way I wanted it. The way it was *supposed* to be. And it worked, man. The audience gave a little collective gasp at the leg lift and then applauded as Hank hightailed it through the female pleasure channel with the Jazz Crusaders smoking. I was so happy.

Afterward, a couple of the teachers were outraged.

"You promised! You said you were going to cut that scene."

"Hey, I made some cuts," I retorted. "I cut the shower head."
"But you promised," they whined.

I smiled. "The audience loved it."

So when the censors, the nut-butters, come around, and if you can get away with it, you tell them whatever they want to hear—they're insane, you realize—and then you just go ahead and do whatever you want. But don't harm anybody, of course. And don't do evil.

☀

Now UCLA itself, the actual schooling at UCLA, was incredible. Jim and I learned the "art of the cinema" from some truly wise and inspirational men. The prevailing philosophy of the time was "art first, commerce second." Today, unfortunately, the equation has been reversed. But back in the sixties we were taught to emulate the French New Wave. Directors like Godard and Truffaut and Robert Bresson. Akira Kurosawa and Kenji Mizoguchi from Japan. And Yasujiro Ozu. Satyajit Ray from India. Fellini and Ermano Olini and Pasolini from Italy. Ingmar Bergman from Sweden. The Maysles brothers and Leacock/Pennebaker from America. Artists, filmmakers, poets all. Men of vision, subtlety, and courage. Men who dared to go against the commercial grain and attempted to make a statement about the human condition. Isn't a probing of the relationship between God, man, and existence more involving than an explosion, gunfire, and a car chase? What kind of film stays with you longer, the popcorn-and-candy movies or an attempt at art? It's obvious. Art wins.

So our teachers at UCLA wanted us to be artists. To strive for technical perfection, of course, but only at the service of art.

One of the teachers at the film school was none other than the fabled French director Jean Renoir, who had done *La Règle du Jeu (The Rules of the Game)*, the son of Auguste Renoir, the Impressionist painter. Renoir the director brought romance to the school; that great and fecund French romanticism. Unfortunately, I never had a class with him. I was about to take his directing class but he had gone. The summer had gone by.

Summer's almost gone.
Summer's almost gone.

Where will we be,
When the summer's gone?

He was there for only one year and I had signed up for the directing class in the fall, but he was gone by the end of summer. However, they brought in a substitute for Jean Renoir . . . and it changed my whole life. None other than Josef von Sternberg! I was actually, in the fall of 1964, taught directing by Josef von Sternberg. The man who directed the incredible Marlene Dietrich movies. The man who *invented* the Marlene Dietrich persona and directed her and lit her and photographed her in *The Blue Angel, Shanghai Express, Morocco, Blonde Venus, The Scarlet Empress* and *The Devil Is a Woman.* Classic films and, believe it or not, American films. (How on earth did he get away with it? Such films are not allowed to exist in the American psychological spectrum. Our field of comprehension is much narrower than where von Sternberg would take us. Of course, eventually they did stop him. Like Orson Welles. The studio system has a vested interest in the way things are *supposed* to be. The American Dream as viewed from the lowest common denominator. That puritanical sense of what is allowed and what is not allowed. And how terribly self-righteous it is.)

So Josef von Sternberg taught our directing class, and it changed my life. He changed my outlook on art. He was the one who took me into that world of dark, brooding film noir, of haunted German Expressionism, and I loved it. He opened my mind to the possibility of making movies that were deeply passionate, mysterious, and psychological. Perhaps even slightly kinky, who knows? I know he had a profound effect on the Doors' music. A music that was slightly kinky and slightly Germanic. After all, the Doors did do Brecht and Weill's "Alabama Song," or "The Whiskey Bar," as it has come to be known. Not exactly a top-forty ditty.

Oh, show us the way to the next whiskey bar. . . .
I tell you we must die.
—Brecht and Weill

The next semester, Jim Morrison took the very same class. An interesting coincidence; the two guys who would eventually, inevitably create the Doors were worshiping at the feet of the same teacher, the great man himself, Josef von Sternberg. The creator of Marlene Dietrich. And maybe that's why the Doors are what they are today.

Von Sternberg took us into bungalow 3K7, the screening room where all the films were shown, and said, "Boys and girls. Students. I'm going to show you *The Blue Angel.* I'm going to show you *Morocco.* I'm going to show you *Shanghai Express.* Watch and learn. In particular, watch the lighting. If anything with my films, I'm most pleased with the lighting. I'll show you how I lit Dietrich when we go to the soundstage. I call it the butterfly light. High up, straight overhead. It casts the shadow of a butterfly under the nose. Of course the cheekbones must be perfect." And with Dietrich they were. A beautiful woman exquisitely lit. She exuded an aura unlike anything I had ever seen on the screen before. An aura of knowledge, sensuality, wisdom, and vulnerability. She had been hurt by love, wounded by love, but she was still a romantic. A person who believed in the awesome, terrible power of love; the overwhelming force of love. In defense she wore a cynical, jaded facade but you could see she was ready to surrender herself; but only to the right other. Only to a very significant other. Her man would have to be a romantic, like herself. Worldly, but still deeply romantic. In essence, an artist. Regardless of the profession, an artist.

She was most radiant in *Shanghai Express,* my favorite film. What lighting and what a performance. Shanghai Lily, a "coaster," as Dr. Harvey calls her. Wouldn't you like to have bedded *that* woman? And Anna May Wong. Brilliant. Von Sternberg took a good-girl actress of Chinese-American B-movies, quickie, boilerplate films, and turned her into the sensuous Dragon Lady. So cool, so beautiful, so dangerous. Her look could freeze you to the bone. And her words . . . slice, you're bleeding. These were the two sexiest women I had ever seen in my life. And I thought, I want to be married to both of these women. This is what I want. I want the Blonde Venus and the Dragon Lady. The two of them were absolutely gorgeous, sensual, stunning, brilliant women. And if I may say so, Dorothy Fujikawa comes as close to putting those two women together as any woman I've ever met. Perhaps that's why we're still married, and certainly why she was the star of my student movies.

And what Dietrich did to me she did to Jim in spades. He was in love with her. Mad for her. That's where Elke, the German blonde in the black négligée on top of the TV set in Jim's student movie, comes from. An homage to la Dietrich. Jim and I discussed her sultry persona in *The Blue Angel* in great detail. I sometimes think Jim even adapted a bit of her smolder for his *own* stage aura.

And of course von Sternberg's *mise en scène* was discussed endlessly. We talked about his lighting, his sets, his filling of the negative space in front of the camera, his stories of men as fools for a blonde goddess, his Orientalism, his exoticism, his languid pace fraught with psychological tension. Just like, as I later came to realize, Doors' songs, Doors' concerts. We didn't know it then in our pot-induced musings, but we were preparing for our art form of the future. For the Doors.

☀

Later that year, at semester break, Dorothy and I hitched a ride up to San Francisco with Judy Raphael, a fellow film student. Her father had given her a new car and we had only a Navy-surplus beat-up Chevy and Dorothy's too-tight-for-an-850-mile-drive Volkswagen. Judy was going to see friends in Berkeley and offered us a spare bedroom in their large Victorian home. We tried to get to San Francisco as often as possible to absorb as much real *city* culture as we could cram into a brief stay, and this offer of free transport and lodging was too good to let slide. San Francisco had a sophistication and an ambience that Los Angeles still hasn't attained. Probably never will. Just to walk the streets of that charming, European-style city made us feel like adults. There was a cosmopolitan air to the comings and goings of the people of San Francisco that gave us a feeling of rightness, a feeling that culture mattered, a feeling that *art* mattered. L.A. was a cowboy town in the middle of the desert. Hot and dry and hicksville. Fascism and racism, however, found the climate most hospitable. The jackbooted motorcycle cops were a Nazi costume designer's wet dream. Midnight blue uniforms, black boots to the knee, helmets and sunglasses, sleek Harley-Davidson between their legs. And virtually all of them Aryan. What a chill they could send up your spinal column. Of course, that shiver of fear is a fascist's delight. They thrive on such misdirected sexuality. But for us, seeing one of those man-machines approaching in the rearview mirror was a sight of terror. They seemed capable of any atrocity. "Oh, God, please don't let them stop me." I held my breath as they came up hard and fast—they always traveled in pairs—and then they passed. And you could breathe and resume normal thought. The evil had gone by this time, but it would be back. Anytime you hit the freeway there was a chance of confronting the evil again. The city fathers must have loved the intimidation of the populace. Keep them in line through fear. Man is basically a beast, a sinner, weak and evil. Give man a chance and he will commit a crime. Man must be policed. What a philosophy! Christ, relax, you guys. Just take a deep breath and relax. Smoke a joint or something but just relax. Please!

In San Francisco it *was* relaxed. That's why we loved it. Everything seemed looser and freer up there. You could be a lover up there. Hell, you could be a loser up there and still enjoy life. In L.A. you had to be a winner, hang the cost—especially in the film industry—and you still do. San Francisco played an altogether different game. It was called . . . elegance. I liked that game better. Much more civilized. Much more sophisticated. Much more *adult*. So off we went in Judy's new car. Off to Mecca. Looking for art. Looking for inspiration. Looking for the new paradigm.

And we found it. And it was Beat. As in beatific. As in Jack Kerouac, Allen Ginsberg, Michael McClure, Gary Snyder, Gregory Corso, and so many other poets. And it was in Lawrence Ferlinghetti's City Lights Bookstore. A little handbill was on the bulletin board in the City Lights Bookstore, and it read: "Poetry! Free Way Reading! Gary Snyder, Philip Whalen, Lew Welch—Welcome Home!" The place—something like the Longshoremen's Hall—and the date. "Hey, that's tomorrow night," I said to Dorothy. "These are real beatniks. I've never seen an actual Beat poetry reading. Have you?" "No," she said excitedly, "let's go!"

Now Jim and I had both read *On the Road*, Jack Kerouac's great tome of freedom. For me it was 1959 back in Chicago. A little paperback edition, back-pocket size, that fit snugly in the red-tagged pocket of my blue denim Levi's. Very rebellious with illustrations of scenes from the book on the cover; kind of a come-on to the potential customer, your everyday, garden-variety teen-angst-rebel. Chicks, car, open road, and a guy in a blue-and-white striped sweater with a bandanna around his neck. Looked cool. But it also looked French to me. And with the name Kerouac, I thought it might be a European existentialist novel. Thank God it wasn't. It was American. All-American! And it was free and wild and hip and cool and dangerous and sublime all at the same time. A cascade of images. The first book I ever read that said, "There is another way to live, kids. You don't have to put on the yoke of conformity. You don't have to become a button-down mind in a gray flannel suit. You don't have to become a corporate entity. You don't even have to remain a Judeo-Christian-Muslim God-is-other kind of person if you don't want to. You can find the Buddha, the Christ within. If you dare. If you have the courage to throw off all convention. All dogma. All orthodoxy. All traditional, time-honored, acceptable, long-standing Establishment codes of behavior." Can you stand free, the book asked. Can you stand alone? Can you stand on your own two feet and shout to the heavens, "I am alive!"? Can you look life square in the eye and say, "I am all things!"? Can you simply say, "I am!"?

That was the challenge of *On the Road*. And that was its promise. To head off into the Wild West and find that one last freedom. The freedom of the mind.

The West is the best.
Get here, we'll do the rest.

I resolved to head west as soon as I could. Jim Morrison did the same. I came from frozen Chicago, he came from swampy Florida; but we both came for the same reason—freedom! I suppose if Jack Kerouac had never written *On the Road*, the Doors would never have existed. It opened the floodgates and we read everything we could get our hands on: *Go*, John Clennon Holmes; *Howl*, Allen Ginsberg; *Gasoline*, Gregory Corso; *A Coney Island of the Mind*, Lawrence Ferlinghetti; *Peyote Poem*, Michael McClure; *Naked Lunch*, William Burroughs; *The Subterraneans, The Dharma Bums, Big Sur, Doctor Sax*, Jack Kerouac; *Letter from Kyoto*, Gary Snyder; *The New American Poetry 1945–1960*, Grove Press.

All mind-benders, soul-twisters, heart-openers, foot-tappers, bone-crushers, eye-wideners, refreshers, inspirers, instigators, and general *fine* things. I suggest you read them all—and there are many more—and get that little taste of the possibility of freedom that Jim and I felt.

So there we are, Dorothy and I, in San Francisco, and an actual Beat poetry reading is taking place. Now the Beat scene is virtually over by this time, '63, '64 . . . except everybody is still around.

There's just not a media hype going on anymore. But the poets are alive and well and still writing and still reading. And they are reading right here and now and *we* are going! Yes! And here's the bill: Lew Welch, who has just come out of the forest after being in solo hibernation—isolation for the last two or three years—is going to read his new poems. Gary Snyder has just come back from Japan after studying Zen Buddhism and Asian culture and calligraphy and *ukiyo'e* and *umeboshi.* He's going to read his new poems. Philip Whalen—yet to become a Zen roshi as he is today—is also reading his new and fierce and wild and inspired poems. What a night, huh? Dorothy and I were definitely going.

The next night we borrowed Judy's car and drove across the Bay Bridge into San Francisco from Berkeley. We arrived at the Longshoremen's Hall and the place was packed! Must have been two thousand people—at a poetry reading. And it was electric! The air was charged with a psychic electricity and the crowd was attuned and energized and ready to GO. There was so much vitality and energy in the air. I thought I was in Russia, early revolutionary Russia, and Vladimir Mayakovsky and Anna Akhmatova and Mikhail Bulgakov were all reading. The house lights dimmed, a hush fell on the room, and Lew Welch took the stage. He started to read . . . and it was sizzling, it was crackling. I mean, it was just amazing. He was trying to be peaceful and gentle, telling about the forest and diving into his soul, and what was going on in there and what was going on all around him. In that beautiful northern California redwood fern-floored forest. But his joy and enthusiasm were palpable. And the audience picked up on it. It tickled their receptor sites and they began to call out to him, "Go, Lew. Yes! Get it, Lew." And once again the electricity took over the auditorium.

After Lew Welch, and a standing ovation, with two thousand people shouting "Lew! Lew!" applauding and stomping for him and Lew grinning and bowing in a stiff, embarrassed, and most charming manner, out comes Philip Whalen. He takes the microphone, sets his papers on the podium, and proceeds to read at the fastest pace I've ever heard. He is smoking. Roaring. Racing. He's riding on the energy in the room and he's definitely breaking the speed limit! The energy of the audience is so intense he's just surfing across the top of it. Borne aloft by static electricity, he's going as fast as he can possibly go. And clear and precise and well enunciated. Nothing is being lost. Ten minutes into his reading, some guy stands up and shouts out, "Read slower! Philip, for God's sake, read slower." Whalen stops the runaway train, pauses, looks at him, and says, "Listen faster!" and just jumps right back in. Tearing on furiously for another half hour. Whew! We were exhausted. But then out came Gary Snyder. Dressed in a Japanese schoolboy's blue uniform, he was absolutely mesmerizing in his Zen-like explorations of man, God, and existence. He was very humble and very intense at one and the same moment. He read for over an hour, stepped away from the podium, bowed to us, and left the stage. A huge roar erupted from the audience. Another standing ovation. Gary came back out, smiled, bowed again, and was gone. The evening was over. Dorothy and I looked at each other, spent. "Wow!" she said. "What a night." I could only nod my head and smile.

When Jim came along with *his* poetry in the summer of '65, I thought, Man, this is going to be fantastic. Jim has that same kind of aura about him that the Beats had. He's got that same literary gift. And he definitely was gifted. He could string words together like no one I'd ever met. Words that would probe your hidden places, your secrets, your joys and delights, and . . . fears.

Words got me the wound and will get me well

But this was all in the yet-to-be. This was all to come off. Off in the distance. Undreamed of. However, the fates did have a sneak preview in store for us. Just a taste of the fortuitous coincidences to come. Just a glimpse of our partnership yet to be. And just two days later.

Playing in Berkeley, on a community theater screen, two days after our poetry intoxication, was the West Coast premier showing of Jean Genet's now-famous, then-infamous film *Un Chant d'Amour.* That's right. Jean Genet, the legendary French Beat/existentialist novelist, famous for *Our Lady of the Flowers, Querelle* (Fassbinder made a film of this novel), the theater pieces *The Maids* and *The Blacks,* and many other writings about homosexuality, depravity, sensitivity, love, anguish, philosophy, and delight in the senses. I had heard of his film; highly controversial, banned in France, it played a few times in New York and was pulled from the Bleecker Street theater by the New York City vice squad. And here it was, in Berkeley. We saw a small ad in the local paper, said, "Holy shit!" and ran out to buy tickets immediately.

And two nights later, there we were. At a Bernard Maybeck–like brown Craftsmen public-assembly facility—must have been part of the University of California complex. Another one of those wonderful redwood buildings that dotted the hillsides in Berkeley. A line had formed, and at 7:45 the doors were opened. We pushed in hurriedly to get seats in the middle. Not too close, not too far back. Just the right spot for this truly "special" event. How they could get away with showing such a controversial film in a community theater I'll never know. I guess it's just the way things are in Berkeley. After all, someplace in America has to be hip besides New York City. And the Bay Area is it.

The room filled quickly. The house lights dimmed slightly at precisely eight o'clock, and a teacher type stepped in front of the screen. He told us we would be seeing "a film by the French novelist and playwright Jean Genet. It is entitled *Un Chant d'Amour,* or *Song of Love.*" A few titters from the audience, a defiant remark or two, "Yeah, man. We know that," and "That's why we're here." A shuffle of feet by the professor, a nervous throat-clearing, and he continued: "But first, an anthropological film from Africa, *The Giraffe Hunt.* A film of the Bushmen. I think you'll find it quite fascinating." And he left the stage. Five or six people applauded. Must have been his wife and faculty members of the Anthropology Department of Cal Berkeley.

So that's how they got the Genet film, huh? It's part of an Anthropology Department screening. Okay, fine. So what? Well . . . let me tell you so what! Here's the first flick: five skinny guys on the plains of Africa stalk a female giraffe for an ungodly long time. They creep and stalk and jump behind a bush and crawl and hunker down and run behind a tree—only four trees in the entire film, a very dry place. Lots of tall grass, however. Finally they creep up on this giraffe, spears at the ready, and proceed to hurl their dull weapons at this poor animal. Three spears bounce off, one sticks in the shoulder, another in the rump. These guys grab the fallen spears and start poking at the giraffe's flanks. Someone draws blood. The audience is disgusted, people are booing. Some reprobate calls out, "Kill the damn thing and let's eat!" Secretly, we *all* hope they do so the film will end. Can we just see the Genet, please?

But no, those spears have only opened flesh wounds. Those aren't killing wounds. The poor animal could maybe bleed to death, eventually, but it's not going to fall now . . . and the movie's not going to end now. The giraffe, goddamn it, runs off! And the five guys follow it! Three with spears—the other two spears are stuck in the animal—and two with long knives. And they run after the giraffe. And it runs, too. Off into the distance. And then the camera begins to run after the Bushmen. Bouncing and bobbling over the veldt of Africa. And we're all running, and it's awful! They run and stop and catch their breath and run again and stop and eat and run and finally it gets dark. They stop and go to sleep and we all sigh in a collective relief. "Thank God, it's over. The giraffe got away." Hell no! The next shot, fade in, the next day. They pick up the blood trail and off they go . . . for the next three days! We were going insane. It was going on for an hour and a half and these five guys are still on the blood trail of this beast. And, you'll love this, the movie is in black and white! No colors of Africa. No gold, no sunsets, no blue sky. Nothing but shades of gray. And even more sadistically . . . it's silent! No music! Nothing. You see, it was an anthropological film. It wasn't made for entertainment. It was made as a study of tribal mores. We were dying . . . like the giraffe. Which finally did. The film finally ended as the five guys began cutting the meat off the bones of this poor, dead animal. What a bummer!

Intermission. Everyone bolted for the door. Air, please! Large throng of people, milling about, pot smoke in the atmosphere. Dorothy and I moved off to the side of the Maybeck building and lit up a number. We inhaled the mild intoxicant, got properly elevated, and moved back inside to our seats in the center. Now, finally, it was time for Genet. The room was packed with people, the lights dimmed, the film began. It, too, was in black and white and silent, but we knew that going in. The newspaper told us. The title, *Un Chant d'Amour*, hit the screen—a big round of applause. *Mise-en-Scene: Jean Genet.* Applause, whoops, shouts! We were ready.

And a tale of homosexual love in a prison presented itself to us. Steamy, racy, extremely sensual. And yet very little actual contact or nudity. It was all desire and the frustration of non-consummated desire. Men in cages. Knowing a lover is in the next cell but being unable to touch the love object. Terrible frustration creating only a deeper desire. The more that physical release was denied, the more carnality was enflamed. And what heat. The screen was practically smoldering. At least a third of the audience was gay. They were in a swoon of lust. Murmuring noises spontaneously erupting from deep inside the body. Little sighs of desire and grunts of want. All inadvertent, of course. A nice counterpoint to the silent film. A kind of human sound track—differs with each showing. Pure chance. John Cage, our great American composer who worked with silence and found sounds and chance, would have loved the film. Hell, John Cage may well have *lived* the film.

Here's a couple of shots: camera dollies past four cells, inmates languishing in various states of deshabille. The first three are white guys—in almost a tableau—the camera moves slowly, languidly exposing each cell and dwelling on each motionless occupant. Caressing each young man, who stares back into the lens. Into us. And of course they were *beautiful young men,* as John Rechy calls them in *City of Night* (the great Los Angeles homosexual novel that lent its title to lines in the Doors' song "L.A. Woman").

Are you a lucky little lady in the
City of Light . . .
Or just another lost angel . . .
City of night.
City of night. . . .

The camera finally arrives at the fourth cell and it's a slender, glossy black young man—dancing his tight ass off. Moving to unheard music. Bopping around his cell . . . and completely naked. Can you see the contrast with the first three cells? What a surprise! And what a fine young man with a fine full member. It bounced about in perfect time with his dancing rhythm, forcing a few people in the audience to actually cry out, "Ohh, my." How happy they were. Another example of the power of the cinema.

Another shot—two inmates, lovers, separated by bars and a thick, dungeonlike wall between their cells. Too far apart to touch. However, one prisoner of love had found a small hole in the stone that went through to the other cell. He put his tongue to the hole, his lover put his tongue to the hole on his side, and in their minds they proceeded to lick each other's bum holes, feeling the air, the vibrations, the heat, and saliva from the other cell. All very discreet but very sensual. And then one of the prisoners put a straw into the hole and proceeded to blow into it. The other inmate placed his cheek to the hole—the straw came just to the edge—and received the breath of his lover in the adjacent cell. He made love to that blowing breath. He let it caress his cheek, his eye, his ear . . . and he was in love. And we, the audience, were getting hot. Homo, hetero—it didn't matter. This was so seductive and sensuous we could all identify with it. That breath caressing our own cheeks, the breath of a lover upon our faces. My hand went to Dorothy's thigh and I became even hotter. And harder. I rubbed her thigh and then placed her hand on my crotch. She held my swollen tool for a moment, squeezed it twice, and whispered in *my* ear, "Later," as she put her hand back in *her* lap. Whew! I was on fire. Genet had done his job.

The film ended—far too quickly, it was only thirty minutes long—much applause, house lights up, I turn to see the audience and who is sitting two rows behind us, a little off the left, but Jim Morrison! At this hippest of hip events in Berkeley, 450 miles from UCLA, who should be there but half the Doors.

I call to him, "Hey, Morrison."

He sees me and grins. "Ray."

"What are you doing here, man?" I ask.

He pauses for a beat. "Well, I've come to see the movie. What about you?"

I smile. "Ditto."

He says, "Some flick, huh?"

I can only nod my head, raise my eyebrows, and say "Whew!"

"Hi, Jim," Dorothy says. "I kind of thought you'd be here." And we both look at her.

Is she psychic, too? I thought.

Jim's head tilts slightly to one side and he does his lazy-boy grin. "Why?" he asks.

Dorothy smiles. "You're hip," she says, and takes my arm. We head out into the Berkeley night. The three of us. Together, as if it were fated. In the same place, at the same time, for the same art. It was simply meant to be.

※

There was an easy camaraderie amongst the heads at the UCLA Film School. A relationship of artists mimicking the bohemian lifestyle of the twenties. We were all dadaists in a way. All a little mad, a little over the top, and all in love with life. John DeBella was a poet. Jim was a poet. I was the jazzer-musician-blues guy. Phil Oleno was the Jungian. Felix Venable was the older, boozier talker. Dave Thompson was the mod rocker. Bill Kerby the intense writer. Kit Gray the consummate eyeball cameraman. Frank Lisciandro was the artistic wanna-be. There was a small New York contingent, but most of the other guys and girls were from scattered places around the country. Very few locals.

Of all the people at UCLA, I would say Jim was the guy I liked the best. Now, I wouldn't say we were "best friends" or anything like that, because I think that's rather a childish concept. I don't think artists of our age group—twenty-something—have a best friend. Except for the work. (The work itself becomes your best friend. That's one of the reasons people become artists. What you do is your friend. We're all basically lonely guys finding companionship and solace in art.) We instead had circles of acquaintances. Groups of people with whom you felt comfortable, with whom you shared common views. In our little circle there were perhaps a dozen or so people whose apartments were always open to you, at any time. You could drop in night or day and find a welcome. People simply went over to each other's "pads." Dorothy and I would be doing something at home on Fraser and DeBella would walk in, maybe with Phil Oleno. Or Morrison would walk in. "Cool, man. Want to smoke a joint? You had dinner yet?" The greetings were always cordial. "What's going on? What do you guys want to do?" Or we'd go over to Jim's place. A very nice apartment on Goshen. He lived by himself, although he had a girlfriend, Mary Werbelow. She was his junior college sweetheart. She had followed him out from Florida. And was now going to school at L.A. City College—LACC—on the other end of town, but she was around with regularity. And, man, what a fox. We're talking nectar here. Hard, tight body. Large breasts, firm and pointy. Long, straight auburn hair. A body and a half and a dancer of sorts—she went on to become "Gazzari's Go-Go Girl of 1965," a nightclub on the Sunset Strip; the Doors played there in 1966. Jim wanted her to stop the go-go-girl, shimmy-shake dancing and go back to school. Continue on with her education; she was taking painting courses and seemed to really enjoy them. But she was seduced by fame and thought being Miss Gazzari's 1965 was the be-

[handwritten margin note: Friend — the Real Answer]

ginning of her show-business career. Unfortunately, it *was* her career. That was all the fates had written on her slate: "Queen of the
Sunset Strip—Summer 1965." Nothing more ever happened. In her
hubris at the time, however, she had constructed grandiose fantasies.
And when Jim told her to go back to school and continue with her
painting, she told *him* to go back to school and get a master's degree.
She told him *his* career was hopeless—she didn't like the Doors—
and his band was going nowhere and he would never amount to anything. I don't think he ever saw her again after that exchange. She
had fallen into the tar pit of Hollywood—"show business," don't you
know—and it destroyed their relationship. She was just too naive,
too beautiful, too foolish to make the right choice. Ten years later I
heard she was a belly dancer at a Greek restaurant in Honolulu, "the
Mad Greek," or the "Passionate Greek," or "the Flaming Greek," or
something equally Dionysian. However, she *had* taken up painting
again, as Jim told her, except the moment had passed. Jim was
dead. It was all too late.

Dorothy and I would just drop in on Jim. Anytime, whenever
we were in the area. He lived between UCLA and Venice, near the
Veterans Hospital complex on Wilshire and San Vincente. And just
a few blocks from the "Lucky U," the UCLA Film School's *numero
uno* Mexican restaurant. All the hip students went there. It was Jim's
favorite, too. We spent many an afternoon at the Lucky U nursing
our meager change into a divine meal. Rosario Carillo was the chef
and he was a genius! His food was inspired. *Chile colorado*, rich and
succulent with beef and spices in a deep mahogany sauce. *Chile verde*,
his pork-and-tomatillo classic, light and green and fiery hot. He also
put the *chile verde* on his burritos. Great, rolled-up flour tortilla tubes
of *frijoles* and meat. The burritos were our main source of nourish-
ment for almost two years. His tacos were crisp and beefy. Tostadas
were warm-weather and luncheon fare. A mountain of salad, atop
chile verde, atop refried beans, atop a crisp fried tortilla. Ambrosia.
And when you were flush, well, shit . . . *chile rellenos!* The best. The
best I've eaten, anywhere. Mexico City, La Paz, Cozumel, Cabo San
Lucas, Cancun—nowhere better than Pancho's—as he liked to be
called. Large, mild *ancho chiles*, stuffed with longhorn cheddar
cheese, dipped in an egg batter, fried on a large short-order grill.
Served slathered with *chile verde* and pork on top, with a side of *frijoles
refritos*, his wonderful Mexican/Spanish fried rice, rough chopped

salad, and three corn tortillas. Wash it down with a Tecate and lime. Heaven. Mexican heaven. We ate there maybe three times a week. I loved it. All the heads loved it. Jim loved it. And it was all fresh and real. Pancho made everything himself, including his beans. I never saw the man open a can. And it was an open kitchen, behind the bar. You'd eat and drink and watch him cook. And I never saw a can. Man, it was good food and good *for* you. What more could you ask from a meal?

Now, Jim had a very nice apartment. Not that it was elaborate or anything, but obviously his mother and father had a couple of bucks. As Dorothy said, "Look, he has an electric blanket. He must have money. Look at his socks. . . ." I said, "Look at his socks?" She said, "These are expensive socks, Ray." She was like Sherlock Holmes. "Okay, honey, if you say so." "He's got money," she said. He certainly had a substantial investment in books. They filled an entire wall of his apartment. His reading was very eclectic. It was typical of the early- to mid-sixties hipster student. Classics—both Greek and Roman—French Symbolist poets, German Romantics, modern novels—Hemingway, Faulkner, Fitzgerald—existential-ists—Camus, Sartre, Genet—contemporary literature—Norman Mailer, especially *The Deer Park,* Jim's favorite. He identified with the character Marion Fay. And lots of beatniks. We wanted to *be* beatniks. But we were too young. We came a little too late, but we were worshipers of the Beat Generation. All the Beat writers filled Morrison's shelves, along with James Joyce and Céline. All the antecedents to the Beat Generation, the same books we *all* were reading. That is what influenced and inspired Jim Morrison. And we borrowed freely from these authors, as homage. For instance, Céline's *Journey to the End of the Night.* One of our songs is called "End of the Night."

Take the highway to the end of the night.
Take a journey to the bright midnight
End of the night.
Realms of bliss, realms of light
Some are born to sweet delight
Some are born to the endless night

(and from William Blake)

God appears and God is light
To those poor souls who dwell in night.

Jim was borrowing and quoting and paying homage to his masters, as I was borrowing quotes from all my favorite jazz and blues musicians, and even a Western classical riff now and then. For instance, the solos in "Light My Fire" are based on John Coltrane's "Ole" from the album *Ole Coltrane*. The same repeating chord structure, McCoy Tyner, comping behind 'Trane—he's in D minor, we're in A minor—over and over. A minor to B minor in 4/4 time. Coltrane's "Ole" is in 3/4 time. You know, like a waltz—1-2-3, 1-2-3—as opposed to 4/4 time—1-2-3-4, 1-2-3-4. When it came time to solo in "Light My Fire," I suggested we quote Coltrane on Robby Krieger's song. It worked so well that Robby and I would extend our solos for upwards of ten to fifteen minutes in concert. It was such a joy to float over that repeating figure and to interact with each other that we never got bored with the piece, even though we played it at every concert.

Other examples: I quote, verbatim, a Thelonius Monk line from "Straight, No Chaser" in the Doors' song "We Could Be So Good Together." The opening organ passage of "When the Music's Over" was inspired by Herbie Hancock's "Watermelon Man." The organ solo in "Take It As It Comes," J. S. Bach. "Break On Through," Stan Getz and João Gilberto's bossa nova album *Getz/Gilberto*. This was one of our favorite "relaxing" albums. John Densmore and I were really into the whole Brazilian samba groove. And this record was the coolest. We'd get high, open the windows on Fraser, light some incense, put *Desafinado* on the turntable, and float away to Brazil. "The Girl from Ipanema" would walk down that beach at Corcovado and we would, indeed, say, "Ahh."

Even the name of the band itself is an homage to William Blake, who wrote in "The Marriage of Heaven and Hell," "If the doors of perception were cleansed everything would appear to man as it is . . . infinite." And Aldous Huxley takes that line and calls his book on mescaline experimentation *The Doors of Perception*. And Jim takes that line and calls the band the Doors.

So Jim's bookshelf was very eclectic, but also standard, de rigueur *Evergreen Review*, New York City hipster, San Francisco, City Lights Bookstore, beat jivester, jivenik, cool cat. In other words, we were all reading the same thing. John DeBella had the same books that Jim had, that I had, that Phil Oleno had, that Dennis Jacob had, and a lot of other guys had. Except Jim had more! A wall of books. And it seems he had read them all; nothing in reserve for future reading. He was able to tell you the author and title of any book he had. He would challenge people, "I'm gonna turn my back. Take a book off the shelf, open it to any page, read me a line—maybe I'll need more, maybe a couple of lines—and I'll tell you the title of the book and the author of the book. If I'm wrong . . . I'll buy the beer. If I'm right, you buy . . . Corona or Tecate." Jim Morrison drank free beer 95 percent of the time.

※

What we did at Jim's apartment was talk. Tecate, a toke or two, and we were all motormouthed. Film, literature, the political situation, the H-bomb (always lurking below the rational level of consciousness), Vietnam, Kennedy/Johnson, and the contrast between elegance and shit-kicking, and music . . . classical, jazz, and rock and roll. Coltrane was discussed, his modal compositions influenced by his tenure with Miles Davis. His repetitive chord changes so well handled by McCoy Tyner. McCoy Tyner's relationship to Bill Evans. Bill Evans's relationship to the piano music and tonal coloring of Claude Debussy. Debussy's lyricism as contrasted to Stravinsky's primitivism in *Rite of Spring*. Carl Orff's *Carmina Burana* as even more basic and primitive. I first heard *Carmina Burana* at Jim's apartment and was transfixed by its power. Big, rhythmic, Gregorian chant voices, ostinato bass lines—very moving. (I recorded it many years later with Philip Glass as producer. We did an electronic transcription of the piece, complete with jazz-rock guitar and rock and roll drums.)

Film, of course, was our main topic of conversation. Here's how the conversations would go. . . .

"I think *Vivre sa Vie* is Godard's best work," says Alain Ronay as he sips an aperitif.

"*Breathless*, Alain," Jim comes back. "*Breathless* is his masterpiece."

"You're both wrong," I passionately object. "*Contempt* [*Le Mépris*] with Brigitte Bardot and Jack Palance and Fritz Lang. *That's* his best film!"

"Could be," Jim agrees.

"It can't be *Breathless,*" says Alain. *"Breathless* is immature. His first work. Too cutty."

Jim sips his Corona (Alain didn't buy this time, he wouldn't play the "Name the Book and Author" game anymore. Jim beat him six times in a row. Alain said *"formidable"* and quit.) and says, "It's supposed to be cutty, man. It's called jump cutting. It may not be correct for the 'cinema of your papa,' but it's correct for *today.* It's at *our* speed, *our* tempo. It doesn't belong to the past. *We* don't belong to the past, not anymore." The hemp was working. Jim was off . . . and getting more loquacious. . . .

"Didn't Kennedy say, '. . . the torch has been passed to a new generation'? . . . Well, that's *us!* We *are* the future. We outnumber those bastards. Sure, they've got the military behind them, but we've got the ammunition." And he held up one of his tightly rolled joints.

I was always amazed at how perfectly he could roll a joint. They were like thin, machine-rolled cigarettes. Like a Lucky Strike or a Camel. Perfect, no wrinkles. I myself couldn't roll for shit. Loose, flat, wrinkled, pathetic. I always let others do it for me; why embarrass myself in public? But Jim's were little works of art. He couldn't make a splice on 16mm film, he became Private All-Thumbs, but he could roll better than anyone. Clean, crisp, tight, perfect little magic bullets of pleasure. In fact, we were going to call the Doors music publishing company Ammunition Music, our motto, "Praise the Lord and Pass the Ammunition." When it actually came time to pick a name we opted out of any dope reference. Things were just too tight in those days. The Establishment was really cracking down on any public drug references. Ammunition Music was just a little too obvious. You know, ammunition . . . get loaded! Potential police problem there.

"They can't kill us all," he continued. "They can ship us off to Vietnam to be slaughtered in an Asian jungle, but they can't kill us all. We've got the numbers." He lit the joint, grin on his face, eyebrows arched like Groucho Marx.

Alain smiled a French smirk and said, "And you get all of that from Godard's jump cut?"

We all laughed at that one. We passed the joint and sat back, relaxed. We stared at the walls, but they weren't blank, as in most students' apartments. One of Jim's walls was a work of art in progress. It was a massive collage. He had cut out photos from *Life* magazine, from *Time* magazine, from fashion magazines, color and black-and-white images. Dorothy said Jim was the first guy she ever knew who bought fashion magazines. She was into *Vogue* and *Harper's Bazaar.* A fashion maven, she's always been into au courant styles. Always keeping abreast of the fashion of the day. Enjoying the changing patterns, the light, the chiaroscuro on the covering of women's bodies. And so did Jim. He would paste models, beautiful women, in surrealistic settings by using other photos as counterpoint, creating a long, continuing collage running the entire length of the wall adjacent to the bookcase. It was like a Chinese scroll unrolled and tacked up on his wall. Except the images were all contemporary. It was a picture story, a picture scroll. I stared at that wall, trying to discern a linear narrative in the images but I never could. The pictures didn't tell a story . . . it was the same thing Jim was doing with his student movie. It was poetry. It was a collision of images. Sergei Eisenstein, again. Here's one section: Marines are lounging about without shirts on. Naked to the waist, very relaxed in one another's company — Genet would have loved it — in a state of easy camaraderie. They're juxtaposed against this beautiful model — Jean Shrimpton — who's looking very seductive, and coming out from behind her is a snake, and the snake moves into an elephant, and then an African scene — Watusi warriors jumping — and then an American basketball player in mid-leap, and another model, arms outstretched, seemingly about to catch him. It went on like that. Beautifully cut and pasted, it was a tripster's delight.

The sun was beginning to set. We had watched the wall long enough. It was time to go. I finished my Tecate, took Dorothy's hand, and said, "Dinnertime. See you guys later." And off we went, out to Dorothy's mustard-colored VW bug, jumped in, and headed down San Vincente, out toward the ocean. Out to Venice. We hit Ocean Boulevard as the sun was beginning to dip into the Pacific. We hung a left on Ocean and ran parallel to the beach. And, man, what a sight! Palm trees silhouetted against flaming tangerine light hovering over slightly-darker-than-azure water. We were at the top of the cliffs, the Palisades, above the beach, with a view all the way to China. Probably could have seen it, too, if the Earth didn't curve. It was that clear. The light was shimmering. The air was warm. The entire atmosphere was soft and gentle. We were high, my baby and me. We were headed home to our little apartment on Fraser. I was enrolled at UCLA, we had great and intellectual friends, and all was right with the world. And the sunset was a spectacular collage of reds and blues and golds.

But best of all, we were in love! We were young and romantic, idealistic and in love. And we had met in an art class at UCLA. Drawing 101. The basic art course. Dorothy had to take it because she was an incoming art major. I took it because I wanted to learn how to draw storyboards like the great Sergei Eisenstein, the Russian director of *Potemkin, Ivan the Terrible, Ten Days That Shook the World, Alexander Nevsky.* A brilliant filmmaker. All stylized and angled. Russian Constructivism on the screen. And his storyboards were works of art. Hard, linear, insistent angles. Dynamic figures in kinetic relationships. Vigorous, forceful juxtapositions. My kind of stuff. "That's the way I want to do it," I said to myself. "I'm going to draw like Eisenstein!" What a boneheaded idea. I couldn't draw for shit. Rendering something in three dimensions on a two-dimensional page is impossible! I could never get a sense of volume or the idea of the vanishing point. My drawings were flat and American primitive. If I had been doing what I was doing a hundred years ago, and had been an eighty-five-year-old woman . . . well, it would have been art. As it was, it was a C-minus grade. I was never going to draw storyboards. The class was a complete waste of . . . but wait a second. Hey . . . who's that cute Japanese chick over by the windows? She's got a great sense of style. Shoulder-length black hair, parted on one side. Sometimes it would fall across one eye and she would brush it back with a saucy little gesture that said "I'm not subservient to anyone." Cute plaid skirts and blouse combinations. Black leotards under the skirt. She probably likes jazz, I thought. Black leotards meant beatnik, intellectual, hip existential chicks. Just the kind I liked. When the teacher called roll I listened for her name. "Miss Fujikawa, Dorothy Fujikawa." She answered "Here" in a very refined voice. Soft yet purposeful. Very elegant and very Audrey Hepburn. I think I fell in love at that instant. The reflected sunlight was streaming through the large bank of industrial windows to the north and she was at a drawing board closest to those windows. She was radiant in that light. She was lovely and I wanted her. And the fact that she was of a different race was even better. It added something exotic to my desire. Although she was a regular American girl from

Dorsey High, third-generation American, grandparents from the old country—same story as your author's—at that moment she was beautiful *and* exotic.

After class, I torqued up my courage and went over to her.

"Hi, Dorothy," I blurted out from my surprisingly now-dry mouth.

She looked up at me, eyes outlined in black, her full, sensuous lips discreetly reddened. "How do you know my name?" she melodically asked.

"I listened for it," I said, and smiled. "My name's Ray."

"I know," came the sphinx's reply.

"You do?"

She smiled. "I listened for yours, too."

Amour, love, romance, sweetness, little fire arrows flying back and forth on the spiritual plane, cupid shooting wildly from heart chakra to heart chakra, hitting bull's eyes.

"Would you . . . uhh, do you . . . uhh . . . need a ride somewhere, or something? I have a car in Lot C, it's very close by," I blurted out.

"No, thanks, I have a car, too."

Oh, shit, rejection. Come up with something else, Ray, quick. "Where's it parked?"

"Lot 12," she said.

"That's on the other end of the campus." I had it.

"It's all I could get. I'm only a freshman."

My mind raced, unbelievingly. Only a freshman? She was as sophisticated and sphinxlike as this and only a freshman? How could this be? How could she . . . ahh, who cares? I just didn't give a damn. Would you?

"Why don't I give you a ride to Lot 12? It's a long walk from here."

"Okay. This is my last class of the day."

"Me, too," I said, beaming. I had made it, we were going somewhere together.

"Let me get my things." She started putting pencils and charcoals into her little tackle box. We all had them to carry our drawing supplies, my instruments of torture and shame. I looked at her sketch. It was good. I flipped a few pages. It was very good.

"Hey, these are good. What's your major?"

She looked at me quizzically. "Well . . . art. What else?"

"I was just wondering. I'm a film major myself."

"Ohhh, the film school," she enthused. "That's cool."

Try to be blasé, Ray. "Ohh . . . it's okay."

"What are you doing in 101?"

I swallowed. "Trying to draw storyboards."

"Let's see," she said as she took my sketch pad.

"No, let's just go. I'm not very good. I can't get the hang of it."
I tried to take it back. She wouldn't let go.

"Come on, Ray, let me see." She smiled. And I melted. What
could I do? She flipped the pages and smirked ever so slightly.

"You probably ought to stay in the film school," she said as she
handed the sketch pad back.

I laughed, half-embarrassed, half-clownish. "Don't worry," I
said. "I intend to!"

She smiled again. Damned Cheshire cat grin of hers. Wise beyond her years. Knowing things.

"Good," she said as she scooped up her supplies. We headed to
the door, out into the corridor of the art department, through the
double doors of the horizon and into the California afternoon. And
she took my arm. Wow . . . Dorothy Fujikawa!

She has wisdom and knows what to do
She has me and she has you . . .
She lives on Love Street

As we drove to Lot 12, I went for it. "There's a new Godard
film opening this weekend. Would you like to go see it with me?"

"Maybe . . . who's Godard?"

Ahh-ha! She doesn't know everything. "A French director. He
made *Breathless*. This new one's called *Contempt*. It's with Brigitte
Bardot. They say she actually acts for the first time in her career," I
smugly added.

"I'll believe *that* when I see it," Dorothy cutely responded.

"Hey, anything's possible," I said, smiling back at her.

"I *have* seen *The 400 Blows*," she said.

"What did you think?"

"I loved it. It was poetry with a camera," she sighed.

"I agree. Brilliant film."

"Who was the director?" she asked.

"Truffaut. He's part of the Nouvelle Vague, the French New Wave, like Godard." I was the grad student now.

"It's a whole movement?" she asked almost excitedly.

"Yeah . . . and Swedish films, like Ingmar Berman."

"I've seen *The Virgin Spring,*" she said.

"You have?" I *knew* she was hip. "Have you seen *Black Orpheus?*" I asked. "That's my favorite of them all . . ."

"I loved it. It was so tragic," she said.

"I loved the *music.* That Brazilian rhythm that goes through the whole thing. It was relentless. It never stopped. And the Greek tragedy set in Brazil . . . just incredible."

"Those are the kinds of films I like best," she said. "Something with some thought behind it."

"That's the kind of films I want to make."

"Good for you, Ray," and she touched my arm. It was like electricity. The "blue spark" that John Doe and X sing about had been set off between us. Ouch! I was burning.

"Here's Lot 12," she pointed out.

I stopped and she got out. "Well," she said.

"Well what?" I asked. Mind on fire.

"*Contempt,* this weekend?"

I grinned my best Steve McQueen at her. "Wanna go on Saturday?"

She gave me her best Audrey Hepburn. "Okay, I'm free then," she said. "See you in class on Friday."

And she was gone. Dorothy Fujikawa. Man!

To support ourselves through UCLA, Dorothy had fifteen dollars a week in child support money from her parents' divorce settlement and I had thirty dollars a week from my weekend gig as "Screaming Ray Daniels," blues singer, with my brothers' surf band, Rick and the Ravens.

My two younger brothers, Rick and Jim, those pups from Chicago who were now living in the South Bay—Redondo Beach, to be exact—had formed a rock band in the then-prevailing style of surf music. Music for the riding of the wild surf, for the hanging of ten, for the crying of "Kawabunga!" Music of the early sixties. Pre–British Invasion. And they had a gig at a beer bar with the ridiculous name of the Turkey Joint West, one block off the beach in Santa Monica. Dorothy loved to ask, "Is there a Turkey Joint East somewhere? Perhaps in Boston?"

Now most of the heads from the film school lived near the beach, in Venice and in Santa Monica. Rents were cheap and it was all appropriately funky. Because I was playing and singing the blues with a surf band—everybody's favorite music at the time, blues and surf—a bunch of the guys who lived close by would come down on a Friday or Saturday night. They would bring dates, get drunk, and howl at the moon. Knowing me, the guy on the stage, somehow gave them license to get rowdy and leap out of their normally cool, artistic, Beat personas and into a Dionysian state of goofy revelry. And Jim Morrison was one of them. Mr. Goofy. A funny, loud, and rowdy drunk, along with Paul Ferrara, DeBella, Dave Thompson, and Frank Lisciandro and his new bride, Kathy, the Madonna from Manhattan. (They were a cool couple. We dropped acid together, and you didn't do that with just anybody.) And when Jim got loose he would shout out song titles at the band, mainly "Louie Louie." We could always hear him barking from the back of the room: "Play 'Louie Louie'! We wanna hear 'Louie Louie'!" And the other assembled reprobates would follow his lead, laughing and sloshing and calling out from their cups. And Jim was in his element, loving the rowdy camaraderie of the whole thing, with his friend Ray onstage singing Chicago blues tunes and his other friends from UCLA blitzed all around him. It was good and raucous fun. We all loved it.

And one night I had the inspiration to announce to the audience, as Jim and the film guys were shouting out requests: "Ladies and gentlemen! We have a special treat tonight. A guest in the audience who just happens to be a very fine poet and a man I'd like to bring onstage and have him help me out in a special version of 'Louie Louie.' Jim Morrison!" And the heads started applauding and whooping like crazy. So did the rest of the crowd. Hell, they didn't care; *special treat,* why not? Jim looked around, gulped once, took a deep breath, and then bounded to the stage. He was ready to rock. All loose and oiled and emboldened. Ready to give it a try.

"Here he is, ladies and gentlemen. Direct from the UCLA Film Department . . . Jim Morrison!" And I handed Jim the mic. And my brother Rick kicked in the opening riff of "Louie Louie," and my brother Jim smash-joined him on piano chords; the drums and bass surfer-stomped the rhythm, Jim let out a bloodcurdling war whoop, and the Turkey Joint West went Dionysian. The fucking place exploded! People hit the dance floor and Jim and I shared the mic and began to sing "Louie Lou-eye, ohh baby, we gotta go!" He was good. And he loved it. He bopped around and sang himself hoarse, what with his whoops and yells and screams and shouts and his untrained vocal cords. But he loved it. I loved it, too. And, man, we had fun that night!

After the set, I joined Jim and the film school regulars at their back table and we laughed and drank ourselves blotto. Jim was so hoarse he could barely talk. His voice was no more than a whisper but he was beaming and making little "heh, heh, heh" laughing noises as we all slapped him on the back for a job well done. That was the first time Jim Morrison ever sang onstage. Who knew it would be far from his last. Maybe only destiny.

chapter four

the beach and lsd

It's late May of 1965, and Raymond Daniel Manzarek and James Douglas Morrison are now college graduates. We have finished our course of studies. We have matriculated into the school of life, from the shelter of academe into the jungle of reality. Expelled from the warmth and security and fantasy of the womb of Westwood into the howling, squalling, riotous, dangerous, psychological madness known as adulthood. What a place to have to spend the rest of your life.

No more leisurely strolls through the sculpture garden debating the fine points of Eisenstein's theory of montage. No more idle hours at the outdoor snack stand—the Gypsy Wagon—in animated discourse on the superiority of Marlon Brando's *One-Eyed Jacks* to John Ford's *The Searchers*. I always found it incomprehensible how USC people could actually prefer *The Searchers* to *One-Eyed Jacks*. Some UCLA students were also afflicted with this lapse of aesthetics. They, of course, were squares, certainly not poets. However, they were entitled to their opinions, even if those opinions were, well . . . lame. And, Lord, how they defended them! With vehemence and ferocity; proclaiming their lack of hipness into the soft afternoon air. Unashamed, unembarrassed, and unrepentant. "I like John Wayne better than Marlon Brando." "He's got a rod up his ass," we retorted. "His walk is ridiculous. Brando flows and glides; from the hip. Wayne lumbers." They were undeterred—"It's John Wayne's best movie!" We snorted in derision, "John Wayne never even *made* a best movie. He's a racist jock. He's a friend of Ronald Reagan's for cri-sake!" Their witty rejoinder, pressed to the limit of their critical abilities—"He's an American, a *patriot!*" We laughed. "Boo, hiss. Why don't you go to USC, where you belong, *fascist!*" That always hurt them. We knew that the phrase "true American patriot"—add "Christian"—was really unspoken code for fascist white supremacist. And they knew that we knew. And there was nothing they could do about it except to call us "Communists!" Morrison always laughed at that one.

"Hey, I love this country," he would say. "I'm proud to be an American. I'd die for this country if I had to. Would you?"

And then he'd get in one of their faces, nose to nose, Marine-style. "Would *you* die? Would you die right *now?* Huh, would you?" Eyes blazing, intense as hell. He was running a number, a put-on.

Or was he? He was so damn sincere. So over the top. So on fire, so hyper that people thought he *was* ready to die. Right there. No brag, no excuse, no quarter.

"I'll die, will you?" The other guy always backed down—hell, wouldn't you?—and then backed away. "Fuck you, Morrison," was the only thing left for him to say.

We'd toss lines from *One-Eyed Jacks* at the retreating figures. "Scum-sucking pig. I'll tear yer arms out. Big tub 'a guts."

⁂

So we were graduates. An M.F.A.—a master's degree—for me and a bachelor's degree for Jim, both in cinematography.

"What are you going to do now?" I asked Jim.

"I don't know," he said. "I been thinkin' about going to New York City."

I felt a slight sinking in my gut. I was enjoying our new friendship. It was just beginning to blossom. He was witty and funny and smart and hip and very well read. And now it would be over. Chances of our meeting in New York were very slim. Chances of our *never* seeing each other again were very good. And that made me sad. Jim was cool and I valued our too-brief association. I was going to miss this pothead, this avant-garde stoner, this rebellious psyche-delic poet pal of mine.

"Too bad," I said. "I'm gonna stay here in L.A."

"I thought you would," he smiled. "You're the golden boy. You couldn't leave the sun."

"You're right," I laughed. "I love this weather. I can't leave it now. Hell, I just got here. Besides, I want to see what destiny has in store for me in Southern California."

"Destiny can be pretty demanding, Ray," Jim said knowingly. "I wouldn't ask too much of it if I was you."

"Shit, man. I'm in charge here," I replied in my puffed-up, "master of fine arts" hubris. "Destiny is an old friend of mine. I'm here in L.A., aren't I? Hell, you're here, too. We made it all the way out to the end of the West . . . didn't we?"

His voice softened and saddened ever so slightly. "I won't be here much longer, though."

And a darkness crossed the bright L.A. light. Destiny was already extracting too steep a price; a separation of friends before a friendship had fully developed. I tried to plant a seed of doubt in his plan, hoping I could dissuade him. "What the hell would you do in New York, man?"

A long pause . . . "I'm gonna try to get together with Jonas Mekas, from Film Culture. Make some poetic films like I did for my student flick."

I said, "Well, good luck to you, Jim. I'm gonna stay here and see if I can become a director in Hollywood. Make some features . . . the way *I* want to make them."

I tried to lighten the mood, and laughed. "It's my destiny."

Jim smiled. "Then good luck, to you, too, Ray. I'll see you around, man." And he was gone.

Smash cut to forty days later. I was at the crossroads. I'm sitting on the beach, down from Fraser in Ocean Park, middle of July. Dorothy's at work. (She had a little job at that time, cleaning computer tape. Big reels, two inches thick. Shuttle back and forth, spewing bits, picking up data, then processing data, then erase the tape. Bits of gunk remain on the supposedly erased tape, need to be immaculate; calling Dorothy Fujikawa. Clean that tape, honey.) She was the only one of us able to get employed at anything. What a profligate bunch we were. Talk about slackers. Man, we were the originators of Generation X-dom.

So we're living on Fraser, Dorothy and I, nice little place above the garage of a California bungalow. One bedroom—rent, seventy-five dollars per month—overlooking the rooftops of Venice; looking out to the beach, the Pacific Ocean, the setting sun, and, ultimately, Asia. An idyllic student apartment. Great times were had there. Great lovemaking, moviemaking—*Evergreen* and *Who and Where I Live*—my design project, which also made it into the Royce Hall Screenings (featuring a lithe and nude Dorothy Fujikawa superimposed on our little apartment. It was shot on outdoor film brought indoors, to give it a golden glow. A most effective look on Dorothy's beautiful body and a color that just caressed her lovely, soft skin). Great conversations were had there with Jim Morrison and John DeBella and Phil Oleno and Paul Ferrara and Dave Thompson and Bill Kerby and a host of heads, and some great acid trips were had there, too.

She's at work and I'm on the beach, working on a tan. Big, lazy guy from the frozen tundra of Chicago is soaking up the rays of that great Aten disc in the sky and having an existential crisis. I'm at the crossroads. My brain is racing. What am I going to do with myself? Here I am, I've got a master's degree in film from UCLA, I want to be a filmmaker—a director—I love making movies . . . and I don't know a single person in the film business! How the fuck am I going to break into this closed circle of Hollywood? The worry continued: I've got a bachelor's degree in economics from De Paul University in Chicago, an M.F.A. from UCLA, and I don't know what I'm going to do with myself. I don't know how I'm going to make a nickel to support us. I want to ask Dorothy to marry me, but I'm flat, busted broke. No jack in the bank and no real prospects. Shit!

I began to walk along the ocean. And everything around me was moving in slow motion, even the waves. And in silence. I couldn't hear a sound except for the high whine of the ghosts that appeared when I entered the crossroads. The ghosts that were now accompanying me on my walk . . . hovering . . . whispering to me . . .

telling me about what the future might be. Trying to instill the fear into me. Trying to panic me. They were insidious and evil. They had turned off the sound on the entire ocean and allowed only their high-pitched squeals to enter my mind's ear, sending cold shivers down my spine. And they swarmed about my head, blotting out the light. But they were also ephemeral. They could be chased away with the blink of an eye, the wave of a hand, and a hard, clear thought. So I swallowed hard, shook my head, splashed some Pacific Ocean on my face, and they were gone. The waves came back up to speed and the sounds of the day switched back on. And, hell, man, the sun was out. It was a fine day and I was no longer afraid. The only decision was, What am I going to do with the rest of my life? And I turned it over to the energy. I thought to myself, I'm in no position to make any decisions. I'll let the energy of the sun guide me. The divine energy. The all-healing, all-encompassing, all-nurturing, all-supportive energy. I went back to my beach towel and just plopped down.

And there I was, just sitting in the sun, being a bum, smoking a joint and trusting in the energy. And who comes walking down the beach, but James Douglas Morrison. The sun is streaming in behind him, the water is glistening, and I see this silhouetted figure walking along in the shallows, the shore break, kicking up water. I can't quite make out who it is, but as he's kicking at the water, diamonds are materializing all around his feet. He's like an Indian deity, like Krishna—the Blue God—creating a field of diamonds from his footsteps, like Sai Baba, a popular guru of the time, materializing ashes from his fingers, but this human figure is producing glittering, ephemeral, now-you-see-them, now-you-don't jewels. He's making diamonds because of the way the sun is hitting the water from behind. It's called backlighting. It gives everything a halo of light; it makes translucent objects shimmer with an inner fire. And the sun is coming in low and hard. It's the beginning of eventide. The great orb is beginning its descent into the waters of the unconscious, into the underworld, where it will pass through the darkness, battling the negative powers, and rise triumphant at the next day's dawning.

And I see this guy, in semi-silhouette, wearing cutoffs, without a shirt, weighing about 135 pounds. Thin, about six feet tall; rail-thin kind of guy with long hair. There was something strangely familiar about this watery apparition. Was this a manifestation of the ocean itself? Did our mother conjure up this solidity? Or was this a projection of my own Jungian inclinations toward liquidity and wholeness? I looked again, with more intensity, and who should emerge from the light, from behind the sun, into my field of vision, into my field of consciousness, but Jim Morrison!

"Hey, Jim. Hey . . . hey, Morrison," I called out. The figure stopped, looked in the direction of the call, and waved back.

"Hey, Ray," and he comes walking over to me, across the twenty-five to thirty feet of sand where I'm sitting off from the shore break. And there, standing in front of me, is the new Blue God, my buddy Jim, transformed. He looked great. He had lost all his baby plump. Dropped thirty pounds. Down from 165 to about 135. His hair had grown out in soft ringlets and he looked not unlike Michelangelo's *David*. Even more like busts I have since seen of Alexander the Great.

"What are you doing here, man?" I asked. "I thought you were going to New York City."

"Nah, I decided to stay here."

"Any particular reason?"

He shifted his weight and played Paul Newman in *Hud*.

"Seemed like a good idea at the time," he said, slyly grinning.

"Well, cool, man." I was happy to see him. "What you been up to?"

"Nothin' much"—now he was James Dean in *Giant*—"tryin' to stay out of trouble."

"Succeeding?" I asked.

"Unfortunately"—he shape-shifted again—"yeah." And he smiled that Steve McQueen in *The Great Escape* grin of his.

We laughed, easy in each other's company.

"I thought you let your apartment go. Where you living now?" I inquired.

"With Dennis Jacob."

"Dennis?!!" (A notorious UCLA Film School, Nietzschean madman. He had been editing his final thesis movie for five years, and had succeeded in cutting three hours of film down to fifteen minutes. Great lighting and camera angles, though. Very Carl Dreyer.) "You sleep in the same apartment with Dennis?!! How can you do it? Isn't he like . . . I mean . . . a slob?"

"I sleep up on the roof," Jim said, allaying my fears for his contamination. "I only go inside to take my meals. He's a pretty good cook."

"Christ, you'd never know it. A good cook, huh?"

"Yeah." He nodded. "Really." He grinned again. "Well, kind of." We laughed, looking out at the setting sun.

And we laughed like soft, mad children.
Smug in the woolly, cotton brains of infancy.
The music and voices are all around us.

"What have you been doing, man?" I asked.

He said, "Nothing. What are you doing?"

"I'm not doing anything," I said. "I've been trying to figure out what to do."

He said to me, "Working on anything?"

"I've been thinking about some film scripts and like that," I said. "What about you, you working on anything?"

"Yeah," he said. "I've been writing some songs."

And there it was! Just like that! It dropped quite simply, quite innocently from his lips, but it changed our collective destinies. Both Jim's and mine and, in a perhaps less significant way . . . even yours, too. "Writing some songs." My psychic antennae twitched. This could be something serious. (By that time—the summer of '65—the Beatles and the Rolling Stones had completely captured the American airwaves. It was known as the "British Invasion" and it was a juggernaut. An irresistible force. It included the Animals, the Dave Clark Five, the Who, the Searchers, Gerry and the Pacemakers, Them, and even the ridiculous Freddy and the Dreamers—the comic relief of the invasion. But riding above it all were the Beatles and the Stones. Good and evil made manifest. We were all in awe of their success, if not their artistic accomplishments. They were *front-page* news! The Beatles tour of America hit the national headlines. They came to New York and the *Los Angeles Times* ran the headline "Beatles in U.S.A." Pandemonium, concerts, riots, chicks, limos, press conferences, flashbulbs, high fashion, *mucho dinero*. Everything a young man could dream of. The *Herald Examiner* ran the banner "Beatles Take Back America!" A Hearst paper, always provocative.

But it was incredible. Youth on the front page. The mod movement had seized the aesthetic consciousness of the entire country. And then the Stones came. Those darling bad boys entered the land of innocence and hysteria. And everything went bonkers again. "Stones in L.A." ran the *Times* headline. And Jim and I and all the hipsters at UCLA saw these headlines . . . and drooled. Those guys were just like us. Early twenties, art students, longish hair, Jagger from the London School of Economics, for cri-sake—like *me*, for cri-sake—and they're changing the world! I thought, I'd sure like to be doing that.)

My mind did a cartwheel at the possibilities. "Songs, huh?" was all I could say because this was beginning to feel like something preordained. Something requiring only an act of will . . . and ability, of course. Ability always comes first. It's the ultimate prerequisite. You must be able to *do it!* You can't simply wish for fame and fortune, you must have some ability. And you must know it in yourself.

So I said to him, "You know what, sing me a song, man. Let me hear what you've been writing."

"Aw, Ray. I don't have much of a voice," Jim shyly responded.

"C'mon, Jim, of course you got a voice. Bob Dylan doesn't have a voice and look where he is. You can do fine. Just go ahead and sing. Like at the Turkey Joint."

"That wasn't the real me. I was drunk then," he said. And he shifted shapes in the sand once again. But this time he was looking for himself. No more playacting. No more character adapting. And straight as an arrow. This was going to have to be the *real* Jim Morrison. And, Lord, he was shy.

I continued encouraging him. "It's just you and me here and I'm not gonna judge your singing voice. I just wanna hear your words and, you know, what you've got in your head." And then softly, "Go ahead, Jim."

That seemed to work. Emboldened, he got up to his knees, faced me, and dug his hands into the sand. He came up with two handfuls and began to squeeze real tight. And the sand started streaming out between his fingers. I saw these rivulets of sand, this waterfall of sand coming out of his hands, like the yogic master Sai Baba, and he said, "Okay. Here's one I have. It's called 'Moonlight Drive.' " And he closed his eyes and began to sing, sand still streaming, and I heard those words for the first time.

Let's swim to the moon.
Let's climb through the tide.
Penetrate the evening that the
city sleeps to hide.
Let's swim out tonight, love,
It's our turn to try.
Parked beside
the ocean on our . . . moonlight drive.

I'm a fish in the ocean, I see the bait. It looks delicious.

Let's swim to the moon
Let's climb through the tide
Surrender to the waiting worlds that lap
against our side.
Nothing left open and no time to decide
We've stepped into a river on our . . . moonlight drive.

Now I take the bait! It *is* delicious.

Let's swim to the moon
Let's climb through the tide
You reach a hand to hold me but I
Can't be your guide

I instantly fell in love with that line. It signifies a loss but also a need for individual strength. We must each do it on our own. "I can't be your guide."

Easy to love you as I watch you glide
Falling through wet forests on our . . . moonlight drive.

I swallow the bait. And I'm hooked. Caught. Seduced. The words have both ensnared and enfolded me. I am secure and warmed by their artistry. I surrender myself to their liquid images. There, on the beach, at the end point, the terminus of Western civilization; watching our great, glowing Father sink into the softness, the blueness of our Mother, I am happy. I know what I'm going to do with my life!

Because as he's singing, I'm hearing an entire recording taking place in my mind's ear! Drums, bass, guitars, backup vocals; and I'm playing a funky organ over the whole thing. Jimmy Smith style, or maybe Ray Charles, or Charles Erland on Gerald Wilson's "Blues for Yna Yna." I'm punctuating the words and filling the spaces with imaginary riffs, blue and cool and mean and funky. The whole track is percolating and bubbling and I'm loving it. And Jim is floating like a blue angel over the top of the whole thing, singing his ass off. But every once in a while he tries to float away, carried off by the inspiration, into the blue canopy, off into the light; but I bring him back with a firm hand on his ankle and a blues line on the organ. And he's grounded again, centered and singing. And, man, we are making great music together.

He finishes with these dark and portentous lines.

Come on, baby, gonna take a little ride
Goin' down by the ocean side.
Get real close, get real tight.
Baby, gonna drown tonight.
Goin' down, down, down.

The chief ghost, the angel of death, brushed my shoulder at that instant, but I feared it not. I was in a rapture of creative imagining and nothing could dissuade me from my goal. This was just too good not to be. This will be. This will happen. Even if we have to do battle with death itself, I thought, my mind racing with possibilities. Besides, with death involved in the process, well, that only adds an urgent edge to the entire construct. And being the LSD ingestors, the acid eaters that we were, death was not foreign to us. The idea was not to be feared, nor was it to be embraced. It was simply a fact of life. The other end of life. The exit point. The terminus. And there we were, after all, at the terminus of the West. So why not "drown tonight." It was dangerous, it was slightly obsessed, and it was pure Morrison.

"Oh, man. I love it! This is incredible. Do you have anything else?" I was glowing. He felt my enthusiasm for his creation and breathed a great sigh of relief. The sand had run out but he was not rejected. His psyche began to swell, a smile crept across his face, and his shyness began to retreat. This was the beginning of Jim Morrison, rock star!

The grin ate up his face. "Yeah, I've got a couple of other things," he said. "One's called 'Summer's Almost Gone.' I've got another one called 'My Eyes Have Seen You.' "

"Whoa, 'My Eyes Have Seen You'?" I whooped. "What a great title. Do that one for me!"

"Okay." His eyes were blazing. We were *both* on fire. "This one's kind of fast."

And he began to sing, not in the booze voice he used at the Turkey Joint, but in a Chet Baker voice. You know who Chet Baker is: trumpet player, West Coast jazz, cool school, played with Gerry Mulligan, handsome young heartthrob of the early fifties. When he sang he had a very cool, soft, mellow voice. And here's Morrison, sitting in front of me, singing like Chet Baker, but even better. A whispering kind of soft. A haunted voice. Jim's real voice.

My eyes have seen you
My eyes have seen you
My eyes have seen you
Stand in your door

And now he gets more intense. The whisper recedes.

When we meet inside you can
Show me some more
Show me some more
Show me some more

He was beating on his thighs for rhythmic accent on the last three lines. Hard, almost tribal. He was intense as shit. I'd never seen this personality in Jim Morrison before, and I loved it. "Show me some more" sounded vaguely like the Kinks but also Latin at the same time. I could do Latin jazz-rock behind it. It would work great. It had never been done before. Chet Baker cool into hard Latin rock. Oh, yes!

He continued, dropping down to the haunted voice again.

My eyes have seen you
My eyes have seen you
My eyes have seen you
Turn and stare
Fix your hair
Move upstairs
Move upstairs
Move upstairs

He was slapping and whacking in rhythm, and I swear he almost began to levitate. He was so into it. And so was I. I was deep inside the structure of the song, creating the bed track for his manic vocal.

"Solo here," I shouted, and began to sing a melody line of my own. Working my fingers over an imaginary keyboard. Latin, jazz, and rock and roll.

"Go, Ray," he enthused, keeping the rhythm on his thigh drums. I finished and brought it down to whisper level again. I knew what he was doing and where the song structure was going. Following him was very easy, very logical. It all made perfect sense. And he began the third stanza . . .

My eyes have seen you
My eyes have seen you
My eyes have seen you
Free from disguise
Gazing on a city under
Television skies
Television skies
Television skies.

And we were off and racing again. I was beating the rhythm now on the sand. The last stanza kept the intensity going. No haunted voice at all. Hard rock all the way out.

My eyes have seen you!

He almost shouted. Strong and clear. Heads turned.

My eyes have seen you!

We paid them no mind. We were in another world.

My eyes have seen you!

And my favorite lines of the song . . .

Let them photograph your soul
Memorize your alleys on an
Endless roll
Endless roll
Endless roll

"Keep it going," I cried out. "Keep the rhythm going." We slapped at our drums, feverishly, like pagan revelers around an ancient bonfire. "We'll do a ride-out and solo and then a long fade." I sang solo lines over the tribal drums. Jim drove me on. "Go, man! Get it," he enthused. And I did. And he did. We rocked that song out over the beach and into the ocean. A long, gradual fade-out that took us into the blue space. And it was finished. Quiet, peaceful, spent.

We both exhaled huge gulps of air. "Whew . . . that's a great song, man."

"Yeah, I kind of like it." And he grinned that sly southern cat grin of his.

I hit him on the arm. "Smart ass," I said. "You gotta sing me some more. Sing me some more." We both laughed.

So he did "Summer's Almost Gone," and I found it sad and melancholic. A song of the end of innocence. Perhaps of the end of love. Perhaps of the end itself. I heard a bolero behind it. A Latin, close dancing–ballad rhythm. It would work perfectly with his lyrics of loss. It was in a blues structure with a bridge.

Summer's almost gone.
Summer's almost gone.
Almost gone,
Yeah, it's almost gone.
Where will we be
When the summer's gone?

And now the bridge, with a Bach-like descending passage.

Morning found us calmly unaware,
Noon burned gold into our hair,
At night we swam the laughing sea . . .

There's the liquid again. Our Mother, the ocean. We were definitely Venice boys. Of the beach. Of the ocean. Both of us.

When summer's gone, where will we be?
Where will we be?
Where will we be?

Indeed, where will we be? We needed the intense energy and light of that high summer sun. We needed the warmth, the comfort, the security. We were two young men, college graduates, about to embark on a grand undertaking and we would need all the support we could muster.

I told him, "Jim, these are the best songs I've ever heard in rock and roll. With your lyrics, what I can do playing the keyboards, playing behind that . . . man, we got to get a band together." And just for fun—as a joke—not in any calculated way, but out of sheer exuberance, I laughed, "We're gonna make a million dollars."

And he looked at me and said, "Ray, that's exactly what I had in mind."

"Cool, man. All right!"

"But who's going to sing?" He was shy again.

"Well, shit. You are, man." I said. "Not me. As of this moment I'm officially retiring 'Screamin' Ray Daniels.' Hell, they're your words. Who could do them better?"

"I don't have a real voice, ya know?"

Time to prop up his ego again. "Your voice is fine, Jim. It's just fine. And it'll only get better with practice." (And that was the truth. He was right on pitch; he didn't waver. His tone was good and he had a strong sense of rhythm. He was in the pocket and his sound was right. He would be fine, as soon as he gained some chops and some much-needed confidence. And that would come. I wasn't worried at all.)

"You think so?"

"I know so." I paused. "But there is one problem."

He frowned. "What, what problem?" I loved the way he stretched out the word "whhaat" with a downward inflection. Kind of singsong. Kinda cute.

"We need a name for the band. We're not gonna call it Morrison and Manzarek, like a folk duo or something."

He laughed. "Or Jim and Ray."

"*That's* cute," I said. "They'd really take us seriously as Jim and Ray."

"Well, we could add 'Two Guys from Venice,' " he joked.

"A pizza duo, like Two Guys from Italy," I said. "I like it." I did my Groucho Marx: "But seriously, folks . . . really, you got any ideas?"

"Sure," he said. "We call it . . . the Doors."

I said, "The *what?* Come on, that's the most ridicu—" and then stopped, mid-word. I flashed on the logic of it. It made perfect sense. Of course! "You mean, like the doors in your mind?" I continued. "Like opening the doors of perception? Like Aldous Huxley?"

"Exactly," he said. "Cool, huh?"

"Ohh, man. Too cool!" I was floored. "That's just too hip." And I thought to myself, You know, the Beatles have the whole teeny-bopper thing. They've got four plucky lads. All happy, peppy, and poppy! Close harmony, terrific. They're as cute as all get-out. No one could ever fault the Beatles for their cuteness. But let's face it, it's lightweight. (This is the summer of '65, don't forget. They were doing "She Loves You" and "I Wanna Hold Your Hand." They had yet to consume the magic substance, LSD.) And the Rolling Stones were doing Chicago blues. And that's all well and good . . . but so what? I can do that in my sleep. They look great and they're doing Muddy Waters. But, hell, I grew up on the South Side of Chicago, so that doesn't really mean that much to me one way or the other . . . bunch of white guys playing the blues . . . I've been doing that since I was twelve years old. In other words, I surveyed the competition and found it vulnerable to a challenge from a different direction. A psychedelic direction.

"Jim, man, with your words and my keyboards . . . there's nobody doing this. What we're gonna do, nobody on the planet is doing. This music, *our* music, is called . . . psychedelic."

"All right, Ray!"

"First order of business is, we got to get you off Dennis's rooftop," I said, leaping to my feet. "You'll catch pneumonia or, shit, *pleurisy* for cri-sake sleeping in that night air."

He slowly rose to his feet, languidly stretching like a cat. "Naw, I won't. I've got a good sleeping bag, keeps me warm."

"Doesn't matter, Jim. The damp creeps in through your nose and mouth. Every breath, it goes down into your lungs. And before you know it, *bam*, pleurisy! End of Doors. Back on the dole. Call Mom and Dad, 'Send more money!' And what if they don't?" I poked him jokingly. "What then?"

"Jesus," he laughed, "what is this, a new script you're working on?"

"Could be, huh? A kind of true-life . . ."

"Here's a title, *Portrait of the Artist as a Dead Dog.*"

"I like it. I'll have to remember that. Maybe I can use it someday." I laughed. "Maybe a book or something."

"Too late, Joyce beat you to it," he rejoined.

"I know, but I like your version better. It's punnier."

"Oww, so is that, Ray."

We both laughed, secure in our art and charged with energy over our newly conceived plan of action.

In that year we had an intense visitation of energy.

The energy had brought us together. It was only a matter of how far we would go and what price the fates would extract for the journey. Little did I suspect back then, back in that light, that they would demand the ultimate price.

I started to walk through the sand, back toward Fraser. "Come on, man. Let's go."

"Where?" he asked.

"Home. You're moving in with me and Dorothy."

"All right, Ray!" he whooped.

And off we trudged. Through that deep, golden sand. Away from the soft blue and toward the land, toward the city, back into the Western Dream.

Now it was time for casual speak. "How did you lose all the weight, man? You look great."

"I wasn't eating," he said.

"What do you mean you weren't eating?"

"I was taking acid and getting high. I hardly ate anything since we graduated." He hit his slab of abs. A good, solid whack. "Hard as nails, Ray."

"Shit, I wish my gut looked that good."

"Well . . . don't eat."

"Can't, man," I said. "I love the sheer, sensual pleasure of it."

"Ray"—and he spoke in that slow, laconic way of his when he wanted to make a point—"you're nothing but a sybarite."

"Guilty!" I laughed. And we walked on through the golden.

A small retaining wall awaited us at the end of the beach separating sand from sidewalk. We approached it and climbed over, and I caught a glimpse of Jim's profile. I don't know why, but this realization waited for that precise moment. He was handsome! His jawbone had come out and it was four-square and straight. He was all-American in his handsomeness. He shed his softness and a hard, lean, angular WASP face had emerged. High cheekbones, hard jaw and chin, strong neck. He was now a good-looking man. No longer a boy. And I thought to myself, The girls are going to love this guy. They are just going to absolutely fall in love with this Jim Morrison. He'll be irresistible to them. He's charming, polite, witty, and handsome as the devil. Irresistible. I had to smile to myself at our prospects. The lyrics are great—they're poetry—and the music is going to be great—I'll handle that. We're going to be spooky, weird, and psychedelic. And on top of it, we've got the best-looking guy I've seen in a long time—since Steve McQueen. It was like a running battle. Who was the best-looking guy? James Dean? Yes, but he was gone in that silver Spyder. So you've got Steve McQueen and now the challenger, Jim Morrison. My bet goes on the challenger. I thought he looked better than the reigning heartthrob sex object, Steve McQueen. "Man, we're going all the way to the top!" I knew it. I could feel it.

Over the wall, onto the street, and up Fraser we floated. Borne aloft by this new dream. We had entered a new reality and it was the fates that had brought us together. It was pure serendipity that he should come walking through the shore break at that exact moment in time. It was serendipity that placed me in the exact spot to *see* him in the shore break. *Fortuna.* Destiny. And we were ready to rock!

We turned up the driveway of the gray Craftsman-style California bungalow and climbed the stairs of our little apartment over the garage. Dorothy was already home. The door was open for some cross-ventilation. I hit the top step . . .

"Honey, I'm home!" I called out.

"Me, too, Ray," she answered.

"Somehow I knew that," I joked as I went in, grabbed her, and hugged her close.

"Oh, you . . . wise guy." She smiled and pressed herself close against me. I could feel her hard, sweet little breasts against my chest.

"Guess who's coming to dinner?" I whispered in her ear.

"I'll bet you are," she grinned.

"That's for later . . . that's our dessert." I flicked my tongue into her ear. She shivered for an instant. I broke off our embrace reluctantly.

"You'll never guess who I brought home."

Jim did a little leap around the corner and into the room.

"Jim Morrison . . . ," Dorothy cried out.

"Hi, Dorothy."

". . . I thought you were in New York!"

He looked at me, grinning. "Didn't we just have this conversation?"

"Sounds familiar," I said.

"What are you doing here, Jim?" Dorothy queried.

"We . . . uhh . . . I'm going to live with you."

Dorothy's almond eyes got very round. "What?!! Why?"

"Let me explain, honey," I said.

"Did you lose that apartment on Goshen?" she asked.

"Yeah, I gave it up," Jim replied.

"And you don't have anyplace to stay?"

"Uhh . . . let me explain, will ya, honey," I repeated.

She looked at me. "Well, Ray, he's got to have a place to stay."

"I know, honey."

"He can't be living outside, he'll get pneumonia or something."

"Ray said possibly pleurisy."

"Exactly," Dorothy agreed. "Something awful, like pleurisy."

"See why I love her?" I asked Jim. "Two people, one mind."

"I can see that," said Jim.

I turned to Dorothy. "And if he catches pleurisy he won't be able to sing."

She looked at me, her head slightly askance. "What is he going to sing?"

I grinned. "Our new songs!"

"Your what?"

"That's what I've been trying to tell you. We're getting a band together. It's gonna be called the Doors . . ."

"Like *The Doors of Perception?*" she jumped in. (High IQ—147. Jim's was 149. What a couple of smart asses. And mine at only 135. Shit.)

"Exactly. And Jim is gonna be the lead singer."

"Whose words?" she wisely asked.

"Jim's—he's the poet."

She paused for a beat, looked at Jim . . . and Adonis registered himself in her eyes. "Ohh." She looked at me, back at him and then back at me. Sizing us up. Judging the cuteness factor. Seeing if we could compete with the Beatles and Stones.

"Works for me," she said, and grinned.

I grabbed her and hugged her again. Jim put on his best happy face and laughed. He was home.

"Wait until you hear the words," I said.

"Good?" she asked.

"Poetry," I said.

"And the music?"

"Jazz-rock . . . and psychedelic!"

"Wow," she said. "Poetry and jazz-rock. Like the beatniks, huh?"

"Maybe even better," I said.

"Uhh, Ray," Jim warned, "we're gonna be good but let's not go that far . . . hubris, you know."

"This is just between us."

"We have to appear humble on the outside," he joked. "Even if we're all arrogant as hell inside."

"Speak for yourself, Jim Morrison," Dorothy rejoindered.

"Hell, I've got enough arrogance for all three of us," I said.

"That's for sure," Jim responded.

"But I'll try to conduct myself with a proper degree of humility . . ."

"Good," he said.

". . . at least in public."

Dorothy laughed. "That'll be different."

We all smiled and the angel from *Jules and Jim* passed overhead.

Jim broke the sweet silence. "Man, I'm hungry!"

"You look like you haven't eaten in a month, Jim." Dorothy said.

"About a month and a half, to be exact," Jim corrected her.

"Let's go to the Lucky U and get some of Pancho's *chile rellenos,*" I said, my taste buds beginning to go bazooka. "I'm starved."

"Pancho's, yes!" said Jim.

"My treat," Dorothy said. "I suppose I'm going to have to support you guys while you put this all together . . . so I might as well get started now."

"All right, Dorothy!" Jim exclaimed.

And off we went. We piled into the Volkswagen Bug and headed into that warm California night. Young, alive, and on fire!

※

Later that night we shuttled back and forth from Fraser to Dennis's apartment on Speedway and loaded Jim's gear into the Navy gray Chevy. Thank God he had sent his books home to his mother and father, who were now living in San Diego. He had only one box of selects. Among them were Joyce's *Ulysses;* Céline's *Journey to the End of the Night;* all of Arthur Rimbaud, *A Season in Hell,* etc.; Kerouac's *Doctor Sax, On the Road, Visions of Cody,* and *The Town and the City;* Allen Ginsberg's selected poetry, other Beats; Norman Mailer's *The Deer Park* and *Advertisements for Myself;* Truman Capote's *Other Voices, Other Rooms;* Tennessee Williams's plays; Carson McCullers's *Reflections in a Golden Eye;* William Faulkner's *The Mosquitoes;* Hemingway's *The Sun Also Rises;* T. S. Eliot's *The Waste Land;* and F. Scott Fitzgerald's *The Great Gatsby.* He also had his electric blanket . . . and his expensive socks.

We put Jim in the bedroom. Dorothy and I moved our mattress into the living room, near the heater. We weren't going to let him have an electric blanket *and* sleep next to the heater. He was already spoiled. Why spoil him any more? Of course, we *all* were spoiled. Indulged and pampered by our parents. Doted over since childhood. We were spoiled brats now on our own. We had cut our ties with polite society and had entered the world of art! Do or die. "Look out, destiny, here we come."

And destiny looked back at us hard and square in the eye and said, in her sweet and seductive voice, "Look out Ray Manzarek, Dorothy Fujikawa, and Jim Morrison, you've now entered my sphere of influence and you have *no* idea what I have in store for you."

So we set up house together. And the mornings came and Dorothy would go off to work. Jim and I would drive her and when we didn't have our usual breakfast of tea and English muffins with peanut butter and honey at home, we would treat ourselves to breakfast at the Snack-O-Rama, Dorothy called it the Snake-O-Rama, on the corner of Santa Monica and Sepulveda. Eggs, hash browns, and whole wheat toast on a paper plate. Sometimes Dorothy and I would share a humongous cinnamon sugar snail swirl, with big cups of hot steaming coffee to ward off the morning ocean damp. And it was a mighty fine snail swirl, too. It was all good, honest food at a price you don't even want to *hear* about today. Man, it was a lot less expensive back then. Of course we made a lot less money, too. Ultimately, isn't the trick called "living within your means"? Don't *want* more than you can afford. Simple, right?

So we would drop her off at work and Jim and I would go on to UCLA, into the music school practice rooms in the basement—little sound-baffled rooms with little spinet pianos—and work on the songs. "Moonlight Drive," "Summer's Almost Gone," "My Eyes Have Seen You," "End of the Night," "I Looked at You"—that silly little ditty that, although a love song to a girl, almost defined our present situation.

I looked at you, you looked at me
I smiled at you, you smiled at me
And we're on our way, and we can't turn back
Yeah, we're on our way, and we can't turn back

(Here's destiny's part)

'Cause it's too late, too late, too late,
too late . . . too late!

And we worked those songs. Cajoled them into shape. Tickled them when they were obedient, shook them at other times, and beat on them when they were naughty. "Go Insane" was both wry and raucous. Faux innocent, mock naïf, and then goofy, South Bay–style rock and roll–blues progressions.

"The Crystal Ship" was a great song to work on. A beautiful descending melody line to which I put a harmonizing and descending chord structure. Moving underneath it, supporting Jim's words . . . and his voice. I put a radical for rock and roll B♭ major 7 as the third chord in the descending phrase of the verse:

Before you slip (Fm) into uncon(Cm)sciousness
I'd like(B♭ maj 7) to have another(D♭) kiss
Another (F) flashing (B♭7) chance (C) at (B♭)
Bliss (F) another(E♭) kiss (F)
Another (E♭) kiss (F)

I knew that the B♭ major 7 chord would cause trouble. Rock and roll's foundation was basic major and minor chords only. You could add sevenths, of course. But only minor sevenths. Hell, minor sevenths were the very foundation of the blues. A dark, mournful chord that carried with it the weight of slavery and oppression. It was the sound of the South Side of Chicago. The sound of rhythm-and-blues radio. The sound of Howlin' Wolf and Muddy Waters and John Lee Hooker, Magic Sam, Jimmy Reed, Sonny Boy Williamson, Little Walter, and a host of black geniuses. The minor seventh *was* the darkness; but the major seventh (a half step up from the flattened seventh) was *cool!* It was jazz, it was cabaret nightclub singers, it was smoke-filled lounges and cool chicks and West Coast mellow. And it had never been used in rock and roll. When we played the song in person during our early years on the Sunset Strip, Carl and Vito and their band of hippie gypsy trance dancers (who prowled the strip from club to club and party to party) did psychedelic, arm-waving, liquid-love slow dancing to it. But Carl or Vito (who could tell) would always complain to me after our set, "Ray, I hate that jazzy chord in the middle of 'Crystal Ship.' Can't you change it?" And then the hippie-harpies would descend on me, agreeing with their leader like a Greek chorus punctuating Euripides' *The Bacchae:* "We don't like it, either. It's corny. It's old-fashioned. It's not groovy. It's just not *with* it. Change it!"

Are their teeth actually sharpening and elongating as they speak? I thought. Am I actually calling forth succubi, Furies, night things? Or are these just lame-ass Valley chicks looking for a know-nothing scene to glom onto, to stick their two cents into, all too ready to agree with whatever the mob, the cud, the herd sanctioned? I opted for the latter, smiled, and said, "Sorry, I like it. It stays." They hissed at me and backed away. Five minutes later all was forgotten as the Strip gypsies came up to me again all a-twitter and said, "Ray, are you guys going to play 'The End' next set? We love it, it's so groovy." I had to smile to myself. "You bet we will, and it'll be special for you guys. Would you like that?" They leapt and fluttered and twittered and all was right again with the world. What a *hazarai* over a B♭ major 7. But, then, it does kind of represent the difference between childhood and adulthood. The sophistication of that jazzlike chord requires a putting aside of the things of a child. And as Yeshua ben Joseph, the great Jewish mystic and heart master, once said, "When I was a child, I spoke as a child, I played as a child, I thought as a child. Now that I have become a man, I have put aside the things of a child."

When we didn't feel like hammering on the forge of those songs, Jim and I would stay home and Dorothy would tool off in the Volkswagen to the only job that our little collective had. When the weather was good—and that was most of the time—we'd head out to the beach. Straight down Fraser, to the water's edge, hang a right, and continue north all the way to the Santa Monica Pier. Pacific coast shorebirds, plovers and sandpipers, would dart in front of us as we walked. Long-legged little things rushing back and forth as the waves would break. Staying just to the edge of the water's farthest point, running rhythmically with the ebb and flow of the sea foam, looking for tiny crabs that would quickly bury themselves in the sand as the water passed over.

As we walked, we talked: of the current rock and roll scene, of politics, of literature, of cinema, of the secrets of female sexuality, and of the fact that we were walking on the end line of Western civilization. Twelve miles out to sea from where we strolled became international waters and the West was over with. The Western dream of expansion and Manifest Destiny ended at that beach. It had emigrated from Europe, beginning in ancient Greece and moving across the European continent to England, outward bound across the Atlantic to the shores of the new continent. The New World. New England. And then, "Westward ho!" the great migration began, eventually covering the entire continent to bring us to the place where we stood. Jim and I on the beach in Venice, California. The West had run out of land. There was nothing left. Beyond us and the great expanse of the Pacific was Asia. And perhaps it was the beginning of their time in the sun. But not yet. Not in that summer of 1965. The sun was shining down on us. We were in the energy and the energy *was* us.

But since the West had ended . . . what about the Western Dream? Was it still viable? Did it still matter? And was it inextricably bound with the three Jerusalem-based religions? Or was it time for a new dream? Some kind of rock and roll dream. Some kind of racially mixed, culturally mixed, religiously mixed, rhythmically based new dream.

> *I want to tell you about*
> *Texas radio and the big beat.*
> *It comes out of the Virginia swamps,*
> *Cool and slow,*
> *With plenty of precision and a backbeat*
> *Narrow and hard to master.*
> *Some call it heavenly in its brilliance,*
> *Others mean and rueful of*
> *the Western Dream.*

These were the kinds of things we talked about as we headed north to the Santa Monica Pier. We were going to Muscle Beach, the exercise area at the side of the pier. The infamous, wicked, and bloated Muscle Beach of yore. Where men of beef and babes of boobs strutted their inflated stuff. Except in the summer of '65, the barbells and the dumbbells were gone. The powers that be had removed the heavy metal due to a controversial morals charge. Gang rape by the beef masters of a beach bunny . . . or perhaps a beach boy. It took place back in the late fifties and there were still legends of buggery and other unnatural penetrations making the rounds. There was nothing left of the golden days but a sign over a small boardwalk bar, proclaiming itself to the setting sun as the official Muscle Beach Bar. What had replaced the weights were free-hand parallel bars, rings, and balance beams. Wholesome gymnastics apparatus. The Olympian ideal. The beef men had moved elsewhere, perhaps to the original Gold's, or Vic Tanny's, or Vince Gioranda's; but definitely indoors, away from the tourists, out of the sun, out of the light, and into a high-protein-enzyme, anabolic-steroid, amino-acid dreamworld. And God bless them in their muscle quest. Personally, I can understand the motivation. It's called "the biggest motherfucker on the entire planet." Mr. Fucking World Biceps *Huge!*

Jim and I, however, were headed to the rings and things. We were going to get ourselves in shape for the coming onslaught on traditional values, the revolution right around the corner. We were going to dip and swing and chin and climb ourselves into fine-tuned psychedelic warriors ready to do battle with the Philistines of the Establishment. We began on the rings. A series of rings suspended from an iron support of semicircles and a top bar running for ten to twelve yards. About ten to fifteen rings, approximately three feet apart. The object was to swing from ring to ring, hand over hand, like a monkey in the trees. You'd hold the first ring, stand on the little elevated platform, leap off, and swing out to the next ring, grab it, and let go of the first ring as you pulled yourself back and forth to gain momentum to grab for the third ring. And so it went, ring to ring, out to the end, turn, and work your way back and up on to the little platform. Voilà! Kids would do it easily. Like little monkeys. Big guys, however . . . well . . . shit, we fell off at the second ring the first time we tried it. And I've got a good grip. Piano hands. But, man, that was hard. And gravity pulling on my arms and shoulders . . . Ouch! Jim fared no better than I. We looked at each other and shook our heads in mutual disgust.

I said, "Jim, we're pathetic. The kids can go all the way out and back and we can only do two rings. What a couple of pussies."

He agreed. "We are a disgrace to college graduates all over America. Ray, you and I have a lot of work to do. So let's get *started!*" he mockingly barked.

"All right," I shouted back. "Let's hit it!"

And, goddamn it, we did. We started a regimen of every other day at the rings, alternated with song creation at UCLA. Jim was coming up with more variations and permutations on his lyrics that required more and more invention on the keys from me. I loved it. He was exploding with ideas, and I was constantly pushing myself to try different and more imaginative chord changes, harmonic patterns, solos, rhythms, funk grooves, blues riffs, and jazz and classical modes of playing to support and embellish his poetry. We were definitely progressing. The Doors were on their way to creating an important body of work. Or, as the potheads used to say, this was some good shit!

At the beach apparatus, we worked our hands almost to bleeding, doing dips on the parallel bars, pull-ups on the chinning bars, push-ups on the low, sand-level parallel bars, and swinging on the damned monkey rings. We stood on that little platform, holding the first ring, and leapt out into space, grabbing for that second ring about a hundred times before we could make it to the third ring. But when we did, we knew it was the beginning of *our* mastery of that piece of exercise iron. The monkey rings could no longer mock us. *We* were becoming the monkeys. And sure enough, in a little under a month, Morrison and Manzarek had become monkey men and were swinging all the way out to the end and back. Like the kids could do it. Except we were the big guys and, goddamn it, we could now do it, too! And it felt good. Hand over hand, ring after ring, with a rocking motion, suspended in air by nothing more than the sheer power of the grip of your hands on metal, moving fast enough to create a cool breeze on your face . . . and we became simian. For a brief moment we forgot being human and stepped back a couple of evolutionary eons to become beasts again. And there was a joy to it. An exuberant joy of simple, pure physicality. It was free of all worry. Free of all thought, for that matter. As we hurled ourselves through space we entered the holy now. We were in the animal mind, in our case the ape mind, and we were having what Joseph Campbell calls a "peak experience." It was as brief as the time it took to traverse those rings, but I want to tell you . . . it was fine!

That afternoon, when Dorothy came home from her computer gig, I couldn't wait to tell her . . .

"Honey, we did it! All the way out and all the way back," I gushed.

She beamed at us. "Well, congratulations, you guys. I'm proud of you."

Jim beamed back. "Pretty good, eh, Dorothy? Pretty neat."

"I'll say, Jim. To be honest, I never thought you two would make it all the way out and back." Dorothy had come with us on the Saturday of our first week's attempts at self-propelled flight. She saw us reach feebly at the third ring while slipping off the second, arms flailing, foolishly falling to the sand. "This looks awfully hard, Ray," she said back then.

"Oh, ye of little faith," I mocked, and then pounded on my chest. "We're the monkey men." Jim whooped like a howler monkey and did his best ape walk. Dorothy laughed.

"Of course I had faith in you guys . . . but those rings are *hard*," she said.

"I'll say, look at my hands," I said, and thrust my hands out, palms up. Calluses and gnarly skin!

"I know about the calluses, Ray. I can feel them on my breasts."

"Dorothy!" Jim mockingly said. "I'm embarrassed."

"Honey, not in front of company," I joked. Then serious . . . "You can? I didn't hurt you, did I?"

She gave me a little push on the arm. "No, you big lug. I was only teasing. Congratulations!"

I beamed, too. "Let's celebrate. Let's eat meat."

"Let's fire up the barbecue," Jim said. "I want a T-bone steak."

Dorothy shook her head. "Payday's not till Friday, Jim." This was Wednesday. We were short.

"How much do we have?" he asked. We started to count our collective moneys and found ourselves with enough cash to buy the trimmings but hardly the steaks.

"Let's go to the market," Jim said. "I'll handle this situation . . . you guys leave it to me." He grinned. And the devil flashed behind Jim Morrison's eyes.

At the market on the corner of Ocean Park and Lincoln we went about our shopping business in a calm and casual manner. The three of us walked behind a shopping cart and ambled over to the produce section.

"Head of lettuce," Dorothy said as she plucked an iceberg from a stack of green and plopped it into the cart.

Dad and me

Jim, Rick, and
Ray Manzarek
as muscle men

My first
piano recital

Me—adolescent
pimples, peach fuzz,
and Mr. B. Collar

The "Hoyne Giants":
Joe Niese is holding the
football. I'm upper left.

A Polish wedding
in Chicago with
Mom and Dad.
I'm sixteen.

Me, the hambone, as Prince
Charming in *Cinderella*
high school play

The Manzarek family:
Ray Sr., Helen, Ray Jr.,
Jim, and Rich

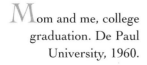

Mom and me, college
graduation. De Paul
University, 1960.

Rick and the Ravens

Me in the first month of my life in California

Screamin' Ray Daniels

Jim, my mom, Dorothy, and Thor the Doberman

The Doors' first
photo session.
New York, 1966.

More jamming and
transcending on
"Gloria" by the Doors
and Them. *Photo by
George Rodriguez. Used by
permission of the Doors.*

Jim Morrison and Van
Morrison onstage at the
Whiskey-a-Go-Go, jam-
ming on "Gloria." *Photo by
George Rodriguez. Used by
permission of the Doors.*

Romeo and Juliet in San Francisco, 1967. *Photo by Robert Klein. Used by permission of the Doors.*

Our wedding, 1967. *Photo by Paul Ferrara. Used by permission of the Doors.*

Into the Mystic, East Coast, 1967. *Photo by Mike Barich.*

A Lincoln dog, D.C., 1967. *Photo by Paul Ferrara. Used by permission of the Doors.*

Reading the Lincoln plaque, Washington, D.C., 1967. *Photo by Paul Ferrara. Used by permission of the Doors.*

San Jose Rock
Festival, 1968.
Jim: "What do you
want to play next?"
Ray: "I don't know,
but first hand me
that joint."
*Photo by Ed Caraeff.
Used by permission
of Ed Caraeff.*

A backstage discus-
sion on the literary
merits of a fanzine.
New Jersey, 1968.
*Photo by Michael
Montfort/Gunter Zint.
Used by permission
of the Doors.*

"Three baked potatoes," Jim said, and dropped three Idahos into a bag.

"Why are you wearing your pea coat, Jim?" I asked. "You catching a cold or something?" It was summer. It was hot, for God's sake.

"Part of the battle plan, Ray," he said enigmatically.

"Broccoli for our iron." Dorothy said as she bagged a big green bunch of B.

"Let's go take a look at the *meat* counter," Jim said, doing a Mae West imitation. "I want to see how three steaks look."

"They look unaffordable, Jim," I responded. "Unaffordable and delicious." I did a W. C. Fields back at him.

Dorothy laughed and maneuvered the cart through the aisles to the beef. Along the way we plucked some Alta Dena milk and butter from the dairy case, Thomas's English muffins from the bread rack, and my favorite, a bottle of Gallo Hearty Burgundy. A damn fine blend for an unsophisticated palate. And my palate was certainly naive. Now it was time for the moment of truth. We were at the meat counter and everything looked great. Lamb chops, pork chops, roasts, and steaks. Lots of steaks. Jim ran his hand over the wrapped packages. Each steak enclosed in its own little cellophane shroud. He stopped at the T-bones, shuffled them around, examined them closely, and made his choice. Three big beauties.

"Let's go," he said, holding the three packages in his hands. Dorothy pushed off. I was next to her and Jim was right behind us. Walking too close to us. We were almost to the checkout and I turned to him.

"Move back, will ya. You're bumping into me." And then I saw it. The steaks were gone!

"Where's the meat?" I asked. And he opened his pea coat and grinned that southern lazy-boy grin of his. Stuck in his pants, under his belt, were the three steak packages! He quickly closed his voluminous pea coat, folded his arms across his chest, and we all moved into the checkout line. Bing, bing, bing, the trimmings were added up. Dorothy paid the bill. The victuals were bagged. I grabbed the two bags and we began to move to the front door and freedom. Jim, wise guy that he always was, stopped and turned back to the cute checkout girl.

"Say, you're not free this weekend, are you? Like, Friday night? I thought we could catch a flick together or something."

My brain went ballistic! We're stealing steaks and he's asking the checkout girl for a date! We're committing a felony or something and he's playing *Cool Hand Luke*. Jesus!

The girl smiled. "Sorry, I'm married."

"Well, didn't hurt to try," said Jim, smiling. "I'll be seeing you again." He never unfolded his arms.

"I hope so," the girl said. "Bye . . . for now."

And we were gone. Free. Piled into the car, raced to Fraser, fired up the grill, baked those potatoes, buttered the broccoli, tossed the salad, and the two monkey men and their patroness ate those charbroiled steaks. Man, it was good!

⁂

Now in and around this time of Jim and Ray and Dorothy living together was also our time of LSD ingestion. It was legal back then. Almost everyone we knew was a pot smoker but very few were takers of soma-LSD-acid! It was simply too dangerous for most—and still is! I would never, and do *not*, advocate the taking of LSD . . . by the emotionally unstable. But I, of course, impetuous youth, took it as soon as it made itself available to me back at UCLA. I reasoned: If smoking grass is as innocuous, harmless, and pleasant as it is . . . hell, why not try some acid, too? The marijuana high was quite delightful and certainly non-addictive. There didn't seem to be any real drawbacks to it other than the damn tars and phlegm in your lungs. The stuff was loaded with tars and resins that you could feel in your lungs and occasionally produced a loose mucous hacking cough. Not a pleasant sound. Thank God nobody smoked pot the way people smoke cigarettes or it would be the lung cancer ward in a quick decade. Nobody could smoke a pack of pot a day. Maybe a joint or two, but that was it. I could never do more than that.

The other drawback was in the operation of heavy machinery. I wouldn't want to operate a bulldozer or a crane when I was stoned. I wouldn't advise anyone to manipulate a wrecking ball while high, either. Hell, you could miss the target. Whoops, hit the wrong building . . . not good. Threshing machines out in a field of wheat could be okay, though. Hard to keep the lines straight, but no potential for real damage. Jet fighter pilots taking off from and landing on an aircraft carrier probably shouldn't smoke grass. Once you're in the sky, it would be quite nice, but not during a precision landing. The reflexes slow down a bit, so whenever your ass is on the line and you need to have split-second physical timing . . . well, don't get high. Wait till afterward and then treat yourself. "It's Humboldt time!" Driving in the Indianapolis 500 is no good, on the street . . . be careful. I don't recommend it. Although, shit, it's a lot better to smoke the weed than drive drunk. How many people are killed and maimed by drunk drivers? You know the answer to that . . . too many! Pot accidents? Sure, there are some; but probably a lot fewer than random, straight-drivered fender-benders. And kids should never do it. Makes them lazy and stupid. And they're lazy and stupid enough already. Kids need discipline and study and practice. They need to develop some expertise before they can kick back and relax. Kids *are* relaxed. That's all they are, all the time.

The negatives of marijuana were few. The positives were delicious. Relaxation, increased perception, color enhancement, delight in food, delight in sex, increased logical brain connections—"Oh, I get it now!" and "I understand" and "I never saw the connection between those two things before" and a general and overall groovy feeling, as we said in the sixties. Of course those logical brain connections are exactly what your religious leaders and your federal, state, and local government officials do *not* want you to make. They'd be out of a job if you actually looked behind the curtain. They definitely don't want you opening the doors of perception.

⚜

Word of a substance called LSD-25 began to spread around UCLA as early as 1963. Rumors and written reports from San Francisco and word of experiments at Harvard by Timothy Leary and Richard Alpert were beginning to tantalize the more adventurous student heads. And the word was . . . "LSD-25 is the new sacrament. It is the new food of the Gods." In Leary's book *The Psychedelic Experience* and in *The Psychedelic Quarterly*, a scholarly publication on psychotropic substances that also came out of Harvard, we started reading about mystical states of consciousness that were being attained by the new "soma eaters," and these were being compared to the enlightened state of the Buddha. To Zen enlightenment. To the attaining of satori. To Nirvana. The exact same things the Beats were talking about. So here's this substance that may or may not actually open the doors of perception.

Well . . . of course I had to try it! And if I was going to try it, you know Dorothy was going to try it, too.

However, our first trip took us nowhere. Nothing happened. Geoff Goodrich had sold me 100 mics, and he was a trustworthy guy; a folksinger–guitar player–filmmaker and completely honest. So I went to him and said, "Geoff, what the fuck, this stuff doesn't do anything."

"What'd you do?" he asked.

"We split the hundred and sat around all afternoon waiting for it to come on . . . never did," I replied.

He said, "That hundred mics was for you. That's a mild dose. I didn't want to give you too much, just see what happens on a hundred. You can't split it. Fifty's not enough to get anybody high."

"Oh," was all I could say. He reached into his omnipresent knapsack and took out two small vials of colorless liquid.

"Here's two one-fifties," he said. "My treat. You take one, give Dorothy the other."

"No, man. Let me at least pay for one," I said as I handed him a ten-dollar bill. A lid of grass was ten dollars, so one hit of acid was expensive in comparison.

"Deal," Geoff said. "Now go home . . . and enjoy yourself." He grinned.

So we took it. Ray Manzarek and Dorothy Fujikawa. Apprentice seekers, beginning bodhisattvas, pilgrims in search of the Golden City. We made a nice setting for ourselves on Fraser, lit some incense, took our 150 each . . . and we were off! Flying on the wings of love . . . to Nirvana, to the Pure Land.

It was absolutely stunning. We were in our little one-bedroom apartment above the garage, looking out over the rooftops of Venice, out onto the setting sun . . . and had entered the cosmic state. It was divine. It was expansive and harmonious and beatific and one. I was alive! For the first time in my life I understood what it meant to be truly alive.

Here's what happened to me on that fateful acid trip. After falling in love with the sun (talk about pure God energy; the closest approximation to the secret of the origin of life is the solar energy coming off that great golden globe that shines down on us all) I was lying on the floor with my eyes closed . . . and I had entered the womb. I had gone back to the womb. Lying there in a fetal position, I had gone back to my mother and was completely safe and secure. I knew I was Ray Manzarek, in Venice and on LSD, but I was experiencing the womb again. I opened one eye to look at the setting sun, but I closed it quickly. I wasn't ready to leave yet. It was not yet my time of emergence. I hadn't cooked enough. The child was still undone. Like bread not yet golden. So I simply lay there, being in the womb. Being in that warm, soft place . . . in that fetal position, just feeling *so* good that I came to a realization. I understood, at that instant, what the concept of being born again was all about. Jesus the Christ says in the Christian Bible, "You must be born again." And I knew what he meant. You must go into yourself . . . all the way into yourself . . . to your beginning, your origin. Into the waters of your unconscious. Into the core of you. A Zen koan asks the question, "What were you before you were born?" Well . . . you must be born again.

And when I finally opened my eyes . . . I had been reborn. I was a new Ray Manzarek. I was the same man but I was the new man. I had left my fears behind. I had left my childhood behind. I had "put aside the things of a child," and I had become a man. A free man on the planet. Completely responsible for my actions. Completely responsible for all of the things I would now do in the future and had done in the past and very possibly—a philosophy I came to later—completely responsible for *everything.* Responsible for the destiny of the planet . . . as all of us, each and every one of us, are. *We* are responsible for this planet. This is our playground. It's *our* sun in the sky and this is our Garden of Eden. We've never lost it. We've only forgotten the key to unlock the door of perception.

Have you forgotten the keys to the Kingdom?
Have you been born yet, and are you alive?

This is what I realized on LSD. This is our playground and we are here to laugh and dance and sing in the sunshine. To sing and laugh and dance and play music in the moonlight. . . . to play drums and to play guitars, to play Vox Continental electric organs as a shaman/poet leads us in a mad, passionate Dionysian revelry around a great, blazing bonfire. *That* is the purpose of being alive. An absolute delight in the senses! And the profound responsibility for being the creators of the world. The tenders and maintainers of the garden.

I closed my eyes again, overwhelmed by the multiplicity of objects. The choices were infinite. The sheer number of things in this universe of ours is beyond calculating. The void is stuffed to overflowing with the objects of our creation. Just look about you. Look up from this book for a second, dear reader. Look around the room, out the window. Lots of things, lots of stuff . . . lots of *life*, right? Now, imagine none of it there. Imagine nothing. A state of nothingness. Close your eyes and imagine . . . nothing.

I was doing time in the Universal Mind,
I was feeling fine.

Imagine you can feel only energy. Outside of you is nothing. You are everything, all there is, and you are rested, relaxed, charged with energy, and ready to create a world to occupy. You are eternity. You are infinity. And now you want some relativity. You want some things to exist with you. You want forms and shapes and flesh. You want to occupy some flesh of your own for the purposes of dancing and singing and lovemaking and feasting. You want all the attendant fears and dangers that go along with being temporal. You're ready for both the fun and the turmoil, the delights and the suffering, the pleasure and the pain. And you have to take both, *of course*. That's the yin and the yang of it. You don't get the sweet without the bitter. And, as I was later to find out, you don't get the highs without the lows. But who would want the one without the other? Life without suffering would be boring. Love without heartache would be sugar syrup. How much goody-goody could you take? Imagine being like the Eloi in H. G. Wells's *The Time Machine*. No, sir. That's not the life we want. We want action, excitement, adventure, danger. We want passion and love. We want to be living, breathing human animals. Conscious and alive!

We want the world and we want it . . . Now!

So go ahead. Make up a world. Make up a universe out of your nothingness. And here's the irony . . . it would most likely be exactly what we have. A blue-water planet, spinning around a sun, filled with green and liquid and sky and clouds and good things to eat and life in thousands of forms and a spinal column, nervous system, and brain for self-realization and male and female for sex and procreation and . . . well, you get the picture. What you'd make is what we already have. And it's fabulous. Let's do it!

And now it was time for *me* to dive back in. Come back into life. I was lying on the floor, on Fraser, in the fetal position with my eyes closed, realizing I was going to be born again, realizing I was going to come out of the womb again, this psychological womb I had gone into; and I said to Dorothy, "Hand me that orange. . . ." It was one of the things I had seen when I briefly opened my eyes and was flooded by sensory input. We had halved an orange and made wedges on a plate; individual segments to refresh ourselves. "What?" she said as I called my love out of the void, or out of some ecstatic reverie of her own. "An orange, hand me a slice, honey," and I held my hand out like a blind man. She placed a cool, moist slice in my hand and I could smell orange blossoms in the afternoon air. I held it up to my nose, eyes closed, and inhaled the intoxicating essence of that orange. The fragrance of that slice was so refreshing and so absolutely delightful. The odor of an orange is simply overwhelming. It seemed so thirst-quenching. So refreshing. I put the slice half in my mouth, holding one end, and licked it. And that orange essence on my tongue just took over, just occupied my mouth . . . I felt my taste buds begin to tingle . . . then I bit into it with my teeth and punctured the tiny flavor sacs of juice. Man, they just exploded! Liquid everywhere. My mouth filled with orange juice. Sweet and tart at the same instant. The juice started to trickle down my throat and I chewed the flesh and swallowed. Delicious. I was completely refreshed. Completely revivified. The energy—the *chi*, as the Chinese say—in that fruit literally brought me out of the womb, gave me birth again. I came to life on that orange. And I opened my eyes and looked at that half slice in my hand and I saw thousands of tiny sacs attached to the central pith of the orange. Thousands of little flavor sacs. Each sac holding a bit of juice. Thousands of little amorphous, Indian-shaped, teardrop, membrane-skinned juice containers in a single slice. Clinging to each other, and all somehow attached to the cottony central pith. And this marvel of construction is repeated in segment after segment after segment. I looked at it and thought, This is the most complex thing I've ever seen in my life. Who made this? My brain paused. . . . God made this. But wait a minute, we're *all* God. I was breathing hard now. Did my mind think of this? Did the mind of all of us think of this? Is this the mind, the Creator at work? Am I the Creator? I had to smile at the sheer joy of my thoughts. Are we all the Creator? Are *we* the Creative Mind? Is the mind of God . . . *our* mind? I had mentally stepped into the fourth dimension. Ouspensky's *Tertium Organum.* The realm of Nietzsche's *Übermensch.* The land of the Arborians.

I'm the freedom man,
That's how lucky I am,
I'm the freedom man . . .

My thoughts raced on: The orange has been put here for our pleasure. The point in occupying this fleshy form we call the body . . . is the pleasure we receive from the body. That's why *we're* here. For our pleasure. The delight and pleasure I received from that orange, the sheer sensuality of it, was absolutely overwhelming, and intoxicating, and . . . joyous!

Lying on the floor, in that little apartment in Venice Beach, that little apartment in which my girlfriend, Dorothy Fujikawa, and I had begun our nest, that little one-bedroom on Fraser Street overlooking the roofs and the palm trees of Venice . . . I had, on that day, entered William Blake's Palace of Wisdom. He had been there, too. And, I was to learn later, so had many others. And so can you. It's our birthright. We are all supposed to dwell in the mansion at the top of the hill (the crown chakra). It's our ultimate destiny. It's cosmic consciousness. Nirvana. Satori. The *kether* of the Kaballah.

Later that afternoon I explained the whole thing to Dorothy and she said, "Let me try that orange."

She took a slice, broke it in half, looked deeply into it, and said, "You're right! There are thousands of little flavor sacs. Look, each one is a unique little thing and they're shaped like those paisley forms on our Indian bedspread."

I said, "Eat it, eat it! Try it! Feel the juice in your throat."

She bit into it and her eyes lit up. "Oh, God. It's so good." She smiled. "Ray . . . we're alive!" She looked at me, "We're alive and we're in love. I love you!"

And I said, "Dorothy, God, I love you, too."

And I took her in my arms and held her and she wrapped her arms around my body in a sensuous, serpentine coil. She had little tears in her eyes, overcome with joy. We stripped our clothes off and made love there on the floor of our nest. Her flesh was all of creation to me. Her legs wrapped around my back as I entered her. She enfolded me and secured me within her. The female gesture: open, rounded, enfolded, entwined. Little moans of pleasure involuntarily passed over our lips as I began the male gesture of thrusting forward. Into the essence of her. Into her depths. And I realized where I was: "My God, I'm inside of you. I'm on the inside of your body."

She wrapped her legs tighter, "I love you, Ray," she said through those beautiful parted lips of hers, "I'll always love you."

I pushed myself into her again, she moaned.

"We're one flesh now," I whispered. "We're Adam and Eve . . ." And we both closed our eyes and gave ourselves over to that deepest and sweetest of all sensual pleasures. We made love into the night and we created the world with our bodies. LSD-25!

Jim Morrison and I never really discussed our LSD trips in any great detail. They were personal, private, and, dare I say it, sacred. There were things best left unspoken between friends, and this was one of those things. However, the knowledge lived in the eyes. There was a certain shine, a luminosity projecting out through the cornea of the devotees. The carbon-arc of the brain was flooding the entire brain pan with holy light and that understanding would radiate outward through the eye sockets. The eyeballs of the initiates were fields of fire, and Jim's were especially radiant. He exuded a glow of energy and spirituality that was warming just to stand next to. There was no need to discuss the voyages because you could *feel* the journeys in the other person's emanations. And, hell, what was there to say, anyway? It was the understanding beyond words. It was the place beyond intellect. It was the proper home of the human animal and it is always there, awaiting our presence, yearning for us to enter the new dimension and cast off our chains.

Break on through to the other side

And Jim Morrison had broken through the closed circle of the ego. He was free. I was free. Dorothy was free. And *you* can be free, too. All you have to do is . . . do it. We're waiting for you, and we very much "hope someday you'll join us." And then we can begin the changing of the guard. The changing of the power structure. The dismantling of the military-government-industrial complex. We can begin the creation of the New Time . . . and the New Man. And the New Garden.

Please, please, listen to me, children
You are the ones who will rule the world

And perhaps that day is just around the corner. Perhaps we're almost there. Why not?

Wake up, girl, we're almost home

Although we didn't share our inner journeys, Jim did share one of his hallucinations with me. He had dropped a tab with Felix Venable at Felix's place in the Venice canals that he shared with his then inamorata, Mary Morhoff. Mary was at work (another good woman supporting her vagabond artist boyfriend), and Felix was flat on his back, unable to move, demanding beer. His voice had an irritating timbre to it and he usually got his way.

"Morrison, you got to get some beer," Felix whined.

"Hey," Jim responded, "I'm not going all the way to the liquor store for a six-pack. It's too far."

"What are you *talking* about, Morrison? It's only a block *away!*" (Sort of nasal-whine that to yourself and you'll get the picture of Felix's voice.)

"Felix, that's an eternity away. I just want to look at the water in the canals, that's all I want to do. It's beautiful."

"Come on, Jim . . . you gotta get me some beer."

"Why don't *you* go, then. And get some beef jerky while you're there. I could really go for a Corona and some beef jerky. Eat some *meat*, you know?" Jim said.

"I can't move," Felix said from flat on his back. "I'm pinned down to the earth and I can't get up. If I had a beer I could get up. You gotta go and get a six-pack . . . if you don't I could be here on this fucking floor forever. You don't want me to *die* here, do you, Jim?"

Jim laughed. "There is no death, Felix. Don't you get it?"

"I'll fuckin' die right here, Morrison," Felix protested. "I swear to God . . . I'm dying right now." Then the odd timbre. "Please, man, get me some beer, will ya?"

"All right already. Just *stop!* Enough, I'll go." Jim was beaten down by the annoying insistency of Felix's will. Felix loved to exercise his will. He was doing it now, even on acid. And that was quite a trick, considering that LSD breaks down mind games and ego barriers . . . but not in Felix's case. Although it *had* pinned him to the floor like a butterfly in a display case, acid still hadn't shut him up. There was a saying at the time: "May the baby Jesus shut your mouth and open your mind." Well, the little Yeshua ben Joseph had a tough goy to crack in one Felix Venable.

Jim continued, "Give me some money and I'll go."

"I don't have any money. Mary's got the money and she's at work. Come on, you buy," Felix begged.

Jim shook his head. "I left my wallet at Ray's. I don't have a cent on me."

"Shit, shit, shit!" whined Felix as he flopped his arms and legs on the floor. Jim later said that watching him thrashing made him think of a big turtle turned on its back. A big loggerhead sea turtle up on the sand, out of its element and stuck on its back. Felix on acid *was* out of his element. He was a boozer. He probably should have just stayed a boozer. LSD was definitely not his substance.

"Why don't we just forget it, then?" Jim said.

Encased in his ego and stuck in his bodily hallucination, Felix said, "No, man, we can't! I can't get *up* unless I have a beer. Go back to Ray's and get your wallet."

"Fuck you," Jim said. "I don't want to walk one block to the store and you want me to walk eight to ten blocks back to Ray's and then come back and buy you beer? Felix . . . go fuck yourself."

"All right," Felix said. "Just go to the store and ask the guy for credit. He knows me."

"Ask who?"

"The chink who owns the store," said Felix, ever the racist. "Just tell him it's for Felix and get a six-pack and some beef jerky. Get me a pony of Ripple, too. Okay?"

"When should I tell him you'll pay him back?" Jim asked.

"He won't ask that, he's cool," Felix replied.

And Jim did it. He went out the door, crossed an eternity, bummed a six-pack of Corona, beef jerky, and a pony of Ripple, crossed another eternity, and walked back in the door.

"Got it," Jim said.

"Thank God," said Felix, still pinned to the floor. "Open one, quick."

Jim did, handed it to Felix, who downed the entire can without taking a breath . . . and sat up! Simple as that. "Whew," said Felix. "I needed that."

Jim could only laugh. "Yeah, I'll bet you did, Felix."

"Did you get the Ripple, too?"

Jim dug into the paper bag, pulled out the pony, and tossed it to the alcoholic-to-be. Felix cracked it and began to walk around the room, sipping the sweet syrup. "Good acid, huh?" he absurdly said. Jim was oblivious. He was back in his spot, viewing the water of the canal and munching on a strip of beef jerky, alternating bites with sips of Corona.

After consuming his snack, Jim turned to Felix. "So when *are* you going to pay him back?"

"Who?" asked Felix.

"The guy at the store," answered Jim. "He seems like a nice guy. He said he knows you."

"Of course he knows me. He gave you the beer, didn't he?"

Jim cocked his head. "He didn't *give* me the beer. You have to pay him back."

"So?" Felix grinned.

"So, when?" Jim replied.

And then Felix looked him in the eye, and his true nature came forth: "Never," Felix snarled. "Fuck him . . . the chink asshole."

Jim was speechless. He just got up, belched one time, and walked out the door. He hung a right on Main and began the ten-block walk north to Fraser. And along the way his own hallucination kicked in.

He said he saw a satyr following him from across the street. A little satyr with horns and pointed ears, a man's head and upper body, walking on two goat legs. A little Greco-Roman satyr. A faun, as in Debussy's *Prelude to the Afternoon of a Faun,* so brilliantly danced and choreographed by Vaslav Nijinsky for Diaghilev's Ballet Russe. Pan, the god of the forest. And this little satyr was popping in and out from behind parked cars and waving to Jim, clowning and joking and making silly faces. Jim later said he thought the satyr was inviting him to dance or to frolic. He said the little forest dweller followed him for about five blocks. Always staying on the opposite side of the street, never crossing over to Jim, but continually beckoning him and smiling and just carrying on as fauns are wont to do. As Jim approached Fraser, the satyr simply leapt behind a palm tree and was gone.

"I was just followed home by a satyr," he said as he walked in the door. His eyes were wild and blazing. He looked not unlike a satyr himself.

"Is it still with you?" I asked, sure that he was on acid.

He looked back outside, behind him. "No, he's gone," he said. And then he silently went into the bedroom, closed the door, collapsed on the bed, and slept for the next twelve hours.

I believe that little satyr was the spirit of his own freedom. On this one acid trip he had been attended upon by both the devil and freedom. Felix was the spirit of human darkness: power and manipulation, selfishness, mendacity, greed. Alcohol brought out these negative traits in Felix and, once unleashed, they completely dominated his personality. At school or when he was sober, Felix was a good guy. He was bright, relatively hip, and older than everyone else. He had a lot of experience under his belt. And Jim liked him as a much older brother or perhaps even a father figure. And what Felix was selling would eventually insinuate itself into Jim's psyche, where it would germinate, take root, and breed a tiny monster. Jimbo. After all, Jim and Felix were of the same ethnic lineage, the same tribe, the same bloodstock, they had the same southern frame of reference and shared a penchant for alcohol. Of course they hit it off. And when Felix spoke, Jim listened. But when Jim drank, in those days, he just got silly. When Felix drank, however, the devil came out. And Jim saw that devil on this particular acid trip . . . looked him in the eye . . . didn't blink . . . turned his back, and walked out the door. Felix was very big on making the other guy blink. Making the other guy avert his eyes from a hard, cold stare. The cowboy/Western man manipulation of power on the psychic plane. The American Indian averts his eyes from a hard, penetrating stare. He considers it to be rude and somewhat crazy. "Why does the white man stare at us in the eyes like that? What's the matter with him, is he insane?" asks the Native American. But the new tribe of psychedelic native Americans, the heads, had gone soft in the eyes. They had become what Jesus had talked about in the beginning of the Piscean age: lovers. "Though shalt love thy neighbor as thyself," said the Galilean. Felix, however, had never gone soft. He was still a hard guy. A power freak. A seeker after dominance. An American. The very traits Jimbo would emulate. But there was no point to Felix's wanting of the power. He had no great ideas. He didn't have a plan. He didn't want to change the world. He didn't want to re-create the Garden of Eden. He just wanted the power! For himself. So that *he* would have it and you wouldn't. In that, he was not unlike Oliver Stone. Felix once revealed the "secrets of the race" to Dorothy. He was drunk and he really shouldn't have told her. He violated the unspoken code by telling an Asian person the secrets of the white man. The booze had clouded his judgment and given him a too loose lip. Dorothy told me of their conversation. It was at a party we all had gone to at Colin Young's house. Colin was the head of the UCLA Film Department, and a very cool Scot.

"You know what you do, Dorothy?" Felix asked.

"No, Felix . . . do about what?" she responded.

He looked about the room, checking for eavesdroppers. "The power!" he said.

"What about it?"

"Do you know how to get it?" he slurred, secure in his privacy.

"What power are you talking about, Felix?"

"The power to the whole thing, Dorothy." And then his eyes lit up, savoring the thought. "The power to rule!"

"Why would I want to rule?" she asked.

"Because you *want* to! Because it's *there*," he blurted.

"What would I do with the power, Felix?"

He looked at her, quizzically. . . . "That's not the point, beautiful. It doesn't matter what you do with it." He sipped his scotch. "It only matters . . . whether or not . . . you *have* it, see?"

"I think I'm beginning to understand you," she answered.

"Do you know how to get it"—more scotch—"in a situation like this party, for instance?" And before she could reply, he was off:

"You look the other guy in the eye, straight into his eyes, hard." Another hit of scotch. "You hold his gaze until he can't take it anymore and has to look away. You make him blink!" And he killed the scotch. "Then you have him." Dorothy said his chest swelled, as if he were reliving a moment of psychic assault and triumph. "Then *you* have the power. He's yours!"

Dorothy looked *him* in the eye and said, "You know what, Felix? We call that kind of shit . . . *mind games.*" And she turned away from him and walked off into the party.

Later, Felix told me how much he admired Dorothy.

"She's got a good mind, Ray, and"—he had danced with her that evening—"she dances like a fucking snake!"

I laughed. "Yeah, Felix. I like her, too."

Now Jim's satyr was a most appropriate hallucination for a Dionysus-like individual. Satyrs are the familiars, the attendees of Dionysus. Also of Bacchus, the Roman god of wine and revelry. They mill about Dionysus, waiting for the fun to begin. They wait for the maenads, those frenzied women who take part in the wild, orgiastic rites that accompany his worship. They wait for the bacchantes. They wait with Dionysus for the rock concert to begin. For the *groupies* to appear! And this particular faun came out of the ether because he saw a *new* Dionysus walking down the street in Venice Beach, California, and he knew the fun was going to start again. Jim Morrison was going to assume the mantle of Dionysus, as had Rimbaud and Nijinsky, Modigliani and Mayakovsky and Picasso, Brendan Behan and Jackson Pollock, Neil Cassady and Michael McClure and Allen Ginsberg and Jack Kerouac, and so many other hard-living artists. Dionysus. The shaken-loose god of the green powers, the resurrection, the rebirth, the fecundity of the planet. And the wildness! *That* was Jim's calling. The wildness. Jim Morrison was the one who would dare to go further than anyone I have ever known. A man who knew no bounds, acknowledged no restraints, no rules, no laws. Only joy! Complete, unfettered, unbounded joy. He spoke of the powers of the earth and the delights of the earth and he had no fear in embracing the wild child in himself.

Wild child, full of grace,
Savior of the human race,
Your cool face.

Jim was able to dive into himself and find the fauve, the wild beast, and actually *become* that free-spirited animal. That Dionysian wild man. He had the courage to embrace that ancient god and enter into a partnership with the bearer of the grapes, the passionate one. Jim had the courage, and very few do. And that embrace was not evil, was not harmful to others, and was certainly not the devil. It was joy!

The new Dionysus was here, and the old cycles and the old gods were about to spin the wheel of destiny again; and the satyr—running down the street—was waving to his new master, just to let him know that he was ready for action. And Jim had been to a liquor store, the modern temple of Bacchus, to buy beer and wine, the libations of the gods. And perhaps the faun saw him there. Looking on from some Olympian vantage point and detecting the ancient stirrings once again, the satyr came back to partake of the rituals. Feeling the vibrations in the ether, this old-time party animal was back for some real excitement, denied him on this continent since the days of Salem and *The House of the Seven Gables.* And here was Jim Morrison, the new Dionysus/Bacchus, ready to lead the new orgy. And it was called . . . rock and roll!

forming the doors

Now it's time to put a rock and roll band together. We've got the lead singer and the keyboard player . . . we've got the patroness . . . what we don't have is the drummer and the guitar player. Someone's got to be the skin whacker/timekeeper and some young genius has to play the role of phallic snake-sliding rib-tickling maestro/fret master. Someone has to be the jungle and someone has to be the gliding angel. Someone has to be Thumper and someone has to be Les Paul/Chuck Berry by way of Charlie Christian. The guitar player *will* be a rocker who knows jazz. And the drummer *will* be a jazzer who can rock. These were my prerequisites. This is what I had to have to make the music I heard in my head.

If Jim and I were going to realize the dream of the Doors, we needed two guys of exceptional abilities. If we were going to create this Doors' something . . . out of nothing but our collective will and imagination, we needed a pair of psychedelic warriors. A brace of fevered, maniacal souls who could plug their spinal column electrical cords into our collective kundalini and not feel they were being strapped into the electric chair at Sing Sing University with Manzarek and Morrison flipping psychic overload switches to full fry! We needed two men of courage and vision. Two adventurers in the void. Two brave and hearty sailors of the psychological sea of dread to accompany us on our mad journey into the unknown.

And they had to play their asses off. They had to have an expertise on their instruments. They had to have studied and logged their too many hours of "practice, practice, practice." I didn't want anybody who wanted to be in a *rock* band or some egomaniacal nut-butters who wanted to be "rock stars." I wanted musicians who loved music; who wanted to play music more than they wanted to fuck. I wanted that same passion and commitment to art that Jim and I were bringing to the table . . . and I wanted them to be heads.

"We need a bass player, too, Ray," Jim said.

"Yeah, I know. But that's the easiest part of it. I want Max Roach on drums and Jim Hall on guitar. That's the hard part."

"We'll find 'em. I can feel it," he presciently said.

"They've got to play like jazz cats and then smash your face with hard-core rock." I was off in my aural fantasy. "I hear the keyboard and guitar interweaving like Escher's Möbius strip. Like Bach but with a rock foundation, ya know? Hard and loud."

Jim smiled. "Bach rock! I like the sound of that."

"Exactly," I said. "And I want it to be dark and moody. Real *misterioso.*" I heard the terror in my head. "But then I want it to explode into the light! I want the sun to shine into the dark corners."

"The dark corners of the *mind,*" Jim added. "We have to take the people *inside* themselves. Those places they're afraid to go into."

I nodded in agreement. "Those places they *have* to go into . . ."

He completed my thought for me: ". . . if they're ever going to be whole."

The angel passed over us again. Silence. What was there to say after that? Jim lit a joint and we passed it back and forth. We were high and we were Jungian. And we needed two more players to complete the diamond. We had the polar axis. We had the line between north and south, between heaven and hell, between good and evil. We had the opposing inclinations of Dionysus and Apollo. My

Apollonian sense of order, fitness, propriety, and harmony as opposed to—or, more accurately, balancing—Jim's wild-man ways. But those two points, when connected, only resulted in a straight line. We had no breadth. We needed the east-west axis to be complete. We need two more suns to occupy *all* the cardinal points of the compass. North-south-east-west. Height, width, breadth, depth. Red, white, yellow, blue, according to the Hopi. The four cardinal points. And when the dots were connected, the form was a diamond.

⚘

I found the other two burning men, our other two suns, in the Maharishi Mahesh Yogi's meditation class, held in the fall of 1965. Transcendental Meditation. It would become all the rage by 1968, when the Beatles went to India to study with the Maharishi in the foothills of the Himalayas. But for me, for now, it was an attempt at a natural high. I knew I couldn't continue taking LSD any longer. I had been to hell on the substance. Of course, I saw heaven first. And I grasped after heaven. I *wanted* heaven. I wanted to be in that state of blissful, energy-infused, intoxicated oneness. I wanted to see the energy waves on the plants and trees and flowers, the Aztec glyphs on the walls of our Fraser apartment; I wanted to be able to feel the tactility of the sunlight, to feel the gelatinous viscosity of the ocean's water, to be able to step in and out of the energy flow of the universe at will. And I *wanted* it. All the time! And when I took LSD again, after seeing and being the oneness of all life, I wanted to feel exactly that way again. That's why I was taking the soma. It made me feel better than anything I had ever taken before. I wanted to feel that way again. In the light. At one with the light. I *wanted*. I wanted to be golden again.

And the LSD said, "Ha-ha-ha! You're telling me what you *want?* You grasping, greedy little pissant! You may know heaven . . . but you don't know hell, boy. *Now* you're gonna find out the *whole* truth."

"I want to go to heaven," I whined. "I want bliss and beauty and peace and love."

"Fuck you. You want? You haven't learned nonattachment? You're still grasping? Go to hell, Ray."

And that's exactly where I went. Into a whirlpool of sinking darkness. Into total ego isolation. Into a cold, frozen place of abject

forming *the doors* ⚘ 133

terror! Complete and total terror. The Frankenstein monster coming after me in my childhood nightmares, unstoppable, inexorable, with no other thought than to crush me to death with blind killing efficiency while I screamed in terror. This recurring dream of my baby youth years was nothing compared to the terror of LSD. Total panic! Blind, senseless fear. The worst possible panic attack. And all because of grasping and wanting and demanding. This young man's heart was in the right place, he wanted joy and love and peace for all mankind. He had become a true Christian, a lover, for the first time in his life. A mystery Christian. A universalist. But not a Buddha. The web of maya had closed over him again, but this time on the deepest psychological level, at the root core of his existence, at the bottom of his beliefs.

I could not surrender my ego. I could not die to myself. And yet that was the only door into what I so desperately wanted. The surrendering of all desire was the only way I could attain what I desired. A Zen koan! I was living a fucking Zen koan and I was trapped in *hell.* I could not crack through the shell of my armor, my ego. I was closed, knotted, encased inside myself . . . and I was sinking. I was being sucked down in a whirlpool of fear and panic. To nowhere. To a place where I would be locked out of the beautiful. To a state of existence where I would not be a part of the divine energy, of life, of light and delight. A place of total isolation. The place called me! And it was hell. It was fearful and it was the absence of God. It wasn't the hellfires. It was the ice. It was the eternal damnation of *me.* The ninth circle of Dante's Inferno. And then I knew . . . hell is ME!

After a night of terror, a dark night of the soul, the chemical wore off and I came back to ordinary reality . . . shattered! The terror had subsided, the panic attack was over, but this novitiate was definitely the worse for wear. I began a psychologically imperative study of philosophy, religion, and mystical thought. I did what Joseph Campbell did, I embarked on the search for self in the literature and mythology of the world. And I was led to India. To yoga and to meditation.

I had discussed my acid bummers with Dick Bock, the head of World Pacific Records. He had signed Rick and the Ravens to Aura Records, the rock subsidiary of World Pacific. I was part of the package as the blues shouter. We cut two or three singles and I be-

came friendly with Dick. He was an older, wiser man and the vision-
ary who had brought the cool jazz West Coast sound to America. He
had recorded, among others, Gerry Mulligan, Chet Baker, Shorty
Rogers, Chico Hamilton, Shelly Manne, and Ravi Shankar. What a
lineup! And now Screaming Ray? Well, I was floored. And he had
also recorded the Maharishi. A two-disc set of lectures. He obviously had an Eastern bent and I felt I could confide in him. I told
him of my profound distress and he gave me the Maharishi's discs.
"Listen to what this man is saying, Ray. He just may be what you're
looking for," he said to me. What I heard was a jolly Indian man with
a giggle in his voice talking about man, God, and existence. I went
back to Dick Bock and said, "He's saying all the right things but
what do I do about my dread?" I was living every day with the remnants of my terror and I wanted it to stop. I was, however, doing a
good job of hiding it from everyone. No one knew, except for
Dorothy. She could sense my psychic distress. And Dick told me of
a class starting up in Los Angeles in which the Maharishi's type of
mantra yoga would be passed on to novitiates and seekers of the
way. A class in meditation. Transcendental Meditation.

"That's it," I exclaimed. "That's what I need, meditation." And
Dorothy and I arrived in Pacific Palisades one evening at the home
of the Keith Wallace family. They were Indiophiles and had opened
their house to the Transcendental Meditation group. A series of six
lectures was to be given by Jerry Jarvis, the director of T.M. West,
and then a mantra would be imparted to you. Okay, I'll listen . . . fire
away.

And the lectures were not unlike the records Dick Bock gave
me, minus the giggle and the Indian charm and lilt to the English
language. Jarvis spoke of life and energy and consciousness and levels of thought and the web of maya and the goal of all human existence . . . cosmic consciousness. It was both eminently logical and
deliciously mystical. The two sides of the coin of life. The yin and the
yang. The duality acknowledged. The attempt would be to rectify
the split in the psyche through meditation. To create the integrated
personality through mantra repetition. Through inaudible sound . . .
through thought waves. To bring us to a state of Jungian wholeness
through the manipulation of our own thought waves by repeating a
Sanskrit word over and over in our minds. Focusing, pointedly, on
our mantra and saying it over and over in our minds twice a day for

twenty minutes, eyes closed, seated and relaxed. And, eventually, the alienation of Western man from nature would be resolved. Id, ego, and superego would merge into oneness. The unintegrated personality would merge its disparate parts into oneness. The shattered schizophrenic—a very American malady—would merge, integrate, and heal himself into oneness. That's what he was selling. And I was buying. I definitely wanted to try it. Wouldn't you?

Now here's the serendipity of the story. Guess who is also in attendance at the Wallace house in the Palisades. John Densmore and Robby Krieger! Doors' guitarist-to-be, Robert Allen Krieger, and Doors' drummer-to-be, John Paul Densmore. But they don't know it. They don't know about a rock band called the Doors and a keyboard player named Ray Manzarek and a poet-singer named Jim Morrison. All they know is that they are looking for something to change their lives. They want something else, something different.

We need someone or something new
Something else to get us through

Amongst a group of approximately twenty people—assorted hippies, older women (always fools for a guru), and a few men in the midst of a midlife crisis—were what I was looking for. The Maharishi's meditation is a discipline that may not give you what you want—but will, more than likely, give you just what you need. And the three of us needed each other. The Doors needed the other Doors. And we found each other in India.

Away, away, away, away, away
in India

Someone had pointed out John Densmore to me and mentioned in an off-the-cuff way that he was a drummer. This was after the fourth lecture, and Jerry was carrying on in much detail about the void, and our relationship to it, and the pure energy. All the marvelous things that Indian mysticism and Eastern spirituality and Zen Buddhism and LSD, peyote, and mescaline open up to you. And I'm nodding my head yes, yes, yes. I agree, that's what I saw. Then he asked for questions and my hand shot up.

"What about the bummers?" I blurted out. "What about the

terror, the stark terror? What about the dark night of the soul?" The collective giggled at my too-flowery imagery. I continued, determined to make a fool of myself . . . and to get some answers.

"What about LSD and its ability to induce the horrors? What is that fear? Where does it come from? What about the terror that exists inside of me; the absolute, sheer terror of being alive!" I was ranting. The class loved it. I even got a light sprinkle of applause amid the smirks and giggles. I was almost going to take a bow but I wasn't doing it to be entertaining, for cri-sake. This was the real shit. This was why I was here in the first place.

And Jarvis was cool. He said to wait until we received our mantra. "Practice the meditation and then we'll talk about your questions. Then you'll begin to understand. Once you've tried it for yourself."

And I replied with the classic impetuous-youth line: "I can't wait until then. I want to know now!"

Everyone laughed at that one . . . and the class was over for the evening. "Two more lectures and then your mantra, Ray," Jerry said as he pocketed his papers from the lectern. We all milled about and I was pumped. I spotted John and went up to him, Dorothy at my side.

"Hey, man, I hear you're a drummer," I said to him.

"Yeah . . . I am. How'd you know?"

"I'm psychic." I grinned.

"You're a bullshitter, too." He grinned back.

"You're right about that," Dorothy said. Always telling the truth. Did she always have to be so damned truthful? We all laughed.

"Well, maybe I am and maybe I just like a good story," I said, grinning back. "But here's what's happening . . . I'm putting a rock and roll band together. My buddy Jim Morrison is a poet and a singer. I'm the keyboard player"—I extended my hand—"Ray Manzarek."

"John Densmore." We shook hands.

"I'm Dorothy Fujikawa," said my baby. "I'm the patroness." She grinned.

"The *what?*" said John.

"Uhh . . . never mind about that," I blurted again. Damned chick and her truths. "We could use a good drummer."

"What's the music like?" he asked.

"I wanna do poetry and rock. Like the beatniks, ya know? Like poetry and jazz." John's eyes began to light up. "I hear a jazz-based thing . . . but in rock," I said.

"Jazz!" he said. "Are you into Coltrane?"

"I love Coltrane. McCoy Tyner is my idol."

"I worship Elvin Jones," he said. "He is the greatest drummer on the planet."

"That's for sure," I agreed.

"What about Miles?" he asked.

"Miles . . . I'm Bill Evans!"

"Man, Philly Joe Jones and Jimmy Cobb . . . that side stick on four, I love that, it's *sooo* cool."

I thought to myself, Great! Here's a guy who knows his jazz. Yes!

To John I said, "That's what I want to do with the band, bring in that kind of stuff. Man, you can do anything in rock today!"

"Cool," he said. " 'Cause I'm not good enough to be a *real* jazz drummer."

"Hell, I'm not good enough to be a real jazz piano player." We laughed at our inadequacies. "I just love the stuff. If we could incorporate that into rock and roll . . . "

"Man, no one's doing that!" he jumped in.

"My buddy Jim has these great lyrics and they're very poetic. We could do all kinds of hip stuff around them."

"Sounds good to me," he said.

And we had our drummer! Just like that. John Densmore. A fop, a jazzer, and a would-be artiste. Perfect!

"We need a good . . . no . . . a *great* guitarist, too," I said.

And here's how the fates work. Sometimes Dame Fortune giveth and sometimes she taketh away. That night she was in a most charitable, giving mood.

John pointed to a guy at the other end of the room talking to the Wallace kid.

"See that guy with the frizzy hair?" he said. "He's a guitarist. Plays great bottleneck. Name's Robby Krieger."

I said, ". . . all right!" and the diamond was soon to be complete. Robby Krieger . . . John Densmore . . . Ray Manzarek . . . Jim Morrison.

However, before we actually formed the magic circle, before Robby joined the band, I plugged John into the remnants of Rick and the Ravens for a demo record session. Along with their high school buddies Vince Thomas, Pat Stonier, and Roland Biscailuz, Rick and the Ravens had rocked the entire South Bay, garnered a record deal, cut a couple of singles with yours truly, Screaming Ray Daniels, the "Bearded Blues Shouter," on vocals . . . and were now going nowhere. Nothing was happening. No record sales, no gigs. Dissent descended on the Ravens. Their deal with Dick Bock's Aura Records was coming to a close and the band had broken up. They had one more single to cut . . . and no band. So Jim and John and I jumped in. We talked Dick Bock into letting us cut a demo record of six Doors' songs instead of Rick and the Ravens' last single.

Of course nothing happened with the demo . . . Robby hadn't come aboard yet. The circle wasn't complete. The diamond hadn't been formed. The power hadn't manifested itself in reality so how could the demo succeed? My brothers decided to give up the hunt and leave the rock world behind. It was the best decision for them. Everything was going nowhere. Why beat your head against the wall of rejection? They bade *adieu* to Rick and the Ravens, the Doors, and the whole damned frustrating thing. Within two weeks Robby was in.

※

We finally assembled on an autumn afternoon at Hank Olguin's house, behind the Greyhound bus terminal in Santa Monica, about four blocks from the Pacific Ocean. The weather was California perfect. Sun everywhere, high seventies, humidity in the low twenties, just enough of a cooling breeze off the ocean to keep it sweet and mild. Everything was golden. And we were all ready for the alchemical transformation. We were going to leap into the alembic, and it was labeled the Doors.

Jim and I arrived in the Navy Chevy. We had an amp and a microphone for him to sing through. I was going to play Hank's acoustic piano. And, wouldn't you know it, it was a big old carved-wood upright. Almost my country German Golem again. I felt good about that, secure. We were going to leap into the void and I was back on Bell Avenue in Chicago with my big protector machine. Full circle. Robby arrived in his VW van, also gray, also German. He hauled in his Fender amp and a Gibson guitar case. I introduced him to Jim. They looked into each other's eyes, shook hands . . . and smiled. The psychic bond was established right then and right there. These two guys were going to hit it off. It felt good . . . the three of us.

And then up pulled a little Singer four-door English automobile, stuffed with drum cases, cymbals, hardware, and John Densmore. It was like a clown car at the circus. How could such a little car contain so much equipment? Well, what it was, was shrewd packing, developed to an expertise over hundreds of gigs. John had played all over L.A. From jazz gigs in Watts, where he was the only honky on the date, to bar mitzvahs in the Valley, where he was the only goy in the entire place. He played everywhere, including lead snare drummer in his University High School marching band. He was schooled and he was versatile. And he was funny. Best of all, he loved jazz.

He and Robby had been together in a band called—and dig this—the Psychedelic Rangers!

Robby was the brainy type. Well-formed cranium, Albert Einstein hair, glasses or contacts depending on the occasion, loose-fitting surfer threads, and a laconic manner. And something behind the eyes that said he was willing to risk everything. Willing to go all the way. Ready to take a chance on anything. Jim loved that about him.

Robby was cool from the git-go. He was well off—from Pacific Palisades—nice home, overbearing father, and a sweetheart of a mother. He certainly shared the overbearing father part with Jim. Hell, that's where Jim's anti-authoritarian bent came from. Rebellion against the father figure. Strictly Freudian. Robby and his non-identical twin brother, Ron, had been busted for pot at Pali High and sent off by Stu Krieger to the Menlo Park Military Academy for a year or so. "Teach those damn kids some discipline." Jim could identify. Robby put in a year or two at UCLA and changed majors six times. He was just drifting. Until today. Now he could begin.

We got everything set up in Hank's living room and it was time to play. Robby tuned his too-cool black Gibson to the piano, Jim said, "Yeah, yeah!" into the mic and through the amp, John went rat-a-tat-tat-splash-whack on his drums, and I tickled the ivories with a riff of Miles Davis's "Milestones." We were ready.

"Let's do 'Moonlight Drive,' " I said.

"Groovy," said Jim.

"How does it go?" asked Robby.

"I'll show you the changes," I said. "It's in G."

"Wait," said Jim. "Before we get into chord changes and that kind of stuff . . . we need some ammunition." And he pulled out a bomber. Like the one in his student movie. Robby's eyes sparkled but John looked apprehensive. Jim lit it, took a toke, and passed it to me; I did the same and passed it to Robby, who sucked on it, filled his lungs with the sweet smoke, and passed it to John. John held it, looked at it, hesitated, and finally conquered his fears. You could almost hear his conscience say, "Come on, don't be a chicken now. Not in front of these guys. What the hell, man. Go for it!" And he did. He stuck that bomber in his maw, pulled on it, and held the firestorm in his lungs. Then he coughed. A big one. The smoke came roaring out but the damage had already been done. John smiled a goofy, stoned smile and said, "That's some good shit." A great collective sigh hit the rest of us. We were *all* stoned. John, Robby, Jim, and Ray. The Doors. High together for the first time. In the late-autumn light of Southern California.

Jim said, "Groovy."

As we finished the joint I showed Robby the chord changes to "Moonlight Drive." They were easy. Mostly G with a few Cs and Ds here and there and a solo in the middle. Robby digested the form in an instant. Another high IQ. And then a "Eureka" lightbulb went illuminati in his brain pan.

"I got an idea," Robby said. "See if you think this works."

He reached into his guitar case, in the little compartment in the neck, and pulled out a weapon! A fucking broken bottle. A mean and evil piece of jagged glass. The neck of a greenish bottle that was all sharp and broken off and could cut a hole in your neck with one quick thrust.

"What the fuck is that?" I shouted. "Is that for cutting someone's *face* off?" I was incredulous. What would Robby need a weapon for? What kind of gigs did he play that he needed a throat slasher in his guitar case? In what kind of neighborhoods?

He laughed. "No, man, it's a bottleneck."

"I'm hip, it's a bottleneck. But what do you need it for? Where the hell do you go that you need to slash at people with that thing?"

He thought that was hysterical. "Ray . . . I don't slash at people with this."

"Then what do you do with that monster?" I asked.

"This," he said as he slipped the bottleneck onto the pinkie of his left hand. "This is what you do with a bottleneck." And he put the glass weapon ever so gently against the strings of his guitar, plucked a note, and moved the weapon up and down the fretboard as he did a tremolo with his wrist. And, *oo-wee*, what a sound! Dark and spooky. A banshee wail. The sound of ectoplasm, the cry of a death bird, the moan of things that go bump in the night. I was amazed. It was so eerie, so unearthly. I'd never heard anything like it before.

And Morrison! Well . . . he went over the top. Kundalini completely uncoiled and raced up his spine. He shivered and jumped to his feet. Or was he lifted by the sound? He said, "Holy shit, Robby, that's the greatest sound I've ever heard on a guitar."

Robby did some extra-fancy spook slides and it was all Jim could do to remain attached to the earth. He was about to start floating again. I had to hold his psyche down, except mine was threatening to disengage from my spinal column, too. Robby's guitar was making our kundalini energy race up and down our bone ladders, and we were tingling and shivering with delight.

"I want that sound on every song," Jim blurted. "I love that sound!"

Robby grinned, pleased with the reaction he had garnered from these "intellectual" college graduates.

"Every song?" he asked.

I jumped in, the voice of reason. "Well, maybe not *every* song . . . but on a lot of 'em. Okay?"

"Fine with me," said Robby. "How about on 'Moonlight Drive'?"

"Let's *do* it!" Jim enthused.

And John did his rat-a-tat burst of nervous energy on the drums. We all took our positions. Jim said "Yeah" into the mic, Robby played a G chord, and I counted it off: 1 . . . 2 . . . 1-2-3-4. And it began. Our first groove. Our first time. And, man, we were on it! We drove that car down Pacific Coast Highway and it was night and the moon was full and we were going for a swim in the Pacific Ocean with our best girl . . . and maybe we were going to drown tonight. Or maybe we were going down on each other tonight. It was the Morrison triumvirate of love, death, and travel. And we were all there. All four of us were in the same space at the same time. An impossibility in physics—two bodies cannot occupy the same space at the same time. But in the holographic universe, on the psychic plane, in the energy . . . all four of us were in one place. And that place was called "Moonlight Drive."

We were inside the song. And we were inside each other. We had given ourselves over to the rhythm, the chord changes, and the words. We had let go of our individual egos and surrendered to one another in the music. Jim and Ray and John and Robby no longer existed. There was only the music. The diamond was formed and it was clear and hard and luminous. The facets glistened in the sonic spectrum like the ragged edges of Robby's bottleneck. We caught the light and we held it. We held it in our heart chakras and it warmed us like sex. The light filled that room and we rode it and we were high on it and we were one with it. We created it and we were one.

We were the Doors.

I'd never felt anything like it before. It was perfect synchronicity. Perfect harmony. Four spirits locked in a love embrace inside the insistent, propelling rhythm. John's drums were carrying us on a trip into the primitive. We were riding his tom-toms into the primeval world. Into the realm of basic instincts. And Robby's bottleneck guitar was snake-weaving us into the fourth dimension, into a higher, expanded state of consciousness. We had gone primordial and cosmic at the same time. And, man, it was fine!

When the song finally ended, a hush fell over the room. An angel passed over again as we collected our thoughts. I was the first to speak.

"Man," I said, shaking my head. "I have played music all my life . . . but I never *understood* music until right now. You guys are amazing."

Murmurs and a laugh or two, nervous and delighted chatter; youthful exuberance poured out. Jim smiled his lazy-boy, Robby tugged at his corkscrew hair, John bounced on his drum stool, shifting his high-pockets butt from left to right to up to down and said, "That was very groovy. I like that tune."

"I love the bottleneck," said Jim.

"Gallo wine bottle," said Robby. "They're the best for slide."

I was in the future. . . . "We're going all the way with this, I can feel it."

"Where?" Jim teased. "In your sphincter?"

John and Robby laughed.

"In my bone marrow, man," I shot back. "And bone marrow doesn't lie . . . can't . . . that's why it's marrow."

Jim laughed. John grinned and snorted. Robby smiled and slid his Gallo glass up and down his Gibson's neck, punctuating my pun like a Vegas pit musician.

"We've got it," I continued. "Like the sax player in *On the Road.*"

"What do you mean?" asked Jim.

I was off and running. . . . "*You* know the section. Kerouac walks into this bar in San Francisco. A quartet is playing and the sax player is wailing. The place is packed and Sal Paradise says, more or less, 'He had it!' And everyone in the joint knew he had it. And he rode it and bobbed and weaved and honked and squealed it out over the whole crowd. And they called back to him, "Do it! Go! Get it, man!" And he did. He was sweating and squatting and leaning into it and pouring it out over the audience and they were taking it all in, every ounce of it. I'm telling you, he had it!' "

I stopped to catch my breath. "And you know what? . . . I always wondered what *it* was. What did the sax player have? What did Kerouac mean, 'he had it'? What? I never knew what *it* was . . . until now!" I looked at the three of them, trying to impart some of the profound depth of what I felt, some of my revelation, and repeated, ". . . until now!"

Jim smiled. "An epiphany, huh, Ray?"

"Now I know what *it* is." I nodded. Then I laughed, partly at my own pretentiousness and partly from my delight. "And *we've* got it!"

And they all laughed. Alive, young, and excited. We were the Doors and we were one.

And we had it!

We played a few more tunes: "Summer's Almost Gone," "End of the Night," "My Eyes Have Seen You." They were all that they were supposed to be. Doors' music. Some fell right into place, others needed more work. But we were there. We were at the crossroads and there was only one possible direction for us to choose. Straight ahead. We threw ourselves into the arms of destiny and she embraced us. She enfolded us under her angel wings and said, "I'll protect you."

We formed a bond that afternoon. A bond that would last until Jim went to Paris. We formed a magic circle. A circle of art and love and energy. A circle of power based on creativity and the regenerative forces of the earth. A circle of inspiration and trust in each other. A circle of trust in the universal energy. Trust in the karmic principle of "as you sow, so shall you reap." The music was hot and hard rock; and we were ready to sow our seed into the belly of the American psyche. We were ready for love. We were ready to give the young people of America, the hip people of America—because it had nothing to do with age, and everything to do with consciousness—something they had never heard before. Psychedelic music by a group called the Doors!

After rehearsal, we walked over to the Santa Monica Pier to taste the swarming life atop those pylons, and feel the sunset. We walked out to the end of that old wooden pier and stood against the railing, watching the lowering sun turn the water an azure blue. The air was soft and warm. Life was all around us. We felt secure in one another's company. It felt good to be together. It felt right. There wasn't even a need to speak. We just let the breeze off the Pacific wash over us. We were being baptized in the air. The new, cleansing sacrament of the Aquarian Age. Washed in the energy of the air. Purified.

Finally, Jim spoke. "This is the end of the whole thing. Right here."

Robby looked shocked. "What are you talking about, Jim? We're just getting started. Everything sounded great."

Jim smiled at him. "I don't mean us . . . I mean Western civilization. This is as far as it goes."

Densmore jumped in. "God, I thought you meant the band. I thought I was fired before I even joined up!"

We all laughed. John the cut-up.

"No, I mean Western man," Jim said. "He can't go any further. This is it. We're at the end point."

We all looked out at the ocean. The angel from *Jules and Jim* passed over us again. Then Robby slyly spoke.

"You know what's out there?" he said as he pointed at the meeting line between the water and the air, the earth and the sky, the temporal and the universal . . . the horizon. "You know what's out there, beyond that line?"

A beat, and then John spoke out: "Asia!" he said. "That's what's out there, man. Asia . . ."

Jim's very words, echoed by John, proposed by Robby. I could only smile to myself. The boy from Chicago had made it all the way across the continent and he now stood at the end point of Western civilization with this new group of seekers. The Doors. The four of us, together, on the quest for the grail. I knew it was going to happen for us. It was inevitable.

As we walked back along the pier, we passed, among others, a fortune-teller's shop. A certain Madame Rozinka who "sees all, tells all."

Jim said, "Let's go in! Have our fortunes told. What do ya say?"

"No, man," I said. "I already know what the future has in store for us."

Robby looked at me. "What?"

I could only smile at my three magicians. . . . "It's golden!"

☀️

Now began a lengthy round of rehearsals and composition. The blade was forged but it needed a long period of tempering. We had to plunge it into many baths of blood and sweat and the waters of the unconscious. We had to harden the vision into reality. That afternoon of magic and epiphany at Hank's house had to be duplicated on a continuing basis, on call and on demand. In other words, we had to be able to do it! Anytime, anywhere.

We started a regimen of rehearsals of three times a week, every week. We worked at Hank's house until the neighbors complained to the police of that dreaded nuisance: "Live music!" People hate to hear a rock band rehearsing. The old farts always blow the whistle and call the cops. It's the drums. The "savage tom-tom beat" of the drums unnerves them. Africa begins to loom and threaten the European ear. Hell, it begins to open the ear to Dionysus—it's been said that Dionysus enters through the ears—and that opens the door to paganism, and paganism opens the door to . . . well . . . a pathetic religion of God-knows-what abominations. Probably . . . sex! And love! And marijuana! Those kids had to be stopped. Those *drums* had to be stopped. Like a B movie of white men in Africa: "Those drums! Why won't they stop?" Some dame or lily-livered guy was always losing it and cracking up because of the native tom-toms. Well, same-o, same-o in Santa Monica. "Those drums!" And the cops arrived, polite, if you can believe that, and shut us down. "No live music, boys. You'll have to do it somewhere else."

Felix was there that afternoon. He came with Jim. I never could figure out why. But as long as he was going to be around, I told him to shoot photos of us. Make himself useful. Document our beginnings. I told him, "This is going to be big, man. Bring your camera and get this on film. The creation of the Doors." He could care less. He listened to the music and didn't get it.

"I don't know, Ray. What's the big deal?" he said after we took a break. "Maybe you ought to stay in film."

"Felix, we've *got* it. We're going all the way. You could have photos of all of this. Get your camera." I hesitated from adding the word "fool." But he never did. He just wanted to drink and play mind games.

"Hey, Jim," he said, turning away from me. "Let's go get something to drink. I'm thirsty, man."

Thank God Jim said, "Later, man, after we finish rehearsal."

"You've rehearsed enough," the incubus said. "Don't you want a cold beer? *Maan* [that whine again], it's too hot for this. Come on, let's go."

"Felix, I said after we finish."

And Felix backed down, but you could see Jim was tempted. The temptation to chuck it all and live the life of a reprobate was the negative side of the Dionysian frenzy. And the frenzy came with a price. Fame and its overindulgences would eventually result in dissipation. A lack of restraint would eventually result in drunkenness. A lack of balance—and God knows Jim had a great sense of physical balance, his psychic balance was his realm of fragility—would lead to . . . madness. If Morrison was going to dance the shaman's dance, he would have to do battle with—and conquer—the demons of indulgence. And Felix was only the first.

And the asshole didn't even like the music. Neither did my good friend Frank Lisciandro, another film school buddy. He didn't think Morrison had it. "What are you doing hanging around with Morrison, Ray?" he asked me. "He's nothing but a punk! You're wasting your time with him." He was incredulous and seemed almost angry. He didn't get it, either. It was beyond him.

Well, the men don't know
but the little girls understand
— Willie Dixon

Later, Frank would become one of Jim's biggest sycophants. He would flatter him and suck up to him and laugh too loudly at Jim's jokes. It was more weakening, enervating indulgence. It was disgusting, but it was the price of fame. When the Doors made it to the top of the charts, Frank finally liked the music. And when Jim put on his leathers . . . well . . . Frank finally got it! But then Jim occasioned that response in many men. And some of them hated him for it. They hated the forbidden feelings that Jim's androgyny would stir up in them. They didn't know whether to beat the shit out of him or grab his tight little buns.

When the cops broke up our practice at Hank's, Felix took the opportunity to put on a display of faux machismo.

"My friend is working on his music here!" he said to the blue men.

"He'll have to stop," came the blue reply.

"He's an artist and he has the right to rehearse."

I thought, Great. *Now* the dickhead is going to defend the music.

"Not here, not now!" The cop was getting angry.

Felix looked him square in the eye. "What's your badge number? I'm putting you on report."

The cop's hand began to reach for his nightstick.

I thought, Oh shit, he's gonna pull that baton and beat Felix's brains into a pudding whip.

I stepped between them. "We'll stop now, Officer," I said to the reddening blue man.

He looked hard at Felix and turned away. "You'd better," he said. "If I come here again, you'll be cited," he tossed back at us as he and his partner left Hank's place. Fuming.

The black-and-white pulled out; Felix turned to Jim and said, "Did you see the way I made him turn away?" Jim nodded. Felix cackled, "He had to back down, didn't he!"

After that, we rehearsed at Robby's house.

※

Stu and Marilyn Krieger were gracious enough to open their house in the Palisades to Robby's new long-haired artiste-pothead-beatnik-existentialist friends. Mr. and Mrs. Krieger had a piano in a recreation room, and that's where we set up shop. Lots of practice and lots of new songs came pouring out. And guess who was also a composer? Robby Krieger! Not only was he the snake man on bottleneck guitar but he was also a tunesmith with a touch of the poet himself. He casually walked in one day after Jim had told everyone to go home and try writing a new song, and said . . .

"I wrote one, came out pretty good, too."

"Way to go, man," Jim said as he punched Robby on the arm, the way guys do as a congratulatory gesture.

"What's it called?" I asked.

Now get ready for this. Here's the fates at work. Here's good karma. Here's the blessing by that angel that passed over our heads. Here's more than we ever deserved and more than I ever envisioned.

"Light My Fire!"

That's all Robby said. Cool as a cucumber. Laid back and California casual . . . "Light My Fire." All Robby had done was write the tune that would become the number-one song in America during the fabled Summer of Love. He had composed the song that would become the Doors' signature piece. An international monster that would be recorded in more than thirty countries. The song that would knock the Beatles off the top of the charts. Hey, we're cool. No big thing.

"I call it 'Light My Fire,' " he casually said.

Jim immediately loved the title. I wanted to know the chord changes and John said, "What's the beat?"

So Robby played it. Sang it in his Dylanesque voice, then said, "I only have a first verse, I need a second one, too."

"You need a lot more than that!" said Densmore the comedian. "It sounds like a Sonny and Cher song. We're not a folk-rock band, Robby," John teased.

Robby got defensive. "It's not folk-rock," he said. He seemed hurt by John's failed attempt at humor.

"Why don't you sell it to the Mamas and the Papas," John continued joking. Going, really, too far.

Jim jumped in. "I like it, man. It's good work," he said to Robby. Robby smiled and John stopped his silliness. He would always back down whenever Jim spoke up. Jim had his number and John was no match for him on the psychic plane. I think John always resented him for that. Even to this very day.

"A minor to F sharp minor is a very cool progression," I said to Robby after he showed me the changes. "I never heard those chords put together in that way before." Robby grinned again. He was proud of his little baby. "But it needs some work," I added.

"Well, I know that," Robby said. He was a reasonable man. "What do you think we should do with it, Ray? How can we make it better?"

And we put it into the Doors' collective mind. We all went to work on it. We hammered it on our forge and everyone had a good idea. Jim came up with lyrics for the second verse.

The time to hesitate is through,
No time to wallow in the mire,
Try now we can only lose,
And our love becomes a funeral pyre.

Words of the burning man, in love, ready to leap into action, into a new life even at the risk of death. You must try at all cost. No fear. The worst that can happen is death; our inevitable end, anyway. The best that can happen, however, is freedom!

John, back to being his cool drummer self, came up with the very cool Latino beat for the verse and then the four-on-the-floor, hard-rock beat for the chorus. Worked like a mother. The contrast between Latin and rock was inspired. He was a great drummer. Always very inventive.

I matched his Latin beat in the verses with a left hand Bolero-like figure and some right-hand Chicano comping à la "El Watusi." We did verse/chorus, verse/chorus, and then it was solo time. And that's where *Ole Coltrane* came in. It was perfect: A minor to B minor.

You could float a solo over that *montuna* for hours on end. And sometimes, in person, it seemed like we did.

Everything was there. The song was great. The parts were now great. The groove was in the pocket. The vibe was inspiring. The tempo was like fucking. The words were elemental. The chord changes were unique. Everything was there, except . . .

"Wait a minute," I said. "How do we start this thing? We can't just jump in on the A minor to F sharp minor. We need an introduction."

"Got any ideas, Ray?" Jim asked.

I paused. "Quite frankly . . . no." I paused again, synapses firing, smoke coming out of my ears, gears grinding. "Why don't you guys go outside for a while. Let me see what I can come up with," I mumbled.

They did . . . and I did. I came up with it. All my piano lessons paid off. All my classical studies came to fruition. All that time chained to the country German Golem in the basement was now put to use. A simple circle of fifths was the answer. The chords were G to D, F to B♭, E♭ to A♭ (two beats on each chord) and then an A for two measures. Run some Bach filigrees over the top in a kind of turning-in-on-itself Fibonacci spiral—like a nautilus shell—and you've got it. "Eureka!" An illuminati moment. They come out of nowhere and you have to be ready for them. You have to believe in them. And you have to act on them. It may seem impulsive but they are probably clues and missives from the better angels of ourselves. Where they come from nobody knows; but I do know what leads up to them . . . "practice, practice, practice."

I called the guys back. "I got it," I said. "Check this out. I'll count it off. John, give me a snare shot on four. Robby, just listen and come in on the A minor. Jim, sing where you're supposed to. Where the first verse starts. Ready?" I was speeding. I was gone. Sweet creativity, what a transcendent state.

1 . . . 2 . . . 1-2-3, CRACK! John shot me with his snare and we were off. Cartwheeling into "Light My Fire." Leaping into history. The song for the Summer of Love. We had it and it was good and it was hot!

chapter six

on the pavement
with our demo

In between rehearsals we walked the streets with our demo, going from record company to record company. We hit everyone in town — all the labels were in L.A. — and got rejected by everyone. Capitol, RCA, Liberty, Dunhill, Decca, Reprise. They all said no. I was shocked! It was a damn good demo, definitely different. A bit raw and undeveloped . . . but good. Good enough for anyone with half an ear to hear the potential in the music. Or so I thought.

But, no. The four of us went everywhere . . . and were rejected. Sometimes Jim and Dorothy and I went alone. The three of us tried Dunhill Records. Lou Adler was the head man. He was shrewd and he was hip. He had the Mamas and the Papas and a big single with Barry McGuire's "Eve of Destruction." He was flush.

We were ushered into his office. He looked cool. He was California casually disheveled and had the look of a stoner, but his eyes were as cold as a shark's. He took the twelve-inch acetate demo from me and we all sat down. He put the disc on his turntable and played each cut . . . for ten seconds. Ten seconds! You can't tell jack shit from ten seconds. At least listen to *one* of the songs all the way through. I wanted to rage at him. "How dare you! We're the Doors! This is fucking Jim Morrison! He's going to be a fucking star! Can't you see that? Can't you see how fucking handsome he is? Can't you hear how groovy the music is? Don't you fucking get it? Listen to the words, man!" My brain was a boiling, lava-filled Jell-O mold of rage. I wanted to eviscerate that shark.

The songs he so casually dismissed were "Moonlight Drive," "Hello, I Love You," "Summer's Almost Gone," "End of the Night," "I Looked at You," "Go Insane."

He rejected the whole demo. Ten seconds on each song—maybe twenty seconds on "Hello, I Love You" (I took that as an omen of potential airplay)—and we were dismissed out of hand. Just like that. He took the demo off the turntable and handed it back to me with an obsequious smile and said, "Nothing here I can use."

We were shocked. We stood up, the three of us, and Jim, with a wry and knowing smile on *his* lips, cuttingly and coolly shot back at him, "That's okay, man. We don't want to be *used*, anyway."

And we were gone. Out the door. I wanted to hug Morrison. What a great comeback line.

Lou Adler got back at us, however. He was one of the promoters of the legendary Monterey Pop Festival and the Doors were never invited to play Monterey. Damn!

We tried Capitol Records. The big tubular tower on Vine Street that has become a symbol of Hollywood and the rock and roll music business. The Beatles were on Capitol! It was the big time. The four of us notched up our courage and entered the circle of glass, demo in hand. The lobby was a two-story affair, vaguely Bauhaus in its austerity and positively Croesus-like in its display of gold records. They covered every inch of wall space. There were hundreds of them. Gold everywhere. A true temple of Mammon. A palace of the temporal world. More gold records than I'd ever seen. More gold records than anyone has ever seen. We wanted in!

A lone receptionist at a desk. Being the oldest, it was my obligation to make the opening gambit.

"Hi, we're a rock band called the Doors," I said with a smile to the foxy little gatekeeper.

"The what?" came her reply.

"The Doors," I repeated.

She looked puzzled. "How do you spell that?"

"D-O-O-R-S."

"You mean like a door?"

"Yes, like opening a door." My smile was fading.

John jumped in. "A door in your mind," he said as he flashed her *his* best Steve McQueen.

She looked at him, even more puzzled. "I don't get it. What door?"

"In your mind," I repeated gently.

"I don't have a door in my mind," she said.

"It's symbolic," Jim added.

She looked at him. "Of what?"

It was the first time I had ever seen Jim stumped. "Uhh . . . of the . . . well, like opening the door . . . in your mind. You dig?"

She just shook her head. And added . . . "No."

It was hopeless. "We have a demo. Can we play it for somebody?" I asked, trying to get to the business at hand.

"Play it for who?" she asked.

I thought I had entered an Ionesco play by mistake. It was beginning to sound like theater of the absurd dialogue.

"Play it for anyone who will . . . listen to it," I stammered.

"I know that," she said. "Like who?"

My brain screamed "Help!" I spoke with great difficulty, trying to maintain an even strain. "Uhh . . . well, like someone in A&R, for instance. Do you have someone who listens to new demos?"

"Yes, we do."

An opening! I pressed my advantage. "Can we speak to that person?"

"No, you can't." It was back to Ionesco.

"Why not?" I repeated.

"You're not allowed to . . ."

My God, it was now Kafka. We had entered the Castle.

"Not without an appointment."

"Can we make an appointment, then?"

"No," came her reply. *"You* can't."

It *was* Kafka.

"Why not?" It came out in a whine. It was actually whining. I was losing it.

She leaned forward and said, "Because we don't accept unsolicited demos." She smiled smugly and sat back in her chair. The winner.

"You mean demos . . . off the street?" Morrison sarcastically asked.

She looked Jim in the eye. "That's right," she replied. "Now why don't you four Doors take yourselves back out on the street . . . where you belong." We were dismissed.

I was getting depressed. When we got back to Fraser I said to Jim, "Maybe we ought to hang this up, man. Maybe you could sell your songs or something. Sell 'em to some publishing company. At least you could make a few bucks that way."

"Raaayy . . . what's the matter with you?!" He was aghast.

"I'm fucking depressed."

He punched me on the side of the arm. "Don't be depressed," he said. "Come on, where's that sunny disposition? Mr. Aquarian Age. Mr. Sun Worshiper . . ." Another punch. "Come on!"

"I'm just not so sure we're gonna make it. We've been turned down by everybody. This is a lot harder than I thought it was going to be."

"You can't give up yet," Jim replied. "Something good's gonna happen. You'll see." He grinned. "I can feel it."

"I hope so," I maudlinly answered.

"We've got an appointment with Liberty Records tomorrow, don't we?" Another punch. "This could be the one!"

"I sure as fuck hope so."

It was the one, all right. The worst one.

For reasons unknown to me, I wound up going by myself. Jim was nowhere to be found, John and Robby had things to do of a more pressing nature, and Dorothy was at work. It was an omen but I refused to read the signs. No one wanted to go on this appointment at Liberty Records. It was with a big cheese, too. A guy who had produced a number-one single by some Ventures-like imitation. A surf-style instrumental hit of twangy guitars with a faux *Twilight*

Zone riff. It had an outer-space name and went to the top of the charts. Strictly cud fodder but still . . . number one. And I was to have a meeting with him. Well, okay!

It was all uneventful until I was ushered into his office. Hell, at least I was in the building; better than Capitol and Ms. Robot the secretary. But then I saw him. Vegas to the max. A swinger. A rat pack wanna-be. The kind of guy who called women "broads," who whored and drank and gambled and corrupted anything he could get his hands on . . . but was also religious. A regular churchgoer and an upholder of the American way of life, who hated all pot-smoking long-hairs. And that was me. He took one look, saw the enemy, and turned to ice. His eyes went colder than Lou Adler's. I was no longer in a shark's den, I was in the room of a man who could kill. A man who could kill *me!* I shivered, gulped, and began my spiel.

"We're a rock and roll band called the Doors. Our lead singer is a poet and real handsome."

He snorted. "Poet?"

"He's gonna be a star." I nodded. "We got some really great material. This is only a sampler. You know, a demo."

"Poet?" Guttural and incredulous. The concept of poetry and rock had never occurred to him. It had no folder in his mental file cabinet, therefore: How could it exist?

I handed him the demo. "Why don't you listen to 'Moonlight Drive,' " I suggested.

" 'Moonlight Ride'?" he grunted as he took the black platter.

"Drive," I corrected.

"Don't get smart with me." Guttural and dangerous.

Ingratiating and humble. "No, sir, it's called 'Moonlight *Drive.*' "

"Yeah . . . ?"

"That's the title. It's there on the label."

"Yeah . . . ?"

I thought I was talking to Uncle Joe Grande in *Touch of Evil.* He looked at the label.

"Where . . ."

"I think it's number three."

And then I caught a break.

"I'll start at the top. I like to listen to the whole thing. Gives me a sense of what it's all about."

"That's good," I agreed in my most agreeableness. "A lot of

A&R guys aren't smart enough to know that." Liar, liar, pants on fire! I wanted to call that one back as soon as it hit the air. But he didn't flinch.

As he put the record on the turntable he spoke to it: "I don't like potheads." He hit the switch and turned to me. "You're not a pothead, are you?"

I gulped again. "No . . . no I just wear my hair long. That's all." Liar, liar.

"Like the Beatles, huh?"

"Yes . . . like the Beatles." I smiled, nodding like a spring-necked doll on the dashboard of a candy apple red '62 Corvette.

"I like the Beatles," he grunted. "They're number one."

"Yes, I like them, too." I said, spring neck bobbing.

Mercifully, the music started. He sat down and listened to the first three songs. "Moonlight Drive," "Hello, I Love You," and "Summer's Almost Gone." His head moved in time to the music and he was really concentrating. I thought he was digging it. He *looked* like he was digging it. I was getting excited. But after "Summer's Almost Gone" he spun around in his chair and jerked the tone arm off the record.

"I hate this shit," he said as he ripped the disc off the spindle.

"Wait, wait!" I pleaded. "Play the last one. It's something like your outer-space hit. It's got a repeating note like *Outer Limits*, real fun lyrics." Ingratiating smile again.

"Yeah . . . ? Like *Outer Limits?*"

I said the right thing. Now he had an association. The cud mind needs something to compare a thing to. It can't handle the idea of something in and of itself. Something unique. It must make a comparison. It must be *like* something else. Now he had a handle . . . and played "Go Insane."

Mistake! When he heard those *fun* lyrics he lost it.

Once I had a little game,
I liked to crawl back in my brain,
I think you know the game I mean,
I mean the game called go insane!

When Jim screamed "go insane," Joe Vegas ripped at the tone arm.

"This is sick!" he shouted. He flung the record at me. I caught it before it hit the ground. "This is pothead stuff!"

"But isn't it kind of like . . ." He wouldn't let me finish.

"Get out of here," he shouted. "Get the fuck out of my office. This is sick!"

I rose, knees trembling. "But I thought you liked—"

"I don't *like* this music." He came out from behind his desk and grabbed my arm. "I *hate* this shit." His eyes were blazing. He was gone.

He roughed me toward the door—"Now get out of here!"—and shoved me out of his office.

"And don't you ever come back here. Fucking pothead!" As he slammed the door I could hear him muttering "Go insane? Fuck me!"

I walked out into the clear California light, depressed again.

⚶

Two days later, Dorothy was fired from her job. She had been re-placed by a machine. All the tape cleaners were now superfluous—victims of automation. Shit.

The next week, when I went to pay the rent with her last salary money, old Oscar the arthritic landlord, who lived in the front house on Fraser, in his wheelchair and darkened living room, which he never left, with smells of dankness and death and mold and old, told me as I placed seventy-five dollars between his disease-locked fingers . . . "You'll have to move out, Ray, you and that bunch up there. This is your last month."

"But . . . why? We haven't made any noise or anything."

"Too many people," came his curt reply. "I rented it to two people . . . you've got four up there now. Can't have it. No, sir, no more."

"But . . ." I was speechless.

"You're out! That's it."

He was right, there were four people now. An Army buddy of mine, Britt Leach, had joined us. He was from another part of my life. I had done my time a few years earlier. I thought I would enlist and get into film (you got your choice if you joined up) before they drafted me and made me a rifle-toting mud hog. Film was filled so I took darkroom still photo instead. I went to Fort Ord in Monterey (John Steinbeck country) for basic training. We looked down on the lights of Salinas on night maneuvers and prowled Cannery Row on free weekends. Then Fort Monmouth, New Jersey, for photog training. And New York City for weekends! I saw Coltrane and Mingus live! *Last Year at Marienbad* and many other art flicks. MOMA and the Met and Greenwich Village. It was fabulous. And then off to Okinawa, where I played jazz with Logan Walker, a great tenor player of Gene Ammons-like girth and intonation. Then Thailand, where I first encountered *Cannabis sativa*. Thai stick! Wow. And back to Okinawa and a week at Clark Air Force Base in the Philippines, and finally home. With a mess o' weed stuffed into my securely locked footlocker. It lasted me and Dorothy a good eighteen months.

Fortunately Jim, Robby, and John got out of their required military obligation. Back in those days, universal conscription—the draft—existed. Everyone had to do two years in the Army or enlist in some other branch of the killerdom. And a war was going on! Vietnam! Fuck!

And they were scared shitless. Being drafted meant the end of the Doors and probably going off to be a grunt in 'Nam. And that could mean death. The ultimate fear. Although Oliver Stone seemed to like the idea well enough . . . the sicko. So when the draft notices came around, Jim stayed awake for an entire week on pills, went down to the draft board, and did a Morrison crazy on them. They let him go immediately—"Unfit for military service." Robby got doctor paper from his uncle in Phoenix saying Robby had mental problems and other brain disorders. They let him go, too. John did a version of Jim's trick and also checked the box labeled homosexual. BAM! He was out that fast! They were free . . . and we could all breathe again.

Britt had come to L.A. fresh out of Gadsden, Alabama, wanted to be an actor—did in fact become one—and needed a place to stay. I had figured two sort-of southern boys could get along in tight quarters, so I let Britt sleep in the bedroom with Jim. They hit it off, no problems, no sweat, no big thing. Oscar, however, blew an arthritic fuse . . . and we were out. Man, I was depressed.

No prospects, no place to stay, no steady money coming in, nobody liked our demo. We had bottomed out. On top of it, my acid-shattered psyche was already fractured. The internal man had collapsed and I was gradually piecing the "new Ray" back together through yoga asanas, meditation, and much philosophical reading. But adding all this external disappointment to my internal turmoil was fate's way of being *too* capricious. The Doors' diamond had been formed through serendipity, through fate's blessings, but now I was being tempered in fate's alembic. The alchemical fire was burning me in its blast furnace and I either was going to be hardened or shattered. It was existential time again. I was at another crossroads. Hell, we all were.

My belief in the efficacy of the energy was being sorely tested. Was I actually going to be able to live in accordance with my psychedelic visions of harmony, love, and trust in the sweet, divine energy of creation? The energy that supports us all—you can call it God's love, if you need to—the energy that *is* us. Could I live in communion with the Christ within? Could I hurl myself into the chaos with nothing but my trust in the energy? Could I leap into the void space and fly? Did I actually believe in the goodness of existence, the divine rays of the sun, the beneficence of mind itself? Could I actually overcome these adversities through belief in the possibility of our *all* becoming the new man?

This was the task.

Here's what happened: The four of us—Britt, Jim, Ray, and Dorothy—needed new places to live. We had one month. Britt moved out about two weeks later. Packed his duffel bag and headed off to a bachelor apartment in Hollywood to pursue his acting dream. Dorothy and I began driving around Venice, looking for something suitable for a young couple in love. We wanted something charming, something romantic. Just a little place, but cool, with lots of character. In other words, exactly what we already had on Fraser. Shit.

We drove and drove, looked and looked. Nothing. Nothing small. Nothing inexpensive. Nothing charming. I was getting very depressed.

However, a phone call came for Jim at Felix's house. Jim had left Felix's number as his; I didn't have a phone. Very few calls ever came for Jim and they were all from his friends. But this time it was different. This call was from Columbia Records! We had dropped off a demo at the front desk and, unlike at Capitol, it worked its way up the ladder, all the way to Billy James, second in command in A&R at the biggest record company in the world. And he wanted us to come in. He liked the demo!

The gray scud over my spirit lifted. The sun was shining again. The depression dissipated. Columbia Records! Oh, yes!

Trust in the energy, my friends.

Jim and Dorothy and I drove into Hollywood, to the 1930s Art Moderne Columbia complex on Sunset and Gower. Streamlined Moderne, à la Raymond Loewy. A nifty set of buildings. I love that style.

We left John and Robby back at their homes, just in case. Didn't want to subject them to any Liberty Records–like scenes. I wouldn't want to subject *anybody* to that long-hair-versus-Vegas-swinger kind of confrontation, let alone a couple of fragile medita-tors with tender egos. Jim and I would scope it out. Dorothy was along for the fun. Hopefully there would be plenty of fun.

We smoked a number in the parking lot and headed into the labyrinth. Eventually we found Billy's secretary, Joan Wilson. She was attractive, blond, and very intelligent. Jim chatted her up. He seemed quite taken. She ushered us into Billy's office and told us to wait. Billy was in the loo. We looked at his gold records. I wanted one of those. A framed Byrds album was on the wall. Billy had writ-ten the liner notes and compared some of their guitar riffs to John Coltrane. I thought that was a real stretch. The Byrds were country, they didn't have any black in them at all. They couldn't play jazz. Hell, they probably didn't even *know* anything about jazz. They were folk-rock, for cri-sake. Country music. For whites only. But, what the hell, John Coltrane had been mentioned on the back of a hit album. *That* was incredible. And that was by Billy James. I felt real good about this meeting.

And in he came. A cool New York dude. He introduced him-self, shook Jim's hand, took mine . . . we looked in each other's eyes and I burst out laughing! He was a head, too. All right! You could see it in his eyes. He grinned back at me, unsure whether I was being sarcastic, putting him on, or what?

"What's funny?" he said.

I stammered something in my hemp haze and then Jim jumped

in to save the situation: "He's just happy to see you. Kind of, you know, high on life."

Billy laughed at that one. "Yeah, I'll bet," he said. "Why don't you all sit down," he offered as he went to his desk. Our demo was right on top. He picked it up and said, "I love this demo."

Three brains went cuckoo. We had never heard those words before from someone who had a desk. Let alone an office . . . not to mention a *secretary.* Wow!

"You guys have got it." (See, I wasn't the only one who thought in terms of the *it.*) "But it's really raw," he continued. "You need a good producer."

"Do you know of any?" Jim asked from cloud nine.

"Sure. They're on staff here. I was thinking of Larry Marks for you guys. He's hip. I'll introduce you to him"—and then he paused for theatrical emphasis, a sly smile creeping across his face—"as soon as I sign you to Columbia Records."

Three people levitated in that office. Ray, Dorothy, and Jim floated up to the ceiling, bounced off the Swiss-cheese acoustic tile, and swan-dived back to their seats. Signed to Columbia?! Holy shit! Our dreams became reality in an instant. Holy fucking shit! Signed to Columbia?!

"I'll have legal get the contract together. It'll take about a week for those suits to justify their salaries," Billy said.

We laughed. Billy James was obviously an anti-Establishment type. He wouldn't kowtow to the powers that be and yet he was sweetly sitting in a position of prominence. He could play the game and still be outside the arena. No mean feat in those days of "counterculture versus the Establishment." Today, of course, it's impossible. If you play the game, you are the game . . . and you love the game. Even if it drives you mad. And the game is . . . slowly . . . driving us insane. We are gaining the world—wealth, power, and fame, the goals of all right-thinking Americans—and gradually losing our souls. The spiritual rot is subtle . . . but inevitable. If you believe in the game, you lose. That's the great irony, the joke of maya. You can acquire all the outward trappings of success—the wealth, the position of authority, the homage of the public, the respect of your peers . . . the power! . . . the sheer giddiness and hubris-inducing tendency of the acquisition of power, power for its own sake—but you must surrender your freedom. Your internal freedom. Your spiritual freedom. You can no longer be a free man on the planet. You cannot be a slave to success and be free. It's really an either/or choice. It's existentialism . . . and the choice is yours: bitch goddess of success or free human being. Slave to the game or slave to no one. Come the millennium, you're going to see a shifting of the paradigm as more and more men and women opt for freedom. That's what we did in the sixties. And that's what's going to happen again in the twenty-first century.

> *I was doing time in the Universal Mind,*
> *I was feeling fine.*
> *I was turning keys,*
> *I was setting people free.*
> *I was doing all right. . . .*
> *I'm the freedom man,*
> *That's how lucky I am,*
> *I'm the freedom man.*

Billy then said, "Is there anything you guys need?"

I laughed. "Man, I'll say. We need some money."

Jim added, "Is there any front money on signing?"

"Sorry, guys, money I can't get you. But anything else? Like, how about equipment . . . can you use some new equipment?"

My eyes lit up. "Yes! What kind, Fender?"

"No, we just bought Vox. You can have anything you want that Vox makes."

"Really?" I gushed.

"Would I make it up?"

Now here's the cool part: Vox made the organ that the Animals and the Dave Clark Five used. The red-and-black Vox Continental Organ. Alan Price played one with the Animals, and he was good . . . and it was very groovy. The black and white keys were reversed and it had two chrome Z-shaped legs. It was sleek and loud. You plugged it into a guitar amp and cranked the sucker. A keyboard player could then compete with those maniacs of loud . . . the guitar players. Volume to equal Robby. And Super Beatle amps. The very amps the Beatles used on television. On the *Ed Sullivan Show*, no less.

Big chromed pre-Marshall monster amps. All the top English groups used them, and we could have them for free?! Yes, Lord, the fates do move in mysterious ways.

"How long would it take to get a Vox organ?" I asked. "Couple of weeks, or what?"

Billy smiled. "Hell, tomorrow if you want. The Vox plant is out in the Valley."

"No shit?"

"Would I make it up?" Billy put on a Lower East Side New York accent. "So go already."

We laughed, stood up, shook hands, grinned at each other like a bunch of potheads, and were out the door.

Billy shouted to his secretary, "Joan, give them the address to the Vox plant and then call Ed Whozits out there. Tell him *the Doors* are coming."

God, that felt good.

We called John and Robby from a pay phone in the lobby. They were ecstatic. We told them to bring the VW van, meet us at Fraser tomorrow, and we'd all head out to the Valley and load it up with Vox equipment.

Robby the realist said, "Vox stuff's not that good, Ray."

"What are you talking about?" I shouted into the phone. "The Vox organ is great! Alan Price plays one."

"I don't know about the organ," Robby said, "but the amps aren't better than Fender amps."

"But it's free!"

"So what?"

"You could get a Super Beatle for free!"

"I don't want a Super Beatle."

"Why not?"

"I'd rather have a Fender Twin Reverb."

"But Columbia doesn't own Fender, they own Vox."

"Well, they should have bought Fender."

"Robby! Jesus Christ, do you have to be so picky? Just be at my house tomorrow morning. Early!"

Jim grabbed the phone. "Hey, man, we got a fucking deal! I want to hear you laughing and singing." Pause. "No, there's no front money." Pause. "I don't know how long the contract's for." Pause. "He didn't say how many albums." Pause. "Billy James." Pause. "I don't know, I haven't read the contract yet." Pause. "I can read a fucking contract." Pause. "Fine, whatever you want. I'll see you tomorrow." Jim hung up, turned to me and Dorothy, and shrugged his shoulders.

"What did he say?" I asked.

"He said we need a lawyer. His father will get us one."

Robby the realist.

The next day we did it. We were in the Vox plant, the five of us, and it was a showroom of the British Invasion. The music of the British Empire ruled the airwaves and we were in the armory. And anything we wanted was ours! We were taken to the display room, where samples of all their equipment were set up for public scrutiny. What a mass of chrome and plastic and wire. There was a brace of Super Beatles, all gleaming and almost six feet tall. The biggest amps I'd ever seen. Riding on their own chromed caster support stands for ease of the wheeling about of those monsters of wattage. There was a myriad of smaller amps in a rainbow of colors. Guitars everywhere—even the Brian Jones teardrop-shaped beauty. There were posters on the walls of all the warriors of the British armada who used Vox—the Beatles, the Rolling Stones, the Animals, the Dave Clark Five, the Spencer Davis Group. And in the middle of this psychedelic cornucopia . . . the Vox Continental Organ. *My* organ. Waiting for me, waiting to go home to Venice.

Everything was irresistible. I would have taken one of each but Billy said not to get greedy. "Just take what you need," he had said.

"Well, I need that Vox Continental and I need an amp," I said to the man in charge, Ed Whozits. I asked Robby . . .

"Should I get a Super Beatle?"

"The speakers are too small, Ray."

"But it's almost six feet tall. How can it be too small?" I asked him.

"It's just a bunch of eight-inch speakers. They break up too easily. Get something with two twelves. It'll hold the bottom better."

He pointed to a black amp low to the floor. "Get that one. It's as close as they have to a Twin Reverb."

"Are you going to get one?" I asked Robby.

"No, I want a Fender."

"Then how about a Brian Jones guitar?"

"Fuck no. That's a piece of plastic junk."

"It looks good."

"So what, it's already been done."

Jim spoke up. "I want a Super Beatle to sing through."

Robby said, "Are you going to carry it?"

Jim paused. "Uhh . . . I'll take one like Ray's getting."

"Two Royalton amps," I said to Ed. "And a Continental."

"I'll take this guitar, too," Robby said. He had picked out a guitar not unlike his Gibson. "I'll use it for bottleneck. I can keep it in open tuning. That way I don't have to go back and forth all the time," he said to me.

"Groovy," I responded, not really sure of *what* he was talking about.

Jim said, "John, anything for you?"

"Forget it, man," John said, "I don't see any drums on the floor, do you?"

"Come on, John, don't get cranky now," Jim chided. "Just because you can't get any free equipment is no reason to sulk."

We all laughed, and of course John sulked because we laughed.

Jim turned to Dorothy. "How about you, Dorothy. Want a Brian Jones Teardrop guitar?"

She grinned. "I want a Super Beatle."

"Are you going to carry it?" Jim asked.

More laughter, even from John. He was okay again. We were all okay. We had our loot!

We went to the loading dock and stuffed the Volkswagen with our new equipment. What a haul. We were delirious. We were floating. Jim made a graceful, slow-motion leap from the loading dock onto the roof of the VW van, landed securely, spread his arms, and proclaimed to the world . . .

"Now we're ready for some gigs!"

the beach house

Eureka! We found it. Dorothy and I found the apartment of our dreams. Right on the beach. Northstar and Speedway. And I mean on *the beach!* The front yard was the sand of Venice Beach. The ocean was fifty yards away from our front window. You stepped out the double Mondrian doors and onto . . . sand! The California dream. A beach house.

It was the downstairs front apartment of an old, dark shingled Craftsman-style two-story duplex home that had been divided into four units. The landlord was upstairs front—the best unit—and we were below him. He was never home in the daytime. We could do anything we wanted without having the whistle blown. In fact, everybody was gone during the day. No one was there, everyone was at work. We could rehearse on the beach! We could crank all that new Vox equipment and no one would be around to complain. Our nearest neighbor was at least seventy-five yards away in another old home on the beach. We were five or six blocks north of the Marina Channel and everything was all spread out. Our neighbor to the south was a praying-mantis-headed oil pump that just kept bobbing its head up and down, endlessly agreeing with everything. To the north was "the bad boys" house. A small group of priests in black took care of a small group of probable juvenile delinquents. We could never exactly scope out the kids because it was too far away to discern any features and thus read any personalities, but it definitely gave off vibes of a halfway house. So there was nothing to interfere with our creation of the dreaded "live" music. We could set up all the equipment in the living room and blast!

And what a living room it was. Fifty feet of glass windows looking out on the beach, the ocean, the setting sun. It was originally the sunroom — back in the twenties and thirties — before the division. It was all wood and glass and warm. What a creative environment. It couldn't have been more sun-infused, more light-washed, more solar if we had designed it ourselves. The wheel had turned in our favor again.

A small bedroom, a small bathroom, and a small kitchen were all connected to the sunroom. It was, essentially, *all* sunroom. The other rooms were an afterthought, a mere courtesy to the residents. Had to eat and sleep somewhere in between bouts of lizardlike sun basking. I brought the guys to see it. They loved it.

"We can rehearse right here!" Jim said.

"We can set up the equipment and just leave it," said John. "I don't have to keep moving my drums back and forth and tearing them down after every rehearsal. This is so groovy!"

"And now that we've got all the electric stuff, we can't play at my house anymore," said Robby. "The neighbors would shit a brick if they heard us wailing."

"Live music!" I mockingly nodded.

"They *hate* live music in Pacific Palisades," Robby finished.

"And well they should," said Jim the trickster. "Can you imagine the caterwauling of untalented rich kids electrified?"

Robby was mosquito stung. "Fuck you, Morrison. I'm not a rich kid."

"Oh, yes, you are," laughed John.

"Well, *your* father's an architect," shot back Robby.

"Yeah, but he's not rich like yours."

Robby thought for a beat. "But he's only been rich for a couple of years now."

We all laughed at the absurdity of that one.

"When can we set up, Ray?" Jim asked, ready to rock. We were *all* ready to rock.

"Yeah, when can I bring my drums?" asked John. "Can I bring them tomorrow?"

"I haven't rented the place yet," I replied.

"Well, close the deal," said Robby.

"Yeah, take it." Jim said. "Don't let someone else get it."

"There's only one problem . . . ," I said.

Their faces fell. A collective pall hit the sunroom.

"What . . . ?" they said almost in unison.

"I can't afford it," I answered.

Another pause. Brain wheels turned.

Robby spoke first . . . "We'll pay for half."

John was shot with an electric arrow. "What?!" he shrieked. "Why do I have to pay for Ray and Dorothy to have a place to live? That's not fair!"

"You're not paying for them, idiot. You're paying for our rehearsal room," answered Robby.

John saw the logic but needed to worry himself a bit more. When he had one of those "hot flashes" it took him a while to subside.

"Damn, it's just not fair," he grumbled.

"It *is* fair, John," said Jim. "If we went to a rehearsal place we'd have to pay for that. Why not pay for this one? Hell, and it's right on the beach."

"Yeah, but Ray gets to live here."

"Do *you* want to live here?" Jim asked.

"No!" he said. "But why should Ray get to live here?"

John could be such a pissant sometimes. Most of the time he was cool; a funny guy, a good guy, but when he got a "surprise" . . . holy shit! Get out of his way. When he got a hot flash he became mean, and vindictive.

Robby brought the subject back to reality. "How much is the rent, Ray?"

"Two hundred a month."

John shrieked again. "Two hundred! That means I have to

pay . . ." The wheels turned but they wouldn't cog together. "I have to pay . . . uhh . . ."

"About thirty-three dollars," said Robby.

"Ohh. Yeah, thirty-three dollars. One-third of a hundred. That's right." And then logic took over. The hot flash passed and his blood rush subsided. "Hey, that's not so bad. I can afford thirty-three dollars. Shit . . . that's not so bad at all."

John was back. The hysterics were gone. Who knows, maybe that volatility is what makes him such a great drummer.

"But can *we* afford a hundred?" I asked Dorothy.

All eyes turned to her, imploringly. She looked around the long sunroom and then out to the beach, as if evaluating both the place and our entire situation. She paused, took in a large breath of air, and said, "We have to. We have no other choice. This is it." She turned away from the window and spoke to the Doors. "This is where you guys are going to perfect your songs. Right here. In this light."

"All right, Dorothy!" Jim whooped.

John and Robby were giddy.

I hugged her. She was so positive that I didn't even worry about the fact that we had only three hundred dollars in our little savings account.

"Maybe my father will give us a loan," she whispered as the celebration began.

"Well, *mine* sure won't. 'The twain don't meet,' you know," I said, remembering my father's line.

"Oh, yes, they do," she said as she hugged me tighter. "We'll make it."

Jim had a six-pack of Tecate. He passed them out, we cracked them, and toasted our new digs.

"To our new rehearsal studio," Jim said.

"Damn right," said John.

"To the beach," said Robby.

"To the sun," I said.

"To the Doors!" Dorothy said.

We touched our Tecates and guzzled our ceremonial brew. We were home. We were together. And it was good.

※

Within a week we had shifted everything out of Fraser and over to the beach house . . . except for Jim.

"It's time for me to get my own place," he said to me. "I can't keep living with you guys."

"There's plenty of room," I said to him. "You're welcome if you need it."

"Thanks, man . . . but . . . uhh, I'm gonna get something for myself. We can't keep up this platonic *ménage à trois.*" He smiled. "It's unseemly."

"Who cares?" Dorothy replied.

Jim shuffled his feet, a bit embarrassed. "Well, to tell you the truth . . . sometimes I feel like I'm your son or something. I don't want to be your kid."

"You're not!" I protested. "You're our friend."

"Yeah . . . I know," he said. "But sometimes, well, you know how it is, Ray."

Now I was embarrassed. I didn't realize he'd felt that way. I'd always thought of us as equals. Even though I was older, I felt he had a great wisdom in his soul. He seemed much older than his years, as if he were privy to an ancient knowledge. As if secrets had been imparted to him and it was his obligation to now pass them along to the lovers of America. And the secrets were joy and passion and intoxication with life. The Dionysian secrets.

> *I was turning keys*
> *I was setting people free*
> *I was doing all right. . . .*

But he was also vulnerable. He was very open and trusting, and of course adventurous. A most dangerous combination. It meant he could easily be seduced. His openness and sense of adventure meant that the forces of evil—the self-destructive powers—saw a potential subject for trasmogrification in James D. Morrison. Just as the satyr saw the reemergence of Dionysus in Jim, so too did the always present, always lurking shadow creatures of destruction see prey in the tender psyche of the lead singer of the Doors. They knew they had the seductive powers of alcohol and fame in their arsenal. They knew that fame would indulge Jim's "bad boy" side, and booze would open the trapdoor to the monsters of his id. The battle would be Manichaean. The power of the light—what he was when we first put the band together: that fine and decent and spiritual poet. That young artist who had combined the American WASP aesthetic with Native American shamanism and had the potential to heal the psychic split in the peoples of this country, and had the potential to become president of the United States. (I felt, back then, that a person from the arts or entertainment had the public access to elevate himself to the White House. I projected we would make our run in 1980. Who better than Jim? Certainly not that fascist show-biz guy who did run in 1980.) That guy. That Jim of light against the power of the darkness—the forces that would destroy all potential, the forces of greed and lethargy and viciousness and sloth and power for power's sake. The evil forces that would deny man his rightful due, his birthright . . . his enlightenment!

But I didn't know that such a battle would take place. I was riding on the first flush of our creativity, the energy of inspiration. It was all blue skies and clear sailing for this Pollyanna. I was having a ball . . . and so was Jim. I'd never seen him happier. Or more full of life and enthusiasm. He was a blazing fire and his heat and light were joyous to be near. He was now my friend and I loved him.

"Have you found anything yet?" I asked him.

"Nope, still looking," he replied.

"Well, if you don't come with us, where are you going to stay?" Dorothy asked him.

"Felix and Phil Oleno have gotten a place together. I'm gonna move in with them."

"Phil and Felix? What about his girlfriend, Mary?" I could feel the potential for disaster. "Is she gonna be there, too?"

"Naw, she threw him out."

"It's just gonna be the three of you?"

"Yeah, what's wrong with that?" He was almost getting testy. "You don't think we can take care of ourselves?"

I felt fate slap me across the face. I tried not to blink.

"I just don't want you to . . . well, you know . . . get in any trouble or anything."

He put his arm around my shoulder in a macho bonhomme-like way.

"Hey, Ray, don't worry about a thang. I'll be fine."

He grinned his best Steve McQueen and I was relieved. Maybe it would be all right.

⁂

It wasn't. Felix was a reprobate and Phil was brilliant but unstable, and the three of them together were incendiary. They drank too much. They indulged in strange chemical substances — Asthmador, belladonna, jimsonweed — just to see what they would do. If they had read about a crazy drug they wanted to try it. No heroin, however. Just weird shit, and the more arcane, the better. It was Jim's "derangement of the senses" phase. He told me about seeing the green lady on belladonna. He started hitting the bottle with Felix. That sot started to impart the "secrets of the tribe" to him. And in a receptive, boozed-up state, Felix's eye contact diatribes began to make sense to Jim . . . or should I say "Jimbo." The jimsonweed had opened the trapdoor to Jim's id, and out had come the character called Jimbo. A good-old boy. A racist. A fat man who liked the power of domination. A monster. A monster of skin. The creature who would eventually take Jim to Paris and kill him.

Unfortunately, I knew none of this at the time. I had never experienced alcoholism before. I didn't know the symptoms or how it began. I didn't know the causes of the disease or its warning signs. But it wasn't just the alcohol, you see. Jim had the shaman's crack. The split. The psychotic leaning into the fissure between ordinary reality and what could be called . . . madness. And the monster could escape through that crack. But so had Jim's angels. And had Jim served a proper shaman's apprenticeship, he could have controlled his demon. But, unfortunately, a proper shaman's apprenticeship had not been served in the West for a thousand years.

And I didn't know the warning signs. The signs of the fissure. I also didn't know the secrets of the tribe. Or that they would matter. And I had *no* idea what derangement was possible under the influence of those weird drugs the unholy three were taking. I saw Jim intoxicated. Out of it. Not himself, but also not yet possessed. It was far too early in the game. The good Jim Morrison — the poet, the artist — was still too strong to be seduced by negativity. But Felix was sowing the seeds and Jimbo was peeking through the trapdoor, and the sleep of reason was going to produce nightmares. Waking nightmares, for me and everyone who loved James Douglas Morrison.

⁂

Dorothy and I took up residence at the beach house, the equipment was set up, and the perfecting of Doors' songs began. It was very powerful to rehearse in the electric mode. It was the first time I was able to plug in with John and Robby and I loved it. And everybody loved the sunroom. Grins all around and great music. All the songs immediately responded to the sun's prodding. We had become the chosen ones, infused with solar energy, warmth, and joy. And the music was smoking. We were hot . . . and we were rocking.

Jim was in great spirits. When he was with the Doors there was no other self but his real self. The real Jim Morrison—funny, poetic, charming, witty, intelligent. The artist. The guy all three of us loved. He didn't "get down with his bad self" when he was around us. He was part of the circle. The charmed circle of the music. In that sunroom, on that beach, he was on the grail quest with the rest of us. We were seeking a cleaner, purer realm. A place of unbounded joy. The realm of enlightenment. The pure land. Buddhahood.

The rehearsals were going great. New songs were being created, and strange and interesting cover songs were being reworked in the collective Doors mind. Robby came in with Willie Dixon's classic "Back Door Man" and we put it into the sifter and came out with what I consider to be one of the great Doors songs. Dorothy had a record of Bertolt Brecht and Kurt Weill's *Threepenny Opera* with a couple of cuts from *Mahagonny* at the end of the disc. It was an original cast recording from 1932. This was her kind of music. She was a twenties and thirties buff. Loved the fashion, the art, and the music of that rich and fecund time between the wars in Europe. We'd play the record on our breaks and marvel at the textural harmonies and orchestrations of Kurt Weill. It was so Weimar. Jim was especially taken with "The Alabama Song." To hear Lotte Lenya and the girls sing in a haunted, broken English:

Oh, show us the way to the next whiskey bar.
Oh, don't ask why,

For if we don't find the next whiskey bar
I tell you we must die.
—Brecht and Weill

Well, it was just too delicious for a southern Gothic boy. He was hooked on the song. He walked around humming it, and one day Dorothy said, "Why don't *you* guys do 'The Whiskey Bar'? As long as you're doing other people's material, you might as well do Brecht and Weill, too."

It struck Jim like a flash.

"What a great idea, Dorothy!" He was pumped. "Let's try it," he said to us.

"Whoa, those are some complex harmonies going on in that song," I protested. "I don't know if I can figure them out."

"We don't have to do it exactly like the record," Robby wisely said. "We'll do our own version."

"Exactly," Dorothy said. "Make it a Doors song."

I was unconvinced. But we went to work on it and, man, was I wrong. Robby divined the chord changes, I put on the "nightmare carnival organ," John gave it a German oompah beat, Jim played Lotte Lenya, and we had it! Another Doors classic.

And now it was time for some gigs. It was time to audition at the local clubs and make a few bucks already. We had enough tunes for two sets. We were ready. Of course we didn't have a bass player—we auditioned two guys and wound up sounding like a cross between the Stones and the Animals. It was not right with a fifth guy. Four Doors, that's all. The cardinal points. The diamond.

So we hit the circuit . . . and were rejected by everyone. Once again—same as the demo. "Too weird . . ." "Can't you play 'Satisfaction'?" "Where's your bass player?" "You're not what we're looking for." "You stink!"

But at a club in the South Bay we found our bass player. The Fender Rhodes keyboard bass. It was sitting atop a Vox Continental Organ, and belonged to the group that was a permanent fixture at this "airport" lounge. It was all black and silver and looked great against the red and black of the Vox. I took one look at it and said, "This is it! This is what I've been looking for." I was playing left-hand figures on the Vox but the sound was too muddy. The Vox was strictly a one-handed instrument; four notes in the upper register were the maximum. Add a left-hand bass line and the sound fell apart. Fuzz crap was what you got . . . the opposite of what I wanted. I wanted clean and crisp and hard-edged stiletto-like shrieks emanating from my red, black, and chrome Z-legged beauty. I wanted a sound to clean plaque off your teeth. I wanted it screaming like a banshee, and then soft and thick and mellow on our ballads. I didn't want fuzz crap. So I didn't use my left hand—well, only sparing little pokes at the lower end. I might as well have used my boogie-woogie Bach-trained left hand to pick my butt or piddle Little Ray for all the good it was doing on the Vox low notes. But when I saw that keyboard bass I knew I had found something for lefty to do other than something of a scatological nature. We didn't get the gig but we got our bass.

We went to a music equipment store the next day, Robby and I, to seek out our new friend. We found it in Hollywood, and it was fine . . . and it was $250. Way too much for a gigless band. What to do, what to do? All chip in? Hell, they were paying rent already. Dip into our savings account? Hell, that was for rent, too. Get the loan from Dorothy's father? We already tried that. He turned us down, said the "twain didn't meet." We were fucked. There was our bass player and he was beyond us. We simply couldn't afford him. I told Robby we'd just have to keep saving until we had the $250. He said, "That could be a long time." He was right. Shit.

We reconvened at the beach house for a rehearsal about three days later. And, lo and behold, in walked Robby Krieger carrying a brand-new, fresh-in-its-box, Fender Rhodes Keyboard Bass! I was shocked, delirious, overjoyed . . . and then worried.

"You didn't steal it, did you?" I asked him.

Robby smiled. "Yeah, I robbed it with my bottleneck. Threatened to carve a hole in the salesman's neck unless he gave me a keyboard bass."

We all laughed.

"No, really . . . ," I said.

"I asked my mom and dad for a loan and they wrote out a check to Wallach's Music City. I got it yesterday."

"It's ours?!" I exclaimed.

"All ours," Robby said.

"I love your mother and father!"

"Good thing they're rich," Densmore joked.

"Fuck you, John," Jim said.

"I'm only kidding. Jesus, can't you take a joke?"

"When I hear something funny, I'll laugh," Jim responded.

"Shut up, you guys," I said, "we've got our bass player!"

I tore open the box. It was brown. The Fender Rhodes Keyboard Bass—brand new—was brown. I didn't want brown, I wanted black and silver. Brown didn't work with the Vox. Brown wasn't sleek. Brown wasn't dynamic. Brown wasn't bitchin'. Black and silver was bitchin'.

"It's brown," I said to Robby.

"It's all they had," he replied.

"I wanted black and silver."

"Those were all sold. Brown is all they had left."

"Oh, sure, the good ones were all sold. I get the dregs." I was looking the gift horse in the mouth . . . and complaining. What an asshole.

"Hey, you got it," Robby said. "What am I supposed to do? They didn't know *when* they were gonna get a new shipment."

"You want him to take it back?" John chided.

"Fuck you, John," Jim said again.

"No, no! It's fine. I'll keep it . . . I'll take it!"

I wasn't going to let this baby go. This was a godsend. Stu and Marilyn Krieger were the greatest.

"How do your mom and dad want me to pay them back? Something every month?" I asked Robby.

"My dad said just make 'Light My Fire' a hit and he'd forget about it."

"No shit?!" I whooped. "Well, let's play and see what this baby *sounds* like!"

I set it on the left hand side of the Vox, plugged it into a spare amp, hit a few notes—the damned thing sounded just like a bass!—and we started "Light My Fire." And, man, it was good! John's cool Latino beat sounded great against a big bottom bass line. The four-on-the-floor chorus had real balls to it now. And the *Olé Coltrane* solo section . . . well, it was hypnotic and ecstatic! The repetitive A minor to B minor triad pattern on a deep, gut-rumbling, chest-cavity-massaging, lower-two-chakras-stimulating bass instrument was incredible. Robby and I floated on that deep bottom, weaving lines of melody in, out, around, and through each other. John whacked away at his drum kit, keeping his impeccable time. Playing with even more fury and abandon now that he had a deep bass line to support him. We kicked that solo hard and Jim went into a rapture. He grabbed a maraca and started dancing around the sunroom, shaking that gourd on a stick for all it was worth. He was into it! We were *all* into it. We played our asses off. We had never sounded better. The keyboard bass was the missing ingredient. Now we were ready to challenge the Beatles. Now we were ready to take on the Stones. Now we were . . . the Doors!

⁂

About a week later, Jim came over by himself. Just to get some sun and laze around on the beach. But something was wrong. He seemed edgy, nervous. He was slightly disheveled with four or five days' growth of beard. Maybe he'd been to the desert again with Felix and Phil. Dave Thompson told me a story of the three of them — he heard it from Phil — going out to the Sonora Desert to look for peyote. They got as far as the California/Arizona border, stopped at a bar for beer and tacos, in Needles or somewhere, and got the living shit kicked out of them by some Chicano bikers after Felix had made another one of his racist remarks. Probably insulting the brown-skinned low riders with a vicious "greasers" and putting a nasty WASP twist on the word "Mexicans." So they got their white boys' asses kicked from one end of the parking lot to the other. Felix later told me that one of the bikers was kicking him in the head as he lay on the tarmac. He said: "I thought, If this spic doesn't stop kicking on my head I'm gonna fucking die right here in Needles." And then he laughed. What an asshole. But he didn't blink.

Jim had cowered near the car with Phil, so he only got a cut over his eye and a few body bruises. Phil came out okay but shaken. Felix didn't look too good when I saw him. And neither did Jim when he came in that day.

"You okay, man?" I asked him.

"Yeah I'm . . . uhh, fine." He wouldn't look me in the eye. "You got anything to drink?"

"Some apple juice, couple of Cokes."

"No, I mean a beer. I'm thirsty."

Shit! That was Felix's line. Jim didn't talk that way. A beer was for fun. You didn't drink a beer when you were thirsty, for crisake. You drank water when you were thirsty. Why was Jim talking that way? Had the psychic transference begun? Did Jim have a new mentor now? Was he going to follow Felix's lead instead of mine? Were the secrets of the blood tribe stronger than the calling to universal brotherhood? Was the combination of weird drugs, booze, and "blood" going to prevail over the new multiracial tribe? Would the future not be attained because of the pull of the racial archetype? Pulling him back into the security and exclusivity of the ethnic tribe. Would he abandon the giant family in favor of a feast-of-friends blood tie?

"Why don't you have some ice water, man?" I said. "I'll get some ice cubes out of the freezer. Make you a big, cold glass."

"Yeah, that could be good." He looked about the room, distracted. I tried to make small talk . . .

"It sure is sounding great." I fiddled in the freezer. "Your songs sound terrific. It's definitely the way I heard them in my head . . . maybe even better," I said with a laugh.

"They're *our* songs, man. They're not mine anymore. I just gave them their first shot. They belong to all of us now."

He seemed better already. I handed him his ice water and he downed it quickly. He *was* thirsty.

"Oww, that burns," he said. "My head hurts . . . I guess I drank it too fast."

"No shit," I answered.

He touched his temples and grimaced. He was hurting but he didn't want to let on. Didn't want to appear to be weak.

"Why don't you sit down, man? Relax awhile," I said.

"Yeah, I think I will. I'll just relax . . . that's why I came over, anyway."

"You're welcome anytime. You know that. Let me see if I've got a joint around here," I said as I fumbled around in the bedroom. I couldn't find anything but it gave him the opportunity to regain his strength as he sat looking out at the ocean.

"Why don't you take a towel and go out on the beach? You could use some sun."

His neck hairs bristled. He had a Marlon Brando hairline in

the back that was now covered with what I thought to be a too-shaggy mane. But still those hairs bristled. He was testy, edgy. Too much revelry . . . and it showed.

Then I, like a fool, pushed it over the edge. . . .

"You know, man, you really ought to get a haircut. Your hair looked so much better about three months ago. Why don't you—"

And he exploded! He jumped out of the chair, threw the glass down—merciful God, it didn't break—and stormed toward the door.

"Don't ever tell me what to do, Ray!" he shouted at me. "Don't ever do that again."

He opened the Mondrian door and then turned and shot me an enraged look. A look unlike any I had ever seen in his eyes before.

"Nobody tells me what to do. Nobody!"

I couldn't believe it. I was shocked, outraged. I thought, What are you hollering at me for? I'm on your side. I'm here to protect you, to see that your art flourishes, to help you stay out of trouble. And then a terrifying thought flashed through my mind for the first time: To help keep you from . . . killing yourself. And a sadness swept over me. A deep darkness with the green thing wrapping itself around my gut. An emptiness. A longing for the sun. He was shattering himself, psychically. He was imperceptibly destroying himself. He was, perhaps, going mad.

He glared at me again. "Understand, Ray?!"

I nodded. "Yeah, sure, Jim. Whatever you say, man."

And he was gone. Slammed the door and was gone. I had just confronted "Jimbo" for the first time.

the sunset strip

Now began our assault on the citadel. We were going to Mecca. Into the eye of the hurricane. Into the very heart of the beast. We were going to audition for a gig at a club on the Sunset Strip. The London Fog. Just down the street from the holy of holies . . . the Whiskey-a-Go-Go.

The Whiskey had all the big bands. One didn't "audition" for the Whiskey-a-Go-Go. If you didn't have a record contract you didn't play there. If you weren't on a national tour you didn't play there. If you weren't hot and racing up the charts, you didn't play there. We couldn't play there . . . yet. We had to start at the beginning, and that was the London Fog, a funky little club with very little clientele, but with "live" rock and roll! And we wanted to be on the Strip; and the London Fog, whatever its shortcomings, *was* on the Sunset Strip.

Jim and I secured the audition, and when the next blue-

Monday night rolled around, we were ready. We had called all our friends from the UCLA Film Department and John and Robby had contacted the meditators. The club was packed with our ringers and we played our asses off. The owner—the absurdly and yet appropriately named Jesse James—was ecstatic. He had never seen so many bodies in his club, let alone on a Monday night. People were dancing, drinks were flowing, the music was rocking, and Jesse James was beaming. He made us play a second set. We knew we were hired. He never suspected a thing.

We started the next week, and as we arrived to set up our equipment, we saw it: a hand-painted banner above the club emblazoned with our name! It read The Doors—Band from Venice and below that, in small print, Rhonda Lane Go Go Dancer. I loved it for its absurdity. There was no other way to bill us except Band from Venice, and the tag of Rhonda Lane, well . . . hello to show-biz land. But, hell, there we were on the Sunset Strip and a cheesy, hand-painted sign said The Doors. The Doors on Sunset! Not a bad first step for this journey of a thousand miles.

The London Fog immediately went back to its usual clientele. A few businessmen, two sailors on shore leave in their angel whites, a couple of prostitutes, an occasional transvestite hustler, a small group of guys and girls from the Valley looking for Strip action—it sure wasn't at the London Fog—and a random hippie or two. But never at the same time. Always scattered over the evening, so that at any given moment there were approximately ten people in the joint. The four Doors, Dorothy, the lovely Rhonda Lane in her go-go cage directly across from us, Jesse James on bartender, a revolving waitress, and two patrons. Jesse said to me after our first week, "I can't figure out why there aren't more people. We were packed the first night you guys played here."

"They'll come, Jesse," I said. "It's just kind of the luck of the draw. Sometimes you're busy . . . sometimes you're not."

"You're right, Ray. That's how it is owning a club."

"I know," I lied. "It's tough." I coughed and cleared my throat. Now for the hard part. "Jesse . . . uh, could you pay us? It's been a week, you know."

"Has it? Well, sure, Ray. But I'm a little short this week. I can't give you the full amount."

The full amount?! Shit, with five dollars a night per man and ten dollars on the weekend, with one night off, the total was forty bucks per guy! Chump change. Slave wages. Peon fodder. Slim pickin's. But what the hell, the Doors *were* on the Sunset Strip.

He gave me $130 that night and continued to stiff us $20 or $30 every week. He was a sweet guy, though. You couldn't get too mad at him; there just weren't any patrons.

So we practiced on the stage. We played our songs and stretched them out and improvised our two sets' worth of material to fill up four sets. "The End" went from a simple two-and-a-half-minute love song to over eleven minutes of Indian raga jam. "Light My Fire" stretched itself to fifteen minutes—complete with poetry improvisations in the middle. "When the Music's Over" came into existence, and that was good for another twelve minutes or more. We jammed on the blues and a few Stones' songs and worked up an obscene version of Them's "Gloria." The long nights were well spent. We were getting good. No mistakes, no gaps in the sets, burning straight through our forty-five minutes onstage. We were high and we were cooking. We were gaining our confidence and Jim was gaining a voice. All that singing was exercising his throat muscles and they were getting strong and thick. His neck was starting to look like a Genet dream on an engorged cock. Heavy, swollen, and veined. His voice was losing that Chet Baker whisper and Morrison the screamer, the shouter, the crooner, the blues man, was beginning to emerge. He was sounding great. We were playing great. We were ready for anything.

And then she walked in the door. Pamela Courson. All freckle-faced and redheaded and creamy white skinned. Fresh out of Orange County. Fresh off the farm of the mind and with a fire in her eyes.

Her dark red hair,
The white soft skin,
Look! She's coming in here.
I can't live through each slow century
of her movement.

She was the dame of this film noir story. The gorgeous, tragic, little wisp of a girl who was destined to become Jim's inamorata . . . and his doomed partner. Juliet had entered Romeo's playground. And death smiled.

Pam was transfixed by the music. She was immediately drawn to it. And drawn to what she saw on the stage. And one guy on the stage was immediately drawn to her . . . John Densmore. He was the first one to spot her and the first one to be hooked by her cinnamon bait. Jim didn't become aware of the predestination until later.

Pam and her girlfriend—a good girl never prowls the Sunset Strip alone—took a table next to Dorothy. Company in the empty tomb. They ordered a couple of drinks and Pam just stared at the stage, transported. I glanced over briefly, pleased to see three actual girls in Jesse's joint. Jim had his back to the club, as usual. He faced us. We worked in a circle. We all looked at each other, just like at the beach house. And, besides, there wasn't anyone in the club to perform for. So he missed her entrance. But John didn't. As soon as the set ended he was on her like ham on rye.

He sat down at her table, ordered a chocolate milkshake–like brandy Alexander—his favorite drink—and proceeded to put the make on Pam. I was at the next table with *my* inamorata, and we watched the attempted seduction with rapt attention hidden behind casual small talk and drink sippings. We were all eyes and ears behind a very cool and completely disinterested facade. We wanted to see John at work, John on the hunt all sniffing and scratching after the unobtainable. And he was good. He fed Pam a most pleasant line and was slowly reeling her in. She was being appropriately coy and they were smiling and chuckling with each other. I thought, This could work out, John may have finally found a girlfriend here.

Jim was at the bar, oblivious to the whole thing, talking to Jesse and the revolving waitress of the week. Dorothy and I soon lost interest in John and Pam's small talk and diverted our attention back to ourselves, where it's been ever since. I don't remember where Robby was.

And then Jesse said, "All right, you guys. Time to make some music. Break's over!"

Jim said, "Come on, Jesse. There's nobody here. We'll play when somebody comes in."

"Nobody's gonna come in unless they hear music playing first. That's why I pay you . . . to play music to bring in the customers. *Capisce?*"

"Yeah, yeah. I understand, *paesano.*"

And Jim headed for the stage. I saw him, kissed Dorothy, went up, and mounted my organ. Robby drifted up, strapped on his Gibson, and squealed his amp.

"Too fucking loud, man," I said.

Guitar players are always doing shit with feedback. They love it, everyone else hates it. I hit a couple of high notes on the Vox in retaliation. Made it shriek. A nasty banshee shriek. Robby was oblivious, didn't give a rat's ass how loud I played. Didn't bother him one whit. Actually, nothing seemed to bother Robby very much. He certainly could maintain an even strain. John and Jim were the volatility brigade. And Jim shouted into the mic, into the darkness: "John, where the fuck are you? Get your ass onstage, boy." Complete with southern drawl. Probably mocking Jesse's slight country twang. "We got's to make music!"

Dorothy said he reluctantly rose, smiled at Pam, and then bounded across the small dance floor and up onto the oddly placed, too-high stage, which had us off in a corner and almost touching the ceiling of the London Fog. It felt as if we were at the fair in the German Expressionist film *The Cabinet of Dr. Caligari.* And of course *we* were the sideshow, complete with cooch-dancer Rhonda in her cage and Jim as Caesar released from his somnambulistic state to become the slayer of young girls' hearts. The whole damned scene at the London Fog was an Expressionist film except for our song improvisations and extensions . . . and Pam.

John was on fire that set. He must have been playing for her, or inspired by her. The set was hot and we were working the magic . . . for an empty club. It was the last set of the evening and who knows what possibilities awaited John after two A.M., closing time in Los Angeles.

We finished the set of fire and John rappelled off the stage, went to Pam's table . . . and she was gone! Oh, disappointment. Oh, rejection. She had taken her soft, cinnamon skin and her lustrous red hair back to Orange County; perhaps never to be seen again. A passing moment, a spark ignited and then all too quickly quenched. Ahh, life . . . how cruel love can be.

But guess what, two days later she was back. Unfortunately, with girlfriend. John didn't care. He resumed his posturing and really chatted her up. Pam stayed the entire evening and was gone again before the last set was over.

Now it was the weekend and she came on both nights . . .

alone. We thought for sure John had made a conquest. Dorothy and I were happy for him. He needed someone, and *this* someone was cute. But on the first night of this fateful early April weekend of 1966, Jim Morrison noticed Pamela Courson. And on the second night he made his move. And she was his. Forever.

John and Pam were in one of the booths, talking, smiling, John having his brandy Alexander, Pam sipping a beer . . . and Prince Charming just slipped into that booth as smooth as a water moccasin slides into a bayou. He bit her on the neck and Trilby was forever enslaved to Svengali. He sat next to her, gave her his best Steve McQueen, and she was his. I don't think she even glanced over at John again. Her eyes were locked on Jim's . . . and she was in love. She probably fell in love with him that first night, standing in the doorway before she even crossed the threshold to her destiny. I have no doubt it was instantaneous on her part and close to warp factor 9 on his. Once their eyes combined, their psyches did a caduceus up the staff of Mercury and their souls sprouted wings. They were mated. Olympian. Cosmic.

John felt Pam's attention disappear, divined the situation, moved out of the booth, and let Pam slip out of his mind. It was hopeless. She was Jim's. Had been from the start. John forgot about Pamela Courson. As far as he was concerned, it never happened. He simply continued to be the best drummer I've ever played with! What a monster on the tight little "mod-orange" drum set of his. That's why he was in the Doors. Because he was a great drummer, a jazzer, and, back then, a spiritual seeker.

We played the London Fog for two more weeks, Pam came off and on, she sat with Jim, transfixed . . . and then Jesse James lowered the boom on us.

"Guys, this is gonna be your last week," he said. "I've got to get a new band in here. You're not drawing flies."

Fate rolls the dice again. Hey . . . you lose. The great, sweeping, all-engulfing depression descended on my head and slipped down into my intestines, happy to be again causing its disemboweling anguish.

Sure, I can talk a good show. But I'll be damned if the fear didn't grab my gut as soon as an opportunity presented itself. Last week! Christ, now what?! my brain screamed.

I looked at Jim. He could only shrug his shoulders. John and

Robby took on the mien of whipped dawgs. We were fucked. I sat down with Dorothy and spilled the bad news, and she put her hand on my forearm, lightly, comfortingly, in that way she has of touching me that says I love you, trust you, I'm here for you.

"Don't worry, Ray," she said. "Something will happen. I know it. You guys are too good for it *not* to happen."

She smiled at me and her warmth wrapped me in an aura of light. God, I love that woman.

And sure enough . . . two days later . . . in walked the booker for the Whiskey-a-Go-Go! Ronnie Harran. A very cute and very hip chick. The club was crowded—wouldn't you know it, Jesse fires us and business picks up—people were dancing! She heard the band, saw the bodies, took one look at the Venice Dionysus and fell in love. Ronnie had good taste . . . and her taste ran to Jim Morrison.

After the set she came up to us, looked at Jim the whole time, and said . . .

"How would you guys like to be the house band at the Whiskey? You'd open for the headliners, two sets a night."

The Doors' collective mind went into mass overdrive. "The Whiskey?! Mecca! House band?! The motherfucking Whiskey?! Wow!" Our brains were ecstatic. Our mouths, however, were dumbstruck. Nobody said a word but the eyes went saucer.

"Well?" said Ronnie.

"Well, what?" said Cool Hand Luke Morrison.

"Can you start next Tuesday?" She smiled at Jim.

"You know what . . . give us some time to think about it," Jim casually replied. "Why don't you come back tomorrow?"

"I will," Ronnie said. "I've got to get back to work now." She smiled at all of us this time and was out the door.

We all proceeded to pummel Morrison's deltoids!

"You asshole," Robby said. "Why didn't you take the gig?"

"What do you mean, we have to think about it?" John said. "We don't have to think about anything, we don't *have* anything, for cri-sake."

"This is the best offer we've ever had," I chipped in. "Why didn't you just say yes? We're finished here on Sunday, we can start at St. Peter's on Tuesday."

Robby jumped back in, "You shoulda said yes! You saw the way she looked at you, she's crazy about you."

Jim shuffled a bit, moved his center of balance to his other hip, and said in his best Paul Cool Newman, "Hey, you don't want to appear overanxious now, do you?" He grinned. "Of course we'll take the gig . . . tomorrow."

We pummeled him again.

"Morrison, you asshole! Jive-ass! Jim, goddamn it," we shouted as we rained mock blows on his arms and back. He laughed. We all laughed. The fates had rolled the dice.

※

Our deal with Columbia was going nowhere. We hadn't heard from them in weeks. We called to set up an appointment with Billy James on Monday to tell him about the Whiskey and our good fortune and to find out when we could begin to record. Well, on Monday, Billy was happy for us but had no date for recording. Something didn't feel right. He had to leave the room for a bit and we sat around, grumbling.

"I don't like the feel of this," Jim said.

"Me neither," said Robby.

"You think something's up?" I asked.

"I don't know," Jim answered. "Maybe so."

John was nosily rummaging about on Billy's desk.

"Hey, look at this!" he shouted. "A fucking pickup and drop list."

"What does it say?" Jim asked.

John read it: "It says we're dropped. They're picking up five bands, I never heard of any of 'em, and they're dropping, let's see, one-two-three-four-five-six-seven. We're number five! Shit!"

Jim jumped up.

"Let me see that drop list."

John handed him the sheet. Jim read it.

"Sure enough," he said. "We're number five."

Billy walked in, saw the jig was up, and said, "I went to bat for you guys. I think you're great, but this is a corporation . . . what can I say?" he shrugged his shoulders, palms up in a Hebraic supplicant manner.

"That's okay, Billy," Jim said.

"We don't blame you, man," I said. "We know it's not your fault."

"I did everything I could," Billy said.

"Hell, you got us all that Vox equipment," Robby said.

"I'll keep trying to get them to record you guys," Billy said, brightening. "You've still got three months on your contract." It was for six months. "If nothing happens by then, they have to pay you a thousand dollars as a buyout."

John whistled. "A thousand dollars?!"

"Just give us a notice of termination now, Billy," Jim said.

"But if we wait three months, we'll get a thousand dollars," John whined. "Maybe they'll even record us yet."

Jim just shook his head. "Wake up, John. They're not going to record us. We're on the drop list. It's a corporate decision." He turned to Billy. "We want our freedom, now!"

Billy nodded, sadly. "Okay, you guys. I'll have paper by the end of the week. But I think you're making a mistake. Take the money."

"Sorry, man," Jim said. "We'll take freedom."

And we were out the door. Columbia artists no more.

⁂

Smash cut to the Whiskey-a-Go-Go. The headlines of our initial engagement week? THEM! Yes, my friends, Van Morrison and Them! Our favorite singer and perhaps our favorite band. "Gloria" and "Mystic Eyes" and John Lee Hooker's "Boom Boom." What great songs. What a great band. And what a wild-man lead singer. Van was a possessed Celt. He was all over the stage. Manic. Arms continually raised in a hallelujah salute to the energy. A ball of black Irish plasma reconstituted as the lead singer of a wandering band of minstrels that had set down beside us on the Sunset Strip of Los Angeles, California. Jim was transfixed by Van. He studied his every move. He put the eye on him and he absorbed. Van Morrison was — and is — the best of the white blues men. No one has that soul, that torment, that anguish. And he displayed it all at the Whiskey . . . and we watched, mesmerized. All of us. I especially loved the way Van would grab the mic stand, thrust it into the air, turn it on its head with the base pointing up to heaven, and continue wailing into the Shure 47. "She got one, two, brown eyes . . . Hypnotize!" Goddamn he was good.

And could he drink. I wish Jim hadn't seen that part of it.

What with Felix imparting the drunken secrets of the race and Van the Celtic Christian blues man idol of Jim's downing copious drafts . . . well, Jim didn't stand a chance. He became enamored of alcohol.

But we all became friends, and the last night of our too-brief week's engagement with the Irish crazies saw us all in a monster jam session. The doors and Them onstage together. Jim Morrison and Van Morrison onstage at the same time! And singing "Gloria"! What a fucking night. The Morrisons were amazing. There was more power coming off that stage than had *ever* been generated at the corner of Sunset and San Vincente. We were rocking and I was at stage left, at the Vox. I'll never forget the picture I saw, to my right, of Van at the mic and Jim with a hand-held mic sitting atop a large amplifier, his head above and slightly behind Van's, both of them bathed in a golden light. And they were gone! They were in another time and another place. They were in the music and they were wailing. We were *all* wailing! It was 1966 and we were young and alive and rocking. The future was ours.

We played the entire summer. And we played with some great bands: Frank Zappa and the Mothers of Invention, the Buffalo Springfield, the Byrds, Captain Beefheart and the Magic Band, the Turtles, the Chambers Brothers, and even the number one band from Mexico, something called the Locos.

It was a time of magic and the gathering of the new tribe. The tribe of expanded consciousness. The Sunset Strip was where the nightly powwow was held. And the Whiskey-a-Go-Go was the sweat lodge. Each member brought his own peyote as needed and the vibrations through that summer were one of peace and love. And the tribe was expanding—long-haired young men and women in soft raiments were everywhere.

> *The soft parade has now begun,*
> *Listen to the engines hum,*
> *People out to have some fun,*
> *A cobra on my left,*
> *Leopard on my right.*

It was becoming a movement. A spontaneous movement of young people and lovers. An eruption of denied forces, a release of suppressed emotions, the reemergence of the ancients of Gods. Of

Dionysus and Aphrodite. Of Eros. Of Wakan Tanka, of Coyote the trickster. Of the Kachinas. And the spirits of our Indian ancestors, the indigenous peoples of North America, smiled at this new tribe of Native Americans. For it's been said that those born on the soil of America are all Native Americans. And the Earth's power sites are always there, all we have to do is feel them. All we have to do is draw the new medicine wheel; the new cross within the circle. For the primordial values do not change over time. The sacred truths are *always* there . . . waiting for us to remember them . . . and reapply them.

Do you know we exist?
Have you forgotten the keys to the Kingdom?
Have you been born yet, and are you alive?
Let's reinvent the gods, all the myths of the ages,
Celebrate symbols from deep elder forests.

"The Doors are hot!" was being said. Word of the house band at the Whiskey spread through Los Angeles. And Jim—"the lead singer is the hottest of them all"—was acquiring a reputation as something unique, something new. A new creature unlike any singer that had ever been seen before on the Sunset Strip. His performances were becoming positively shamanic as he reinvented the gods before our very eyes. The entire band celebrated the ancient symbols of the forests as we immersed ourselves in the waters of our collective unconscious with a music that was at once primordial and future bound. The Doors had coalesced. We were there. The band could enter the energy at will. We were one. Jim and John, Ray and Robby.

And the two young guys, John and Robby, plugged in to a musical transcendence they had never known before. And they were hooked! They loved it. They loved the power of the music, the ego-boosting adulation of the crowd, the lights, the fantasy, the energy, the chicks. The sex! And they wanted more. More of everything. We all did.

And Jim himself was magnetic. What a great joy it was to play with him. He was driven, and his passion drove the band to new heights of fervor. John and Robby and I were right there with him, ecstatic. Carrying him, supporting him, sometimes even leading him. Sometimes taking him to places of which he had no precognition.

Our musical inventions created new realms for him to enter, and he was always able to conjure elegant words and fiery emotions to match our tonal explorations. We were all there for each other. Driving and pushing each other into unknown territory. Into the new world that was founded upon the ancient world. The New Age. And it was happening every night at a sweaty little boîte on Sunset Boulevard called the Whiskey-a-Go-Go.

Jim was also acquiring a reputation as the reigning sex symbol of the Sunset Strip.

The men don't know
But the little girls understand
— Willie Dixon

They loved him. He was so damned handsome, lean, sexy, and snaky that he was irresistible to women. And he was polite, well mannered, and an intellectual. What woman wouldn't want that in a man? Isn't that the perfect combination . . . sex and brains? That's what I want in my significant other.

They stood at the front of the stage, devouring him with their eyes. The maenads—with their mod bangs and flat-pressed hair and Courreges boots and bell-bottom slacks and ribbed poor-boy tops— had found their Dionysus. And their offering to him, their god, was themselves. It was like something out of Herman Hesse's *Steppenwolf*. Jim had opened the door marked "all women are yours," and he was inundated. With their perfumed bodies and nubile flesh they were equally irresistible to him. And, as their god, he had the duty to service as many of his worshipers as humanly possible. And he tried mightily. Wouldn't you? He was a very ardent lover. And very busy. He took his godlike position seriously. It was an obligation he did not shirk. But how he managed to balance Pam Courson and Ronnie Harran and Joan Wilson in and amongst all the maenads, I'll never know.

※

We were having a great time. The summer was per the Doors' master plan . . . and four long-haired rock and roll acidheads were in a state of near-perpetual euphoria. Hell, we were even getting paid. Union scale: $135 simoleons per week—per man! I could pay my own rent. Dorothy and I even got a phone! We were flush. And very happy.

And then Jim laid a bomb on me. (It's always got to have its up and down, doesn't it?)

Middle of July. Almost one year to the day that we first sat together on the beach in Venice and he sang those songs to me. A warm and balmy Southern California night. Scent of flowers, night-blooming jasmine, in the air, mixed with eucalyptus sweet camphor. Moon at three-quarters' full and Leo astrological energy giving everything a little extra charge of excitement. A good night to be alive.

And after the first set Jim said to me, "Ray, I've got something I want to talk to you about. Let's go outside, where we can be alone."

"Sure, man," I said. "You holding?"

He grinned. "Yeah, I got a little number."

"Done deal," I said, and we headed off into the alley behind the Whiskey and walked a block up the street.

We stopped under a big eucalyptus tree and the smell was intoxicating. Jim produced one of his perfectly rolled joints and we lit up. The sweet smoke invaded our lungs and worked its subtle way into our psyches, making them warm and secure.

"Now, what's up?" I asked him.

He casually flipped the roach into the darkness and said, "We've got a problem."

I thought he was kidding. "What, that was the last joint?"

"No, man. I'm serious."

"We don't have any problems. Everything's jake."

He hunkered down and rested his back against the enormous tree trunk. I joined him and we looked like two Okie farmers squatting in the dry earth of the 1930s dust bowl Depression.

"Not quite," he said. "We've got a big problem."

"Jim, what?!" I was incredulous.

He took a deep breath, looked at me, and said, "We've got to get rid of the drummer."

My brain went into a panic.

"What?! Why? Don't you like John's drumming?"

"No, it's not that . . ."

"He knows the tunes." I wasn't even listening to him. My brain and mouth were racing in disbelief. "He keeps a real solid beat. He knows jazz and shit. He's good!"

"Ray, it's not his playing . . ."

"Well, what then?"

"His drumming is fine . . . I just can't stand him as a human being."

The reverb unit in my head went on multiple feedback: Shit, oh shit, oh shit, oh shit!

"We've got to fire him," he said with finality.

"Now?!" was all I could say.

"As soon as we can find another guy."

I rested my reverb unit against the tree. We hunkered in silence, the 1930s dust swirling around our feet. The soil baked and parched . . . like my brain. Then it was my turn for a deep breath. . . .

"It's too late, Jim. We're stuck with him," I said softly.

He looked at me, imploring me.

"It's not! Come on, Ray, we can get somebody else."

"We're on our way, man. This is the unit. The music's too good to change it now. It would break the circle."

"I don't want to do that," he wisely said. "I just want to get rid of him." He looked into the soft, warm night and shook his head. "He gets under my skin, man. Rubs me the wrong way."

I laughed in agreement. "Yeah, I know what you mean. He is abrasive, but what are we gonna do? He's the card we were dealt."

"Fuckin' deuce of spades," he sneered.

And then I remembered the revealing little incident that happened when I first introduced Jim to John. A minor incident, nothing really, but obviously filled with portent.

"Jim, this is the guy I was telling you about. The jazz drummer, John Densmore," I said back then. Jim smiled, extended his hand, and looked into John's eyes. John took Jim's hand, said, "Hey, man," and quickly turned his gaze away. He could not tolerate Jim's penetrating stare. It was too much for him. He had to avert his eyes. Jim's soul-searching shamanic look had penetrated the core of John Densmore's psyche and John couldn't be comfortable with that. Perhaps he was unsure of himself or perhaps, even, he had something to hide. Was I reading too much into it? Were my acid-infused eyes reading too many psychological revelations into a brief encounter? I thought so at the time, but not now. Jim knew it, too. And I don't think Jim was pleased by what he saw. Even back then.

"Man, you're the older," I tried to reason with him. "You're a college graduate, he's not. You're more mature and a lot wiser than he is. Think of him as your dumb kid brother. You've got to bring him along."

"Oh, shit," he said.

"Use your maturity to help him, Jim. Help him grow up."

"Ray! *I'm* not grown up, for Christ's sake."

"More than he is."

"Oh, shit."

"Just try to overlook it when he pisses you off. You can do it, I know you can."

"Sometimes I just want to strangle him."

I laughed. "Come on, you can do it. You're his big brother now!"

He hit me on the arm. "Fuck you, Manzarek. You're always the goddamned peacemaker."

"Someone's got to be." I grinned. "With you two hotheads."

He rose up from his hunker and stretched his long snake limbs. "All right, all right . . . shit. But I'm not gonna like it, Ray."

And, you know, he never did.

We continued playing the Whiskey. Jim didn't talk about terminating John Densmore anymore, but he did continue his remarkable sexual balancing act. Although Pam seemed to be slowly winning out as his main squeeze, there was an overabundance of other female companionship. Actually, this was the pattern that continued throughout their entire relationship. Pam was number one but always at the head of a list of a continually revolving top ten. Maenads, you know, need their god. Spiritually and physically. Orgasms *are* required. Demanded, even. And our priapic snake man always tried to rise to the task. Even later, when Jimbo took control and alcohol made his flesh too weak to answer the demands of the multitude, his spirit of sexual adventure was always willing. But for now, filled with youthful potency, in the first flush of his Dionysian powers, Jim was a happy man. And the bacchantes were well serviced . . . and extremely satisfied. They must have been. They kept coming back.

And the music was growing in fascinating directions as we

worked the magic on a nightly basis in front of a very receptive audience. A gathering of the tribe that urged us on, supported us, encouraged us in our explorations of the unknown zone.

There are things known and things unknown.
In between are the Doors.

As the vibrations intensified, the audience in that sweat lodge on Sunset became more delighted. They always wanted us to take them higher, to a new realm, to a psychic state they'd never experienced before. A new land of intensity and passion. The audience in that summer of 1966 was no different from an audience today. The thing we demand from our artists is passion. We crave intensity of experience. We are glutted with stimulation, with a surfeit of sensory titillation; we're in a frenzy of consumption, a frenzy of choices, we're in a crackhead meth-freak zone of "gimme." We want it all! And we've got it all! They give us everything. The entertainment conglomerates and the consumer goods industries have supplied our every need. But we feel unfulfilled, vaguely unsatisfied. Something's missing from our modern lives.

Something's wrong, something's not quite right.

And that something is what the powers that be, the Establishment, as we called them in the sixties, don't ever want you to have. Passion and intensity. We want a passionate life lived in a state of ecstasy. A life of intensity and deep emotions. An existential life in which every moment counts. A real life.

But we're not allowed to have that. Because if we did . . . we would be free. If we were given the passion and intensity we so desperately crave, we could open the doors of perception ourselves. We could step out of the closed circle of our psychic bondage and be free men and women on the planet. Beholden to no one and responsible for everything. And that is exactly what the Establishment doesn't want you to have . . . freedom. For then we would gain *wisdom* and we wouldn't put up with the crap that corporate America is feeding us. We wouldn't buy their junk. Their junk products and their junk entertainments. It would be the end of civilization as we now know it. We would demand passion and intensity and art and a saving of the planet. We wouldn't accept the meth-head bonehead frenzy we now live in. We would demand peace and love and beauty and truth. We could create the new Garden of Eden. We could become the new Adam and Eve and begin the world again. And that's why the powers that be must stop the "counterculture." It's a battle of lifestyles. It's the lovers versus the salesmen of junk. It's the poets versus the manufacturers of crap. It's the dancers versus the bringers of war. It's the song makers, the earth tenders, the new gardeners of Eden versus the military/industrial complex. And beware, my friends, they are relentless.

> *Dead cats, dead rats, did you see what they were at?*
> *Fat cat in a top hat,*
> *Thinks he's an aristocrat,*
> *Thinks he can kill and slaughter!*
> *Crap! Well, that's crap!*

They must be stopped or we are all the losers. The earth itself is at peril. Our mother is dying and we are going mad with choices of consumption. Stop it! Simplify!

※

And then we were fired from the Whiskey-a-Go-Go. Jim had pushed the envelope beyond the pale. We had entered the forbidden zone. We had become intolerable, anathema, a pariah to the management of the club. And all in one night!

Jim had spoken in public the forbidden phrase: "Father, I want to kill you. Mother . . . I want to fuck you." So what? *Oedipus Rex*, right? He was doing *his* variation on Sophocles' play *Oedipus the King*, which was very popular in the late fifties and early sixties in intellectual/psychological/artistic circles. He was giving voice in a rock and roll setting to the Oedipus complex, at the time a widely discussed tendency in Freudian psychology. He wasn't saying he wanted to do that to his own mom and dad. He was reenacting a bit of Greek drama. He had been involved in the production of *Oedipus Rex* back at Florida State University, just as he had been involved with Tennessee Williams's *Cat on a Hot Tin Roof*. It was theater! It was all make-believe. (Or was it?)

But Phil Tanzini, co-owner of the Whiskey, along with Elmer

Valentine and Mario Magliori, certainly didn't think it was playacting. It was real to him and it was *verboten!* That night we had given an absolutely inspired performance of "The End," a mesmerizing performance that had brought the collective audience to a state of near-suspended animation. The dancers had stopped serving drinks, even the go-go girls in their cages had stopped their shimmy-shake routines. There was stillness and a hushed suspension of time in the collective mind of the club. Only the hypnotic drone of the keyboard bass, the delicate cymbal punctuations of the drums, the low snake slides of the guitar, and the words of Jim Morrison continued on in their relentless descent into madness. Into the darkest recesses of the human psyche. Into the heart of darkness. For this was the night that Jim Morrison said, for the very first time . . .

The killer awoke before dawn,
He put his boots on . . .

John and Robby and I had never heard these words before. We were stunned and delighted. Jim was in a very esoteric reality that night, an LSD-enhanced, non-ordinary state of reality, and he was inspired. Whether he had preconceived these new words or was inventing them on the spot, I'll never know . . . but we were with him. We were attuned to every nuance and we were ready for anything as we followed him into the unknown.

He took a face from the ancient gallery

That line was my clue. An ancient Greek drama mask.

And he walked on down the hallway

He took on a psychological mask and began to explore the corridors of his psyche. The audience was at a standstill, virtually hypnotized. Morrison was in a different place, a shamanic place, and we all watched him, entranced.

He went into the room where his sister lived
Then he paid a visit to his brother
And then he . . . walked on down the hallway.

Jim had a sister, Ann, and a brother, Andy. Now it was getting personal. He had gone from the Billy the Kid killer to an ancient Greek drama mask to his own brother and sister.

I was fascinated. I thought to myself, Where is he going with this? How's he going to conclude this new, scary brilliance? He had constructed a labyrinth and the rules of drama demanded that he find a way out. And Jim was nothing if not a good dramatist. He would never leave us lost in a labyrinth of his own construct. He would resolve it, and the three of us were behind him, seeking to make music as hypnotic and compelling as his words.

And he came to a door
And he looked inside;
Father?
Yes, son?
I want to kill you!

Oh, my God. He's doing *Oedipus Rex*, my mind flashed in recognition. It's brilliant, But I now knew what was coming next . . . and it was dangerous. But there was nothing I could do to alter the destiny of that moment. And, besides, I wouldn't want to. Why alter the high drama . . . it's the very reason we had all assembled inside that "ancient and insane theater: to propagate our lust for life." The audience was his now. In the palm of his hand. Hypnotized. The music had short-circuited all rational, conscious thought and the electric shaman was taking the audience on a journey into the beginnings of Western civilization. John had hit a couple of drum explosions on the "I want to kill you" line and his tom-tom cannons had frozen the assembled multitude. There was absolute stillness. And then he screamed . . .

Mother, I want to . . .
Fuck you!

And we all exploded! Drums, organ, guitar in a frenzy of volume and smashing and shrieking and screeching. The sounds of chaos, of hell, of an orgy of madness. We assaulted our instruments; demented monks releasing all the gargoyles from our repressed souls. We flailed away as Jim leapt and gyrated like a satyr. Like *his* satyr. And the satyr had come to join us on that Dionysian night, free again to revel in the ancient rites. And the trance was broken for the audience. They were released. The dancers began to spiral again, joining Jim in fantastical corkscrews. Moving in a frenzy to match the ear-assaulting volume of the music. The go-go girls shimmied for all they were worth from the depths of their fellaheen hips. The waitresses began their balancing act again, carrying drink-loaded trays through the audience of chaos. The bartenders poured again. The club was alive again.

And then John upped the ante and took the rhythm into a twice-as-fast meter. (That's why we couldn't fire him.) And we broke into the double time. The whirling became dervish frenzied. The dancers were ecstatic. Jim was gone . . . the faun was now onstage, leaping about on his little split hooves, priapic and intoxicated. Robby and I were racing to keep up with John, driving and pushing each other faster and faster until we had no place left to go and exploded in an ejaculatory climax! An aural orgasm. A smashing explosion of come. We shot our sonic wad out onto the heads of the collective and anointed the faithful with holy chrism. Jim, or the satyr, shrieked into the microphone, "Kill, fuck, kill, fuck!" and Phil Tanzini went ballistic! People say he was in a booth in the back and leapt up, shouting, "He can't say that! The goddamned motherfucker can't say that! It's obscene! The fucking son of a bitch!" He came out of the booth like a mad bull. Raging, snorting. He was on a mission of decency. This swinging Vegas rat-pack wanna-be was going to defend God, motherhood, the Church, and the American way of life in one grand gesture of defiance vis-à-vis the "counterculture." He was going to nail Morrison and that way-the-fuck too-loud band! The Doors? . . . Bullshit!

We finished "The End" with a delicate and gentle good-bye: a good-bye originally intended for Mary Werbelow. The music was soft and fragile, with a bittersweet sense of loss. Jim's voice was rich and warm as he sang,

This is the end, beautiful friend.
It hurts to set you free,
But you'll never follow me.
The end of laughter and soft lies.

The end of nights we tried to die.
This is the . . . end.

And we left the stage . . . to thunderous applause. We reached the graffiti-rich dressing room and collapsed onto the funky third-hand couches. We were postcoital spent. It was a delicious exhaustion of the psyche and we were proud of our prowess. We sat in near silence, grinning. And then the gates of Pamplona were opened and in it charged! Picasso's Minotaur! The raging bull himself, Phil "Tough Guy" Tanzini!

"You filthy motherfuckers," he shrieked. He was hysterical. A mean little man, screaming. "You guys are all sick. This is the sickest band I've ever heard." He swept the room, pointing at each of us. "You're all fucked . . . too much pot! You goddamned fuckin' hippies."

"We're not hippies," Jim protested. "We're artists."

Phil wheeled about, nostrils flaring, snorting.

"You are the sickest of the bunch, Morrison!" He was apoplectic. "You can't say that about your mother, you asshole. You filthy fucking, *sick* motherfucking asshole son of a bitch! You can't say that! About your mother?!"

"But, Phil," I tried to play peacemaker again, "he was doing *Oedipus Rex*. You know, Greek drama. A play."

"Greek! Greek?!" he screamed. "What the fuck, I'll give you Greek in your asshole, you jack-off. Fuck you, Greek."

He turned back to Jim. Veins popping in his neck and forehead. Steaming, enraged.

"You're fired! You shit. You finish up this week . . . and you're fucking fired! The only way you'll ever get in this club again is to pay admission at the door! And that goes for all of you sick fucks! You understand me?!"

"Sure, Phil," Jim said. "But . . . do we still have a bar tab?" Jim gave the bull his best shit-eating grin.

I almost lost it on that one. What a wise-ass.

Phil snorted at Jim and stormed out, finally speechless. However, our nights of madness and transcendence at the Whiskey-a-Go-Go were over. It was, indeed, the end.

chapter nine

sunset sound studio

Bur once again the fates intervened. The ascent on Olympus would not be deterred. We had signed a recording contact with Elektra Records just three days earlier. Jac Holzman — superhip long tall drink of water Gary Cooper Greenwich Village New York City folk label gone rock record maven — brought us under his corporate wing with a very liberal three-record-album guaranteed deal. He also gave us a very lousy 5 percent royalty and . . . he took the publishing; Nipper Music. Shit. But it was a guarantee of three albums of Doors music, recorded and on the streets. For the people to hear.

And that's what we wanted. We knew once the people heard us we'd be unstoppable. We were making our music for the people. To turn each other on. Both us and them. The transcendental elevation of the psyche through the manipulation of sound waves. We knew

what the people wanted: the same thing the Doors wanted. Freedom. And three full albums of songs was even more than we had at
that time. We could record every tune in our repertoire and still have
another album left to create new works. It was great. And it was exactly the kind of artistic freedom we were looking for. Jac said, "You
guys do whatever you want, we're behind you. Just don't put in any
obscenities. I can't release it if it has obscenities. They'll yank my license." Fair enough, we'd get around it somehow. Jim could figure
out something, he was the word man. But *what* was he going to do
about this new development in "The End." It *had* to be in there. It
was brilliant. Shit, it got us fired. It had to stay. We'd work it out.

The next night Jac brought the fifth Door to meet us. Paul A.
Rothchild. The coolest, hippest, most intelligent producer on the
planet. Paul was street and college. Paul was us. Paul was a head.
Paul knew his Bach, Mingus, and Monk, Sabicas, Jim Kewskin Jug
Band, Arthur Rimbaud, and Federico Fellini. And he had produced
the Paul Butterfield Blues Band and Love! And he was ours. Our
producer. Jim and Paul hit it off immediately. I loved him the first
time I looked into his eyes. Robby's favorite album was the Butterfield platter. John was in love with Love. Man, too cool. The team
was assembled. And then Jac said: "Guess who's coming to work at
Elektra as head of our new West Coast office . . . Billy James." Well
shoo-fly pie and apple pandowdy! How's that for rolling sevens and
elevens on the crap table of existence? We were all together.

Three weeks later we were in the studio. Sunset Sound in Hollywood. And we met the sixth Door. Bruce Botnick. Enfant terrible
engineer. A good and decent man with ears of gold. We're still together. We'd all still be together if the fates hadn't turned vindictive
and taken Jim and Paul from the magic circle. But any thoughts of
the demands of destiny, of the price of immortality, were far from the
minds of Les Six. We were making a record! Rothchild would run
the studio, Botnick would run the sound, Jim and Ray and John
and Robby would run the changes, and the communal mind would
run the magic. And the four horsemen charged through that high-
tech pleasure dome. We roared and we rocked. We went liquid and
snaky. We went into the fire of Agni and into the waters of Jung's
unconscious. We paid a visit to Dr. Freud and the Maharishi Mahesh Yogi. Miles Davis, John Coltrane, Muddy Waters, and Willie

Dixon joined the party, urging us on, inspiring us to play beyond ourselves. Acting as our gurus, our idols, our fathers. And it was good. Very good.

We were in a frenzy of creativity. All six of us were operating on the plane of inspiration. But if one of those six is inclined to Dionysian excess . . . well, frenzy has been known to lead to chaos. And of course it did.

Fortunately, Jim was out of the sphere of influence of Felix. He had made his break from that reprobate and never saw Felix again once we started at the London Fog, because Felix's drunken motormouth retelling of the same stories over and over had become unbearable to Jim. Felix had taught him the secrets of the blood tribe but Felix was, let's face it, an insufferable boor. And a loser, to boot. Jim finally realized it and walked out, never looking back. Jim then lived with a succession of UCLA friends, both male and female, sleeping on couches of males and in beds of females, until he moved in with Ronnie from the Whiskey. That lasted till we were fired, and then he and Pam got a little place together in the Hollywood Hills.

Although Felix was now cut from this film noir flick of ours, the damage had already been done. The attitude had been implanted and it blended seamlessly with Jim's own psychological tendencies. And the combination was lethal. The wild child had his license. There was no reason to hold back. All his inner feelings were valid and there was no reason not to manifest them in reality. Be they joy *or* rage. And he knew he would be forgiven any excess. He was just too charming and too damned much fun to be with for us to ever hold a grudge against him for more than a couple of hours. And he knew it. He'd give you that sly grin of his, and you were hooked. You were his. A fool for his charm. And with your acquiescence came all the more reason for the next outrageous episode. And the drinking didn't exactly help the situation, either. Jim was definitely seeking the palace of wisdom through the road of excess. And he was enjoying every intoxicated moment. Of course, in the end it killed him. But for now, in Sunset Sound, with the Doors, making our first record . . . he was having the time of his life. He was ebullient and smiling and laughing and witty and singing his ass off. We were in a trance of creativity and joy. And then up popped the devil. Jimbo!

It was during the recording of "Light My Fire." We were rocking. We were on it and it was burning. It was definitely going to be the take, and it was the *first* take. John was whacking his skins with a fury. Robby was all cool and liquid and hip. I was pumping the Vox and the keyboard bass right in sync with their metaphysical metronomes. Jim was floating over the top of our rock-solid foundation like a butterfly with the singing sting of a bee. The first two stanzas were smack in the pocket. The steam was rising. And then we hit the solos. I started . . . and the magic was with us. The diamond within the magic circle was functioning sweetly and perfectly. The muse of music heard our call and joined us in the studio. She was sitting on the edge of my red and black and chromed Vox Continental and she was grinning. And she was a fox, too. Euterpe. A fifth-century B.C. fox. I was entranced, fingers flying, soloing madly. And then out from his vocal booth came Jim Morrison, maraca in hand, doing his American Indian shaman's dance. He must have seen the muse, too. She had him in a rapture. He started bopping and hopping around the main room, where Robby, John, and I were set up. Weaving in and out between the instruments, the amps, the baffles and us. Grinning like a fool, hopping on one foot and then the other; doing an ancient dance of the earth. Treading down on the earth and connecting himself with the living core of the planet. Connecting with the rhythm of the song and the rhythm of the earth. Making those two rhythms become one in his body as we were *all* doing at that instant in infinity. The four Doors had locked into the primordial energy of the globe. We were Native Americans and Jim was the shaman of the tribe, leading us, circling about us, encouraging us, pushing us on. And then he saw it!

A TV set. Plugged into the wall, the rabbit ears antenna up and splayed . . . and on! An image on the screen. In the recording studio, facing the control room. It was discreetly off to one corner. But it was on! And it was tuned to a baseball game! And it stopped Jim dead in his tracks. The modern world had imposed itself on his ancient ritual. Robby, John, and I were oblivious. We were in the solo section. It was our turn to shine. And we were smoking. I had finished my solo and Euterpe had floated over to Robby's guitar amp, seductively settled in, and lovingly placed her hand on Robby's crotch as he charged into his solo. Jim, however, was frozen. He stared at the TV set, incredulous. Why? his brain screamed. What is that thing doing here? Why is it on? We're making magic and a goddamned fucking TV set is tuned to a fucking *baseball* game? He was beginning to ignite. His anger was beginning to boil. Soon it would reach critical mass and then who knew *what* he might do.

Here's why the set was on. The L.A. Dodgers were in the thick of the pennant race. Bruce Botnick was a Dodgers fan. The legendary Sandy Koufax was pitching that day. Bruce was a huge Sandy Koufax fan . . . so he brought a portable TV to the studio to sneak an occasional glimpse at the game. In between takes, of course. It should have been in the control room with him and Paul, but the reception was bad in that electricity-filled control module . . . so it went in the corner of the studio, facing the huge glass control-room window, rabbit ears up, picture on, sound off. Bruce could see it from his command chair behind the recording console. He was a happy man. He was making a record *and* watching the Dodgers.

Jim, however, was not a happy man. His psychic space had been invaded by a foreign element. A demon had interrupted his shaman's dance, and he was pissed. He slowly bent down, picked up the TV, and stood to his full height, facing his reflection in the huge control-room window. Robby, John, and I became aware of the TV set at that moment. The music continued but our concentration had been broken. And then we became aware of what he was going to *do* with the TV set. For me, looking over my shoulder at him, it all took place in slow motion. He raised the set over his head, ballgame still flickering, paused for an instant, and with the look of a maniac, hurled the TV at the control-room window! Oh shit, I thought. That window is gonna explode like a bomb. And the set flew through the air, ever so slowly, waiting for the shattering impact. Botnick and Rothchild saw the missile coming and ducked under the console. The three of us stopped playing and tried to reach out to Jim to stop him, but it was too late. And then *impact!* The set hit the glass . . . and bounced off! The window didn't shatter. It was tempered glass. Instead, the TV shattered. It sparked as it hit the window and sparked again as it hit the floor, the screen cracked, a little puff of blue smoke came out, and the TV set died. It went black right there on the floor of Sunset Sound. Right in the middle of the solo section of "Light My Fire."

There was silence in the room. The muse quickly fled. The three of us stood up from our instruments and went to Jim's side. He was staring at the shattered, smoking TV set as if he couldn't believe what had happened. As if he were saying to himself, "Who broke this TV set? Surely, not me." The maniac was gone and he looked like a little boy again. And before anybody could speak, Rothchild burst into the room. "Jim!" he cried. "What the fuck are you doing? You could have killed us in there!" Botnick was right behind him. "My TV." Jim didn't raise his eyes from the shattered set.

"No television sets while we're making music," he softly said.

"But that was *my* television set," Bruce said.

Jim now looked up and met Bruce's gaze. "No TVs, you understand," he intently said.

And Bruce understood the look in Jim's eyes. He backed down and didn't say another word. Paul saw the look, too. He didn't like it. He looked at the four Doors and said, "Let's all go home. We're not going to be able to make any more music today. Jim, go relax. Unwind, will ya? Everybody be back here at two o'clock tomorrow. We'll pick up where we left off."

And with that he marched off. And we all slowly filed out of the studio as Bruce gently picked up his dead TV set.

～✻～

But, by God, the next day was business as usual. It was time to *get* it. And get it we did. The incident from the day before was completely forgotten, or at least not spoken of, and we launched into two rousing, spirited takes of "Light My Fire." The take we chose to put on the record had a marvelous solo by Robby. It's always been overlooked, but I think it's one of the best extended solos I've ever heard in a rock and roll song. He was flying and inspired. The muse had joined us again and we were *all* inspired. Jim was in and out of his vocal booth, doing his shaman's dance and shaking his maraca with manic glee. There was no TV set this day . . . nor would there ever again be a TV set or any other distractions in the studio when the Doors recorded. I mean, after all, this was serious business. John was a powerhouse behind his drums. An exploding metronome. My solo was dictated by the muse and just kept building and building in an ever-upward movement until it climaxed in a rhythmic three-against-four, with John and me in perfect sync in a percussive three-pulse against the basic four-pulse rhythm of the song. After Robby's solo we did the same thing, with Robby joining us for maximum band power, pounding and pounding it until we finally released it into the cartwheeling intro passage that brought the song back to the beginning A minor chord for the last two verses.

And then it was Jim's turn to take over . . . and he gave it his all. Especially the last verse and chorus. He was filled with the power of the song and just burned through that "funeral pyre" and his final "Fire!" was chilling. Delivered with all the strength and intensity he could call up from his hidden depths. It put the final exclamation mark on seven minutes of music that would—little did we know at the time—go down in history.

We went into the control room to listen to the two takes and it became a party. Pam was there with a couple of six-packs, Dorothy was there, Rothchild had a girl, Robby had brought a female friend, Jim had brought a half bottle of Jack Daniel's, and the control room was at full capacity and full volume. The speakers were blaring the playback at us, the alcohol was being consumed, a joint was being passed, and we were all *muy contento*. The Doors, in the studio, at last.

After choosing one of the takes and setting aside an appropriately long time for party, glee, and general ya-ha, it was time to get back to work. We were going to tackle the "Alabama Song" next, Dorothy's choice of thirties Berlin cabaret for the Doors. Paul had brought in a strange device called a Marxophone. It was a turn-of-the-century autoharp with little hammers attached to the base that allowed you to lay it flat and play it somewhat like a keyboard. It gave off a ringing, jingle-jangle sound, all tinny and old-timey. It was a great choice for the song. We recorded the basic track, Jim put on a perfunctory guide vocal—he would get the master vocal later—and after a few passes and sound adjustments we had it. I put on the Marxophone overdub and we were done for the evening. "Light My Fire" and the "Alabama Song," a good day's work.

Jim was in a great mood. Everything was going extremely well. We were in a unique, existential moment; the recording of our first album. A moment in time, an event in the life of a band that can happen only once. And this was *it*. And it was going great. So great in fact, that Jim thought to himself, I think I'll drop a little acid. He was riding the waves of "Light My Fire" and wanted to add more euphoria to his euphoria (his tragic flaw). So during my overdubs he popped a tab, of course without telling anybody. He just sat in the control room with Pam listening to the tinny sounds emanating from that weird, hot-rodded piece of Victoriana I was playing and placed a tab of acid on his tongue and washed it down with a gulp of beer. Folks, trouble was coming.

The LSD was slow to come on. Rothchild said, "What a great day. Let's all go home and do it again tomorrow." We began to straggle out of Sunset Sound, feeling very content with the world, the music, and ourselves. This existential moment was everything we had hoped it would be. The muse was with us and we were capturing the essence of our songs on tape, for all time, for all the people. The world could now hear Doors' music on record. It felt good to be alive.

Jim and Pam were the last to leave. Bruce turned everything off and the three of them headed for the parking lot. Jim said, "See ya, Bruce," tossed the keys to Pam—"Why don't you drive, Pam"—slipped into the shotgun seat, and the acid kicked in. Bam! Boiing! Ba-*room!*

They drove for a while. Jim wanted to be part of the "soft parade" on Sunset; the stream of cars and young people. Young people in their soft and luxurious raiment. He was in his element, the American West. He was young, gifted, and white . . . and he was blitzed out of his brain. Pam later said he was hanging out the window and singing at the top of his lungs. Singing "Light My Fire" for the multitude. She had to pull him back in lest he tumble out of the car and splatter himself on the street of dreams. And when she did, his mood changed. A premonition of danger came over him. A dark scud descended on his over-amped psyche.

"We've got to go back to the studio," he said.

"Why, Jim?"

"Something's wrong, I can feel it. Turn around!"

"Jiiimmm," whined Pam. "Let's just go home."

"This is serious, Pam. Just make a U-turn, right here. Now!"

"In the middle of Sunset?"

"Now! Do it!"

And he jammed his foot onto the accelerator on top of hers. The car leapt forward. Pam started spinning the wheel hard left to avoid hitting the car in front of her and they fishtailed into the opposite lanes, miraculously missing everything à la Neil Cassady, and sped off back to Sunset Sound, Jim's foot still mashing Pam's into the metal pedal.

"Jiimm . . . why are we doing this? Do you want to get us killed?"

"Do you want us to lose our tapes?" he shouted.

"Why would you lose your tapes?"

"Because there's a fucking fire in the studio!" He was raving. "Now drive, will ya? Go!"

Pam had no choice but to believe him. He was *that* intense. She barreled down Sunset and screeched into the parking lot, and Jim was out of the car in a flash. But the gate was locked! He climbed the fence — "scaled the wall" — and leapt over the security chain-link. He raced to the back door and it was open! He was in and running down the hall. He threw open the door to the studio and sure enough . . . he was right. Red. Everything was red! His mind was racing. Holy shit! What do I do? Nobody's here. They don't even know about the fire. It's all up to me.

And then he saw it. A fire hose in the corner. An old-fashioned hose and nozzle with a red valve crank on the side. Must have been left over from the forties or something, but it looked efficient. Jim ran to it, pulled the hose free, and cracked the valve, and the fire snake sprang to life. Water spewed onto the red. That burning, devouring red that was going to eat up our tapes and destroy the wonderful music we had just made. All of our work would be consumed by that terrible red. All of our efforts would be for naught because of that vicious, terrible, evil red. But Jim was there to save the day! He would save our music and our instruments. He would save John's drums and Robby's Twin Reverb and my Vox Continental and the multitrack tapes and . . . well, everything. And so he sprayed the red. Aiming the hose this way and that, covering the room with liquid. But the damned red wouldn't go away. It just kept glowing and throbbing and pulsating. That red. That evil, devouring red wouldn't succumb to the water. Why? What kind of fucking fire was this? What kind of hellfire of sulfuric damnation wouldn't be extinguished by the semen-squirting, phallic monster Jim held in his hands? What the fuck was this RED?!

Well, my friends, it was the work light. In the center of the room, on a stand, with a little screen cage around the bulb was a red work light. The kind they had in the movie studios back in the forties. A red work light. No fire, no flames, no danger to the tapes, no nothing. Nothing but red from the red work light. Jim's psychedelic eyes had, of course, seen a whole conflagration. We had both read James Baldwin's *The Fire Next Time* and *this* was the next time! But, by God, Ensign Morrison was there to save the U.S.S. *Bonhomme Richard* in a most prescient and heroic manner. Out, damned red! The waters of the unconscious would obliterate all evil.

And then *he* realized what the red was. Holy shit! Turn the hose off, quick! Everything's okay. Mission accomplished. Now get the fuck out. Fast!

He cranked the valve shut, dropped the hose on the soggy floor, and hauled ass. Through the door, down the hallway, out the exit door, and over the chain-link fence. Huffing and puffing, he ran to the car and jumped in.

"Let's get the fuck out of here!"

"Was it a fire, Jim? Did you put out the fire?"

"Yeah, I put it out. Now go!"

"But, Jim, your boot . . ."

"What?"

"It's stuck in the fence."

Pam pointed to the chain-link fence. And there it was. His left boot. On the other side. Its toe wedged between the links. Impossible to get out from the parking lot side. Jim would have to climb the fence, extract the boot, put it on, climb the fence again, and then beat his retreat. He only considered that possibility for an instant.

"Fuck the boot, let's go."

The next day, Paul received a call from one Tutti Cammarata, owner of Sunset Sound, and was asked to come to the studio to survey some water damage . . . and to see whether or not he could identify a boot that was found at the scene of the crime. A boot that was wedged, absurdly, in the chain-link fence at the rear of the property. Paul did, Paul could, Paul called Elektra, and Jac Holzman said he would pay for the damages. They were actually slight, Jim kept his hose hysteria in the studio with our equipment—he never got into the control room—and Paul called each of us to cancel the session for that day. He told us the story of the water and the boot. But he never told Jim that he knew what had happened. And the next day it was business as usual. We finished recording the album in four more days and left Sunset Sound . . . still intact and still standing.

We asked Paul where he wanted to mix the record.

"You guys are booked into Ondine for the whole month of November, aren't you?" he asked.

We nodded. Billie Winters, one of Jim's occasional amours, had booked us, two weeks earlier, into the most prestigious and hippest discotheque on the planet. She was friends with the owner, Brad Pierce, and he was buddies with Ondine's number-one denizen . . . Andy Warhol.

"Well, that's where we're going to mix," Paul enthused. "New York!"

n.y.c. — the heart of the beast

Honey, get packed. We're going to the capital of the world," I said to Dorothy when I heard the news about Ondine.

"Where's that?"

"Baby, we're going to New York!"

Dorothy squealed and wrapped her arms around my neck. "New York City?"

"Yep. Billie Winters got us a gig at some hip new club. They say it's Andy Warhol's favorite hang."

"For how long?"

"The whole month of November."

Dorothy squealed again and kissed me hard on the lips.

"I love you," she said.

I wrapped my arms around her lithe body. "I love you, too," I said as we smothered each other with kisses.

"I knew this was going to work," she softly said as my tongue darted in and out of her mouth.

I stopped for a moment. "You mean us, or the band?"

She smiled. "You big jerk, I mean the whole thing!" And she buried herself into me.

And we made love. There in that wonderful glass-enclosed beach house. In our little bedroom, on the mattress on the floor, looking out on the ocean and up into the clear blueness of the sky canopy. We dissolved into each other. And it was long and sweet and good. But it was one of the last times we would make love there.

We gave up the beach house—it had done its work, our apprentice days were over, "Light My Fire" existed, our first album was in the can, and we were going to New York. We put our books and our few summer clothes into storage. Jim simply packed a bag and left Pam to attend to their apartment on Norton Avenue. Robby and John, who were still living at home, simply bade adieu to Mom and Dad. And on the morning of October 31, 1966—All Hallow's Eve—we all boarded a plane at LAX for the big show. We were going into the heart of the beast. To the Big Apple. And we were going to teach those sophisticated, jaded, intellectual, decadent New Yorkers what psychedelic was all about! They had seen everything . . . but they had never seen the Doors. And we were ready!

Or so we thought.

We fell into the phantasmagoria of New York City on the very first night. We checked in at the Henry Hudson Hotel on West 57th Street—our attorney, Max Fink, had arranged for and prepaid our rooms—and immediately headed for the club on East 59th. We walked all the way down 57th and Dorothy and I thought we were in heaven. People, energy, life, sophistication, luxury, elegance, knowledge, worldliness . . . everything a budding aesthete could ask for. This was the big city! We were not in cowboy L.A. anymore. We were in the center of the world, the true *axis mundi.*

And we entered Ondine. Or rather, should I say, we fell into Babylon. There should have been a sign above the door, All Things Are Permitted Here. Or perhaps, Enter, and Be Free. Or All Flesh Is Good. It was Halloween night and the denizens had disguised themselves. Everyone was in costume. Devils and witches, angels and sailors, Playboy bunnies and crones, ghouls, fiends, reprobates, dandies, and beauties.

All strange order of monsters
Hot on the trail of the woodvine
We welcome you to our procession

What a show. What a spectacle. A small, nautical-decor boîte stuffed with fantasy. Engorged with role playing and psychological gamesmanship. Jim was home. You could feel it in the atmosphere. You could feel it in *him*. These people, this city, would allow him to adopt any persona of his choosing. Any mask, any role, any game. It was all permitted. It was all *encouraged*. And it was just what he wanted. Here, finally, was the opportunity for a serious debauch. This was mind games. This was domination. This was sexual power and it began with a cafe au lait Playboy bunny undulating up to Jim and asking him, "Are you guys the band from California that's supposed to start tomorrow?"

Jim looked her up and down, his eyes finally settling on her fine and bulging breasts. "Yeah," he said. "How'd you know?"

She giggled, "You don't look like you're from New York."

"Well . . . you don't look like you're from the Playboy mansion, either," the retort meister said.

"This is an authentic bunny costume," she pouted. "I got it from my girlfriend. She *works* as a bunny."

Jim shifted his gaze from her breasts to her ass. "I'm not saying it's not the real thing. You're just a little out of alignment."

And he put his hands on her divine rear and proceeded to slightly adjust her little white puff of perky tail fur. She squealed with delight.

"There," he said. "That's better. You were starting to list to one side."

"You're outrageous," she cooed. "What's your name?"

He took her arm and began to lead her off to the bar. "James," he said. "James Phoenix."

He'd always wanted to use that name. He felt Morrison was just too mundane. No mystery. He actually wanted to change his name for the album. I said no way. I wasn't going to let him change that all-American Jim Morrison. That was the name of the heir apparent. The prince. The king-to-be. James Phoenix was the name of a rascal outlaw. That name could never become president of the United States. And that's where this was all headed.

Dorothy and I just shook our heads as "James Phoenix" walked off into the Fellini side show, an African-American Playboy bunny on his arm. Robby and John were simply stunned by the whole thing. Their mouths were at half mast. But they did see the chicks, and the women were fine.

One of them came up to us. A chick in a sequined evening gown. A very beautiful young woman, but with small breasts and not exactly the right hourglass figure. She looked at us and laughed.

"What did you guys come as . . . bumpkins?"

And she sidled off. Still laughing. And from the rear the truth presented itself. She was a man. No hiding those angular hips in that sequined skin.

Dorothy said, "That she's a he."

"Fuckin' faggot," snarled Densmore.

"These people are amazing," said Robby. "I've never seen anything like this."

"And we're going to play here for the next month!" I burbled ecstatically.

The four of us just looked at one another and grinned. We were *all* home. And "Knock on Wood" came on the sound system and the club erupted. Everybody started dancing to Ondine's "song of the month." What a show. What a spectacle. We had entered the gates of Babylon. Strange days had found us!

The next night it was our turn. We were going to burn them down. We knew the people of New York were still into R&B. It was a soul and funk town and it had the best dancers on the planet. The regulars at Ondine were the snakiest, hippest undulators on a dance floor I had ever seen. But they didn't know trance dancing. They didn't know psychedelic. And completely unawares, they were about to get an *overdose* of psychedelic music from our four tripped-out acidheads from the benign, soma shores of Venice Beach, California. Our Jungian rockers in that strictly Freudian town. Our transcendental meditators in the temple of Mammon. The Doors.

We mounted up at about nine-thirty P.M. on that Night of All Souls after the Witches' Sabbath. I lit a couple of sticks of incense that I had wedged into the Vox between the chrome Z legs and the English red body. The sweet smoke immediately began to change

the atmosphere. A tranquillity descended. An expectancy, an anticipation of the unknown. But without *fear* of the unknown. More the
imminence of the joy of discovery. An adventure was about to begin
and we all knew it.

And we launched into "Backdoor Man." The music pumped
snakes out into the club. The rhythm was solid and grounded. Jim
let out a few guttural, primal grunts that hit the collective audience's
lower three chakras and the dance floor filled immediately. He had
them. The New York maenads were his. Dionysus had entered
Babylon, and his new followers were released from their chains. The
New Age could begin. And then he began to sing . . .

> *I am a backdoor man,*
> *Yeah, baby, I'm a backdoor man,*
> *Well, the men don't know*
> *But the little girls understand.*
> *— Willie Dixon*

And the satyr cackled. That damned little satyr had followed
Dionysus all the way across the country and stood off in the corner
watching the East Coast maenads—the daughters of Undine the
water nymph—undulate. And he was drooling and cackling and
hopping on those silly little hooves of his and he was in love. New
York girls, rock and roll music, the hippest nightclub in the city . . .
what more could a libertine reprobate ask for? The party had begun
and he was there!

The party lasted for thirty days and thirty nights. The nights
belonged to Dionysus but the days belonged to Apollo. Dorothy and
I explored that city from the Battery to the Museum of Natural History—the great and dark and lodgelike American Indian hall, where
Joseph Campbell had his first epiphany. We walked for blocks and
blocks in a state of amazement and euphoria. Everything was there.
All the art one could possibly digest. Galleries, theater, dance, music,
the cinema, museums. All the best. And . . . shopping! Shopping to
drive a woman mad. The fall fashions by the world's great designers
were there for the purchase. It only took money, and lots of it.
Dorothy the fashion maven was in designer heaven. But unfortunately she could only look. There was barely enough money for
breakfast and lunch. Dinner was free for employees at Ondine; Lon-

don broil, french fries, and string beans every night . . . but it was damned good London broil, succulent and tender, and the fries were crisp, and the string beans were nicely buttered.

When we weren't getting our fill of cultural, Western civilization sophistication, we were mixing the album with Paul Rothchild at a small studio Elektra Records had set up in their office. And it was sounding like a mother. Paul was doing a brilliant job. His ears were as golden as Botnick's and he had entered the space of serendipity where he could do no wrong. He had received the "great visitation of energy" and he was twirling pots and goosing faders like a man possessed. The sound he was coaxing out of the speakers was dark and mysterious. Definitely psychedelic but with the California air of freedom. The sun was always shining. The light was always illuminating the dark and shadowy corners. There was mystery but there was nothing to fear. Dionysus and Apollo had come together. They had fused themselves into Doors music. And we were ecstatic. Rothchild's mix was more than we could have imagined. It was going to be a hit. I knew it. I could feel it in the ether. My receptors had been plucked by the muse of music. We were on our way and there would be no turning back. And the fates said, "You wanted success, Ray? Well, here it comes. Here are your desires, fulfilled. But are you prepared to live with the consequences?"

And lying in wait for Jim Morrison, waiting to begin the mad, downward spiral of consequences, was none other than the fantasist of the Factory himself . . . Andy Warhol.

It was love at first sight on Andy's part. He knew the real goods when he saw it. And he saw it in Jim. To Jim, Andy was merely the entrée into decadence. The benign De Sade. The giggling Caligula of the Lower East Side. He held the keys to that gathering of quasi-artistic but beautiful young people known as the Factory—Andy's great loft of silver foil, silk screens, and anything goes. Jim was down there within the first week of our opening at Ondine. He loved it. He loved the games, the role playing, the attitude. The challenges to go further, to go beyond the self-imposed, societally sanctioned bounds of psychic control. To go beyond the pale. And Jim—like Kurtz (Brando again) in Coppola's *Apocalypse Now*—was born to go beyond the pale.

And so was Nico, the Valkyrian angel of death. Nico was the singer in a Warhol show called Exploding Plastic Inevitable with the Velvet Underground as the band. She met Jim and went gaga. And she would push his buttons at every opportunity, in a deep and Germanic-accented voice. . . .

"*I'm* going to take another von. Vhat's the matter, Jeem, are you afraid?" the Valkyrie would say to the California Dionysus, who would always respond to the challenge.

"Afraid? Shit, I'll take two!"

"Jeem, you are crazy. That's why I loff you."

And they would retire to a silver-foiled room for more. More of everything. More drink, more pills, more sex—evidently, she gave great head, understanding the proper use of the tongue on the underside of the penis, especially that supersensitive area at the base of the head where that small crease attaches to the shaft, that crease that when lightly licked and flicked with a moist, soft tongue produces shudders of ecstasy in the male of the species. And she wasn't ashamed to do it. To bring her man to climax and not remove his penis from her mouth. To hold it close and take it in even deeper at his moment of consummation. To not deny him the warmth and moisture of her mouth as he ejaculated. To swallow his semen and wait for his member to soften and recede back into itself. Only then would she take her lips away, look up at Jim, and smile. . . .

"Did that please you, Jeem?"

Jim could only nod in pleasure, being speechless at the intensity of his ejaculation. The pills and booze were melting together in his brain, obliterating his will to power and replacing it with a will to pleasure. Andy's world was a pill-head scene. Amphetamine uppers and barbiturate downers. They were plentiful and constantly proffered. And they were loved by Andy's minions. There was pot, of course. There was pot everywhere in those days. But this was an alcohol-and-pill scene. And that was not a combination that opened the doors of perception. The holographic universe did not exist on pills and booze. It was strictly body pleasure. Now, God knows, I love my body pleasure, too, but this was too much. The denizens of this pleasure dome had gone too far. They were intoxicants without enlightenment. Inebriates without vision, much as today's crack-meth-bonehead, speed freaks and narcoleptic heroin hounds are dope addicts without a clue.

At the Factory it was all pleasure without consequences. An ultimately enervating pleasure that could only weaken and debilitate. This was not a Nietzschean romp in joy and light and passion. The Factory did not leave its partygoers strong and clean and infused with enthusiasm for life; for the beauty and passion of nature. For the divine warmth and radiance of the sun. There was no desire on the part of the denizens to begin the world again, to create the new Garden of Eden, to transcend ordinary reality, to enter the New Age. The debauchery itself was enough. It was not liberating, as such intoxication should be. It didn't open the doors of perception. It did not break through the walls of the Judeo-Christian-Muslim myth into freedom. It did not charge the psyche with energy. It was merely an end in itself. The pleasure was the end and no other action was needed. No other action was necessary, or even desirable. It was the realm of the cynic, the ironist. A realm of sophistication, of knowledge, of worldliness . . . but without the sun. It was perpetual pleasure and perpetual darkness.

The door to the foil room opened and Andy's head peeked in.

"Oh, you're finished," Andy lisped. "I was hoping I could watch."

"Andy, you always vant to vatch," Nico boomed at him.

"Too late, blondie," Jim laughed. "You'll have to wait till next time. And even then I don't think I'll let you watch."

"Oh, please, Jim. I won't be in the way," Andy begged.

"Well . . . I don't know. You'd have to sit in the corner."

"I will."

"And you'd have to not say a word."

Andy's eyes were beginning to brighten. Maybe he was actually going to be allowed to watch.

"I'll be real quiet, Jim. I won't even breathe."

Jim laughed. "Breathing is okay, Andy. I don't want you to suffocate yourself. But you'd have to beg."

"I can beg, Jim. I will . . . if that's what you want."

"On your knees?"

"Of course, if that's what you want."

"That's what I want, Andy. And I want you to practice."

Andy grinned. "I know how to beg on my knees, Jim. I'm a Catholic."

Jim laughed. "So was Ray. You'll have to meet him."

"I'd like to."

Nico spoke. "The blond von? Vith the glasses?"

Jim nodded. "Yeah. The organ player."

"I vould play *his* organ."

Jim patted his Valkyrie. "His girl is here, Nico. He's practically married."

"So vhat?" the blond beastie said.

"Are you coming back tomorrow, Jim?" Andy drooled.

Jim's demeanor changed. He looked at Andy, hard and mean. The game belonged to him now. He rose above the miasma of the pills and the booze and snarled, "Get on your knees, Andy."

"What?"

"You heard me. Now!" Jim barked.

Andy dropped to the floor like a shot. He became the Catholic supplicant.

"Now beg," Jim demanded.

"Now?" Andy queried.

"Fuckin' beg, Andy!"

"Oh, please, Jim, let me watch. I'll be good. I'll be quiet. I'll do anything you say."

Jim laughed. "Hey, you're good at this, Andy."

Andy smiled. "I'll do anything, Jim."

"Do more," Jim snarled.

"Please, Jim," Andy whined. "Let me watch, please."

Jim stood, zipped up his pants, kissed Nico on the cheek, and walked to the silver foil door.

"Please, Jim . . ."

Jim glanced down at the kneeling Andy, whose eyes were cast up to heaven, looking entreatingly into Jim's.

Jim smiled back at Andy. Slyly, a sadistic glint flashing behind his eyes. "Fuck no, Andy." And he was gone.

Anyway, that's the way he told it to me.

※

We finished mixing the album, finished the gig at Ondine, Jim finished his debauch at the Factory, and *we* were gone. Back to the golden coast. Back to the light-infused soma land that we all loved. It felt good to enter the warmth again. The air of California enfolds you, rather than slaps you in the face like New York air. But, man, we had a good time. Everybody grew up. We even realized our pant legs were cut too high. Brad Pierce, owner of Ondine, once asked us, "Are you guys worried about a flood in here?" What the fuck was that supposed to mean? "Of course not," we said. He laughed. "Then why are your cuffs cut so high up?" And they were. About two inches above our ankles. Bumpkin style. "I've got to teach you guys how to dress," he said. "We're going down to Le Dernier Cri and get you cowpokes some threads."

We bought four suits at the hippest men's boutique in the Village. God, we looked good. Mod style, cool cut, long pants, a break in the cuff. Four very cool Miles Davis guys. I loved it. I still dress that way. Issey Miyake and Rei Kawakubo. Jim burned a hole in his jacket with a cigarette and threw the whole damned suit away within a week. John and Robby were simply too embarrassed to dress up. They were California guys and could only be comfortable in casual clothes. They rarely wore their duds. Brad Pierce never got through to them. Nor did the world of fashion. Jim, of course, didn't need a boutique of French fashion, he was going hell-bent for leather. And it worked. Man, did it work!

Now, some people say Jim saw Gerard Malanga in a pair of leather pants at Andy's Factory. Others say Gerard Malanga copied Jim Morrison's entire persona, *including* the leather pants. Who knows? I personally never saw or met Gerard M. I was never even *in* the Factory. But in Oliver Stone's movie *The Doors*, Oliver most erroneously has all four Doors at Andy's loft. He wrongly portrays Jim as asking us to stay with him because he fears something untoward is going to happen to him. Jim's afraid it's going to be a life-altering night. And he wants our support. But Oliver has us abandon Jim. Oliver "Bonehead" Stone has us turn away as Jim is entreating us to stay with him. To help him. Jesus Christ, Oliver, do you think I'd leave Jim if he asked me to stay with him? Do you think I'd abandon my friend in a time of need? Do you think I'd walk away from a friend who was entreating me for help? But you would, wouldn't you, Oliver? You'd walk away from anybody. Your pleasure and power above all things . . . right, dude? So get your facts straight, Mr. Two Face. Grow up and see it like it really is, you fascist. Anything for a plot point, ehh, Oliver?

There, I feel better now. I had something stuck in my spleen.

the *doors* hits the street

In January 1967 the album was released to the public. It took its time building momentum. The first single, "Break on Through," was getting some airplay in L.A. Probably because we were constantly on the phones calling the AM and FM rock stations to request that "boss tune from the Doors, 'Break on Through.'" At the behest of the record company, we acted like teenagers, requesting our latest "fave rave," disguising our voices, acting silly, and calling over and over from Elektra's office. Billy James watched us with a shit-eating grin. It was his idea and he liked it. We had all our friends and Jim's groupies calling, too. And it worked, sort of. "Break on Through" made it to number twenty-five on the top local AM station, KRLA. One had to have AM play in those days. AM ruled the airwaves. FM was hip, eclectic, and underground . . . and in three years *it* would rule. But funny, I never heard the goddamned thing on the radio. I was always listening to the right stations at the wrong time. Or is that the wrong station at the wrong time? Damn it, you want to hear your song on the radio and I was always missing it. And the only song the radio would *play* was your single. Nobody played album cuts. It simply wasn't done. FM played deliciously off-the-wall singles but they didn't play album cuts. They weren't allowed to. It was singles only. Consequently, the only Doors song I could hope to hear on the radio was "Break on Through" until Elektra released a new single. And *that* was going to be . . . "Light My Fire."

Here's how it happened. Elektra was getting requests from all over the country for "Light My Fire." Radio was calling, saying, "Give us the single!" At home, a local D.J. friend of ours—Dave Diamond—told us in the last week of January (he knew before anybody), " 'Light My Fire' is your hit, guys. Get it out." The only problem was that it was six minutes and fifty seconds long. Singles had to be three minutes. Code, gospel, written in stone . . . three minutes. Never, anathema, blasphemy, never almost seven minutes. Not from a new group, anyway. "Who do you guys think you are, *Bob Dylan?*" He had "Like a Rolling Stone." It was long. FM played it. "But you guys aren't Bob Dylan. He's famous, and you're not. And we demand three minutes."

Shit. Everyone wanted "Light My Fire" and it was too long. And "Break on Through" had run its course . . . it never broke through. It made it to 106 on the *Billboard* National Hot 100—101 to 110 was called bubbling under. We made it to only a low simmer on the Hot 100. We needed a hit. We needed some chart action. We needed national airplay. We needed "Light My Fire."

Sure, we were developing a following. We were getting gigs, lots of gigs. Up and down the state and in L.A. We had money to pay the rent. Dorothy and I had moved into an apartment on Sycamore in Hollywood, around the corner from Grauman's Chinese Theater. A nice, cozy little apartment in the middle of the Hollywood freak show. For an evening's entertainment we would walk down Hollywood Boulevard to Vine Street and come back up to Sycamore on the other side of the street. What a show! Especially with a touch of cannabis intoxication. Hippies, gypsies, weirdoes, freaks, tourists, and prostitutes prowled the Boulevard. It was a most eclectic promenade. We passed metaphysical bookstores, strip joints, Musso and Frank's restaurant (since 1914), movie palaces—the Egyptian and the Pantages—Frederick's of Hollywood's crotchless panties store, taco stands, a "British Invasion" imported record store, the Hollywood Wax Museum of stars and horror, Pickwick's huge and great bookstore, Greek gyros and hummus stands, Indian food, pizza parlors, hamburger joints, the Church of Scientology building with free tests on their tin can *engram meter*—"just walk in, folks"—DeVoss clothing store for mod threads, boot shops with the latest winkle pickers, and cool chicks' shops with English fashions and go-go shimmy fringe dresses (not unlike the outfits from the Roaring Twenties). It was a circus. It was almost New York. We loved it.

But the Doors still needed a hit single. And one day in April, Paul Rothchild called all of us and said, "Guys, I'm going to do an edit." He was going to cut and paste—before computers and the digital realm this was an incredibly difficult and laborious task; it was like surgery, an actual cutting of the tape and splicing of the desired sections back together again. But the hardest part was making the decision of *where* to cut, what to save, and what to toss away. Fortunately, we had a brilliant producer in Paul and had confidence in his instincts. They wouldn't fail him . . . or so we hoped. After all, he was going to attempt a quadruple-bypass open-heart surgery on "Light My Fire." He was going to cut and slash almost seven minutes of music down to three. I envisioned hundreds of cuts to do a *Reader's Digest* condensation. Little slits. A measure or two here, a phrase there. Bits and pieces being excised to maintain the integrity of the composition and yet achieve the necessary radio running length. Frankly, I didn't see how it could be done. I could imagine Paul Rothchild and Bruce Botnick laboring over the cutting block for a month.

Two days later Paul called us and said he had it! "What?!" was our response. "How does it sound?"

"I'm not going to say a word," Paul said. "Come down this afternoon and we'll play it for you. I want *you* guys to be the judge."

And at two o'clock we all arrived at Sunset Sound ready to attend the results of the surgery.

"How did you make all those edits in just a couple of days?" I asked Paul.

He grinned. "I'm not saying anything until you hear it. You don't expect me to give away my hard-earned professional secrets, do you, Ray?"

He was a sly devil. Always was.

"Now I want all of you to sit down and pretend you're listening to the radio," Paul said. He loved creating a mind scene, a psychic scenario for us to enter into, and he was good at it. It usually worked. "You've never heard a song called "Light My Fire." You're just digging the radio and the groovy tunes that keep coming. You don't know anything about the Doors, never heard of them. You're seventeen and you're in Cleveland."

"Oh, no, not Cleveland," Jim joked. We all laughed. "Sentence me to Devil's Island for twenty years but don't tell me I'm living in Cleveland . . . please."

"Sorry, Jim. Cleveland it is," said Paul. "*And* you're seventeen. You don't know shit from Shinola. You've got no brains and a perpetual hard-on . . . *and*, and this is the important part, you buy singles."

"Duhh . . . okay . . . play the song." Jim went teenage.

"All right," Paul continued. "So the radio says to you in your permanent state of sexual fantasy, 'Here's a new song by a new group called the Doors. They call it "Light My Fire." ' "

And he pointed at Bruce, who hit the play button on the two-track. And out it came on those great Sunset Sound speakers. Big and full and fat and very crisp on the top end. Man, hearing your own music in a studio playback setting . . . it is sweet. So the organ intro hits and then Jim starts to sing and the entire first verse and chorus go by and there are no cuts! Into the second verse and still no cuts. What's going on here? I thought. Where are the edits? The second chorus, no cuts. Now the beginning of the solos. We vamp a bit and just before I begin my solo—BAM!—we're at the end of the solos and the cartwheel organ intro repeats itself and Jim begins to sing the third verse. The solos were gone! The best part of the song—the true raison d'être of the piece—was gone! No Ray, no Robby. No mystical trance-inducing, Coltranesque soloing. No Bach-like interweaving of guitar and organ. No sexual simulation building to an aural orgasm. No fuck, no solo. Shit!

And the rest of the song played itself out as we recorded it. The fourth verse and chorus came on the speakers and Jim was singing for all he was worth. We were playing like men possessed and it was great. A great song and a fiery performance. Robby Krieger's first composition was brilliant . . . but Paul had cut the guts out of it. I thought there was going to be delicate surgery but instead there was disembowelment with a dull blade.

Robby was the first to speak. "I hate it," he said.

"I hate it, too," I joined. "You've cut the solos. That's the whole point of the song."

John said, "It's not that bad. I can live with it."

Jim was mute, in shock, I suppose. Paul began his rationale.

"You never hear solos on AM radio. Only short ones, no more than eight bars. Listen to any Beatles tune, short and cute solos."

John interrupted. "George Harrison doesn't even play them. Eric Clapton does."

Jim looked at John. "How do you know that? The Beatles invite you to one of their sessions or something?"

"I read it in an English music magazine," John said. "Why would they lie?"

Jim could only snort, "You ought to try reading a book instead."

Paul continued, "Just think of it as a song. It's a great song with a quick little break in the middle."

"Like a Beatles song," said Robby, now beginning to warm to the idea.

"Exactly," said Paul. "A hit single. A good melody, you can dance to it, regular verse-chorus, verse-chorus structure, a little instrumental break in the middle, and then repeat verse-chorus one and two. Man, I'm telling you, they'll play it on the radio."

I was even beginning to see the logic of the edit.

"If I didn't know the solos were there, I'd think it was just a groovy new tune," I said. "Especially the part about 'Our love becomes a funeral pyre.' Being seventeen in Cleveland, I'd love that part. Ohh . . . spooky!"

Jim jumped in. "And if I dug the single on the radio and went out and bought the album and played 'Light My Fire' . . . I'd get a whole new trip! A real bonus. *Solos*, in the middle of the song where there weren't any solos before! It would be like magic."

"Exactly," exclaimed Rothchild.

"There'd be the short version on the radio . . . and the *long* version on the LP," said Robby, almost convinced. "But I still hate it," he laughed.

"Of course you hate it," Paul said. "I cut your solo. But does it sound like a hit single?"

Robby grinned. "Man, it sounded like a hit single the day I wrote it."

That was the arrogance of the Doors in action. And Robby, for all his shyness and quietude and seeming humility, was really an arrogant and opinionated S.O.B. He still is, God bless him.

"Sounds like a radio song to me," John said.

"It's gonna be a *famous* radio song," Jim said. "I predict a monster hit."

"Whoa, man, how big?" I asked.

"I'm not saying for sure, Ray. But I think . . ." And then he felt the air in a mock mystic manner as if he were the Great Kreskin. He was goofing in the ether. Then his eyes lit up. "Maybe . . . number one!"

We all whooped. "The Amazing Kreskin has spoken," I said, doing my best Ed McMahon imitation. "It will be number one!" Rothchild was ecstatic. His brutal butcher cut had worked. We were all yelping and hollering.

"Play it again, Bruce," Robby said.

"One more time," said John, imitating Count Basie on "April in Paris."

And on it came, on those magnificent speakers, in that cocoon of a studio. The butterfly was born . . . and it was rocking. The edit came up and Robby and I were hit in the gut by a low blow, but we smiled through it. The damned slashing was going to get us some radio airplay. Paul had done it.

"When does it go to number one?" John yelled at Jim.

"It had better be by the summer, John . . . or we're fucked," Jim said.

"We're not gonna be fucked, we're the Doors!" Robby shouted over the pumping music.

"Fuckin' A! Robby's right," I said. "Light My Fire" hit the last chorus and Jim was blaring at us over the speakers. "We're going all the way. I knew it from the beginning." I hit Jim lovingly on the arm. "I knew it when you first sang me those songs on the beach, man."

Jim grinned. "Well, here we go, Ray. I hope you're ready for all the way."

"I am . . . are you?" I hollered.

"Fuckin' A!" he shouted. And we all laughed as the organ intro did its loop-de-loop at the end of Robby's song and John put his signature button on the tail of "Light My Fire."

Jim turned to Dorothy. "What do *you* think, Ms. Fujikawa?"

"I don't like losing the solos" — Dorothy paused for emphasis — "but it sure sounds like a famous radio song to me." She grinned.

"All right, Dorothy!" Jim shouted. And it was done. Unanimous agreement. Paul and Bruce were glowing.

※

I finally heard a Doors' song on the radio. Dorothy and I were headed out to the beach, driving on Sunset in the VW. We had hit the curves of Westwood — all early-May green and tree lush on a glorious warm spring day. And we were headed west, to the beach, to soak up some Aten rays in Santa Monica. And on it came! "Light My Fire." Rocking out of the little German radio! We started screaming. Full-throated screams. I banged on the steering wheel. Dorothy was bouncing up and down in her seat like a pogo stick. More screaming.

"It's us! It's us!" I yelled.

"It's 'Light My Fire'!" she shrieked.

"We're on the fucking radio!"

"I love it!" she said, and grabbed me around the neck and kissed my cheek for all she was worth.

I cranked the radio and went careening around those Sunset Boulevard curves with a cute Japanese chick hanging on my neck and my band's rock and roll song blaring at me in the lush sunshine of Southern California. My friends, it doesn't get much better than that!

And in the third week of July 1967, "Light My Fire" became the number-one song in America. That psychedelic band of acid-head, Jungian, shamanistic, Dionysian, Indian meditators had made it to the top of the *Billboard* Hot 100. We had even knocked the Beatles out of first place. Rock jock DJs all across America were playing the single in heavy rotation. A day didn't go by when "Light My Fire" wasn't heard at least four times a day on *some* radio station in America. And that little 45 RPM disc was flying out of the retail record shops. To get to be number one you simply had to sell more records than anyone else. And we did! That week and for the next few weeks to come we sold more records than any other artists. Including the Beatles and the Rolling Stones. We were ecstatic. And Jac Holzman and Elektra Records went completely ballistic. They even had to contract new pressing plants to meet the demand. They had a plant on the East Coast and one on the West Coast . . . but the heartland had responded big-time. Jac had to employ a plant in Michigan and one in Nashville to supply vinyl to all the chains in the Midwest and the South. Elektra was simply overwhelmed. They had never had a number-one record before. We were all virgins who had spilled a bit of precious red blood in a wonderful coupling on our nuptial couch at the top of the charts.

Lying on stained, wretched sheets
With a bleeding virgin,
We could plan a murder
Or start a religion.

san francisco

The floodgates were open. The Doors were hot and offers for gigs were many. Nineteen sixty-seven was a great performing year for us. We played San Francisco for the first time. Talk about psychedelic — that whole city seemed to be on acid. Our first weekend up there coincided with the legendary Human Be-In. The first love-in. The first great gathering of the tribe. Fifty thousand heads in Golden Gate Park. More long hair and love than had ever been brought together before. Of course the Doors were there. We *had* to be there. We were in the swirl of it and, man, it felt good. Hippies everywhere. No aggression in the air, no power trips, no mind games. Just, dare I use the now-archaic word, *love!* Just fucking L-O-V-E. It could be done back then. Today it would be considered naive and corny, old-fashioned and a bit imma-ture. But of course, it's the one thing we're all looking for, the one thing we all so desperately desire. And the irony of it is — in this era of irony—we can't find it! We're going mad because we can't find love. We're over-amped and hyperagitated because we can't find love. What an age of anxiety we live in. If only we could relax. Huh?

Music was being pumped out over the audience from a temporary stage through the Grateful Dead's huge P.A. system, and people were whirling and twirling and swaying and sashaying everywhere. Indian clothes, tie-dyed jeans, beads and jewels, long flowing hair, head bands, soft suede moccasins, bare-breasted women. A fantasia of colors and forms and bodies and music. Music from the Jefferson Airplane, Country Joe and the Fish, the Grateful Dead, Quicksilver Messenger Service. Poems and prosody from Allen Ginsberg, Gary Snyder, Michael McClure, and Timothy Leary. What a spectacle! We had never seen anything like it. Jim, Robby, John, and I all believed that it was the beginning of a spiritual revolution. A revolution of consciousness. The true revolution of Jesus Christ . . . a revolution of love. For that one afternoon, in that park, in San Francisco, a gathering of lovers had taken place. And it is one of the sweetest memories of my life. Kundalini had broken free of the chains of the lower three chakras and worked its way up to the collective heart of the assembled multitude. Consequently there was a great outpouring of love and compassion and beauty. We were all alive! And we knew it, and it was good.

> *Behold, how good and how pleasant it is for*
> *brethren to dwell together in unity!*
> *—Psalm 133*

That evening was our first set at a San Francisco psychedelic ballroom. The Fillmore, Bill Graham's pleasure palace. We were the opening act behind the Sopwith Camel and the headliners, the Young Rascals. We took the stage to a light smattering of applause and a few scattered boos after Bill Graham's announcement of "Ladies and gentlemen, from Los Angeles, California . . . the Doors!" You see, San Francisco didn't like L.A. Too plastic, not a real city. And here was a band being featured as *coming* from L.A. And calling themselves the *Doors?* Well, how pretentious and how very plasticene. "Boo, hiss!"

We heard it, and we didn't like it. Got the dander up. As we mounted our instruments, Jim whispered to me, "Let's start with 'When the Music's Over.' "

"No," I protested. "Too slow, we gotta do something fast."

Jim insinuated his hand into the air, the psychic air. "It'll work, Ray," he said. "Just play the shit out of the intro. You know how." He turned to John and Robby. " 'When the Music's Over.' " And before they could protest, I smashed the Vox volume pedal to the floor and attacked the keys. The notes began to weave out into the audience. The power in my right hand contained all the energy of that afternoon at the Be-In. It was alive and electric. An entity unto itself. The opening passage, with its subtle variations, was burning its way into the crowd. Take this, San Francisco! The intro was more powerful than I had ever played it. "Here's what we do in L.A. and you ain't seen nothin' like us." And I had them. I cajoled and screamed and rocked and seduced through my fingers, into the keys, out of the amps, and into the hearts and brains of the soon-to-be converted faithful.

Oh, ye of little faith
—Matthew 8:26

And then I brought in the left hand on the piano bass. It was deep and rumbling and seemed to come up from some underground fissure. It was from the depths of the earth, from the unconscious of the multitude. And it was hypnotic. It demanded surrender. I pumped my left and right hand together, working contrapuntally and swirling the notes and sounds in a spiral around the Fillmore's light-show-patterned walls. A swirl of notes and projected colors, all moving and undulating together, and the audience was gone. All skepticism about L.A. . . . gone. All doubts about a plastic band from Southern California . . . gone. They were receiving what they had come for . . . transport. The music was now in control of their destinies, the liquid light show followed the lead of the organ and filled the auditorium in a glowing wash of melting colors, and the audience was ready for a trip . . . with the Doors.

And then John came in with the drums. Cannon shots on the toms and rifle cracks on his snare. Sharp reports and ominous thunder. Off time, out of meter, working against my repeating left hand.

It was brilliant. It created an anticipation, almost an unease; a waiting for the next passage. Almost a *need* for the next passage. You knew it was coming, you just didn't know when. And then he kicked it in. The cue for Jim and Robby to enter. A rat-a-tat-a-tat-a-tat pattern and everything exploded! Jim screamed into the microphone like a hellhound. Robby smashed an E minor chord on his Gibson with the volume knob set at *kill*. John crashed on his Zildjian cymbals like the Persian army in full attack mode and I smashed a corresponding E minor chord to Robby's. It was like a battle on the plains of Har-Meggido summed up in one note. It was apocalyptic. And the audience went into full-on frenzy. They were shocked out of their trance and immediately started dancing. With the band in full-bore rhythm the entire audience took up the call to passion and joined us in the pulsation of the song and danced for the next twelve minutes of "When the Music's Over." And they loved it . . . and they loved us. At the conclusion of the piece there was wild applause and whoops and shouts of delight. The boos had been replaced by the all-American high-pitched squeal and howl of approval. "Who-*eee!*" We had been accepted.

⁂

We played the Fillmore many times after that. Bill Graham was always a gracious host to us, although he could be—when he flipped his rage switch on—the meanest man in San Francisco. I saw him freeze a gaggle of hippies at fifty paces with a mere shout. At a sound check one afternoon, four or five inquisitive hippies had worked their way into the Fillmore and were moving about in the shadows, giggling, at the far end of the auditorium. Bill Graham was on the stage with us when he suddenly picked up intruder vibrations. He peered into the darkness, locked on target, and let out with a blood-curdling yell, "Hey, you motherfuckers! What the fuck are you doing in here?!"

The terror-stricken hippies went petrified. *I* went frozen. Jim, Robby, and John went flash-freeze immobile. It was the loudest, angriest noise I've ever heard come out of a human mouth.

"If you're not with the Doors, and I know you're not . . . then GET THE FUCK OUT OF HERE! NOW!"

They were off like a shot. Bats out of hell, fluttering a blind and hasty retreat. And Bill turned to us, his character completely changed back to the nice Bill, and said, softly and oddly personally, "Those darned hippies, they want everything for free. They don't seem to understand, I'm running a business here. I've got to pay people, support people. *You* guys want to get paid, don't you?"

We were allowed to breathe again. "Sure, Bill." "Of course, Bill." "Yeah, it's a business, Bill," "We understand, Bill." Our heads were bobbing like dashboard Madonnas. We didn't want Bill to holler at us like that, and he never did. Hell, he even went on to produce the movie *The Doors.* After he saw it he called me and said how sorry he was for how badly it turned out. That was a ballsy thing for him to do. He was a real mensch. And he was the only one who had the courage to tell me he was sorry for having participated in that filmic fiasco. Although I did run into Kyle MacLachlan, and he said, "You know, Ray, you were right. The script really wasn't any good and neither was the movie." I had to thank him for that. After all, he played me.

In addition to the Fillmore, we also played Chet Helms's Avalon Ballroom. Another psychedelic light-show-infused venue. Chet was the opposite twin of Bill. Chet was the good guy. The nice guy. Bill was the hard, tough, mean but fair guy. A no-nonsense exterior with a heart of vanilla pudding. Bill and Chet both believed in the coming New Age and were doing everything to expedite its dawning . . . in spite of their vastly different personal styles. We loved them both and played many gigs for them both.

It seems we played with just about everybody in San Francisco: the Jefferson Airplane, Country Joe and the Fish, the Steve Miller Band, Doug Kershaw, Chuck Berry, Junior Wells, the Sons of Champlin, the Sparrow (soon to be called Steppenwolf after John Kay read the book by Hermann Hesse), Canned Heat, the Clearlight, the Jim Kweskin Jug Band (Robby's idols from his Back Bay Chamber Pot Terriers jug band days), Moby Grape, the Grass Roots, Tim Buckley, the Seeds, Tim Hardin, Richie Havens, James Cotton, Procol Harum, and those lovable freaks who personify San Francisco and the psychedelic love movement, the Grateful Dead.

The Dead's support system was enormous. They had huge amps and many roadies, old ladies and groupies and yes-men, personal cooks and gophers and gurus and soundmen and manager types. Consequently, they had no need for normal human intercourse and/or discourse. They were completely insulated. It was a little world of its own and they were perfectly content to remain inside . . . with you locked out. I never did get to know any of them. I barely talked to any of them. I did try to communicate with their organ player, one "Pig Pen," but that turned into a complete fiasco.

Here's what happened.

The Doors and the Dead are playing together at some outdoor festival–type gig. The Dead are the headliners (it's early '67). They have a fucking *wall* of amplifiers. It's like the wall in Fritz Lang's *Destiny*. It dwarfs any human standing in front of it. And drum sets, two of them. And guitars everywhere. And . . . a Vox Continental Organ! Just like mine. Set up stage right. Just where I set up.

They have a sound check in the afternoon and it takes forever. They noodle, they fool around, they play out of tune, they try to tune up . . . but fail . . . and finally play a song. Vocals are out of harmony, guitars are tuned to some arcane, eccentric mode that each musician has kept as his own private secret, not telling the fellow next to him what the mode is, and the rhythm section is at cross purposes with each other, laying down what seems to be two separate and distinct rock beats that have no relation to each other. In other words, it's a typical Grateful Dead song/jam. They finish and, to them, everything seems fine. The musicians begin to leave the stage and the roadies lovingly gather up all the guitars. Everything else has to stay exactly where it is. The drums are not allowed to be moved. Pig Pen's organ must not be moved. Fritz Lang's wall of Destiny is *impossible* to move.

For our sound check—and performance—John's drums will have to be set up on the floor, in front of the existing pair of drum risers. No riser for John. The Dead have taken both of them. John's pissed, as well he should be. I take the opportunity to run up to Pig Pen. I don't know whether to call him "Pig" or "Mr. Pen." Mister sounds a bit formal between long-hairs and "Pig" sounds like an insult. I opted for the all-purpose, ubiquitous "man."

"Hey, man," I say, bounding onto the stage before he retreats into the womblike miasma of Dead sycophants. "I'm the keyboard player with the Doors."

"So? . . ." He's slow and unenthusiastic.

I extend my hand but he doesn't take it. Actually, he doesn't even really see it. His pace is slow.

I try to be jolly. "I play a Vox Continental just like yours."

"It can't be moved," he says.

"I know that." I smile, hoping to somehow communicate with this fellow musician. "What I want to ask is . . . instead of bringing my organ onstage and placing it in front of yours . . . I simply use yours."

"You wanna what?" He *is* slow.

"I want to use your Vox. I play the exact same thing. I'll just set my piano bass on top of your organ and it'll all be simple and easy. Nothing has to be moved."

His head starts to shake back and forth. He isn't liking the idea. But he is understanding the idea. I'm thankful for that. I press on.

"If I have to bring my organ up, I'll have to set it up right in front of yours. I play on the same side of the stage, just like you."

"So . . . ?"

"Then there'll be two Vox organs on stage. One in front of the other. It'll look ridiculous. People will think, 'Why are there two identical organs onstage? Why doesn't the guy from the Doors play the one that's already there? Why did he have to bring up a duplicate organ?' You see, man, it's absurd."

Wrong word. Pig Pen didn't like that word. His face scrunched up. *Absurd* was not a word that was used in the Grateful Dead camp. Too revealing. Too pointed. Even too inner-directed. The Doors, at least Jim and Ray, used the word freely. After all, isn't the post–World War II second half of the twentieth century totally absurd? Do we have to *add* to the absurdity? Isn't the whole point of psychedelics to break down the walls of absurdity and reestablish a divine intuition amongst the human species on this good earth? Well, of course it is. And the Grateful Dead is supposed to be psychedelic, but here I am having an absurd conversation with a person called Pig Pen. Man!

"Nobody uses the Grateful Dead's equipment," he finally said. It was like the Dead party line and he had it well memorized.

"I'm not asking to use the Dead's equipment. I know these amps are all custom built for you guys. We'll use our own amps. And we'll use our own drums."

"Damn right you will," Pig grunted. He was getting testy.

"I know every drummer has his own setup. But the Vox organ . . . it's generic."

"What . . . ?"

"They're all the same! Yours is just like mine. They're identical. It would be so clean and easy if I didn't have to bring mine up."

I gave him my best back-slapping smile of camaraderie. "What do ya say, man? Come on, can I use your organ?"

He paused for a couple of beats. Nice dramatic moment, I thought. Then the hammer . . .

"No way, Jack. I told you, no one uses the Grateful Dead's equipment." And he turned and lumbered off, into the miasma.

I gave his retreating back a peace sign and muttered to myself . . . "Share and share alike, ehh, brother?" Then more loudly to his rear end girth . . . "Peace and love, man."

He didn't even hear me. He was lost in his own little world. His very secure little world.

It was an absurd encounter. Ionesco would have loved it. It was like a scene from *Rhinoceros*, his absurdist play from the fifties. Here it was 1967 and nothing had changed. I didn't know whether to laugh or cry.

※

We also played at Marty Balin's club, the Matrix. A cool and intimate place to do some experimenting with arrangements and poetry placements. We included a couple of cuts from our Matrix engagement in the Doors box set.

We played with Marty and Grace and Paul's band, the Jefferson Airplane, at the Cheetah on the pier at Ocean Park in L.A. It was an ancient structure that looked as if it had been built somewhere in the early twentieth century. Back then it was called the Aragon Ballroom. It was all wooden and warm and archaic on the inside. It looked like something from the movie *They Shoot Horses, Don't They?*, a Depression-era tale of marathon dancing and the pushing of the human body beyond its limits of endurance to win a few dollars' prize. And there *we* were, the most spoiled and indulged generation in American history, making ephemeral mayfly noises in the night. What a country.

Jim unveiled his "tightrope walk" at the Cheetah. He balanced himself on the very edge of the stage and did his shaman/Indian dance from one end of the boards to the other. The damned stage was a good eight feet off the floor and Jim was teetering precariously. I was worried. He had an innate sense of balance, a great inner grace, but this was dangerous and he was intoxicated with the music. The rhythm of the drums had sent him into the alternate zone, where the WASP boy no longer held dominance. The Indian was now in charge and he was dancing and riding on that tightrope for all he was worth. It was quite a sight but I was nervous for his safety. If he fell, he'd splatter on the floor, and eight feet was a mean fall when you're all crazed with arms akimbo. And sure enough— BAM—there he went. He slipped, and I saw him fall off the stage in slow motion and I thought, Oh, shit! But at the last instant he pushed off with his foot from the stage apron, gained his balance in the air, and turned a splayed falling into a swan dive. And damned if the audience didn't raise their arms up in a kind of mass adoration and catch him over their heads. He balanced there for a second, borne aloft by his devotees, by his own grace, and by a communal act of will. Then he jumped lightly to the floor, ran to the side of the stage, and bounded up the stairs to his place at the microphone. The band didn't miss a beat, Jim came in on cue . . . and stage diving was born. At the ancient Aragon Ballroom.

We played with the Airplane again at the Birmingham High School Psychedelic Fair. I don't know how those kids got it past the school establishment, but it was a real trip-fest. There were booths and bands and color and lights and general San Francisco "be-in"-style love and looniness. Far too free and far too advanced in con-sciousness for a high school in L.A.'s San Fernando Valley. But those kids pulled it off and it was a memorable weekend. Hell, they had the Doors and the Jefferson Airplane. That didn't happen again until we went to Europe together in September 1968.

Another great high school gig was at Beverly Hills High, with those icons of the fifties, the Coasters. "Yakety Yak" and "Mother-in-Law" and "Get a Job." What great tunes of my youth. However, there were only two original members left of the quintet. It was sort of a pickup shtick. But the chubby, animated one was still there. He was always the entertaining one, moving about, making silly ges-tures and google eyes on the various variety TV shows during their heyday. But by 1967 they were a nostalgia act, and the now even more chubby one was letting it all hang out. He was giving Little Richard a run for his money. He just didn't care anymore, he was stylin'. He was bejeweled. Rings on every finger. Bracelets on both wrists. A huge and sparkling peace medallion around his neck—he was definitely a part of the "love thang." He loved the idea of peace and love and tolerance of all races . . . and all sexes. And he was playing it for all he was worth. And he immediately fell in love with Jim Morrison. He took one look at Jim and it was instant love. Or should I say lust. He followed Jim around backstage before the concert like a puppy. Jim, at his most tantalizing and demonic best, completely ignored him. He never spoke a word after a cursory "how do you do," and drove our poor boy mad.

They finally had to play their set. The backstage dance of lust came to a finish, and the Coasters took the stage . . . and wowed the audience. It was a greatest-hits show and "Chubby" was at the top of his form. All that desire resulted in a charged performance. He was high-octane and burning. What a showman.

We took the stage next and gave a very hot and intense performance. The kids at Beverly High were intellectual and hip. They got it right away. They were a great audience. Again, how we got to perform inside an official high school auditorium I'll never know. A band of subversives like the Doors? Playing their Dionysian music in the halls of academe? It shouldn't be allowed. Ever. Once again, the kids had slipped it past the officials.

The powers that be were simply not yet hip to psychedelia. They didn't know that they were supposed to hate the counterculture. Hell, they didn't even know what the counterculture was. They do now! And for them it's a battle to the death. A battle for the control of the destiny of America, For the control of the hearts and minds of the populace of America. God, I sure hope the fundamentalist fascists don't win. I hope the lovers win. Don't you?

back to the beast

We went back to New York in August to be presented with the official top-of-the-charts *Billboard* Hot 100 plaque. "Light My Fire" had done its work. It was the number-one song in America. We were now "official" and Elektra was gaga. They put on a wingding at the Delmonico Hotel. A press reception and party with gourmet hors d'oeuvres and open bar. In the wine cellar. What a mistake. Jim Morrison and an open bar, in a wine cellar, being honored by official representatives of the music establishment. Mistake!

Everything went smoothly for the first two hours. The presentation was made and the Doors posed for photos with everybody, holding that damned plaque and grinning into the gaggle of photographers that kept flashing big blinding strobes at us. And Jim started drinking. The entire Elektra staff had to have a picture with the Doors. From big honcho Jac Holzman and his lovely sweetheart of a wife, Nina, to Steve Harris, head of promotion, to all the secretaries and mailroom boys and flunky gophers. And Jim kept drinking. And then the disc jockeys. All the boss jocks who had gone on the edited version of "L.M.F." and helped break the band in the Big Apple had to have a picture, too. And the strobes kept flashing and Jim kept drinking. We were moved from table to table and people just stood up and photos were taken and we moved on to the next batch of unknowns. Who were these people? I swear, I think we took photos with the commissioner of sewers and the chairman of the Fulton Fish Market. And Jim kept drinking.

Finally, we were finished with the photos. Everyone who wanted it had been serviced by the Doors. Now *we* could eat and drink and laugh and goof and bask in the acceptance of our creation. Robby was beaming. His song, his little baby, had been embraced by all of America. He was the composer of the number-one song in America and he was radiant. He had even met a girl in New York. Lynn Veres. A platinum-haired, effervescent fox. And she was with him at Delmonico's . . . even more reason for Robby to beam. John was simply overwhelmed. He was proud and happy but decidedly out of his element. New York City was just too sophisticated for University High's lead snare drummer in the marching band. But that afternoon, he was on cloud nine. It was good to see him so happy. It's an emotion that seems to have eluded him in the last decade. I don't know what happened to the funny, puckish lad of the Doors salad days but he's rarely seen today. And I miss him.

Dorothy and I were beginning to get loose and goofy ourselves. Dorothy, not being a drinker, was approaching early blitz stage by her second martini. No one drank "martinis" back then, but my little sophisticate had heard about the concoction of gin, vermouth, and an olive in the fifties, and now it was her turn to try that deadly yet deliciously dry combination. She was cute as hell in her intoxication. And saucy! She had a cutting wit that the booze enhanced, giving her conversation a biting edge that had me in stitches. Or perhaps the gin and tonics that I was consuming on that hot August afternoon were putting the silly spin on *my* brain. But everything she said seemed funny to me. We were having a grand time . . . and Jim kept drinking.

Andy Warhol was there with a short stack of support personnel from the Factory. Jim was sitting with them in a banquette of

The Lizard King, damn right! 1968 photo shoot. *Photo by Paul Ferrara. Used by permission of the Doors.*

Jim at the Harry Houdini mansion ruins, Laurel Canyon, 1968. *Photo by Paul Ferrara. Used by permission of the Doors.*

Mr. and Mrs. Manzarek

James Dean at the Observatory, 1968. *Photo by Paul Ferrara. Used by permission of the Doors.*

Himself in Russian poet shirt, Hollywood Hills, 1968. *Photo by Paul Ferrara. Used by permission of the Doors.*

Waiting for the Sun recording session, 1968. Paul Rothchild in Borsalino hat.

Waiting for the Sun recording session, 1968. *Photo by Paul Ferrara. Used by permission of the Doors.*

"Screaming Ray" background vocals on "Hello, I Love You," 1968. *Photo by Paul Ferrara. Used by permission of the Doors.*

Flash Gordon in China—at home, 1968. *Photo by Paul Ferrara. Used by permission of the Doors.*

Relaxin' Krieger. At home in Malibu, 1968. *Photo by Paul Ferrara. Used by permission of the Doors.*

The UCLA Film School grads at a press conference. Europe, 1968. *Used by permission of the Doors.*

The auteur and guitar god. Europe, 1968. *Used by permission of the Doors.*

A low-angle, Orson Welles shot. Europe, 1968. *Photo by Paul Ferrara. Used by permission of the Doors.*

The shaman's dance, 1968. *Photo by Paul Ferrara. Used by permission of the Doors.*

Europe, press conference, 1968. Bored. *Used by permission of the Doors.*

Quetzalcoatl and the shaman, Mexico, 1969. *Photo by Jerry Hopkins. Used by permission of the Doors.*

Supporting the Colossus in Mexico at the Forum Club, 1969. *Photo by Jerry Hopkins. Used by permission of the Doors.*

The Doors at the Lucky U. *Photo by Henry Diltz. Used by permission of the Doors.*

The Manzareks in Mexico, 1969. *Photo by Jerry Hopkins. Used by permission of the Doors.*

Venice beach, *Morrison Hotel* photo session, 1969. A rejected cover shot. I wonder why. *Photo by Henry Diltz. Used by permission of the Doors.*

Jim on a plane to the East Coast, 1969. *Photo by Paul Ferrara. Used by permission of the Doors.*

Krazed Krieger, 1969, *Morrison Hotel. Photo by Henry Diltz. Used by permission of Henry Diltz.*

A happy drummer…at last. *L.A. Woman* session, 1971. *Photo by Henry Diltz. Used by permission of Henry Diltz.*

"The path of excess leads to…?" *L.A. Woman* session, 1971. *Photo by Wendell Hamick. Used by permission of Henry Diltz.*

Doors minus Morrison, 1972. *Used by permission of the Doors.*

Left to right: Robby and Lynn, Julia and John, Ray and Dorothy— married and liking it! Europe, 1973.

Dorothy, Ray, Pablo, and Marmalade

manly burgundy, wine bottles lining the wall behind him. I joined them briefly as Andy was presenting Jim with a pink-ribboned gift box.

"This is for you, Jim," Andy sweetly said. "In honor of this day."

"Well, thanks, Andy," Jim responded in a mock macho tone pitched a good octave below his normal speaking voice lest there be a confusion or the slightest doubt concerning his sexual orientation. No need encouraging Andy, after all.

Jim undid the ribbon, opened the box, and took out his gift. A French froufrou phone. A telephone that the beheaded Louis XVI would have used to call for help had the telephone been invented in the age of Versailles. It was white with faux gold encrustation. The receiver rested in a precariously high golden cradle and the dial was solid gold. The whole fucking thing was plastic and it was ridiculous. Jim could only stare at it in disbelief. Was it a put-on or was Andy serious? What would Jim possibly do with such a silly object? Was he supposed to take it back to California with him? What on earth did Andy have in mind giving Jim an ersatz eighteenth-century French telephone?

The gaggle of Factory workers all applauded when they saw the phone. They thought it was a perfect memento. There were oohs and ahhs all around that manly burgundy banquette. Jim put the phone back in its box.

"Thanks, Andy," he said. "It's . . . uhh . . . just what I've always wanted," he slyly smirked.

I almost lost it right there. Almost sprayed my gin and tonic out over the table like a bit of vaudeville shtick from the old Milton Berle show. "Just what I've always wanted?" Jim the joker.

Andy was most pleased. His hollow, dead, void-filled eyes almost twinkled — if those pools of dank permissiveness ever *could* twinkle.

"You can talk to God with it," Andy absurdly said.

I took that as my cue to leave. That was enough Factory woo-woo for me. Jim stayed and continued drinking, but damned if he wasn't maintaining an even strain. It was great to see him in control of his Courvoisier consumption instead of Courvoisier's usual vice versa. Consequently Jimbo was nowhere to be seen. That redneck stayed hidden in New York City. He never made an appearance at the big show. Too sophisticated. Too worldly for a good old boy. Had Jimbo made his presence felt and attempted any of his mind games with the New Yorkers, well, he would have received better than he could have given. And since it was always a battle for domination, a sort of shit-kicker's *Triumph of the Will,* and Jimbo knew he couldn't win against this uptown competition, he did a Br'er Rabbit and "he lay low."

As I walked back to the table where Dorothy was entertaining Lynn and Robby, and nursing her third martini, I noticed the composition of the crowd had changed. The nabobs were gone, the commissioner of sewers and his entourage were gone, the director of the Fulton Fish Market was gone. The *industry* was gone. All those people we posed with were gone. All the adults were gone. They had done their business and quietly slipped away. The Delmonico Hotel's wine cellar was now occupied by nothing but heads! Billy James was holding forth at a table that was sharing a joint. Danny Fields, Elektra's East Coast publicist, was doing the same at the other end of the room. The open bar had done its work and everyone was looped. Now it was time for some pot. And, man, out it came. That sweet smoke started to fill the wine cellar and the noise level rose to about ninety on the decibel meter. The party was a success and no one was there to supervise. It was all young people. And that meant people from forty on down, if they were hip. And what remained in the wine cellar that hot August afternoon in *Nueva York* at the Door's number-one-record party was nothing but hipness.

Now that the party had reached a proper level of intoxication, it was time for Jim Morrison to take control. He rose to his feet from Andy's banquette and called out in a most stentorian voice,

"Waiters . . . more food! More trays of those cute little . . . whatchacallits. My people are hungry!"

The assembly applauded him. Emboldened, he strode across the room to Danny Fields's table and gave Danny a big kiss on the cheek.

"Hi ya, Danny. How ya doin', man," Jim said as Andy glared across the room in a fit of jealousy and envy. Why should Danny Fields get a kiss from Jim? Why not me? I gave him the God-phone.

I sat with Dorothy, surprised that Andy's eyes could register *any* emotion. They always appeared empty to me yet sinister in an excessively permissive way.

Jim flopped down into a chair next to Danny and stretched his arms over his head, luxuriating in his success. And then his hand touched a wine bottle in the rack. His brain flashed and his hand closed over the neck. He hauled it out, placed it on the table in front of him, and shouted out, "Waiter, a corkscrew! And wineglasses for my friends!" He was the rogue pirate, the captain on his ship. "We're thirsty!" And waiters scurried about, carrying trays of canapés to the tables of hungry potheads, a corkscrew and wineglasses to Jim, and all manner of booze concoctions from the open bar as the decibel level pushed up to ninety-five. We were having big fun in the big city. It was drugs, booze, and rock and roll!

Jim popped the cork on his vintage French bottle and sloshed wine into the glasses at Danny's table. He took a quick gulp of his and made a sour face.

"Needs to sit for ten more years," he opined and leapt up, corkscrew in hand, and headed for Billy's table.

"Billy, my man, you need wine on this table!" And he pulled another vintage bottle out of its resting bin, popped the cork, and slammed it down on the table. "Drink hearty," he said and moved off to another table.

Oh shit, I thought to myself. He's going to pull an expensive vintage bottle of wine for every fucking table of boisterous, hollering New York heads. I didn't know *what* to do.

Dorothy saw what was going on, too. "He's gonna pull a bottle . . . for every fucking table," she slurred at me, the martinis doing their work.

Lynn cried out, "Wine for everybody, Jim."

Robby joined her. "Yeah, we're all thirsty!"

I said, "Shut up, you two! You're real troublemakers, ya know?"

Dorothy hit me on the side of the arm. "You're not in charge here, Ray."

Robby and Lynn laughed. "There's nothing you can do about this."

She was right. What could *I* do? "Well, then fuck it," I said. "I'm thirsty, too!" And they all laughed.

Jim got to the next table and pulled two bottles this time. "More wine for my men," he shouted as he slammed the bottles on the table. Someone took the corkscrew from him and deftly opened both bottles. Jim bowed to the bottle opener and moved across the room to Andy's banquette.

"Wine, Andy?" Jim asked.

"Yes, please, Jim," Andy hissed.

Jim went for the wine rack, but to get at it he had to climb up on the table and reach behind the banquette. He was knocking glasses over and stepping in the hors d'oeuvres and just about to grab more wine from the racks when the manager of the wine cellar burst into the room, saw Jim standing on the table, and rushed across the room, grabbed him by the leg, began yelling at him, and shouted, "Get down! Young man, get down off the table. Where do you think you are?"

"I'm in the wine cellar," Jim responded as he pulled his leg free, "and my people are thirsty . . . aren't you?!" he shouted to all of us. And the entire room responded back with shouts of "aye" and "right on" and "More wine" and general hubbub and cries of merriment. The manager was having a fit. He'd never seen anything like this. Mayhem in the wine cellar. "Who's in charge, here?" he shouted.

Jim grabbed two bottles of wine, held them over his head, and declared, "I am!"

And the place broke out in a roar. The intoxicated heads were beside themselves. It was us versus the Establishment and we were winning.

"Aren't there any adults here?" the manager whined as he scanned the room. He realized he was completely outnumbered and began to flee as random "boos" were tossed at him. Everyone cheered as he exited the room, Jim jumped down off the table, presented Andy with the two bottles, and moved on to the next table. The din had become a roar. Chaos reigned. We were having a grand time in the Big Apple. Man, what fun.

But within five minutes the police arrived. The jig was up. Such Dionysian revelry could not continue in the Delmonico Hotel wine cellar—although what could be a more appropriate place for an afternoon bacchanal, I ask you. Police whistles were blown, nightsticks were drawn, and a sweep of the room began. It was mean and orderly on the part of the cops, and chaotic and stumbling on the part of the revelers. It was, perhaps, one of the first confrontations between the counterculture and the blue muscle-arm of the Establishment, which would culminate in the Chicago police riots at the

Democratic National Convention and the murder of four college students by the National Guard at Kent State University. *That* madness was yet to come. For now, at the Doors "number one in America" official *Billboard* plaque presentation party . . . it was all fun and games. We were all laughing and goofing and carrying on like a mob of sillys as the blue men, rather embarrassedly, cleared the room. They felt extremely foolish having to drive a group of young people out of a four-star hotel for excessive fun. But they did their job, and we tumbled out onto Park Avenue and into our waiting limousines. Police rousting hippies who climbed into limos? It didn't compute in cop mind. But it was so and it was done. The party was over. And Jac Holzman was sent another Jim Morrison bill for damages.

And the French phone? Later that evening, while driving in the limo with Andy and Danny and Robby and Lynn and a couple of Factory workers, Jim rolled the window down when he saw a couple of winos sharing a paper bag at a stop light in the Village. He stuck the box with the phone out the window and said, "Hey, man. This is for you guys." One of the winos quickly grabbed the box as the limo began to pull away. Robby said he saw the guy open the box, take out the froufrou phone, and just stare at it, and then at the disappearing limo. Jim rolled the window up and smiled. Andy never said a word. Nor did he ever get to watch.

⚜

We played at Forest Hills with Simon and Garfunkel, a popular folk duo of the time. They were the kings of New York and we were the opening act. And it was terrible. In that very prestigious tennis center of the U.S. Open we had the worst reception of our entire career. The audience hated us! They had come to see smarm and were instead getting rock abyss from the opening act. And they hated it! Boos, catcalls, heckling, jeers, and whistles assaulted us as we tried to weave a little night music around their empty heads. But they didn't want electric, they didn't want Jung, they didn't want the Doors. They wanted their soft boys. They wanted to be coated with honey-tongued harmonies. They did *not* want intensity. It was ultimately a battle between soft folk-rock (very nice, very inoffensive) and West Coast psychedelic jazz-rock. We lost. Badly. Jim said it was the worst gig he had ever played and the worst audience he had ever experienced.

But we had also played Ondine again and another very hip club called the Scene. It was run by the equally hip Steve Paul. We even played there with Howlin' Wolf. What a double bill! The Doors and Howlin' Wolf. It was such an honor to be performing on the same stage with one of the legends of the blues that I almost had a heart chakra overload. The blues-loving boy from Chicago, playing with "the Wolf," in New York City?! Man, it doesn't get much better than that.

So as bad as Forest Hills was . . . *we* had the underground. *And* the number-one song in America. And it was now time to play it on national television. On the *Ed Sullivan Show!*

Paul and Bruce flew out from L.A. to handle the sound for us. After all, the *Ed Sullivan Show* was "live" and we weren't about to turn the mixing of our sound over to some old TV union guys who could care less about how some rock group called the Doors came off on national television. Hell, Steve Lawrence and Eydie Gorme were on the show that Sunday. *That* was their kind of music.

We wanted everything to be right. This was the real deal. This was Ed Sullivan. A national institution. Elvis had been on in the fifties. The controversial performance that was shot only from the waist up. "You can't show a wiggling pelvis on national television," came the edict from network. The Beatles had been on. The Rolling Stones with Brian Jones's angelic hair and Mick Jagger's full and sensuous lips were on. The Animals were on, the Kinks were on, the best of rock had been on—and now it was the Doors' turn.

We were loaded for bear. Paul and Bruce would run the sound, the band was primed, rehearsed, and ready to kick ass. And . . . Jim Morrison had his leathers! Yes. The black snake bone had been born. The black mamba. The shaman dipped in black liquid licorice. The leather Adonis. The man was all in black with a white poet's shirt underneath. And no underwear. Was he ready? Did he look good? Oh, my, yes! He looked great. He was going to pierce the hearts of the collective TV audience with black arrows of Eros. Dionysus was about to become manifest on the television screens of America. We were ready to rock, and the satyr was drooling.

Now, leather and snakeskin were something Jim had talked about for quite some time. He loved Marlon Brando's look in *The Fugitive Kind* and wanted to be the young drifter, both sensitive and poetic. He wanted to be the character who said, "They say a woman can burn down a man . . . but I can burn down a woman." And "My natural body heat is higher than other people's. More like a dog's." He identified with that role. Hell, he played that role in real life. He adapted the garb and the persona of that handsome young drifter into his own personality projection. And he threw in a bit of classic western Americana . . . leather pants. Like Jack Palance in *Shane.* Like a gunfighter, all cool and dangerous and slightly evil. Except Jim was a slinger of words, not hot lead. He could shoot out the most meticulously crafted phrases as easily as the demented, inbred descendants of indentured servants could squeeze off a couple of rounds from a Colt .45. He was a word man . . . not a gun man. A lover, not a killer. An American aristocrat, not white trash. And he looked great in leather. And when the ladies saw him on TV and saw the bulge in his crotch, they were pierced through the heart chakra. They were slain by love/lust. His American maenads. When they saw, on national television, what appeared to be the head of Jim's penis, the glans penis, straining against its black leather enclosure, they knew he had no underwear. It was just leather against shaft . . . and their imaginary hand was in between. And they loved him.

We did a sound check that Sunday afternoon and everything was jake. Paul and Bruce placed the mics and the sound was hot and crisp. The set was a bunch of doors—looked corny but passable. John and I had put some flowers on our instruments—looked meditative and quasi-mystical. Robby was wearing a naval-jacket-smart outfit. I had on a summer suit and sandals. John had on a kind of yellow sport coat and mod turtleneck thing. And, of course, black mamba man was handsomely dressed in black leather.

And then they dropped the bomb. We were in the dressing room, relaxing, sipping a beer, chitchatting idly when Himself walked in. Ed the Sullivan. We quickly hid the beers—no drinking in the dressing rooms—but he didn't notice, and said, "You know, you boys are really handsome. But you'd look a lot better if you'd *smile more.*"

And he turned and walked out the door. We were speechless. It was Ionesco again. Another absurd statement tossed out into reality. And the irony of it . . . Mr. Stoneface himself was telling *us* to smile.

And virtually on Ed's heels came the one-man bomb squad. The producer, who said, "Boys, we've got a little problem."

My brain screamed, Oh shit! Problem? Shit! What problem? What can possibly be wrong? Shit!

Jim glared at the producer, "What *kind* of problem?" he snarled.

"Well, network has sent down an edict." He spoke in his most official yet conciliatory manner. After all, he didn't want to upset the "boys," but network's will *must* be obeyed. "It seems you can't say the word *higher* on national television."

John spoke up, "So what's that got to do with us?"

"You have the word *higher* in your song."

"Where?" John asked.

The producer spoke as if to a child: ". . . 'girl we couldn't get much *higher,*' " he said as he scanned his clipboard.

John got it. "Ohh . . . so?"

The producer repeated himself, more forcefully this time. "So you can't say the word *higher* on national television!"

Robby spoke: "So what are we supposed to do?"

"Change the word," said the producer.

Jim muttered "Fuck you" under his breath.

The producer whirled around and shot a mean look at Jim. "What did you say?"

"I said 'to what'?" Jim lied sweetly.

"Ohh . . . uhh . . . wire, or liar . . . or something. I don't know. *You're* the poet, make something up," the producer said.

I liked that. At least he was acknowledging Jim as a poet. But change the word? I didn't think so.

Jim was about to get very angry. You could see his face redden. He was about to tear the producer a new hole for his anal sphincter, somewhere in the middle of his chest. I quickly stood up and said, "Why, sure, sir. We can do that."

The band was shocked at my acquiescence. The producer was very relieved. He smiled at us.

"Very good, boys. I'm sure you'll have a great show." He headed for the door. "And be sure to smile more like Mr. Sullivan said," and he was gone.

Jim glared at me, *"Raay,* I'm not gonna change the word for those assholes! What do you think I am, a fucking sellout?"

"Of course not," I said. "You're not gonna change the word. You're gonna do the song the way you always do the song. Say the fucking word *higher.*"

John spoke up. "But you just said we wouldn't."

"John, I lied. So what?"

"You shouldn't lie," he said.

"It's okay when you're dealing with morons, John."

Jim laughed. "Or evil." He was relieved. "But how do we get away with it?"

My tone became conspiratorial. "Okay, we do the song like we rehearsed it. You sing 'girl we couldn't get much higher' the way you always do. We do the short solo in the middle. John, I'll nod to you for the three against four and then the intro again, and then we *kick ass* on the last two sections! And we're done. Simple."

Robby spoke. "But they said we couldn't say *higher.*"

"So what," I said. "We say it anyway."

"But they're gonna be really pissed," Robby said.

"We just tell them we got so excited and so nervous being on national television, on the big-time *Ed Sullivan Show,* that . . . we forgot!"

"I am nervous," said John.

"See, so it's not even a lie," Jim said.

I continued with my co-conspirators. "We just say we were so nervous, and we've done the song this way forever, at least a thousand times, that we just forgot and it came out! What can they say? Hell, we're just *boys* anyway."

"But they have a censor button," said Robby.

"They'll bleep us right on the air," whined John.

I smiled. "Oh yeah? Guess who's working the sound."

Robby grinned. "Rothchild and Botnick!"

"The regular guys won't be *near* the board. Hell, they'll probably take a cigarette break when we're on and won't hear a goddamned thing."

"All right!" Jim shouted. "That's a plan. Let's *do* it!"

Robby and John said, "Yeah!" and we slapped our hands together in a group high five. The Doors' communal mind had gone conspiratorial. We were going to flip the bird at the Establishment. On national television!

This is not how Oliver Stone portrays the incident in his moron movie version. He had the Doors fighting amongst themselves to change the word. Well, *this* is the way it *really* happened, Oliver. And if you would have had the brains to show the Doors fighting the Establishment instead of going for the overused cliché of rock band fights amongst themselves as the lead singer tries to retain integrity while the rest of the band wants to sell out . . . well, perhaps you'd have had a better film, ham-hands.

And the way Val Kilmer says *higher* in the flick! Ha, give me a break, Oliver. Jim would never have been so crude, or so obvious. He was elegant and a *poet*. Or did you miss that subtlety?

My friends, you can see the actual performance of "L.M.F." on the *Ed Sullivan Show* on the Doors' home video, *Dance on Fire*, from Universal. Take a look at it and see how Jim Morrison actually said the word *higher.* Much more finesse than was shown in the movie.

Oliver, didn't you even look at *Dance on Fire*, for God's sake?

So . . . where was I before my spleen had to vent again?

Ahh, yes, New York. Well, we did the song on national TV as we had conspired to do it. The word *higher* just slipped by like it was greased with pure Canadian creamery butter. We played the shit out of the song and Jim was magnificent. His performance was blood stirring. He was every girl's wet dream and every guy's idol of emulation. You either wanted him for your boyfriend or you wanted to be like him. He was great. *We* were great.

And when we got back to the dressing room, sweating like hog boys from the lights and the excitement, there was the producer, waiting in whine for us. I'd never heard a grown man whine before.

"You said it!" He was almost sobbing. "You said *higher!* On national television!

He couldn't stop the whine. I almost felt sorry for him, but it was my time to put part two of the conspiracy into operation.

"You promised," he said to me. "You promised you wouldn't say the word *higher*"—and he turned to Jim—"but you did! Why?"

I was on. "You see, sir. It's like this. We were so nervous, being on the *Ed Sullivan Show* . . . on national television"—I pitched my voice up a half dozen notches to a boyish register and spoke rapidly, excitedly—"with millions of people watching us . . . well, we were so excited . . . we just, we just . . . forgot!"

Like Pig Pen, he wasn't buying it. His head cocked at a querulous angle and his face scrunched up as if he were smelling a three-days-dead rodent.

I sensed I was losing the game and rushed on: "We've done it the same way for at least . . . a *thousand* times . . . and to ask us to change it just before going on *national television*, well, we just forgot!"

"But you *promised*." He had to get one more whine in before he got mad. He turned to Jim again. "I'll tell you what, mister smart-ass." Now he was mad. "We were going to book you for six more shows! Mr. Sullivan liked you. He wanted you back for *six . . . more . . . shows*." He turned to me. "You know what that would have meant to your *career?*" I thought to myself, Shit. And then Jim spoke. It was Cool Hand Luke again. He shape-shifted in his leathers and coolly said, "Hey, man. So what? We just *did* the *Ed Sullivan Show*."

That stopped the producer dead in his tracks. He was silenced. He looked at Jim, the black angel in his black leathers, waved his hand in exasperation, and muttered a disgusted "Ahh." And then turned on his heels and stormed out of the room. We never saw him again. Or anyone from network, or Ed himself. Nor were we ever asked back. But, hey . . . we had just *done* the *Ed Sullivan Show*.

strange days

On the first day of our recording sessions for our second album, *Strange Days*, Paul and Bruce had a surprise for us. Well, actually for Robby and me—this was decidedly out of the province of our two Sagittarians. Paul called the two of us into the command module of the starship *Sunset Sound*, pointed to a big new Ampex tape recorder and said, "Check this out, you guys!"

"What is it?" Robby asked.

"A new Ampex!" Bruce said.

"I can see that, Bruce. What's the big deal?"

Paul jumped in. "It's eight tracks, man!"

Robby got it immediately. *"Eight* tracks? No shit?"

"Here it is, brother," said Paul. "Your wildest dreams come true. A quantum leap in technology."

"And *we* have it for the new record!" Bruce gleefully said.

"Wow, eight tracks. That's groovy," said Robby.

Now it was my turn to exult, "You mean we can do everything we did on the first album and still have *four* more tracks for over-dubs?"

"Exactly," said Paul.

"Holy shit," I said. "We could do anything!"

"Exactly," said Paul.

"Well, let's get started," I said. "I got a million ideas."

Robby laughed. "So do I!"

"What do you want to start with?" Paul asked.

Robby and I looked at each other and almost spoke simultaneously. . . . " 'Strange Days,' " we said.

And thus began our plunge into the laboratory. We were making a record, making music, but we were also mad scientists manipulating the aural spectrum for our diabolical creations. What fun! And what wonderful material we had to work from: "When the Music's Over," "You're Lost, Little Girl," "Horse Latitudes," "Moonlight Drive," "Unhappy Girl," "People Are Strange," "My Eyes Have Seen You," "Love Me Two Times."

Jim's and Robby's songwriting abilities were in top form. They were churning out small masterpieces and the group mind was arranging and manipulating their creations into a fine new block of Doors songs. American songs. Songs from the terminus. Songs from the end point of the West. From the meeting point of the continent and our mother, the sea. Songs from the end of the Western Dream of expansion . . . but songs from the *new* dream of the expansion of consciousness. The new global dream. The music of the new man. The overman. The lover. The dreamer. The caretaker of the new Garden of Eden. The poet. The warrior. The god-man.

And it belongs to everybody. We are *all* the new caretakers. We are all the *Übermensch*. We are all the poets of the New Age. My friends, we are *all* the lovers. And as soon as we realize it, the divine age will begin. As soon as we cast off the bonds of orthodoxy, the delight will begin again. As soon as we can break the conservative chains around our hearts and conquer our fears, the freedom and joy will begin again. Like Adam and Eve, we will be lovers in an earthly paradise again. And it only requires the courage to try an unorthodox approach. To go with something a little different, off the beaten track. The courage to follow the dictates of your heart. To trust your emotions, your instinct for the good. And *that* will invariably lead you to love. The divine Christ within you. The radiant heart chakra. The one.

So we took the energy and went to work. The recording went smoothly and quickly. No TV sets in the studio, no fires that needed to be extinguished. Just sonic creativity. For instance, one of the first uses of the Moog synthesizer in rock. Paul Beaver brought his huge modular Moog system into the studio and began plugging a bewildering array of patch cords into the equally bewildering panels of each module. He'd hit the keyboard and outer space, bizarre, Karlheinz Stockhausen–like sounds would emerge. He would then turn a mystifying array of knobs placed in rows around the patch cord receptacles and more and different space would emerge. He did this for about a half hour and we sat as if at an electronic music concert by some mad German composer. Who knew what he was doing? And then he turned to us, all huddled in the control room, and said, "If you hear anything you want to use, just stop me."

"Well, yes," Paul said. "Actually, that sound you had about three sounds back was very usable. Could you go back to that?"

"Which sound was that?" said Paul Beaver.

"That crystalline sound," Jim jumped in. "I liked the sound of broken glass falling from the void into creation."

"Which sound was that?" said the Beaver.

"A couple back from where you are now," Rothchild said.

"It reminded me of the Kabbalah," said Jim. "*Kether,* the I AM, creating duality out of the one. All crystalline . . . and pure. You know, *that* sound."

"Did I make a sound like that?"

"Sure," Jim said. "A couple back."

"Just go back to where you were," said Rothchild.

And Paul Beaver began to unplug and replug patch cords, and twist little knobs, and strike the keyboard, which emitted strange and arcane and unearthly tones that sounded nothing like the Kabbalah or *Kether,* the crown of the *Sefiroth.* None of the sounds he was creating sounded pure and crystalline. And then we realized . . . he couldn't *get* back. He couldn't get back because he had no idea where he had been. He could only go forward, on to the next patch. Ever new, ever forward. You had to stop him as soon as you heard something you liked. He *was* a mad scientist.

Finally, with Paul Beaver ripping and tearing at his cords and twisting knobs at an increasingly furious pace, sweat dripping from his forehead, ungodly shrieks emanating from his keyboard, Rothchild shouted out, "Stop! Wait a second. Just stop there." Paul was breathing as if he had just run the 200-meter hurdles. It was his idea and it was turning into a fiasco of "sonic creativity." He had to get the control back or Paul Beaver would drive us all mad. Even as he appeared to have driven himself mad. The possibilities were endless. The permutations were infinite. And the Beaver seemed as if he were going to try them all, as we watched, going slowly insane.

"Just stop, Paul. That's a good sound there. I think we can use that."

A great sigh of relief emitted from the Doors group mind. We used the electronic wind sound Beaver had created on "Spanish Caravan" and then another sound on Jim's voice—with Jim striking the keyboard as he sang each word like a mad space captain himself—on the title cut, "Strange Days." What an experience of electronic mayhem. Into the infinite!

Another bit of over-the-top creativity in the studio was my playing of an entire piano track backward on "Unhappy Girl." I overdubbed a piano part with the multitrack tape put on the Ampex upside down. Everything came into my earphones backward. The entire song started at the end. Fortunately, it had a good, steady beat for me to follow . . . backward *or* forward.

I wrote out the entire score, measure by measure. It was an insane idea. And we were doing it just so we could have a piano part with that odd *thwuck* at the beginning of each note. Almost a sucking sound before the chords kicked in. It was the decrescendo at the end of the note, the diminution of the sound coming in first rather than at its proper place at the end. It was an interesting effect. And, besides, in that moment of recording we had a great visitation of energy . . . so why not try it? So I did. And by God it worked.

I sat at the piano and put on the headphones, and Bruce flipped the tape and hit the red "record" button. I was on a separate track—one of the four extras—so it didn't matter if I made a mistake. And we were off. The song started on the button at the end, and the beat was steady but the sound was bizarre as shit. The whole song was backward, including Jim's work vocal. I started reading at the lower right and listened to the time of John's drums as hard as I could. One line went by, it seemed to be working. On to the next line up from the bottom of the page, and it was still working. I was counting measures furiously and the harmony of my piano against the backward song in my headphones was not clashing, so I must have been in the right spot. Or so I hoped. The next line went by and then I was at the top. At the far right-hand side of the top line. Only a few more measures to go. I was reading, counting, and improvising furiously. My brain had gone incendiary. If the music would end at the beginning as I counted my last four beats of the first bar, I would have done it. And, goddamn, it did! As I finished, the music in my headphones finished. I had done it. I had played the entire song backward and in sync.

I took off my cans, turned to the control, and said—to much whooping and applause from *mis compadres,* "Bruce, Paul, please . . . don't ever let me do that again."

Next we rocked out on "Love Me Two Times," Robby's great blues/rock classic about love and loss, or multiple orgasms, I'm not sure which. I played harpsichord; a most elegant instrument that one does not normally associate with rock and roll. It worked like a champ. We used a bass player for the first time on *Strange Days* and for all the subsequent albums to come. The Fender Rhodes keyboard bass just didn't record that well. It lacked the high-end pluck of a bass guitar string. It had plenty of bottom and was great in person, but in the studio it lacked articulation. Doug Lubahn, a member of the band Clearlight, came on board as our fifth Door bottom man. I showed Doug the bass parts that I was playing with my left hand and then he put his own spin on them. And he did a brilliant job, too. He was a real pleasure to work with. A solid bass bottom that John locked into immediately, and a good human being.

Then we attempted "Horse Latitudes." It was one of Jim's poems. Something he told us he had written when he was sixteen years old. I never believed it. The words were too mature. It was about the doldrums, the area of becalmed winds in the Atlantic Ocean, and the throwing overboard of horses to lighten the load in the days of transatlantic sailing ships bearing cargo from the Old World to the New.

When the still sea conspires an armor
And her sullen and aborted currents
breed tiny monsters . . .

True sailing is dead.
Awkward instant and the first animal is jettisoned.
Legs furiously pumping their
stiff, green gallop.
Heads bob up, poise delicate, pause, consent
In mute nostril agony,
Carefully refined and sealed over.

The horses are tossed overboard, they swim in the ocean with a stiff, green gallop until they eventually exhaust themselves . . . and sink in quiet agony beneath the still sea.

The group mind decided on a musique concrète score to accompany Jim's impassioned reading of the poem. He recorded his part first and then we all took to the studio, including a friend of ours from UCLA, Alain Ronay, and Robby's brother, Ron Krieger, his nonidentical twin. Ron helped us out in the early days with equipment hauling and general roadie stuff, and was an all-around good guy, albeit slow of foot and brain. We jokingly called him "Lightnin' Krieger." Robby got most of the IQ of that split ovum of Marilyn Krieger's, but Ron was always cool. We had him in the back of the studio as part of the "yelling brigade," along with Pam and whoever else happened to be walking by the studio that day. There were at least a half dozen of them and they were to scream their heads off on the phrase "Awkward instant" and keep screaming until the end of the piece. They loved it and did a horrific job.

I was going to play the inside of the grand piano. The lid had been opened on the seven-foot Yamaha and I took a pair of John's mallets and started pounding on the strings while applying and releasing the damper pedal. It was the sound of chaos. Random and mad. I had Alain join me with a pair of soft-tipped mallets of his own. Together we beat the hell out of those bronze strings in that great harp set inside that elegant instrument.

Robby conjured strange and eerie death sounds out of his Gibson and John and Jim sat on the floor slamming coconut shells on the parquet to simulate the sound of horses's hooves on a deck.

Bruce hit the red "record" button and we went into it. We pounded and plucked and eeried and screamed and slammed out our version of fear and chaos and drowning and death in the Sargasso Sea . . . in a studio on Sunset Boulevard in Los Angeles, California.

A studio that had become a becalmed sailing vessel somewhere beyond the West Indies, in the nineteenth century . . . and *we* were the
crew on board that death ship.

We did two takes. It was impossible to do any more. It was too
psychically exhausting. We had to break free from that tomb, that
chamber of horrors, that recording studio. We all fled into the light
of Sunset Boulevard; the revivifying light of Southern California.
And we left the Sargasso Sea behind us as we shared a joint and
drank beers concealed in paper bags. Within an hour we had flushed
the chaos and disorder out of our psyches. Paul and Bruce had
stayed behind to begin their alchemical manipulations of the two
takes we had performed. They were going to apply advanced electronic techniques to the tracks to add their own bit of death and anguish to the brew. And did they ever. When we finally went back
into the control room we heard such caterwauling and such banshee
howling that was definitely *not* of this earth. We were amazed at the
horror those two sweethearts of ours had generated. Bruce could
only grin like a demented ax murderer and Paul cackled like a furnace stoker from hell. They had gone mad with eight tracks but they
had produced brilliance. The inspiration continued, unabated. All
was well in Sunset Sound, and all was well with the Doors.

And the last song left to do was "When the Music's Over." For
this one we would not use a bass player. This one was going to be à
la the Whiskey-a-Go-Go. Live. Like the first album. Just Jim, Ray,
Robby, and John. No overdubs. No mad, lab-coated-scientist absurdo backward piano overdubs. Just the four Doors. Pure Doors.
And Jim was very excited. This is the way he loved to record. We
lay it down, all of us, together. Existentially. Either we get it or we
don't. The moment of truth for *all* of us.

Personally, I thought the moment of truth was always with us.
Every take was its own little "ultimate act of creation." We were creating a new universe every time we put on the headphones. Jim,
however, didn't necessarily see it that way. If the truth be known . . .
he mainly didn't care for the overdub process. It was too laborious
for him. It was the musician's raison d'être. It was "birdman" stuff.
Robby and I exulted in the overdubs. What profound fun the extra
four tracks enabled us to have. But it wasn't "word man" fun. Poets
need talking. Preferably in bars with alcohol-oiled tongues all
greased and lubricated for the advent of the *bon mot*. He wasn't hav-

ing his kind of fun in the studio; consequently, he wasn't always there. Until, of course, it was time for his vocals. And then he was a monster of creativity. He loved to sing. He loved the sound of his own voice in his headphones with a little reverb from Sunset Sound's live echo chamber and a touch of Elvis Presley slap-back tape echo. Bruce made him sound big and full and fat in the cans and Jim loved it. He sang his butt off, ripping and tearing at his vocal cords until he got the take to his demanding standards. Sometimes he would walk out of the vocal booth virtually unable to speak . . . but grinning like a Cheshire, knowing he nailed the vocal part.

But when guitar or keyboards or the occasional percussion overdubs were going on, and they did take some time, Jim was off at some bar, usually Barney's Beanery or the Palms on Santa Monica, knocking back a few cool ones and searching for the apt phrase with the ne'er-do-wells-of-the-week club.

"When the Music's Over," however, demanded his presence. It was improvisational. We needed Jim there, to follow him, to weave the music around his words. We couldn't create the tapestry without him. And he knew it and was most excited. This was going to be fun. We had played the song virtually every night onstage at the Whiskey, and Ondine, and the Scene, and the Fillmore, and the Avalon, and now we were going to put it down on tape. Yes! One time for the ages. We were *all* excited.

The day of the recording came. John and Robby and I got there early—one o'clock for a two o'clock call—and started fiddling and tuning and tweaking our instruments. We were like a 100-meter relay team, all twitchy and antsy, waiting for our anchor. Our Carl Lewis, our Jesse Owens. We stretched and twisted and loosened ourselves. Killing as much time as we could with sound adjustments by Bruce and Paul of a minuscule but important nature. We were primed and ready for the starting pistol. The sound was perfecto, the incense was lit, the lights were appropriately dimmed . . . and no Morrison. It was two-thirty and he hadn't shown up yet. I nursed a beer, John and Robby had apple juice, Paul and Bruce paced in the control room, and the hands on the wall clock slowly rotated. Two forty-five . . . three o'clock. Shit! Where was he? He's the one who was all excited and now he's an hour late.

"If he's not here by three-thirty, I'm going to call the session," Paul said through the talk-back.

We were slammed!

"Wait a minute," I said. "I want to play."

"Me, too," said John.

"I'm ready to go," said Robby.

The disembodied talk-back voice came on again: "Go where?" it said. "Jim's not here . . . and he's probably not going to be here. You can't go without him."

"Oh, yes, we can," I said.

John and Robby looked at me most quizzically.

"What do you mean?" Robby asked.

"We know the song. We know what he's probably going to say . . . where he's probably going to come in."

"Well, maybe," said Densmore.

"I don't know about that, Ray," said Krieger.

I shouted to the control room, "Bruce, set up a vocal mic for me on a boom. I'm going to do a guide vocal and we're going to *play* this fucker." I turned to the guys, "Okay? What do ya say?"

They brightened. "Well, shit. Why not?" Robby said. "Let's try it, then!"

John fluttered his sticks and whacked at his drums. "I'm game," he said. "Let's go for it!"

"Okay!" I said. "I'll try to approximate where Jim would come in and I'll sing the words I think . . . he'd probably sing."

"If he was here," John said wryly.

"Asshole, he'll *probably* show up tomorrow," Robby said. "After *we* get the take."

"And he's the one who was all hot to do it live," John said.

"Asshole," Robby said again.

Bruce quickly set up a microphone on a boom stand in front of my organ/piano bass station. Paul had me do the standard. "Testing, testing. One two three testing," and then a few yells for volume, "Hey! Hey! Yeah! Yeah! Testing."

The disembodied said, "Is that okay in everybody's cans?" John, Robby, and I all nodded. "Well, let's get it, then. 'When the Music's Over,' take one!"

And we dived in. I started with the long organ intro, then John came in with his machine-gun splatters, bending the time and holding back the first ejaculation, until it was time for the release. Finally, he hit the rat-a-tat pattern and Robby exploded in! I shouted as

Robby hit a big E minor power chord and the piano bass boomed into action. It was a magnificent explosion. We rode the repeating pattern, vamping for the vocal entrance, for the words to begin. I was almost tranced out by the mesmerizing figure we were playing . . . and then I realized . . . *I'm* the singer. And "Screaming Ray" came back from his self-imposed limbo state. I leaned into the mic. . . .

When the music's over
When the music's over
When the music's over
Turn out the lights
Turn out the lights
Turn out the lights

And Robby and John were right with me, hitting the variations of "turn out the lights" just as they would if Jim were singing. It felt good. This was going to work. And we were playing with an intensity I hadn't felt in the song since the Fillmore. We were on a mission. We had something to prove and, man, we were storming on it. We were hot!

The first two verses and the chorus . . .

Music is your special friend,
Dance on fire as it intends,
Music is your only friend,
Until the end.

. . . went great. But now the improvisational parts were coming! This was going to be the task. This was going to require mind-melding of the highest order. This was going to be virtually impossible . . . but we sucked it up and went for it anyway. Robby and John were right with me.

Cancel my subscription to the resurrection,
Send my credentials to the house of detention,
I got some friends inside.

We were doing it! And I dived into the next phrases:

The face in the mirror won't stop,
The girl in the window won't drop

And then the "Scream of the Butterfly." What I thought he'd say and where I thought he'd say it; with Robby and John in perfect sync. The communal mind of the Doors was honed and operating. I even think the muse had joined us. I think she was standing off in the corner, undulating slowly to the beat, but I didn't have time to pay attention to her. I was too busy . . . and the real monster bear was coming up. I closed my eyes and said Jim's Native American words.

What have they done to the earth?
What have they done to our fair sister?
Ravaged and plundered and ripped her and bit her,
Stuck her with knives in the side of the dawn,
Tied her with fences and dragged her down.

Pause for air, for breath. Let a few measures go by, then continue . . .

I hear a very gentle sound,
With your ear down to the ground . . .

The band got very soft. For the "gentle sound." And for the impending explosion to come. I waited . . . stretched it . . . paused . . . hoping this was where Jim would feel it . . . and finally shouted out . . .

We want the world and
We want it . . .
Now! . . . Now?
NOW!

And all hell broke loose. Feedback banshees on the guitar. Atonal Schoenberg screaming chords on the organ. Cannons and bombs and cymbal lightning from the drums. And we played our wanting of the world like the possessed patriots of freedom that we *really* were. No wonder the Establishment was afraid of us. We had gone Dionysian! Pan was with us. The maenads were with us. The muse Euterpe was with us. Her sisters Calliope and Terpsichore and Polyhymnia had joined us. And they were all whirling and dancing in a delirium of ecstasy, of exhilaration, of joy. We were in the divine moment and all pretense was abandoned. We were our real, naked selves and we were playing our instruments with our souls. Everything was on the line, and because it was . . . everything was alive. That's the reward you get when you make the leap into the void. Into the energy! And the ancients are just waiting for us to "reinvent the gods, all the myths of the ages." And then they'll dance with us. And we need that dance of love now more than ever.

And for a moment, we had it in that studio on Sunset Boulevard in the fall of 1967, and it was good.

The wild solos concluded themselves, and Robby, John, and I brought the music back down to earth. We vamped on the repeat of the opening passage and I sang the concluding . . .

When the music's over
Turn out the lights

and the final chorus . . .

Music is your special friend,
Dance on fire as it intends,
Music is your only friend,
Until the end.

A retard . . . a pause . . . and then one last explosion to finish the piece. A Densmore button on the explosion and we were done. Eleven minutes of music. On the fly, on the natch, in the space. We were spent. There was no reason for another take. We had done it and now all we could do was wait for Jim. For the moment of truth.

⁂

The next day he arrived at the studio at two o'clock. Right on time, but a day late.

"Oh, man. I thought it was supposed to be today." He grinned. "Did I miss a day?"

What a liar! He was so full of baloney and malarky and hooey and bunkum that you couldn't get mad at him. Especially when he smiled. And he was smiling white enamel that afternoon.

"I guess you guys got the track already, huh?"

"Yeah, we got it, Jim," said Robby. "Now *you* gotta go sing it!"

"How am I supposed to know where to come in?"

Robby grinned back at him. "That's for *you* to figure out."

John smugly added, "We did our part . . . now you do yours."

"But I wanted to sing with you guys."

"Then why weren't you here yesterday?" John said, and everybody in the room leaned forward. We all wanted to hear his flapdoodle excuse. The man could really feed the bull when he had to. And the bull was now hungry.

"I, uhh . . . uhh . . . I had some personal business."

That was it? No filigrees, no arabesques.

"Like what?" said Krieger the skeptic.

"Robby, that's what I said . . . it's personal. You understand?"

"No," Robby said.

"Well, I'm not gonna tell you. It's personal."

Robby waved his hand at Jim like the producer on the *Ed Sullivan Show*. "Ahh" was all he could say.

"Well fuck where he's been, let's just make a record," said Paul the pragmatist Rothchild.

Jim turned to Paul, relieved but still worried. "But how am I gonna know where to come in?"

My turn. "I'll guide you through it. Don't worry. Just sing it like you feel it. Where you think you should come in . . . come in . . ."

"Easy for you to say, Ray." He grinned again.

". . . and where you think you should lay out . . ."

"Yeah, I know . . . lay out."

"Exactly!" I said, and grinned back at him. He seemed to feel more secure.

"Okay, man. I'll try it. But I can't guarantee the results."

"Just feel it, man. You'll get it fine. I know."

He headed out to the vocal booth, put his cans on, Bruce hit "play/record," and I'll be damned if he wasn't in the pocket, in the groove, in the space. He was hitting all the cues, all the pauses. He was singing like me. Or, I had been singing like him. Either way, he was in it. And he was great. And he got it in two takes! Eleven minutes of singing and screaming and poetry and passion . . . and he nailed it in two takes. It was an impossible task but he got it. All the pauses and all the entrances, he nailed them. As if we were all doing it together.

And on the psychic plane, we were.

※

In mid-September our first royalty check arrived. Bob Greene, our recently hired accountant, called me in to his office and handed me an Elektra Records check. He sat back and grinned.

I quickly looked at the amount and said, "Wow! Fifty thousand dollars! That's what, twelve thousand and change for me? I love this . . . talk about easy money. Man, 'Light My Fire,' huh?"

Bob laughed. "Take a closer look, Ray."

I did and it said $50,123.75 in big, official, stamped-in— actually cut-in—perforated numbers.

"It says fifty thousand. Split four ways that's twelve K apiece. Do you have *my* check ready? I want to show it to Dorothy."

"That *is* your check. Look at the name."

And then I saw it. The official check with its Elektra Records logo and corporate address and eye-dazzling, multicolored, cut-in $50,123.75 was made out to one RAYMOND MANZAREK! Holy shit. *My* check . . . for me? My eyes did a Froggy the Gremlin "boiinng"!

Jim, in his wisdom, said we should—when it came time to fig- ure out who wrote what and how to divide up our yet-to-be-realized loot—simply cut the pie four ways. He said it would be easier and incur no bickering. There would be no talk of "Why don't we do my song," and we'd never fight over money. He was right. We never did fight . . . about money.

"This is mine?" I stammered.

"All yours, Ray."

"This doesn't get divided four ways, like everything does?"

"Elektra already did that. They send a check to each individ- ual, not the group."

"I don't believe this. Was 'Light My Fire' *that* big?"

"This is only up till the end of June," Bob said. "You get a roy- alty check twice a year. End of June, end of December. If you like this one, wait until you see the *next* one!"

strange days ※ 267

"Man, I don't believe it. Let me take this home and show it to Dorothy. She'll freak."

Bob grabbed the check from me. "Oh, no, this is going right into the bank. I'm not taking any chances. What if you lose it?"

"I'm not gonna lose it. I'm responsible."

He became official and fatherly. "Ray . . . this is going into your account, now."

"Okay, okay. I'll just tell her, then."

"Good. And while we're discussing Dorothy . . . it's none of my business, and please don't take offense, but . . . do you plan to stay with her?"

What the hell was he getting at? "Yes," I said. "We've been together about five years now. Why shouldn't it continue?"

"I'm not telling you what to do . . . but, uhh . . . if you marry her, I can split your income and save you a *lot* of money in taxes. Especially with December's check coming."

And there it was. Cards on the table. I no longer had any excuse *not* to ask Dorothy to marry me. I was now flush. I could support a wife. Hell, I could spoil a wife. I could support her in a manner to which she'd *never* been accustomed. It was time to bite that damned bullet of responsibility. It was time for the final commitment. Marriage. I had tossed the coins for the *I Ching*—the Chinese divination *Book of Changes*. I had asked the question, "Is Dorothy the woman for me?" The coins, in unbelievable synchronicity, fell to six consecutive broken lines! The second hexagram in the *Book of Changes*. The female principle. (The first hexagram is six solid lines; the male principle.) It meant, not only was she the woman for me—she was, for me, the ultimate female.

I arrived at our apartment on Sycamore in a total dither. I was almost shaking.

"Honey, I just got my royalty check from Elektra," I said as I walked in the door. "Guess how much."

She scrunched up her face in her too-cute way, thought hard, and said, "Around, ohh, ten thousand?"

"That's what I thought, too." I said. And I just stood there. Grinning . . . and dithering.

"Well . . . ," she said. "Did you just eat a canary, or what?"

"Get ready for this . . . *fifty . . . thousand . . . dollars!*"

"For the Doors?"

"For Raymond Daniel Manzarek!" I said.

She squealed and grabbed me. "We're rich!"

I wrapped my arms around her, lifted her in the air, and spun her around. "We sure are," I said. And she smothered me with kisses.

I stopped spinning and just held her, in the air, off the ground. "Now I want to ask you a very serious question," I said. She went limp for an instant. The kissing stopped. She seemed almost worried. . . .

"What, Ray?"

I swallowed the canary, grinned again, and said, "Will you marry me?"

She shrieked and said, "I do!"

We both laughed and started spinning and kissing and hugging and holding and clinging and laughing and kissing some more.

"I will," she said, laughing and kissing and crying all at the same time. "Yes . . . I do!" And she was mine.

And we were.

And we did.

And we still are.

⁂

Two weeks later *Strange Days* was released. We moved all around the country, playing and promoting the new album for the people in Des Moines, Iowa; Denver, Colorado; New York, New York; Tulsa, Oklahoma; Danbury, Connecticut; Nantucket Beach, Massachusetts; Baltimore, Maryland; Selinsgrove, Pennsylvania; Berkeley, California; the University of Michigan homecoming dance (What a disaster! Jim got drunk, John and Robby stormed off the stage in a fit of pique, I played guitar until the football players—men of great bulk in black broadcloth—and their diminutive dates in pink taffeta started booing and throwing paper cups of punch at the two stoners on the stage playing John Lee Hooker Chicago blues. It was a total fiasco but Jim Osterberg, a.k.a. Iggy Pop, was there and it changed his life. The sheer outrageousness and audacity of Jim Morrison convinced Iggy that a life of anarchic rebellion was the only way to fly . . . and he's been doing it ever since.); Williamstown, Maryland; UC Santa Barbara, California; San Diego, California; Vancouver, British Columbia; Corvallis and Eugene and Portland, Oregon; the Fillmore and

Winterland, San Francisco; Hunter College, New York; and Washington, D.C. Jim's mother and his brother, Andy, were at that concert.

Now, the first time I spoke to Jim about his parents, back in Venice, on the beach, he said, "My parents are dead."

I was shocked.

"You mean, you're an orphan?"

He hemmed a bit. "Well, you know . . . it's like, uh . . ."

"How long have they been dead? Since you were a kid, or what? I mean, who raised you?"

"Ohh, my parents raised me."

I breathed a sigh of relief.

"Thank God for that." I paused. "I'm sorry, man. They died just recently, huh?"

He nodded.

"What happened . . . a car or something?"

"No, nothing like that."

My mind went dramatic.

"Jesus, it wasn't . . . it wasn't a *murder*, was it? Or suicide?!"

"No, man. Don't be silly."

"I'm not being silly, just tell me . . . I mean if you want to."

He looked away. Kind of turned his back to me.

"It hurts, doesn't it?"

He didn't respond. He just looked out at the water, then he spoke softly, to the ocean.

"They're not really dead."

I couldn't hear him over the roar of the waves. "What did you say?"

He turned to me.

"They're not dead. I just made that up."

I couldn't believe it. What a thing to say about your family.

"Why?" was all I could muster.

He hemmed and hawed again. "I just . . . I, uhh . . . I don't want to see them." And then the real shocker. "Ever again."

And I began to understand. Must have been some kind of intolerant, antagonistic upbringing. Nothing like my family's nurturing, encouragement, and love.

"What does your father do?"

"He's in the Navy. . . ." He shuffled his feet, embarrassed. "They just made him an admiral. He's in Vietnam."

And there it was. Death. Vietnam. Military. Professional killers. Admiral! No wonder Jim was conflicted.

"Military, Jesus. Must have been hard on you, huh?" I said, softly.

"Fuck yes, he was."

"You want to talk about it?"

He started to walk along the beach. "Not really."

I didn't say anything. I just walked with him, in case he needed a friend. A shoulder.

"He was real strict," he finally said. Probably glad to unburden some of the weight. "He ran the house like he ran his ship. When I was a kid he was the captain of the *Bonhomme Richard*." Jim laughed. "They called it the *Bonny Dick*."

I laughed, too. *"That's* funny . . . the pretty dick."

"We had to be all shipshape and correct." The blockage was slightly opened. "We had to call him 'sir' and my mother 'ma'am.' He wouldn't stand for any fucking around; no goofing off."

"And your mother?"

"She had to go along with him. I mean . . . he was her husband, after all."

And then he closed up. The blockage back intact. Holding in the anger, the fears, the resentment, the demons. We walked on in silence, Jim kicking at the water . . . and his memories.

He later told me that his grandfather on his mother's side, in contrast to the Morrison clan, was a civil liberties lawyer in the thirties. A defender of Communists and liberal causes. Jim was proud of that. I'll leave it to you to divine which DNA helix, which genetic strain, which side of the family produced . . . Jimbo.

Back in D.C. Jim gave our crew strict orders to keep his mother away from him. The task fell to Rich Linnel, a promoter friend of Robby's and Bill Siddons, our surfer roadie. They did it only too well. He never spoke to his mother that night, but at least she got to see her son perform. Her husband, Admiral Steve, never did. I don't know that they ever spoke but there is a rumor that Jim had talked of visiting his parents and letting bygones be bygones once he came back from Paris. Today, his mother loves him dearly. I suppose she always did. I think even the Admiral is proud of his son . . . in spite of his being a poet.

And then came New Haven! Busted! December 9, 1967 — arrested right onstage. Captain Kelley and a brace of his blue meanies hauled Jim Morrison off the stage, roughed him up behind the curtain, where another half dozen evils in blue were waiting, and carted him off to the hoosegow. Into the slammer. For breaching the peace and inciting a riot! Of course the blue men were the only ones who rioted. This highborn son of military aristocracy; this arrogant, snot-nosed college punk; this pretentious, anti-war peace-nik, dope-smoking, commie-pinko, sarcastic son of a bitch pressed every one of their buttons and they went over the top. He had no respect for the police—just because they had maced him in a bathroom before the show, just because he was making out with a girl and refused to stop and received a full blast of mace, that was no reason for him to call them "little blue men in their little blue suits and their little blue caps" from the stage. Just because he had been blasted with tear gas and was choking and crying his eyes out, that was no reason for him to say, "I thought their motto was 'protect and serve,' the fascists!" Just because a doctor had to attend to him and the girl and flush their eyes with saline solution; just because the concert had to be delayed for an hour because Jim could barely breathe, just because it was a violation of his civil liberties and rights as a human being, it was no reason for him to bait the police and call them "little blue pigs." That was too much! That was when they they charged the stage . . . and stopped him.

And for good measure they also arrested, in the backstage mêlée and ensuing commotion at the stage-door parking lot, Michael Zwerin, jazz critic of the *Village Voice*, Yvonne Chabrier, a *Life* reporter, and Tim Page, a noted photographer just back from assignment in Vietnam. The New Haven blues were doing a fine job of shooting themselves in the foot and cutting off their toes.

Jim spent a couple of hours in jail, had his mug shot taken, nursed a few lower body bruises, and was finally released when Bill Siddons made his bail of $1,500 from the night's receipts. Eventually the charges against Jim and the three journalists were dropped. Insufficient evidence.

※

So, obviously, it took a while for Dorothy and me to get around to tying the knot. We had our license and blood test and whatever else

of official paper was needed to make it "legal" for God, man, the na-
tion, and the IRS. All we had to do was set a date and pick the place.

We didn't want to do a traditional wedding with formality and
whiteness of the bride. Dorothy wasn't hung up on having that "one
perfect day" that seems to obsess today's young women. In the sixties, the young people of the world were trying to create a new tradition that had to do with personal involvement, commitment, and
freedom. The ceremonies would be *our* ceremonies. *We* would create
the set, setting, and words of our new joining.

I asked Dorothy, "Do you want to do a ceremony on a hillside
or by the ocean or something?"

"Not really. Do you?"

"No . . . not particularly. It'd be too embarrassing."

"God, yes! I couldn't stand in front of our friends and recite
some kind of 'I love you truly' vows."

"What about your relatives . . . and mine?"

"Ray! . . . No! I'd die."

"Me, too," I laughed.

"But you can get up and play in front of thousands of people.
You're not embarrassed then."

"I can hide behind the music. *This* would be you and me naked.
We'd be standing there, exposed to the world, and everybody would
be going, 'How cute, don't they look sweet, aren't they adorable!' I
don't want to be *adorable*. I don't want my mother and your mother
crying."

Dorothy agreed, "I just couldn't do it. I couldn't stand everybody just *looking* at me like that." Then she laughed. . . . "I guess I've
smoked too much pot. Am I paranoid?"

"Hell no! You're realistic." I thought for a second. "And what
about the *reception?*"

"Ohh, God. And then we have to feed them?"

"Sure. Wedding equals food and drink. Hell, they'll want
champagne and smoked salmon."

"Caviar!"

"Something sumptuous and luscious."

She scrunched up her face again. . . . "Well, they can't have it.
That's just too much. I'm not going to put on a show for them and
then treat them all to a feast, too."

"So . . . what do we do? Time's a-wastin'! We have to do this before the year is out."

She paced the floor, thought a bit, and said, "City Hall!"

"You mean, just go downtown?"

"Absolutely. This is a governmental function, isn't it?"

"Well, yes."

"We're doing this for the legality of it, aren't we?"

"No," I protested. "I love you. I want you to be my wife."

She smiled shyly. I loved her like crazy when she smiled like that. All shy and vulnerable, as if I had touched some deep and private part of her. "I am your wife," she said.

I took her in my arms and held her tightly. "But now it's going to be a legal commitment, on paper, before the whole world."

"So let's go legal. City Hall."

"When?"

"Hell, let's do it tomorrow!"

And we did. With Jim and Pam as best man and maid of honor. On the judges' lunch hour. There was a large waiting room adjacent to the judges' chambers and it was filled with what must have been seventy-five couples and their attendants. Fifty Chicano couples, twenty-four black couples, and one mixed-race hippie couple. Us.

Eventually, the judge's herald—who would call out a couple's name and lead them into the sanctum as they alternately wept and giggled—got around to us. "Manzarek and Fujikawa" came the cry. We rose, the four of us, and I'll be damned if I wasn't shaking ever so slightly. I was nervous and Dorothy was nervous. I could feel her arm shaking as I took it for our triumphal march to the gallows. This was it. The real deal. Marriage! And there was no turning back.

I looked at you, you looked at me.
I smiled at you, you smiled at me.
And we're on our way, and we can't turn back.
Yeah, we're on our way, and we can't turn back
'Cause it's too late, too late, too late,
too late . . . too late!

Jim and Pam were right on our heels, grinning like fools. No pressure on them. Just fun. It was good having them there. They were a fine couple. And I really needed Jim's support in this extreme moment of truth.

My mind goes blank at the enormity of that moment. I remember a man in black, white haired, in a paneled room. He asked, "One ring or two?" "One," I replied. I had purchased, from a novelty store on Broadway that morning, a large, garish snake ring with a glass ruby on its head. It was something a cholo biker or his mama would wear. I thought it would lighten the mood, sort of disrupt the official solemnity.

Jim and Pam signed in as official witnesses and the words began. The judge read from a book, quickly. I don't remember the phrases. They were standard. We both said, "I do." And he said, "You may place the ring on your bride's finger." And out it came. *El serpente grande!* I lovingly placed that monster of silver and black and red on my wife's finger and Jim Morrison almost fell to the floor with laughter. He grabbed his mouth and doubled over at the sight of the ring. Pam hit him on the side of the arm. The judge didn't blink. "You may kiss the bride," he said. We kissed. She was mine. I was hers. "Next!" said the judge. The herald checked his list, opened the door, and called out into the bullpen of remaining couples, "Sanchez and Obregon!"

We went off to Olvera Street, the old Mexican "City of the Angels" thoroughfare. It was the first street in L.A. and was now a delightful collection of shops and restaurants. This was going to be our reception.

"Margaritas all around, *por favor*," Jim called out as we took a table on the patio under a hundred-year-old grape arbor. "We have newlyweds here and we want food and drink!" He was beaming. Dorothy and I were beaming. Pam was glowing. We were radiant with love and warmth and joy. And four big margaritas hit the table with chips and salsa.

"To the newlyweds! May you dance together forever," Jim toasted.

"Forever!" repeated an ebullient Pam.

And we downed those frost-salty concoctions of tequila, triple sec, and lime juice, the cold hitting the back of our throats as the sweetness of the triple sec tickled our tongues. The burn of the tequila worked its way down our gullets and settled tranquilly in our stomachs, adding an internal blush to our festive revel. We were happy. We were young, successful, in love with each other, and all things seemed possible on that twenty-first day of December, 1967.

"Food!" Jim cried out. "More margaritas and food for my people."

"Enchiladas for me," shouted Pam.

I took up the cry, "I want *chile rellenos* . . . with *salsa verde!*"

"Enchiladas for me, too," shouted my bride. "Cheese enchiladas, with a little *chile colorado* on top."

"Me, too!" shouted Pam. "Put whatever Dorothy said on mine, too."

The waitress in her ruffled Mexican peasant outfit came running up with another round of drinks and, smiling and laughing with the gringo newlyweds, took our order.

"*Carne* for me!" said Jim. "I want beefsteak and beans and rice . . . and guacamole. . . ."

"And tortillas, *maíz* . . ." I added. "*Mucho* tortillas."

The waitress spun on her heels, her skirt flaring in a saucy fandango, and raced off, giggling.

"I feel great!" I said as I dipped into the second margarita.

"That didn't hurt at all," said Dorothy, beaming.

"No, Mrs. Manzarek," I said, "That didn't hurt a bit." I kissed her and Pam squealed.

"It was so *easy,*" she said. "I didn't know getting married could *be* so easy. Did you, Jim?"

Jim coughed and dived for the chips and salsa. "Uhh, no . . . no, I didn't, honey," he mumbled under his breath, caught. He knew what was coming. She was going to be on his case to marry her for the next three years. "Jiiim, it's so easy. Remember how Ray and Dorothy did it?"

"Hey, Ray. You're ready for another one, aren't you?" Jim quickly asked. "I'll just go inside and get our waitress," and he was gone like a shot. Out of harm's way, before Pam could utter another word about the ease of knot tying.

So we drank and ate and laughed into the late afternoon. Four young friends, in love with life.

The next night we played at the Shrine Auditorium. With the Grateful Dead, again. Our honeymoon was a weekend with the Doors and the Dead. Psychedelic lights were everywhere. Of course the Dead played too long and out of tune, as they usually did in those days. And when the Doors finally took the stage, Jim dedicated the entire set to "the newlyweds." It was a fabulous night. Halfway through the set I brought Dorothy up onstage. Jim announced "Mr. and Mrs. Ray Manzarek!" I kissed her, she blushed from ear to ear, and the band and our roadies all laughed and applauded. And the entire audience joined in and applauded as "the newlyweds" held each other tightly.

The next night the cops busted the whole damned thing. Shut us all down. Shut down the Shrine. No arrests . . . just shot the bacchanal to pieces. "No more music!" the blue meanies said. It seems the promoters were in violation of multiple city ordinances, so L.A.'s finest took the opportunity to harass the hippies once again. "No more music! Clear this facility . . . now!" And that was it. Shut down!

And that was the end of 1967!

In that year we had a great visitation of energy.

waiting for the sun

Now we needed a place to rehearse. We no longer had the beach house in Venice, and Robby's parents had moved to an ersatz Frank Lloyd Wright house that was not hospitable to kick-ass rock and roll. We needed something professional. A piece of commercial property that would allow us to have creative space *and* an office. I scoured the West Hollywood area, being central to everybody, what with Robby and John now out of their parents' homes and sharing digs in the Hollywood Hills, Jim and Pam ensconced on "Love Street" in Laurel Canyon, and Dorothy and me in our cool, new house that we had purchased in November with the 50K royalty check. Two bedrooms with a swimming pool, a paneled living room, a newly remodeled kitchen, *and* a fish pond! For $49,500. Corner of Vista Grande and Hammond. A hip little area later to go totally gay. But we were there pre–boys town and it was cool. The deal was consummated at about the same time our marriage was consummated. Me . . . house and a wife. Far out!

And then I found it. Our rehearsal space. Corner of La Cienega and Santa Monica. Little two-story building. Large room downstairs, two rooms upstairs. Perfect. Music on the first floor, business on the second. Elektra was half a block away on La Cienega, Duke's—the great health-food-style coffee shop/restaurant—was a block west on Santa Monica, the legendary Barney's Beanery was a block east on Santa Monica, right across the street was the Alta Cienega Motel—where Jim spent many a night after fights with Pam—and the Phone Booth—a topless bar where Jim also spent many a night . . . resulting in many arguments with Pam that resulted in his spending many a night across the street at the Alta Cienega Motel.

We immediately moved into the Doors' "workshop." Bought a couple of desks, a file cabinet, lounge chairs, a small refrigerator, and a couch for the upstairs office. A pinball machine and another couch for the rehearsal room downstairs. Siddons moved the equipment in, set it up, and we were a go. We fired Bill Siddons and hired Vince Treanor—a Boston pipe organ fanatic and electronics genius—as our equipment manager and immediately rehired Siddons as the Doors' official *manager*. Bill would now be responsible for all the phone calls coming in. He would deal with Elektra in terms of publicity, promotion, and distribution. And he would book our gigs. We would tell him what to do and he would tell us what requests and gig offers came in during the week at our Friday band meeting. It was a big job for a twenty-two-year-old surfer, but he was up to the task. And Vince was a godsend.

We brought in Leon Barnard to handle the press and, eventually, after a few mistakes, Kathy Lisciandro as our secretary. She, of course, was running the whole show within three months. And a fourteen-year-old kid named Danny Sugerman kept coming around. Jim took a liking to him and made him the Doors fan mail answerer. I thought the kid was sharp. A high IQ. Good work habits. He eventually became our manager . . . some ten years later. And he still is. Even if he is prone to take a walk on the wild side every once in a while.

So the office upstairs was staffed and humming. Downstairs was for art. And the four of us dived into the songs for the third album. "Hello, I Love You," "Love Street," "Summer's Almost Gone," "Wintertime Love," "The Unknown Soldier," "Spanish Caravan," "My Wild Love," "We Could Be So Good Together," "Yes, the River Knows," "Five to One" and "Not to Touch the Earth." We worked on "The Celebration of the Lizard" but it kept resisting us. Its time for the birthing process was not upon us. The lizard needed a longer gestation in its egg. But we did manage a very intense completion of the "Not to Touch the Earth" section, including Jim's infamous line . . .

I am the Lizard King,
I can do anything.

The press loved it. It was their new hook for him. Jim would now be known as "the Lizard King." There was "the King" — Elvis — and "the Lizard King" — Morrison. Easy, neat, a buzz phrase, a no-brainer. Hell, the people loved it, too. Lizards, snakes, and reptiles tapped right into the Judeo-Christian mind of all real Americans. And here was Jim Morrison, the beautiful, androgynous lead singer of that rock band that the press called "the Kings of Acid Rock" and the "Kings of Orgasmic Rock," calling *himself* "the Lizard King." It was perfect. They couldn't resist it. It pressed those damned Freudian buttons and gave the country a cold shiver shot right up its collective spine. Kundalini rising!

We recorded the album at TTG in Hollywood. It was located next to Stan's Drive-in, a car-hop fifties anachronism of Suzie Q fries and patty melts and cherry lime rickeys. Hot-rod eating, California style. Good stuff. I filled up on plenty of those corkscrew Suzie Qs during the making of *Waiting for the Sun.*

So did the execution rifle squad we brought in to open and close the bolts on a dozen M-1s for the firing-squad shooting of Jim in "The Unknown Soldier." They were all empty, of course. Paul rented the rifles and we called a bunch of rock writers, including Paul Williams of *Crawdaddy* and Richard Goldstein of the *Village Voice,* to come and take part in a Doors' recording session . . . to actually be on a song. They immediately cottoned to the idea, and when they got to the studio and saw real rifles, they flipped. They opened and closed those bolts, pointed those weapons at everything in sight, shot each other with ammo-less clicks of the hammers, and ate Suzie Qs and drank Cokes like a bunch of little kids. Writers with guns! And they were going to be a firing squad that kills Jim Morrison? Man, they loved it. The rock writers were a rare breed in those days. Actual intellectuals. And they were all writing at the top of their form.

The album was fun to record. The ballads were sensitive and beautiful. The rockers like "Five to One" were insane hard-on, over-the-top crunchers and all was well with the creative process . . . except for Jim's drinking.

It was starting to become excessive. He would say, "I'm depressed, let's go get a drink," or "I feel great, why don't we get a drink." Too much booze and too much Jimbo. He was hard to live with when that redneck came out. That hillbilly/cowboy/honky/-trailer-trash creature was not the Native American–inspired poet whom I knew and loved. Jimbo was another personality altogether—a mean and desperate man. A man of roughness and crudeness. A man on a hell-bent-for-leather quest for domination, power . . . and kicks. Jimbo was Felix's Frankenstein monster, the destructive golem. And he was Jim's doppelganger. An evil homunculus brewed up by the immersion of Jim Morrison in a wash of grain alcohol. And the blood secrets of the tribe. And Jimbo attracted scum like flies to feces. Or did he seek them out? Out of some need for validation of this alter ego. A need for companionship in his dissolution. Or did they simply, serendipitously find each other? Like finding like in this holographic universe of vibrating entities. Even as Jim and I had found each other on the beach in Venice, in the sunlight, in what was beginning to seem like a long time ago.

This time he found Freddy and Wes. They were musicians. Wes played keyboards and Freddy played, I don't know what, probably skin flute. They lived on a ranch. Outskirts of the city. They had guns. Jim would go out there and drink and shoot the guns. It was Charlie Manson time. He was at the crossroads, and Jimbo was winning.

You got to meet me at the crossroads,
Meet me at the edge of town.
Outskirts of the city,
You better come alone,
You better bring your gun,
We're gonna have some fun.

And fun they had. They were an odd trio, however. Jim would have had nothing to do with these two. But Jimbo loved them. I wouldn't be surprised if Jimbo was trying to start a new band like the Doors. But this time a negative-energy band. An opposite, mirror reflection of what the Doors were. An incompetent, loose, and lazy band of boozers . . . who couldn't really play their instruments or write poetry or sing very well. A band without discipline, without talent, and certainly without love. But, man . . . they would have been good at messing with your mind. Shit, they would have been as good as Manson.

And one day Jimbo even brought his drinking buddies to TTG. To a Doors' recording session. Not a good idea. Rothchild would have none of it. No boozing in the control room, no sarcastic asides, no loud guffaws, no mind games. Paul let them stay a couple of hours and then took Freddy and Wes aside and read them the riot act.

"Get the fuck out of this recording studio and never come back here!" He was seething.

"You can't throw us out."

"The fuck I can't! This is *my* recording studio. I'm running these sessions. I'm the producer and you're out of here!" shouted Paul.

"We're Jim's friends, he invited us."

"Friends? You're not his friends. You're destructive assholes. You'd bring the whole fucking thing down."

Rothchild had their number. They *would* have destroyed the whole thing. Hell, Jimbo wanted to destroy the whole thing, too. He wanted to push us as far as he could until we snapped. Until he broke us and we said, "That's it! We quit. We can't take this anymore. We want to play music and you want to play *mind games?* What the fuck is your problem? Are you fucking insane or something? Let's just break the band up and go our separate ways." That's what Jimbo was after. Jimbo wanted to destroy the Doors. And when he couldn't, he eventually took Jim to Paris . . . and destroyed himself.

But we didn't know about Jimbo back then. We didn't know about alcoholism and the meanness it carries with it. The insane, destructive behavior that lurks in every bottle of Jack and Wild Turkey. Waiting for the right personality to set free the obsession.

The right chemical makeup and the right psychological profile to allow the demons out of the bottle. To allow the spirit possession to take place. The Native American was susceptible to the powers of rum, and the redneck knew it. It was outlaw Jimbo's task to kill the shaman. It was always the white devil's task to kill the natives, and Jim had become a Native American. Born of the soil of America. Reborn of the spirit of the shaman. And Jimbo was out to destroy that man. And the Doors, if he could.

"We are *too* his friends," Freddy continued. "We take him out to the ranch, and he rides the horses . . . and he shoots guns . . . and he . . ."

"Jim doesn't fucking ride horses," I said.

"Yes, he does, man. *You* just don't know him," Freddy rejoindered. "Not like *we* do."

And there was the line being drawn. Sides were being chosen up right then and there. Jimbo, Freddy, and Wes on one side, Doors on the other.

"Guns!" shouted Paul. "You assholes let him shoot guns?" Paul glared at Freddy. "Are you crazy?"

"He likes to shoot guns. He likes being with us . . . better than being with *you* guys. He told us!"

I was stabbed in the heart. Jim liked being with them better than us? How could he? . . . Why? What had we done to him to make him feel that way? To say that? I was destroyed.

You see, I just didn't understand. Had *any* of us understood that personality transference, that psychic split, we would have been able to deal with it. But as it was, we thought it was Jim. And it hurt.

"I don't care what *he* likes," Paul forcefully said. "You two are history in *my* recording studio. Now get the fuck out and never come back."

And Freddy and Wes slithered out, hissing meanly, never to be seen again.

⁂

Another night, Jimbo—being deprived of his cowboys—brought a foxy lady to the studio. Sable Sperling and her pink Jaguar convertible. We watched them pull up. What a mod-sixties machine. And then they attempted to get out. "Holy staggers, Batman." They were more than boozed out. This was wiggle-wobble, rubber legs. This was downers!

Sable had on a miniskirt that was almost even with her lamb pit. She had great legs, except for what appeared to be a huge birthmark on her right thigh, and a skimpy little top that showed off her pre–plastic enhancement melons to their full ripeness. She was a fine figure of a woman . . . but a real ditz. And they staggered in. Jim clutching a bottle of Wild Turkey, Sable clutching Jim.

Now, this was supposed to be a vocal night. We had planned on Jim getting two songs, "Love Street" and "Summer's Almost Gone." Not too difficult a night's work. Easy, actually, for Jim Morrison. Impossible for Jimbo. Especially Jimbo on downers.

When the down duo walked into the studio, Sable opened her purse and put a baggie of colored pills on the recording console. Jim offered us all anything we wanted. Pills, booze, Sable. No takers.

"How many of these have you popped, Jim?" asked Paul.

Jim slurred heavily, "I don't know . . . maybe ten . . . maybe twenty . . ." An evil grin. "Maybe thirty."

"Oh, Jesus," was all Paul could say.

"He didn't take thirty," offered Sable. "He's just a big fucking liar. He lies about everything." She went up to him and gave him a sloppy lewd kiss to match her lewd speech. "That's why I love him."

Jim pushed her away. "I got work to do," he said. "I gotta sing!" And he howled like a wolf.

"What do ya wanna sing, Jim?" I asked him.

"What am I supposed to sing?"

" 'Love Street.' "

"I don't wanna do 'Love Street.' "

" 'Summer's Almost Gone'?"

"Nah . . ."

Robby spoke up, "You gotta sing something, Jim, it's vocal night. We planned on it yesterday, remember?"

Jimbo didn't remember anything. He had a memory, a life, only when released from the bottle, and last night there was no bottle of Wild Turkey. Ergo, no Jimbo.

"I don't remember saying that. I just wanna sing."

"What?" asked Robby.

" 'Five to One'!" And he howled again. "Yeah!"

"Well, shit, man. Get out there and do it!" said Rothchild. "If you feel that good . . . give me a great take."

"Yeah!" shouted Jimbo. "I fuckin'-A will!"

And he cracked the bottle of Wild Turkey, put his hand in the plastic baggie, grabbed three or four multihued pills, and before anybody could stop him, slammed those suckers into his mouth and washed them down with a quick splash of fine Kentucky bourbon.

"Yeah!"

And he staggered out of the control room to the Neuman vocal mic set up in the center of the main room with baffles and a music stand, and earphones, and a little table on an Oriental rug with soft, moody down lights for the right atmosphere. It was a very nice arrangement that Bruce Botnick had set up. Very conducive for singing. Jim put his bottle on the table and the earphones on his head, and slurred into the mic, "Yeah! . . . Yeah! . . . More echo!"

Paul looked at Bruce and said, "Fuck the echo, call the paramedics."

"Now?" Bruce asked.

"Now," said Paul. "Tell them what's going on here, don't use any names, but tell them where we are, we got a guy on downers and booze, and we're gonna call them as soon as he hits the floor."

"After what he just took that should be about ten minutes," said Bruce.

"Exactly," said Paul. "Now go call them and put them on standby, so all you have to say is 'Come now!' "

And Bruce went into the office to make preparations for the saving of Jim's life.

And Jim sang "Five to One." And I'll be damned if he didn't get the take. His rhythm was a little off in the "get together one more time" section—he came in on the wrong beat—but it was such an impassioned performance that we put it on the record. And the healthy young son of a bitch kept drinking and never did hit the floor. Of course, a few years later he was dead because of nights like this . . . but for now that return phone call to the paramedics never had to be made.

I was in the bathroom as Jim was onto his third take and Sable spilled into the men's room. She had broken a heel and was listing to port. She had also popped a few more pills before Paul stashed the

baggie in his briefcase—no one was getting any more of that poison—so she lurched about like a novice deckhand on a December
North Atlantic crossing.

"This is the men's room, Sable."

"I can't find the fucking ladies' room. Is it okay if I go in here?"
Slur city. Christ, lay off the downers, babe.

"Sure, Sable. Who cares?"

"I don't care." She smiled at me. A most seductive smile, come
hitherish in a tawdry way.

I looked her up and down. A nice piece of work . . . but totally
gone and blowzed out. And then I noticed her thigh. It wasn't a
birthmark. It was a bruise. All blue and almost green at the perime-
ter, and red and raw at the center. It had about an eight-inch diame-
ter and it looked like it hurt like hell. Or would have without the
downs.

"Jesus, Sable. What happened to your leg?" I asked. "Did you
get in an accident or something?"

"No, nothing like that," she slurred, with *that* coming out of her
numb, lewd lips like "thash."

"Did you fall off your high heels, then?"

"No, nothing like that."

"Well, what . . . ?"

"Jim hit me with a fucking board."

We sent her home in a cab. Jim, too.

☼

In the summer of '68, *Waiting for the Sun* became the number-one
album in America. "Hello, I Love You" became the number-one single the same week. And José Feliciano's Latino version of "Light
My Fire" was racing up the charts. It was number thirty on the *Billboard* Hot 100 that same week. It would become numero uno in
about four more weeks. We played the Hollywood Bowl on the
Fourth of July weekend and filmed the entire concert. Paul Ferrara,
a UCLA Film School buddy, was our director of photography. The
concert was sold out. The Stones were there. It was a big success. If
you're interested, you can see a video of the performance. It's
called—appropriately enough—*The Doors Live at the Hollywood Bowl*
and it's on Universal Home Video.

Everything was going great, and then Jim walked into the office one day and said to me—the hammer was about to fall again—"Ray, I wanna quit."

I couldn't believe it! We had the number-one single and the number-one album. We were realizing our goal. The dream we had together on Venice Beach in the summer of '65 was a reality. All the hard work had paid off. We were there. On top. It wasn't a dream, a fantasy of two college guys who wanted to be like the Beatles and the Rolling Stones. It was reality! We *were* like them. And this was just the beginning. The cinema was next. And then politics. Man, we had a long way to go. And he wants to quit? My mind went blank. I couldn't even think. Could you?

"Why?" was all I could manage to say.

He paced the room. Kathy was at her desk, jaw unhinged. Leon was at his PR desk, staring. Unbelieving.

"I just can't take it anymore," he finally said.

I was incredulous. This was *easy.* Rock and roll was the easiest and most lucrative thing I had ever done. And what an art form! What a great way to make a living. We were doing everything we wanted to do, creatively and artistically. The future was ours . . . and it was unlimited.

"What are you talking about, man? This is easy."

He looked at me. He looked tired. His eyes looked tired.

"I'm tellin' you, Ray, I can't take it."

"But we don't tour that much. It's not like we're on the road for months on end." I began to pace the room as Jim flopped down on the couch. The tension was sucking the air out of the room.

"Want a beer, Jim?" asked Kathy.

"Yeah, Kathy. I need one."

Kathy ducked into Siddons's room, to the mini-fridge, and rushed back with a Tecate.

"We go out for a weekend or so and then we come home," I said. "Four, five gigs at the most, and we're back in L.A. We don't go out more than every other week. Do you think we're working too hard?"

"No, man. It's not that . . . it's . . ." He glugged the Tecate. Left me hanging there. I jumped into the void space. I needed to fill the silence. I was panicking. We all were.

"The recording studio is easy. It's not too hard making records, is it?"

"No . . ." He drank again. He seemed to need it. He drank as if his body, or some deep place in him needed the alcohol.

"Man, this is everything we worked for, Jim. We're there! And this is just the beginning."

His head slouched down. He half mumbled under his breath, "I don't think I can take it anymore."

That stopped me. It froze me. I could only stare at him. He finished the beer, far too quickly. Finally, I spoke.

"But . . . why, Jim? What's wrong?"

His head slowly came up. Our eyes met.

"I think I'm having a nervous breakdown."

Kathy gasped. Leon dropped his fan magazine to the floor. They didn't say a word.

"Oh, man. No, you're not. You're just drinking too much. It's starting to get to you."

"No, Ray. I'm telling you . . . I'm having a nervous breakdown. I want to quit."

Panic attack again. My heart was racing.

"You can't quit. Not now!"

"You guys can go on without me. Get another singer, or something."

"I don't want to work with another singer. I wanna work with *you*. Jesus Christ, Jim, I never said this before . . . but, I love you."

He looked up at me again. Through those too-old eyes.

"I love you, too, Ray."

"Well, Christ, let's not break it up now. I'll tell you what . . . let's give it six months. If you feel the same way then, we'll break the band up."

"And you'll go on without me?"

"Jiiimm"—I was sounding like Pam—"I don't want to think about that now. I just want you to feel good." I sat down next to him. Put my arm around his shoulder. "You're not having a nervous breakdown, you're just tired. You gotta stop burning the candle at both ends."

He smiled for the first time. "Yeah, I guess I do get a little excessive."

The tension was broken. The air came back into the room. Kathy, Leon, and I laughed.

"Just a bit," I said.

"Okay, six months," Jim said. "But I tell ya, Ray. I think I'm having a nervous breakdown."

Kathy finally spoke. "Jim . . . go home and go to bed. Just let Pam take care of you for the next couple of days. You need to rest."

"Yes, Mother," Jim responded.

"And don't drink," I added.

"I don't know about *that*, Ray."

And he stood up and headed for the door. "Don't call me for a couple of days, Kathy."

"I won't, Jim," she said.

And then he looked at me, and his eyes became vulnerable. "I don't feel so good, man." And he was out the door.

After he left, I thought, Freddy and Wes. Guns and booze. I'm not gonna let him break the band up because of too much drinking and craziness with ne'er-do-wells. And pilled-out Jaguar rich-girl trash. Fuck them. He's got work to do and he's going to do it. He's got a gift like few others have and he's going to share it with the world. He belongs to the people. To all of us. He's not going to dissipate his poetic gift with guns and whiskey and downs. I won't let him stop writing and singing to throw it all away on side arms, black beauties, and firewater. Nervous breakdown? Bullshit!

Now, however, I realize he *was* having a breakdown. It was an impending psychological split. Jimbo was trying to take over. To destroy the band. To kill the shaman. To silence the poet. Jimbo, with the help of those cowboys, was seeking dominance. He was trying to obliterate the Jim Morrison I knew and create a new, degenerate persona . . . Jimbo the shit-kicker. Jimbo the evil. Jimbo the dogman.

That day in the office, Jim knew he was in a battle for his soul. He knew he was up against a formidable opponent. He just didn't know *whom* he was fighting. All he could feel was that he was being torn apart. Ripped in two. And he came to us for help. Jim didn't want Jimbo to take over but he was losing the battle on his own. If only I had known then what I know now. I could have helped him.

But I was so caught up in the moment, in the joy of it all, in the thrill of riding to the top of the charts, in the giddiness of realizing our dream, in the delight of being flush for the first time in my life, in the exuberance of being the number-one band in America . . . that I never wanted it to end. I wanted the high, the rush, the trip to last forever. I was hooked. I was so in love with the dream that I wanted it to go on and on and on. Into infinity. Into the mystic. Forever. Wouldn't you?

europe and *the soft parade*

In the next six months, Jimbo made only sporadic appearances. Jim abandoned Freddy and Wes and their arsenal and took up with Paul Ferrara, Babe Hill, and Frank Lisciandro. If he was going to have a Doors substitute, this trio was at least more life-affirming. Paul and Frank were from UCLA. They were artists. They were good men. Degeneration was not their goal. Art was. And Babe, who was Paul's buddy, was a roly-poly, jolly dude with a good heart, a thirst for firewater and an unfortunate nose for trouble. Jim and Babe really hit it off. So well, in fact, that an Ingmar Bergman *Persona* trip began to happen.

They were all going to work on the editing of the footage Paul had shot of the Doors on the road. They were going to construct a documentary film. A full-length, ninety-minute feature. A rock and roll documentary to be shown in art house movie theaters. That was the publicly stated reason for their bonding and for the rental of an office/editing space in the inappropriately named Clear Thoughts building just down the street on La Cienega. Clear thinking was *not* what was going to be done in that editing room. It was going to be a clubhouse. A hangout for Jim's new little gang. For the next faux Doors.

You see, he wanted drinking buddies and the Doors just wouldn't drink together. We'd make art with him but we wouldn't carouse with him. We'd make him famous but we wouldn't go on a midnight creep with him. And as the success and fame came too easily, Jimbo wanted action! And that began and ended with booze.

Sure, we'd have a couple of beers together during rehearsal . . . but the hard stuff, forget it. I was a gin and tonic with a lime man. Bourbon did nothing for me, except in a mint julep. Jim was a brown spirits man, exclusively. A real drinker. Kentucky bourbon and Tennessee whiskey, brandy and cognac. John and Robby were ayurvedic pear-apple guys, so there was *no* barroom communication with them.

I tried to drink with him on occasion. The last time was in New York City. One of those Irish Shamrock bars on Sixth or Seventh in Midtown Manhattan. Vaguely tawdry and bummy. Kerouac-like. A place for *men* to drink and talk. Also a place for rummies and alkies. If you had the wit, you could kill an evening in a bar like that. If not, you could kill yourself.

We had played a gig or done a television show or given a press conference or . . . I don't what. But we had time to kill and a gig the next night in New Jersey. Robby and John were off on a juice fast to cleanse their colons of compacted fecal matter or some such macrobiotic excess, so Jim and I headed for the Shamrock. I was going to drink brown with him that night. Brown for brown. At Kerouac's bar. Like a couple of Beat acidheads on the road of life. A shot of Jack Daniel's and a small tap-beer chaser. Chicago style. Workingman style. Like men, ya know? Like poets and artists and musicians with *cojones*. Macho drinking. Drinking to loosen the tongue. Drinking for the sake of alcohol. Not for taste or refreshment but for intoxication, and what might happen or be said before the blackout came.

And, man, we knocked 'em back. Hard and fast. And we waxed philosophical and probably—although I can't remember—solved the world's economic, spiritual, ecological, and population problems. And the shots kept coming and the chasers kept appearing. And I got totally shit-faced. And I can drink. Hell, show me a Polish guy who *can't* drink and I'll show you Chopin. But I couldn't keep up with Morrison. He had obviously been in training, working on his endurance. I had the form but I didn't have the stamina. He was ready for fifteen rounds, I had to bail at twelve.

I looked up at the clock. Blur city. Now, refocus, Ray. Up high. On the wall. Distance vision. And I got it . . . two A.M. Whoa, no wonder I'm looped. I told him . . .

"I can't go on, man."

"I understand."

"I'm snookered, man."

"Shit, me too," he laughed.

"It's my bedtime, man."

"So let's go."

"That's just it, I don't know if I can make it across the street."

"Don't worry, Ray. I'll hold you up."

"I don't need to be held up. I just don't know if I can make it across the street."

"So, I'll hold you up."

"I don't need that. I just need to see if I can stand."

"Go ahead, man. I'll hold you up."

"Jesus, is that all you can say?"

He started giggling. "Yeah . . . I'll hold you up."

"Fuck you. I'm standing up now. Don't hold me, all right?"

"What if you fall?"

"I'm not gonna fall . . . I'm just worried about crossing the street. You understand?"

"Yeah." He laughed and his elbow slipped off the bar. He hit his chin on the rail. "Ouch! Motherfuckin' bar."

I stood up as he rubbed his chin. I made it.

"Hey, I'm standing."

"See? You'll make it."

I was holding on to the rail and then *my* hand slipped. I sent two half-filled beer glasses flying, spilling suds all over us, the bar, and the back-bar display of liquor. Jim grabbed me before I hit the floor.

"I gotcha, Ray. See . . . I told ya. I'll hold you up."

And we headed for the door. Out onto the now-empty Manhattan streets, a cold wind in the air. Burning in the face. The cold help-ing to focus the mind. We had to cross the street and stagger down a block to the Windsor. And damned if we didn't make it. And it was cold. We giggled and staggered and laughed and stumbled our way down the avenue to the safety of the hotel, through the revolving doors—that was tough—and into the warmth of the lobby. We made it! And I didn't fall. And neither did Jim. Although I came close a couple of times and he *did* hold me up. And he was drunk, too. But I was blotto.

"I don't know what room I'm in, Jim. I can't remember."

"Do you have your key?"

I searched my pockets. "Yeah, I got it."

"Well, look at it. Does it have a number?"

I couldn't see shit. Close vision. Focus the eyes on the palm of your hand. You can do it, Ray. Close in. "Yeah . . . 1814."

"That's your room number."

"That's fuckin' clever of them, ya know?"

"Come on, get in the elevator." He half carried me in and pressed floor eighteen. "Go to bed. I'll see you in the morning." He smiled. "We got a gig tomorrow, remember?"

"Ohh, shit!" was all I could say. "Where you goin'? Aren't you goin' up?"

"You can make it from here. I'm gonna get a cigar." And the doors closed. I don't remember going to bed.

The next day I woke up with one of the worst fucking hang-overs of my life. Mean and hard in the head with bad nausea in the gut. I could feel my blood rushing into my brain with each heart-beat . . . and it hurt. My blood hurt my brain. It was too aggressive. Couldn't it be subtler? Did it have to do such wild racing and coursing through my veins? I staggered to the bathroom, drank a glass of water—my mouth had gone Mojave—and immediately threw up in the toilet. That helped. The nausea subsided a bit. And then the phone rang!

"Are you ready to go, Ray? We'll be leaving in a half hour," said a too-cheery Bill Siddons.

"It's fucking morning," I mumbled. "Why are we leaving in the morning?"

"Sorry, Ray. It's two o'clock in the afternoon."

"Ohh, shit." I hung up.

Somehow I made it downstairs. Everyone was milling about in the lobby . . . except for Morrison! Ahh-ha! I thought to myself. He's as bad as I am. Maybe worse.

"Where's Jim?" I asked Siddons. "Isn't he down yet?" Hoping he wasn't. Hoping that he couldn't take it, either. Hoping that he had a killer hangover, too.

"Oh, he's in the bar with Tom Baker."

I couldn't believe it! In the bar? How the fuck could he do it? I had to see for myself. I went in and sure enough . . . there he was. With another Irish reprobate. The star of Andy Warhol's *I, A Man;* Tom, A Baker, as we later called him. I staggered up to them. Jim saw me, turned, and gave me a big smile. "How ya doin', Ray?"

"I'm fucked, man. How about you?"

And then came his unbelievable reply: "I'm fine, man. Why don't you sit down and have a drink with us?" And he downs his beer. I was incredulous! How the fuck could he do it?! Last night we drank drink for drink. I was completely wasted. Dying of angry blood in my brain, my stomach on the verge of purge. And he's at the bar? Having another? Impossible!

That was the last time I drank with Jim Morrison.

※

In September we went to Europe. With the Jefferson Airplane. What a double bill! Psychedelic West Coast acidheads take on the Old World. The Doors and the Airplane. In London. At the Roundhouse for the first gig. The place was packed and all the rock nabobs were there. Even the Sir Paul to be. And the Glimmer Twins, Mick and Keith. But without Brian, of course. They had destroyed him by then.

The Roundhouse was an ancient railroad engine turnabout and it was the hippest venue in London. It was positively psychedelic. And that was a stretch for mod London. They were still very Carnaby Street. The swirling colors and amoeba shapes of psychedelic intoxication had not yet taken over as the "next hip thing." But it had at the Roundhouse. Liquid light projections. Guys and girls in Gypsy caravan garb. And 100-year-old dust everywhere. Man, it was funky. But we New World hippies didn't care. We were going to comply with Diaghilev's request and "astonish them." We were the real goods and we knew it.

The first night the Doors opened the show. It was a great performance and Jim was in top form. He manipulated that audience like a puppet master and was himself manipulated by various shamanic entities. He was at once possessed and in complete control. And he looked great and was straight-arrow sober to boot. He was in his motherland and he was going to show them what he could do. What secrets he had discovered. What lessons from ancient lands he had unearthed. And he wowed them. Our playing was brilliant and Jim black-mambaed the audience back to its pre-Christian, Briton/Celtic roots. And BBC Television was there, capturing it all on videotape. If you want to see us at the Roundhouse, it's available for home video rental on Granada Television and it's called *The Doors Are Open.*

The second night we followed the Airplane. They were inspired, and the beautiful Grace Slick sang like a possessed angel while Paul Kantner drove the band demonically through their repertoire. I'd never seen them better. And then it was our turn. And we did it again. The muse came — Euterpe in her soft, Greek robe — and blessed us with inspiration. The flames of Advent licked our foreheads and we were off. A journey into the unknown. And those neopagan English freedom seekers were right with us. We could have constructed a new Stonehenge with the collective energy being generated in that dusty old roundabout. What a grand night of Dionysian revelry.

Let's reinvent the gods,
All the myths of the ages,
Celebrate symbols from deep, elder forests.

And when the celebration had finally concluded, when the music was finally over and the venue was cleared of bacchantes, the Doors left their backstage dressing room sanctuary and headed out onto the streets of London town. And it was dawn! The sun was rising. We had played the entire night away and it was a new day. And we were in London.

It was good to be alive.

And then came Amsterdam. Jim simply passed out in the dressing room. A half hour before we were to hit the stage, Jim hit the floor. Too much fun, too much jet lag, too much hash, too much booze. Coming out of Germany that afternoon — after two lackluster days in Frankfurt—Bob "the Bear" Hite of Canned Heat gave Jim a small block of hashish. Just for fun. A kindly present. Something to share with the rest of the band. At the airport, Siddons said, "We're going through customs. This is Germany. If anybody's holding . . . get rid of it. And I mean now!" Jim fumbled in his pocket, took out the block of hash, looked at it for an instant, smiled to himself, and popped it into his mouth. He chewed it up and swallowed. He bought a quick beer and washed it down. It was gone! He wasn't holding. What had been intended for four guys and then some was consumed by the Doors' lead singer alone.

The Lebanese shit came on later in the day, after being mixed with far too many of those cute little airplane bottles of booze. Courvoisier and Chivas and Bailey's Irish Cream and a German schnapps and God knows what else. A lethal blend. And it hit him like Mike Tyson hit the skinny Spinks brother. Bam! Over and out. The end.

Jim had done a whirling dervish onstage with the Jefferson Airplane. They were singing "Somebody to Love" and Jim, hashish kicking in, joined them. He sang with Marty, danced with Grace, and egged the band on to a faster and faster tempo. They obliged—Paul later told me he thought it was all a big joke on Morrison's part—and Jim danced furiously, got caught up in mic cables, hit the floor, extricated himself, got back up, and dashed madly off the stage. He headed for the dressing room, opened a Heineken, drained it, and slowly slumped to the floor. Bam. Over and out. The end.

Siddons panicked. He held a mirror under Jim's nose to see if he was breathing (a premonition of Paris?). He was. Vince called the hospital for an ambulance. It arrived as the Airplane finished their set. The meds wrapped Jim in a rubber sheet, put an oxygen mask over his nose and mouth, and carried him out on a stretcher. Like a fucking cadaver. Pale and green and dead looking. And we're on in twenty minutes! A quick equipment changeover and the Doors are supposed to take the stage at the Royal Concertgebouw, Amsterdam, Holland. A beautiful, classical venue. Mozart had been played there. Bach, Beethoven, and Brahms. And now the Doors, minus Morrison.

Vince made an announcement to the audience.

"Jim Morrison will not be able to perform tonight. You can have your money back. Or, if you like, you can have the Doors . . . minus Morrison. It's your choice."

And that cool and hip Dutch audience began clapping in time and shouting, "Play Doors! Play Doors! Play Doors!" And it built to a thunder. No one wanted their money back. Vince moved Jim's vocal mike slightly stage left—exposing John to full view—to Robby's area. I already had a vocal mic set up and the three standing, surviving, sober Doors took the stage to a roar from those Dutch intoxicants. And we played and sang our asses off. Robby and I handled the vocals—rather well, I might add—and John, center stage for the first time in his Doors career, flailed away with demonic glee at not having Jim Morrison standing in front of him, hogging the spotlight. That night the spotlight belonged to John, and his starved, voracious ego loved it! His drumming was furious and fine. The guitar and organ solos were inspired . . . and the audience loved it all. We made it. Whew!

The next day there was a photo of John, flailing away, on the front page of one of the daily papers. He was in heaven. Beaming. His ego bloated and became insatiable. For a day, he actually thought *he* was the star. Delusions of grandeur.

Jim got out of the hospital, rested and ready to rock. No hangover, no damage. He didn't remember a thing after being onstage with the Airplane.

That afternoon we left for Copenhagen. Played a great concert the next night, a TV show the day after that, and Stockholm, Sweden, for two exceptional sets and the conclusion of our European tour.

We all went back to London. Robby and John and Siddons and Treanor split for the States. Jim and Pam took a flat in Belgravia for a month. Pam had secured it through an agency (another premonition of Paris) and stayed there, separate from the Doors tour. Dorothy and I visited them. It was squire Morrison and m'lady Courson. Swell digs. Nicely furnished in the English overstuffed chintz style. A fine reading chair for the squire and a charming dressing area for m'lady. It came complete with books in a vitrine, pots and pans and plates and flatware in the kitchen, and linens in a huge cupboard. It overlooked a small park. It was absolutely charming. They should have stayed there. They should have kept that flat instead of going to Paris.

They invited us over for breakfast. It was the most adult thing I ever saw Jim and Pam do. I was so proud of them. They were a couple. A man and a woman, a unit, making breakfast for their friends. We talked offhandedly about the tour and the current cinema and the vastness of the collection at the British Museum while the squire and his lady prepared rashers of bacon, fried eggs, toast with imported strawberry jam from Poland, and French roast coffee. It was all delicious, and so matter-of-fact, and so civilized. They were both to the manor born. They seemed quite at home and quite happy. It was the calmest and happiest I'd seen Jim since his "nervous breakdown." He was content, satisfied . . . and we never spoke again of breaking up the Doors.

Dorothy and I left for Los Angeles two days later. Within the week, Michael McClure, noted Beat poet and playwright, had joined them to discuss Jim's playing the role of Billy the Kid in a film adaptation of Michael's play, *The Beard*. They clowned around London together and then made drunken plans to visit the Lake Country and pay homage to the grave of Keats. They never quite made it. A little *too* tipsy, don't you know. Michael had read a manuscript of Jim's poetry that had been lying about the Belgravia flat and loved it. He suggested Jim publish a small, literary private edition of *The Lords, and The New Creatures*. Something personal, for friends.

> *Snakeskin jacket*
> *Indian eyes*
> *Brilliant hair.*
> *He moves in disturbed*
> *Nile insect*
> *Air*

It was a good time for Jim.

⚛

It was not a good time for America, however. Bobby Kennedy had been assassinated. Martin Luther King had been assassinated. There were riots in the streets of Chicago at the Democratic Convention. Young people were trying to stop the war and eventually the old people, the warmongers, would be killing *us*. Kent State University was the scene of a slaughter. The National Guard fired their rifles into a group of antiwar demonstrators and killed four students and wounded thirty. It was the beginning of the end of the dream of peace and love and equality. We realized that our own fathers would kill us. Jim *acted* out his Oedipal problems in "The End." It was a catharsis. But this was reality! And they would shoot us if they had to. The fascists were winning. And then they elected Richard Nixon. We began to rot from the top down. And then Charles Manson worked his evil voodoo on a group of runaways who became killers themselves . . . disemboweling Sharon Tate and the others at Roman Polanski's house. It was a despicable act. An act of madness. And we began to rot from our white trash roots up. Things would never be the same again. The war in Vietnam had driven the country mad. And there was no way out. We bear the burden of that madness even today. We are less than we could have been. The powers that be have put the fear into us. And we are their slaves. Except this time they have put the chains inside our brains. They control our imaginings, our desires. Our hearts are bound. Love does not prevail. And our dreams of the future are materialistic and, therefore, mundane. The Establishment has won. The fascists have won. The religious fundamentalists have won. For now!

I tell you this . . .
No eternal reward will forgive us now
For wasting the dawn.

We began the lengthy recording process of the Doors' fourth album, *The Soft Parade*. It was to be a sonic extravaganza, with horns and strings augmenting our basic guitar, keyboards, and drums sound. We were going to bring in jazz cats, country-and-western pickers, and classical players. Had synthesizers been more advanced, more user-friendly back then, I would have scored the whole thing myself. But after that Paul Beaver episode with the monster modular Moog, well, forget synths.

So off we charged . . . into "Tell All the People," the song that finally caused writer's credits to be attributed to each composition. Jim didn't want to say Robby's line "get your guns, follow me down," and Robby refused to change it. Jim didn't want people thinking he was advocating violence, so he said, "Well, let's make sure everyone knows you wrote it, Robby." That was the end of the composing credits "All compositions by the Doors." But we also had Robby's hit single "Touch Me"; a jazz-rock-inspired "Do It"; a country rocker—by way of Muddy Waters's "Got My Mojo Working"—called "Easy Ride"; Jim's autobiographical (and acknowledgment of Danny Sugerman) "Wild Child"; the jazzy, atonal, country-and-western "Running Blue"; the classical "Wishful Sinful"; and the very unusual four-part suite, "The Soft Parade."

I enjoyed the hell out of the production of the album. John didn't. He said Rothchild was pushing too hard, demanding too many takes, becoming too much of a perfectionist. Maybe he was . . . but it worked. I especially enjoyed working with Paul Harris on the arrangements for the tunes that were going to get a sonic wash of horns and strings. Harris did a beautiful job. Robby was indifferent to the process.

And Jim was elsewhere. Off editing with his three new "friends." The three UCLA Film School graduates—bachelor's degree in cinematography—were going for their imaginary master's. Jim and Ferrara and Lisciandro, assisted by Babe "the Blue Ox" Hill were going to cut the Doors documentary and take the film world by storm. They had become puffed up and arrogant—hubris had reared its ugly head again, as it so often does with the semi-talented. They had taken to calling themselves the "Media Manipulators." Now, Frank and Paul were old buddies of mine from UCLA. We had taken acid together. They were good guys and I was happy to see Jim hanging with them instead of Tom, A Baker, or Freddy and Wes. At least they were pursuing art. But "Media Manipulators"? I don't think so. I'd seen their student movies and they had a ways to go. But at least it was keeping Jim off the streets, and their editing suite was right across the boulevard from Elektra Records' new recording studio on La Cienega.

We were the first group to record there. We were all excited at the prospects of breaking the cherry of a brand-new, state-of-the-art recording studio. And we thought it was going to be for free. Hell, Jac Holzman built the damned place with the profits from Doors' record sales. Everybody called the new Elektra facility on La Cienega "the house the Doors built," so why shouldn't we record for free? Besides, it was an in-house studio. It would be for all Elektra artists. Outsiders could hire the studio at the going rates, but Elektra's own people could record there anytime they wanted and for free. Right? We were excited. Wouldn't you be?

Bullshit! No free time. No freebee recording sessions. Everybody paid. Strangers or family . . . everybody paid. However, Jac did say . . .

"Boys, I'll tell you what I'm going to do. For you . . ." And you could see the calculator in his head whirring. You could see that he wanted to be generous to us, he was on the West Coast now, he wore love beads, he had grown his hair long, he was not a crass materialist, he was a new man who believed in peace and love for all races, religions, creeds, and nationalities. But he was also from New York.

"For you . . . a ten percent discount!"

I almost snorted in his face. Jim just spun around on his heels, unable to face Jac. Robby rescued the situation as John tried to figure out how much a 10 percent discount would be.

"Uhh . . . thanks, Jac," said Robby. "That's great of you. We really appreciate that. Thanks again."

Jac beamed. He was proud of his New Age generosity and proud of the fact that he hadn't let the Doors play him for a sucker. He had it both ways, in his mind, and he was a happy man. We shook his hand and got the hell out of there as fast as we could. Beat a hasty retreat to the Doors' workshop across the street, killed a six-pack of Tecates, smoked a joint, and had a good laugh at Jac's "generosity." Oh, well, it was a great facility nonetheless. And *The Soft Parade* became one of our most innovative albums. Even if it did take an ungodly long time to complete. Perhaps too much "quest for perfection."

※

We did the Smothers Brothers' television show. "Wild Child" and "Touch Me," complete with horns and strings from the Smothers Brothers' pit band. We brought in Curtis Amy to lip-sync his brilliant solo on the ride-out. Everything was a lip and finger sync except for Jim. Rothchild and Botnick had made a mix of the songs without vocals. Jim had to sing live. He had to give an inspired performance on demand. Right then and right there. National television! Do it again, man. Be brilliant again! Summon up all your talents and abilities and psychic courage and be brilliant. Pay no attention to the artificiality of the surroundings. Pay no attention to the fact that the rest of the musicians are just goofing and playing to a prerecorded track. Pay no attention to the cameras in your face, the excessively bright lights, the cue to "go!"—just deliver brilliance. And, by God, he did! He was strong and handsome and masculine and sensitive. His tone was in great form. He was right on pitch and his voice was in a fine roundness, all rich and deep. His reading of the "I'm gonna love you" bridge section, the ballad section, was positively crooner like. He had approached his idol, Frank Sinatra, in mellow television romance pipes. It was cool. He was cool. We were all cool, but most of all, Curtis Amy. He was the coolest.

You can see the performance on our home video *Dance on Fire* on Universal.

And you can also see Robby's black eye. Jim and Robby both got punched out by some anti–long hair, hippie-hating rednecks a day or two before the TV show. Wearing long hair in those days was dangerous. It meant you were against the prevailing order of things. Against the war in Vietnam. Against the "decent, wholesome Christian values that have made this country great!" And, therefore, you had to be killed. Like the American Indians. Kill the hippies, kill the Indians . . . kill anything, as long as the white man prevails.

So Jim and Robby took a few blows for freedom of expression at a bar down the street on Santa Monica Boulevard. Unfortunately, Robby took one in the eye and it turned black.

When we got to the TV studio, the makeup people were aghast.

"You can't go on television with a black eye," said one.

"It's all black and blue and purple . . . and even green!" said another.

"Ewww, it's disgusting," said the campy male.

"Leave it," said Robby.

"What do you mean, 'leave it'?" said campy.

"I don't want any makeup."

"You have to have makeup. You simply have to."

"Everyone has makeup."

They were like a trio of harpies, hovering around Robby.

"Not me," said Robby. "I want people to see my black eye. It's kind of a badge of honor."

"It's disgusting!" said campy.

"Good. Leave it," said Robby.

"You can't just . . . leave it," said one.

"You must let us cover that eye for you," said the other.

Jim spoke up. Black snake to the rescue.

"Hey. If he doesn't want makeup . . . he doesn't have to wear any. Now leave him alone."

And they backed away. Very unhappy. Very disappointed.

And Robby Krieger went on national television, on the *Smothers Brothers Comedy Hour,* with a black eye. It was a first.

※

In between recording sessions for the album we played some monster gigs. Our first basketball arenas. The L.A. Forum—home of the Lakers—and Madison Square Garden—home of the New York Knicks. We took the horns and strings from the sessions with us. It was quite a spectacle. Very untypical for the Doors, but what the hell. At the Forum we had a Chinese classical musician play a pipa for the audience. They didn't get it. And we had Jerry Lee Lewis play his country set for the audience. They didn't get it. When we took the stage with the horns and strings—Curtis Amy on sax, George Bohanon on trombone and two jazz friends of theirs on trumpet and baritone sax plus violins, viola, and cello—they didn't get it. They only wanted "Light My Fire." That's all they knew and that's all they wanted. What a lame audience.

Jim was growing increasingly disgusted with audiences like that. They came for a show and not the music. They came to watch Jim become the "wild man." They didn't want intense psychic acts in the ether by the black-leathered lead singer. They wanted a freak show, a geek show, as the band played its most famous songs. Jim's reputation for outrageousness had set up an expectation in the minds of the cud types in the audience. And they didn't care squat for a Chinese lute player or a country-and-western singer—even if he was "the Killer"—or a jazz saxophone or a string quartet. They wanted visual antics. Wild, crazy shit. Mad dashings about the stage and amp leaping and rafter hanging and all manner of absurdo crap. Well, that's not why Jim and I formed the Doors. We wanted a rock band that could play jazz and blues and classical music with poetry floating over the top. An aesthetic little quartet. A hard-rocking, loud-as-hell, electronic, plugged-in version of the Modern Jazz Quartet. John Lewis and Milt Jackson on acid. Percy Heath and Connie Kay on hallucinogenics. Crazed but concise. Precision and abandon. Controlled compositions and free-form spontaneity. *That's* what the Doors were all about. And the audience was coming to see a freak show. What a drag. Jim was becoming increasingly bummed out with the audience's expectations of him. And it all culminated a few months later . . . in Miami.

※

But before the madness came a Buick car commercial fiasco. They wanted "Light My Fire" for a television commercial. But not for a big-ass Buick boat machine. Rather, for the neat little Buick Opel. A cute four-cylinder two-seater. Like a little Corvette but with a fuel-efficient engine and easily over forty miles to the gallon. It was both ecologically correct and stylish. I thought it was a use of technology geared toward the New Age. Lighter, smaller, cleaner, more efficient. Using our brains to save the environment while maintaining a lifestyle and standard of living we really couldn't live without. I wanted a simpler, more natural way of life but I wasn't a Luddite. I didn't want to abandon all technological advances. And here was one that made sense. A cool little car. And they wanted "Light My Fire" to sell it on the tube.

At the time, there was not a lot of rock and roll on television. There were no all-music channels on cable where you could see the latest hot video by the latest flavor-of-the-month rock band. Hell, there was no *cable*. Only the three networks and four or five local outlet stations. And hardly any rock and roll. Only on a couple of Saturday-morning local teen dance shows. And then on network *Ed Sullivan*. And that was·it. Our psychedelic, subversive rock music had not yet permeated the visual spectrum. That was to come much later. In our present era.

So to be asked to use a rock song over a commercial for a new, sharp little machine was at once lucrative *and* subversive. We could get "Light My Fire" played again on national television. We could get rock and roll on a medium that had very little to do with rock music. We could make a few inroads in the changeover of consciousness. Or so I thought. Back then. Back when I was a naïf.

I approved the request posthaste. So did Robby and John. Jim was nowhere to be found. He was on one of his now more frequent disappearing trips. Probably off cavorting with Jimbo. Or perhaps locked in *battle* with Jimbo. Wrestling for control. Fighting for the destiny of the entity christened James Douglas Morrison.

When he finally did show up a few days later, the Buick commercial was a fait accompli. They needed a yes or no immediately. We said yes and signed paper. Jim freaked.

"You can't have signed without me!" he yelled.

"Well, we did," I said.

"Why, man? We do everything together. Why'd you do this without me?"

"Because you weren't here," said Robby.

"So what? Couldn't you have waited for me?"

"Who knew when you were coming back?" added John.

"They needed an answer right away," I said. "So we signed."

"It's not like it's a typical Buick road hog or something," said Robby. "It's a cool little car."

"Gets real good mileage," said John.

"Four cylinders," I added. "A sports car. Two-seater."

"Fuck you!" shouted Jim.

A silence filled the rehearsal room. Jim had never screamed like that before. He was enraged. And he looked wasted. He looked as if his nerve ends were frazzled. He looked as if he had been doing things he shouldn't have. And now he was paying the physical price for his excess. And he looked shattered. He was clearly not in control of himself . . . or his emotions. He stomped around the room, agitated, hyper, angered.

"Fuck you guys!" he said again. "I thought it was supposed to be all for one and one for all. I thought we were supposed to be brothers!"

"Jiiim, we *are*, man!" I said in feeble response to his strange and terrible outburst. "Nothing has changed."

"You weren't here," said Robby.

"Everything has fucking changed, Ray!" Jim said. "Everything!"

"Why? I don't understand. Just because we signed a contract for a fucking song . . . why has everything changed?" I asked him.

And then he came back with a line that really hurt me. Hurt John and Robby, too. Stabbed the Doors in their collective heart.

"Because I can't *trust* you anymore," he snarled.

"But it's a good little car, man," protested John.

"It's fucking industry! It's corporate! It's the devil, you asshole." Jim glared. "You guys just made a pact with the devil."

"The hell we did," said Robby.

"Oh yes you did, Robby. He seduces you with cute little gas-efficient cars. He shows you what you want and then he puts a little twist in it. Makes you say yes to him when you know you shouldn't. . . ." He paced the room, manic. "But you go along with it because the deal's just too good. It tastes too good." And then he looked at me, "It's too much *money*, isn't it, Ray?"

"Fuck you, Jim." I was getting pissed, too.

"I know you, Ray. You're only in it for the money."

Another knife in the heart. Was this actually Jim saying these things? Did he really believe what he was saying?

"Well, I'm not in it for the fucking lifestyle, man," I snarled back. "I just wanna make music. And if we can make some money at it . . . that's cool with me."

"Lots of money," Jim sarcastically said under his breath.

"What'd you say?"

"You heard me."

He was really pushing it.

Robby jumped into the fray. "Why weren't you here, man? A big decision had to be made and you weren't here, again!"

"Where do you go all the time?" asked John.

"Wherever I want!" Jim shot back. "And it's none of your fucking business. You understand?"

John turned his eyes away from Jim's penetrating glare. Unable to confront him. Unable to say what was really on his mind. Hell, none of us could confront him. None of us had the psychic strength to call him on the carpet and read the riot act to him. It was probably just what he needed. Maybe even what he wanted.

"No one tells me what to do, John. You got that?"

I jumped in. "Nobody's telling you what to do, man. We just want to know how come you're never around when you're needed. Where the fuck were you?"

"We called everywhere," added Robby.

"You weren't home, you weren't at the Alta Cienega," I said. "We called Barney's, the Palms, the Garden District . . . you weren't at the Whiskey, Mario hadn't seen you in a couple of weeks."

"Even Babe didn't know where you were," said Robby.

Jim erupted again. "Hey! This isn't about where *I* go." Then, pointing an accusatory finger, "This is about *you* guys signing a contract without me."

A silence filled the room again. Jim had broken out in a sweat. I felt cold and clammy. The evil green thing began wrapping its tentacles around my stomach, probing for weakness. I didn't like this. I didn't like this at all.

I felt bad, hurt, misunderstood. Here I was trying to hold the whole damn thing together. Trying to be the adult. Jim had abandoned ship. He was over the top, gone. The Ray and Jim show from Venice no longer existed. I was the oldest. I had to try to maintain the dream, hoping he would snap out of this phase he was in. Hoping that it *was* a phase. An aberration, a momentary aberration. Hoping that he would come to his senses and we could resume our grail quest together. The four of us. The Doors. Brothers in the void. Supporting and nurturing one another. Hell, keeping one another alive! And we had so much more work to do. More music and poetry. Theater—Jim and I had talked of a multimedia theater project with actors and dancers and rear-screen projections and recitations and Doors' music—the "Magic Theater" of Hermann Hesse. Films, directed by me, starring Jim, music by Robby Krieger and John Densmore. And finally politics. The takeover of America by the lovers! He had to snap out of it. He had to come back to his old self. His *real* self.

"Well, it's too late," said Robby.

Jim wheeled on him. "Oh, yeah? We'll see about that. I'm gonna smash a fucking Buick to dust on the stage." He was perspiring more profusely now. "It's gonna be part of my new act. 'Smash a Buick to Smithereens.' We'll see how they like that. And then I'm gonna get Abe to sue their asses. For big fucking bucks, Ray. For a lot more than their shitty little contract. Then let's see if they still want to use a Doors' song to sell a sports car."

He was pacing and sweating and clearly out of control. He stormed out of the rehearsal room and rushed up to the offices, barged into Siddons's room and told Bill to get our new, young hotshot lawyer—Abe Sommers—on the phone. When he did, Jim got on the line and hollered at Abe to do whatever he could to stop the contract.

"Threaten them with a lawsuit," he shouted into the phone. "Tell them I'm gonna smash a Buick with a sledgehammer onstage! Tell them anything! But *stop* the fucking *contract!*"

And in three days, Buick backed out. They simply decided they didn't want to go with a rock and roll ad campaign after all. Nothing against the Doors or their music, you understand. They simply shifted demographic focus. It was done, finished. And Jim grinned from ear to ear. He had exercised his will against the corporate establishment and he was a contented man. He made them back down. Hell, he made them back all the way out. It felt good. And he wanted more.

And that was called . . . Miami.

miami

The Buick incident was behind us. Jim's tantrum had passed and he was back to his usual creative, witty, intellectual self. The Doors were a unit again. We were hard and heavy into the recording of *The Soft Parade* and playing gigs around the country. We were being creative and productive. Jim was also working on the editing of our film footage with his faux Doors substitute trio. Everything seemed to be going smoothly. And then the Living Theatre came to town.

Julian Beck and Judith Malina led a very avant-garde troupe that engaged in "confrontational" theater. A form of in-your-face, antagonistic, urgent, and angry performance art. They wanted to shake their audience awake. Awake to the suppression of the system. Awake to the evils of the military-industrial complex. They wanted freedom. Liberation. And their new play was called *Paradise Now*.

Jim was hooked immediately. The Living Theatre was in town

for six performances. He bought tickets for all of them. He went to *every* show. And he saw young New York theater people who looked like him, confronting the audience just as he did onstage. But they went further. They went even further than Jim. They took their clothes off. They were stark naked in most cities. However, the police in L.A. let them know ahead of time that they would be busted if anyone went nude. So the young players stripped down to jockstraps and bras and panties as they ranted their pleas for freedom. For *Paradise Now* they shouted, "I am not allowed to travel without a passport, I am not allowed to bathe in the sun, on the beach, as God created me . . . naked before the world," they implored. "I must pay taxes to support an unholy war against people who only want to unite their country. I don't believe in the war in Vietnam!" They were in everyone's faces, including Jim's. "We demand freedom! We want the Garden of Eden! We want paradise . . . now!"

Jim was mesmerized. He even joined the troupe onstage for the last performance. Ranting and raving himself. Leaping about the stage and shouting out his cries for freedom . . . and power. "We want the world, and we want it now!" He was exhilarated. He loved this confrontational theater. And then the idea struck him. He was going to do the same thing! He was going to confront *his* audiences with these cries for freedom. He was going to confront the Doors fans! And he was going to do it at our next gig. And that was . . . Miami.

It was a hot, southern, Tennessee Williams night in Dade County—the County of the Dead—Florida. Fifteen thousand people had been shoehorned into a decommissioned naval (appropriate) seaplane hangar that safely held ten thousand. The audience was moody and restless. The air was humid and slightly fetid. It smelled of the swamp. Of rot. There was an agitation in the mob. An expectation. They eagerly, almost hungrily, awaited the "Kings of Acid Rock." "The Kings of Orgasmic Rock." They were keenly aware that the "Lizard King" himself was going to take the stage that night. Their own Florida native son was returning to his mother state after undergoing a metamorphosis in the crazed hippie land far off to the West. They didn't know *what* to expect. And Robby, John, and I had no idea of what Jim was planning. He never said a word about a "confrontation" with the Miami audience. And he certainly never said a word about taking his clothes off.

And that's exactly what he tried to do onstage. He was overly fortified with alcohol. He had used the spirits to screw up his courage, but he had gone too far and was all semi-sloppy-drunk. But, Lord, was he ranting! He was at once berating the audience for their cudlike acceptance of both authority and the status quo, and at the same time imploring them to love one another . . . and him.

"Love, love, love," he shouted. But he also shouted, "You're all a bunch of idiots! How long are you going to let them rub your face in the shit of the earth?" He was livid and apoplectic. "Maybe you like it. Maybe you love getting your face stuck in the shit. Maybe you love getting pushed around." And the band played like maniacs. Making unearthly noises. Making the sounds of tormented slaves. Of souls in hell.

"You're all a bunch of slaves!" he continued, inspired by our sonic anguish. "Letting everybody push you around. What are you gonna do about it? What are you gonna do about it?" He said it over and over and over, as if he had gone insane, screaming a mantra to himself and to the world and maybe even to God. "What are you gonna do about it?!" And we crashed on our instruments as the audience pushed and shoved against the rickety, temporary scaffolding stage. Attempting to get closer to him. To touch him. To be somehow electrified by the placing of hands against his energy. Seeking the blue spark. I felt the stage begin to list. It was going to go. I knew it was only a matter of time. We were in a near riot situation. And, quite frankly, I loved it. It was Jim at his drunken best. If he *was* going to be a rummy, at least *this* was a boozer with balls. With something to say. Even if he was completely mad. John, of course, hated it. But he stuck it out to the bitter end and played like a possessed madman himself.

And then Jim's mood abruptly changed and he was talking about love again. "Hey, I'm not talkin' about no revolution! I'm not talkin' about no demonstration. I'm not talkin' about no riot in the streets. I'm talkin' about dancing. I'm talkin' about love your neighbor! [Sound familiar, sound like the rabbi from Galilee?] I'm talkin' about grab your friend. I'm talkin' about *love!* Love, love, love!"

And so it went. Back and forth. Between love and hate. At one point Jim dropped a clue as to the Living Theatre inspiration for this chaos. "Now listen," he said to his assembled multitude, "I used to think the whole thing was a big joke. I used to think it was something to laugh about. And then the last couple of nights I met some people who were doing something. They're trying to change the world, and I wanna get on the trip. I wanna change the world!" And the audience cheered and shoved and swirled in the fetid heat of that overstuffed seaplane hangar in the County of the Dead. It was *Suddenly Last Summer* and Sebastian was about to be devoured. And the band played on. Into that crazed night.

"There are no rules! There are no laws!" he continued. "Do whatever you want to do! Do it! Be free!"

And we tried "Touch Me" and "Love Me Two Times" and "When the Music's Over." But the audience didn't care. They just wanted more! More of everything. More chaos, more madness, more show. More ranting and raving. More insanity. Jim had become a crazed prophet in the desert at the dawning of a new age. Calling for each of *us* to become the Messiah. There would be no leader this time around. No second coming. No *moshiach* this time around. The Piscean Age was over. Aquarius was dawning. And we would all have to live as our *own* authorities. Beholden to no one but the Creator. And we are *all* the Creator. Aren't we?

"I'm talkin' about havin' fun," he shouted. "I'm talkin' about dancing. I want to see you people dancing in the streets this summer. I want to see you have some fun. I want to see you roam around. I want to see you paint the town. I want to see you wring it out. I wanna see you shout. I wanna see some fun. I wanna see fun from everyone!" And he started to take his shirt off as the audience screamed their approval and solidarity with this John the Baptist of the New Age. I thought, Oh shit, he's gonna get naked. It's so fucking hot in here, the drunken skunk is gonna take all his clothes off. And I knew *that* was a bust.

"Vince, stop him," I shouted to our equipment chief. Vince divined the situation immediately and wrestled with Jim in front of the multitude. The shirt did come off but the pants stayed on. And, oddly, there were boxer shorts beneath the leather pants. Jim was wearing cotton boxer shorts. And the top was up above his navel as the leathers rode his hips. It was not a good look. Why was he wearing those stupid boxers? He quickly folded them down to the top of his leathers and jammed them in. And then he said the fateful line.

As he was stuffing his boxers into his leathers he said . . . "Hey, any-body want to see my cock?" The audience roared its approval. Lions were going to eat Christians.

"Oh, I see. You want spectacle, don't you." He was on to them and the lust of their eyes. "You didn't come to hear a pretty good rock and roll band play its music. You came to *see* something, didn't you?" A surge in the wave of humanity forced itself against the scaffolding, and the stage moved ominously. The crowd had become an amoeba, filling every available space around us. If the stage were to collapse, it would crush hundreds of people. They would be pinned and wedged between metal bars and crushed by the weight of amplifiers and speakers and instruments and roadies and musi-cians and wooden planking. And the ship of fools' deck was listing, hard. We had left Tennessee Williams country and entered the pages of Nathanael West's *Day of the Locust*. And Jim continued over the roar of the lions.

"You came to see something greater than you've ever seen be-fore. You want to watch, don't you?" They shouted their agreement. "You came to watch me *do* something. You didn't come to listen. You didn't come to listen to *music*. You came to the circus!" He paced the stage with his shirt in one hand, dragging it, and the mic in the other. "Well, what can I do? What can I show you?" He placed the mic on its stand and held the shirt in front of his crotch. He had the idea. He was going to top the Living Theatre. "How about if I show you my cock? How about if I whip it out . . . right here!" And he began fum-bling behind his shirt, as if he were opening his button fly. No one could see a thing. His shirt covered everything. "Okay, I'm gonna show it to you." And he fumbled some more and appeared to take it out of his pants. And then he took the shirt in both hands, holding it like a bullfighter's cape, in front of his groin. "Okay, watch now . . . here it comes!" And he pulled the shirt/cape quickly aside — *swish* — and then back in place. "Did you see it? Did you see my cock?" Again the lions roared. But they hadn't eaten their Christian meat, yet. "Do you want to see it again? Watch close now." And Manolete did another pass with his cape. The shirt was whipped away and then back in place, concealing everything. Exposing nothing. "There, I did it! Did you see it? Are you happy now? Want to see it again?" The audience went mad. They roared, howled, surged, pushed, crushed, and screamed. The stage bobbed and shook and listed. The musicians pounded and flailed. Great fear was in John's eyes, but he kept playing. Robby's face had gone pale blank, but his guitar kept howling. I was caught between fear for the crowd, fear for Jim's possible arrest, fear for my own safety, and a crazed, rebellious exhilaration. *This* was what rock and roll was all about. I was experiencing the end times. The end of this damnable kali-yuga. It was the apocalypse . . . now!

"Now, look close, I'm only gonna show you my cock one more time," he shouted into the mic. And he moved back from the lip of the stage. Back to John's drums, all the while holding his cape in front of him. And then he did a pass. And a great "Olé!" rose up in my mind's ear. The *corrida* roared and applauded. "Olé!" And the bastard did it again. The bull charged and Manolete swished his cape and the crowd roared. And nothing could be seen! Nothing! That son of a bitch Jim Morrison had teased and taunted and cajoled that crowd into believing he had shown them his cock. Hell, he had hypnotized them. He had created a religious hallucination. Except this time the Holy Mother or her crucified son was nowhere to be seen. This time it was snakes! The audience saw snakes where there were no snakes. They saw his cock—and swear to this day that they saw his cock—where there was no cock. The lying dog Jim Morrison had conned them. Had conned *us*, had conned the whole damned County of the Dead.

Folks, he never exposed himself. But it's become a myth, hasn't it? It's become an American rock and roll myth. And it's a lot more fun to believe the myth, isn't it? So we do.

And Manolete's cape became Jim Morrison's shirt as Jim stopped playing Lilly St. Cyr and got dressed. He slipped easily into his sleeves after appearing to put his tool away and rebutton his pants. And it was done. We broke into "Light My Fire." The crowd loved it. It was the song they had come to hear and Jim Morrison had hypnotized them into believing they had seen his cock. It was everything they wanted. The only thing left for them to do was to devour the band. It was now time for the blood sacrifice of Dionysus and his musicians. And they began to surge onto the stage as Jim called to them, "Hey, come on. I need some love. Come on up here and love my ass. Come on! All those people sitting way over there, man. Why don't you all come down here and get with us, man. Come on! Everybody! Come on. Come on down here. Get closer! We need some love!"

And they followed his orders and began to take the stage. It listed more. It was going. The ship was sinking. And the security force—University of Miami football players and a handful of Dade County police—took up defensive positions and began shoving and throwing the stage climbers back into the audience. Bodies were flying everywhere. Chaos reigned. Jim was ecstatic. John had left the stage, unable to take any more. Robby was holding his guitar close to his chest to prevent its being destroyed in the mêlée. And I played the riot. I smashed and pounded on the Fender Rhodes and jammed the Vox pedal to maximum volume as I mashed on the keys. Someone had to score the collapse of Western civilization. And bodies kept hurtling and charging and flailing about. Jim even got into the act. He pushed a security guy off the stage! Not the kids, but a security guy. What an anarchist. One of the beef monsters saw it happen and grabbed Jim and threw *him* off the stage. Oh, shit, he's gonna break his neck, I thought. But the inventor of the stage dive was saved once again. The maenads caught the flying Dionysus and gently lowered him to the ground. Whereupon, he began to dance with them in a swirling vortex that shape-shifted into a snakelike conga line as Jim worked his way through the crowd, his followers behind him. And that damned satyr was there, too, cackling and hopping on his goat hooves. What a night for that little beast. Exactly the kind of action he had come back for. And Jim headed toward the stairway that led up to the second-floor dressing room. He hit the stairs, the security held back the snake line, he rushed up, stood at the top step, waved to the crowd, and disappeared into the sanctuary of the dressing room. "Dionysus has left the building!"

My job was finished. I stopped playing as, sure enough, the stage listed to starboard and very slowly pointed its nose down to the ground. It was all in slow motion. No one got hurt. And everyone had a grand time. What a concert! What a night! What craziness!

Of course there would be a price to pay. The authorities would not allow the Doors—those damnable self-proclaimed "Kings of Acid and Orgasmic and Lizard King Rock"—to have that much fun and create a mass hallucination in fifteen thousand young people, and think they could simply walk away from such madness scot-free.

Oh, no! Someone was going to pay for unleashing snakes and maenads and satyrs. And that someone was . . . Jim Morrison.

⋇

We were busted four days later. We were all in the Caribbean. Jim, Robby, and John in Jamaica, and Dorothy and I on the French island of Guadeloupe. My wife and I did Adam and Eve naked-in-Paradise walks on a deserted beach at the end of the butterfly-shaped island. We stood naked in the soft azure shore break and watched a baby octopus in a tidal pool expand and contract itself as it swam from rock to rock, flaring its tentacles like an unearthly underwater alien. It was beautiful. Rainbow-hued reef fish darted through the crystalline pools, and the sky was filled with great, rolling cumulus clouds. Huge cotton-candy puffs of whiteness set against a penetratingly clear blue sky. It was paradise.

"I love you, Mrs. Manzarek," I said as I wrapped my arms around her supple, golden body.

"I love you, too . . . husband." And she kissed me. Her essence kissed me. The *I Ching*'s female principle kissed me. It was overwhelming.

And I became the male principle. And we made love. On that deserted beach, somewhere below the Tropic of Cancer.

> *Tropic corridor,*
> *Tropic treasure,*
> *What got us this far to this*
> *Mild equator?*

Our marriage was truly consummated. And we were finally having our honeymoon. Dorothy and I ate fresh-caught lobster, flambéed in cognac, and drank planter's punch. We bought little trinkets in the charming capital town of Pointe-à-Pître. We stayed at L'Auberge de la Vieille Tour, an old sugar mill converted to a *luxe* resort hotel. We basked in the sun and in the soft, sensuous love of each other's arms. It was paradise.

And then the phone call came. "You're busted," said Bill Siddons.

"How can we be busted? We're in Guadeloupe," I said into the French phone. "Where are the other guys?"

"In Jamaica," said Bill.

"Well, how can we be busted? We're free. We got away. They didn't bust us in Miami . . . how can they bust us in the middle of the Caribbean?"

"It's after the fact, Ray. They didn't take out warrants until yesterday. They're claiming that if they would have arrested Jim at the gig there would have been a riot," said Bill.

"There *was* a riot!" I shouted into the phone. "That's bullshit. They're lying dogs. We drank beers with the cops in the dressing room after the concert. Nothing happened."

"I know. I was there. I even paid one of them fifty bucks for the hat he lost onstage."

"You mean the hat Jim ripped off his head and threw into the audience?"

"Yeah, that one."

"Christ, they devoured that hat like sharks on a wounded tuna."

"Yeah, the audience loved the whole show."

"So did I . . . it was crazy."

"John didn't like it, though. He's pissed."

"When isn't he?"

We both laughed at the foibles and anguish of John Densmore, Doors' super drummer and resident whiner.

"So what do we do?" I asked Bill.

"Finish up your vacation and then come home."

"Home? I thought we had Jacksonville next."

"Not anymore. They canceled."

"Well, what's after that?"

"Nothing. They're all canceling."

We had booked our first real tour. Miami was the first gig of a twenty-city jaunt across the country. We had never done more than four gigs in a row. This time we were going to barnstorm the entire country. Siddons had been planning it for weeks. He had been working like a dog and had done a superb job. And it all fell apart. Like falling dominoes. One after another. They all canceled. The way Southeast Asia was supposed to fall to the Communist hordes, our tour fell.

Public performance permits for the Doors were revoked in Jacksonville, Philadelphia, Providence, Toronto, Pittsburgh, Detroit, Cleveland, Cincinnati, Salt Lake City, Dallas, Houston, Boston, Syracuse, and all the rest. We were personae non gratae. We couldn't play anywhere. We had caused an outrage and the press had a field day. Jim was on the cover of *Rolling Stone* magazine in a mock-up western-style wanted poster. "Wanted in the County of Dade (the dead). For: Lewd and lascivious behavior in public by exposing his private parts and by simulating masturbation and oral copulation. A Felony: Jim Morrison of the Doors." Articles appeared slamming the "dirty Doors" in every city we were to play. It seemed the entire country was outraged at Jim Morrison's penis. His male member had driven them irrational. (Pan and that damned little satyr again.) "Rallies for Decency" were convened in the name of "decent, wholesome, traditional Christian values." Thousands attended. None was quite so spectacular as the one held at the Orange Bowl in Miami, however. It's rumored that upwards of fifty thousand people attended the rally hosted by Jackie Gleason (notorious reprobate) and Anita Bryant (homophobic orange juice queen). Local bands provided the music in between the speeches exhorting the youth of Dade to keep their flies zipped. Hell, they could have had the Doors. All they would have had to do was ask us. We would have played. Bigger crowd than we had in the hangar.

Well, it was all a fiasco. We went home and entered the doldrums ourselves. We sat around doing nothing. We watched the charts, and *The Soft Parade* did so-so. A lot of radio stations refused to play the Doors. Jim hardly spent any time editing film with his trio of "Media Manipulators." He was bored with the laborious process. He mainly drank with Babe down at the Palms. He was even beginning to look like Babe. He seemed to be adopting a new persona. He sported a full, bushy beard, and the high-caloric booze consumption was packing on the pounds. He was beginning to look like a disciple of Bacchus. No longer a lean Dionysian. No longer the young god of resurrection. Of rebirth. Of freedom and rebelliousness. Of the dark and green and fecund powers of the underground.

It was beginning to seem as if Jim would never be that again. It was time for me to do something to save him. To *try* to save him. If that was possible.

At rehearsal, I talked to John and Robby. Jim was off, who knew where, with Babe.

"We have to confront him," I said. "We've got to sit him down and tell him to stop drinking. Face-to-face."

John breathed a huge sigh of relief. "I've been waiting for you to say this for a long time, Ray."

"Well, it's time now." I said. "*I* was waiting for the real Jim to come back. I thought it was all a phase he was going through."

"It's no phase, Ray. It *is* Jim," said John.

"I don't know if the guy you knew will ever come back, man," Robby said. "But we have to try something . . . before it's too late."

"I'm going to call a meeting for the four of us."

"Where?" asked John.

"We shouldn't do it here," said Robby. "Too many ears."

John said, "Can we do it at your father's house, Robby?"

"Sure. If we can get him there."

"I like that idea," I said. "It's quiet and your father's vibes are there. It's serious."

"It's not gonna be easy," John said.

"Jim's not gonna like it," Robby said. "If he shows up at all."

"He'll show up." I said. "He has to."

We resolved to confront him that week. And it was a hard resolution to make. The sixties were a non-confrontational time. You didn't get in someone else's face. You let everyone "do their own thing." *Whatever* that might be. An entire generation didn't want to become authorities with one another. Saying "do this, don't do that." That was bullshit. That was for the Establishment. For the fascists, the military, the generals, the admirals, the organized religions, the industrialists, the politicians. For Nixon, our new president. For all of them. *They* would tell you what to do. Hell, they *loved* telling other people what to do.

But not the new people. Not the psychedelic people. We left each other alone. Free to go about our own business in our way. Free from moral confrontations.

And here we were. Robby, John, and Ray. About to confront our friend, our singer, our poet. About to confront Jim. It was anathema. It was scary. But it had to be done. And there was no support group to help us. No twelve-step, no Musician's Assistance Program, no detox, no Betty Ford clinics, no nothing. None of that existed yet. Only AA, and that was for old winos and left-over fifties rummies. Strictly skid row and *Days of Wine and Roses* types. We were on our own.

The next day, I told Jim. I put on my best serious yet friendly tone. No one else was around.

"We want to have a meeting, Jim."

"Sure, man. Let's meet." He was too friendly. Too damned agreeable. He was Jim. "When?"

"How about tomorrow?"

"Fine. 'Bout two o'clock?" I nodded. "I'll tell Kathy to fill up the fridge. You want Tecate or Corona? Ohh, and some juice for our meditators. Maybe pear-apple. John's starting to like that. And Robby will go along with whatever John wants." He laughed.

I almost laughed, too. Here he was being pleasant, civilized, and magnanimous. And I'm going to bust his ass. Shit. I put back my serious face.

"No, man. Not here . . . Robby's father's house."

"Ohh." His demeanor instantly changed. "This is serious, huh?"

"Yeah, I'm afraid so."

He got it immediately. He instinctively knew what was up. And his voice got very soft.

"Okay, Ray. I'll see you there." And he was gone. I saw him cross Santa Monica and turn into the Alta Cienega Motel, where he now kept a permanent room. Sort of an escape hatch. He would spend the rest of the day and that night alone with his thoughts.

The next day, the three of us arrived at one-thirty and Jim was on the dot at two. We went out to the patio, sat at a table, and began our confrontation.

All I could think of was my first encounter with Jimbo, when he yelled at me, "No one tells me what to do!" Would that happen again? Or would it be worse? If we said to him "You've got to stop drinking or we're going to quit," he'd probably say, "Fuck you! I quit!" After all, Jimbo was looking for any excuse to break up the band. That was not the tack to take. We had to be supportive, not threatening. There was no need to give him an ultimatum. That was just what Jimbo was waiting for. And no one, including Jim, wanted to break up the band. We all loved what we did. It was sacred to us. But not to Jimbo.

We all looked at each other across the table on that pleasant California afternoon. A great tension was in the air. Jim tried to smile, to make a little small talk.

"This is a nice patio. I like the whole backyard."

"My father and mother really like it here," Robby said. "I told them it's too big for two people."

"Maybe they think you and Lynn are going to move in with them," Jim laughed.

"There's enough room for Ron, too."

We all laughed. Grateful for anything that would short-circuit the electrical web of anxiety that had enveloped the four of us. But it wasn't going away. Not that easily. And we lapsed back into silence. And into paranoia. A dark, electrical paranoia. An evil thing.

Someone had to speak. I was the oldest, it was up to me to begin the inquisition. My heart was racing. All our hearts were racing. The Doors' communal mind was in a state of panic. You could feel it at that table, racing through our brains, our spinal columns. "Uhh . . . listen, man," I began. "The reason we . . . uhh, called this meeting is because . . . uhh . . . well, we're all, uhh . . . concerned . . . about . . . your drinking." There, it was said. And almost immediately the weight began to lift from our collective psyches.

John jumped in. "You're drinking too much, Jim."

Robby spoke, wisely. "It's ruining your health, man. You don't look healthy anymore."

Jim nodded. He knew he was busted. And he knew we loved him. His voice was almost imperceptible.

"I know," he said.

"You gotta stop drinking so much, Jim," John said. "You're really hurting yourself."

"You're killing yourself, man," I said. "The booze is killing your spirit."

And he looked at me . . . a deep sadness in his eyes.

"I know I drink too much, Ray." And then he looked at John and Robby. "I'm trying to quit."

And that was it. That's all we needed to hear. "I'm trying to quit." That's all he had to say. That's all he *needed* to say. The tension was broken. The electrical paranoia dissipated back into the subterranean evil it had crept out from. The afternoon light flooded the table and we all nodded and smiled at each other. No Jimbo. No screaming. No ultimatum. No fear.

"I know I drink too much. I'm trying to quit."

But he never did. He couldn't. It was beyond him.

We didn't know it at the time . . . but it was the beginning of the end.

chapter eighteen

the aftermath

Jim turned himself in to the FBI in Los Angeles. Five thousand dollars' bail. They had become involved because of Jim's going to Jamaica. It seems that that was unlawful flight across state lines to avoid prosecution, even though he had been in Jamaica three days *before* the warrants were issued. They opened a file on him, too. And on Janis and Jimi and John Lennon and all the other rock and roll, left-wing pinko players. It was definitely "us against them." The lovers, artists, and poets against the powers of the Establishment. We lost. They won. And here we are today . . . waiting for the end of the world. Waiting for the first or second coming of the Messiah, depending on whether you're a follower of Jewish or Christian mythology. Waiting for the end times. Waiting for the apocalypse. Waiting for death. The death of all things. And while we wait, the only thing we've accomplished is the death of joy. We've succeeded only in killing our euphoria. We live in a garden of earthly delights and we're slowly dying of ennui, whimpering about our impotence and inability to change anything. We're Adam and Eve in the Garden of Paradise . . . and we've forgotten it.

> *Have you forgotten the keys to the kingdom?*
> *Have you been born yet, and are you alive?*
> *Let's reinvent the gods,*
> *All the myths of the ages,*
> *Celebrate symbols from deep elder forests.*
> *We need great, golden copulations.*

We could take it all back at a moment's notice. We could reclaim our joy. We could reclaim our natural, God-given birthright to joy and delight and happiness and adventure and danger by merely stepping into the energy. By trusting in the energy. By trusting in "the Father," if you need to call it that. The Essene rabbi of Jerusalem called it that two thousand years ago.

> *I and the Father are one.*
> *—John 10:30*

And so can you be. So can we all be. All you have to do . . . is do it! Immerse yourself in the energy. The divine energy of creation.

> *Please, please listen to me, children,*
> *You are the ones who will rule the world.*

And perhaps we will. Perhaps one day the world *will* belong to the lovers. I'd like that. Wouldn't you?

≈

Things were not going well. However, the Doors' film footage was finally cut. Paul Ferrara said a screening would be held at a little professional screening room in Hollywood. We all went down. Robby and John, Dorothy and I, and the entire office staff, including our gopher/fan mail boy, Danny Sugerman. And, of course, the "Media Manipulators," Jim, Paul, Frank, and Babe. The faux Doors.

We took our seats with eager anticipation. What had they come up with? What had three UCLA graduates and the beer-barrel polka man produced? Would it be good . . . or would it be not quite adequate, as were their UCLA student movies? I was willing to give them the benefit of the doubt. After all, they had thousands of feet of footage. They had enough raw material to cut together a very exciting feature-length documentary film. And they had the Doors. And Jim Morrison while he was still in his Dionysian persona! The *real* Jim Morrison. But I was skeptical. I knew their work from school.

The room darkened. The screen glittered with light. "Strange Days" played on the sound track, and we were off. There were some great shots. Paul was an excellent cameraman. But it was a jumble. There was no rhyme or reason to the juxtaposition of elements. It pinballed from one thing to another, jumping about randomly, as if decisions as to form and content had been made under the influence of some new, stupid drug. I later learned that this was exactly the case. Cannabinol was the intoxicant of choice at the editing sessions. Cannabinol and alcohol, a lethal combo as far as artistic judgment was concerned. Jim wasn't trying hard enough to quit. He was back to his pre–Doors, Phil and Felix, belladonna modus operandi. Except he was getting too old to do that again. It didn't play well with a public figure. It didn't work with a man of responsibilities. But then, perhaps, Jim was seeking to rid himself of those responsibilities. Now I realize he was trying to throw off the mantle of stardom. He wanted it, he attained it, and he found it too heavy. The very thing he wanted was the thing that destroyed him. How ironic. How tragic. The success we so ardently dreamed of at the beach in Venice was the very thing he was now trying to shed. And, ultimately, it would be the thing that would finish him.

And the film came to a close. With a very nice boating sequence of the Doors on a two-masted sailing ship, somewhere off the coast of Maui. Out of Lahaina, the great whaling port of the Hawaiian Islands. The music was glorious. It was *Venus* from Gustav Holst's *The Planets*. It worked like a charm. It must have been Paul Ferrara's idea.

But the whole thing was only forty-five minutes long! And fifteen minutes of those forty-five were "The End" from the Hollywood Bowl. And it was slightly out of sync. I looked at the blank screen as the lights slowly came up. I was incredulous. That was it? Forty-five minutes? All that footage and you faux Doors, drinking buddies, "Media Manipulators," could come up with only a forty-five-minute cut . . . fifteen minutes of which was a single live performance? That's all?

There was a polite smattering of applause. We filed slowly, languidly out of the screening room. I couldn't bring myself to say what I really thought. Guys, this was a waste of time. None of you receives your master's degree with *this* exercise. It's only half a feature. It's even too short for a one-hour television special. What the fuck do you do with a forty-five-minute film? Enter it in some third-rate film festivals . . . Kuala Lumpur or Vladivostok? Well, that's exactly what they did. The Atlanta Film Festival. Jim and Frank went down. Received an honorable mention plaque in the documentary division. They were very proud, very puffed up. Public acknowledgment of their filmmaking abilities. Jim was so filled with himself that he hired Frank and Paul and Babe to do another film: *Hwy*. The story of a hitchhiker killer. One of those delightful proto-American types who hitchhike out in the wilderness, somewhere beyond the gates, somewhere east of Eden, and then kill you for your car if you're charitable enough to stop for this vermin. And Jimbo was howling with anticipation. It was a part he was born to play. It *was* Jimbo.

The Doors had paid a weekly salary to the faux Doors trio. That was now over. We had pulled the plug after the screening. "Thanks very much, you guys. The dole is over." But Jim picked up their nut at the same time as he was paying for Pam's hippie-dippy clothing shop on La Cienega. Themis it was called. It was costing him plenty, considering that peacock feathers were being used to cover the entire ceiling. *That* bit of excess luxury was thought of in an opium haze by one of Pam's advisers. She had surrounded herself with an unsavory group of very fashionable, very languid, very downer boys. They were very pretty things. Some were even prettier than Pam's girlfriends. They were all, both faux male and female, helping her fill her shop with sensual delights. And they were spending Jim's money. Rapidly.

She has robes and she has monkeys,
Lazy diamond-studded flunkies

To support these "artistic" endeavors, Jim was drawing against future royalties. He was in debt to his own band. Ultimately, the

Doors paid for everything. He had zip in the bank. Money was spilling from between his fingers like the sand that he had held clenched in his fists when he first sang "Moonlight Drive" to me on the beach of Venice, back a long time ago.

It was not working out the way I planned it. He had not turned the corner as we thought he would—as he *said* he would—at our "confrontation." It was, as John said, *not* a phase. Jimbo was still present. The madness was still present. And it was slowly taking over.

I was aching inside.

I wanted to say to Jim, "Forget about all this cash-guzzling nonsense. Come home. Just come home to the rehearsal room. We'll take care of you. All you have to do is write your poetry. Robby, John, and I will take care of you. We'll never fail you. We'll never make bad art with you. We won't allow *you* to fail. Just come home. You've wandered enough. You need to rest now." But I never could. When I'd look in his eyes, I would see both of them. Jim and Jimbo. And I was afraid. I had never dealt with anything like this before. I didn't even know what it was. I was lost . . . but we carried on. Knowing the music, the joy in the music, would transcend all of this.

※

We finally got a gig. PBS television. An hour-long show called *Critique*. A show of performance and interview with the artist, and a panel discussion of the artist's worth by New York journalists. We played "Tell All the People," "Back Door Man," "Wishful Sinful," "Build Me a Woman," and a powerful version of "The Soft Parade." A song of the anguish of Jim's internal life. His turmoil. His need to rest. His need for succor.

> *Can you give me sanctuary?*
> *I must find a place to hide,*
> *A place for me to hide.*
> *Can you give me soft asylum?*
> *I can't take it anymore.*
> *The man is at the door.*

We played the hell out of the song. We were all on top of it, rocking with a controlled fury. It was good to play in a public setting again. Good to be the Doors again. And this was a very prestigious PBS show. It usually featured classical and jazz musicians. We were only the second rock group to be asked to appear on *Critique*. The other was the New York Rock and Roll Ensemble, obviously an artsy group, with a name like that. So we played with our best fury and precision. Jim was extremely focused. Really on his game. You see, Jimbo didn't come to New York. Outclassed, don't you know. In New York, Jimbo would stay hidden. He was waiting for other places. Other times. He was waiting for Paris.

You can see our performance and interview on the Universal home video, *The Soft Parade*. We didn't include the panel discussion. Frankly, it was pedestrian: Richard Goldstein of the *Village Voice* was the moderator. "Rosco," the D.J. from WNEW, was insightful. Al Aronowitz, another writer, hated the Doors. He said our music was inconsequential, wouldn't last. He was from the Freudian, Bob Dylan-is-the-best, New York folk-rock school of critics. They simply couldn't allow themselves an immersion in the Jungian waters of the unconscious. They couldn't "drown tonight." They refused to "swim to the moon." Too liquid, too opalescent . . . too feminine. They were still beholden to the patriarchal religion. As was Freud, vis-à-vis Jung. Arorowitz had a long way to go. Patricia Kennealy was the last panelist. She was also a well-known writer. She simply fell in love with Jim. Madly.

※

Another gig came in. Mexico City. A bull ring, fifty thousand people. We were going to play for something like fifty cents per person. For the students. For the people. We *all* went down.

> *Went down south and crossed*
> *the border.*
> *Left the chaos and disorder back there,*
> *over his shoulder.*

Everybody took their girls and wives. Lynn and Robby were soon to be married—and they still are. John brought Julia Brose, a hip, blond clubette who would soon become *his* wife. We were all happy for John. Julia was cool and made a great wife and hostess; we even used to hang out at their house. "Let's go up to John and

Julia's and shoot some pool." Julia would always have drinks and food and pot for the gang. It was fun. I'd never seen John happier. Of course, it didn't last. He's onto wife number three now. I brought Dorothy. Jimbo had taken a backseat for a while, so Jim was in good form. He brought Jerry Hopkins, a writer for *Rolling Stone* who was doing a post-Miami profile.

We had a great Doors' family time in Mexico. Bill and Vince were there, too. Had to be. No performance without Vince, and Bill collected the pesos. We went to the pyramids of Teotihuacan and the magnificent Anthropological Museum that had been opened especially for us. A private tour. Arranged by the son of the president. A small group of fifteen or so young people walking amid the art and statuary of an ancient civilization. The great stone sun calendar of the Aztecs. The jaguar god. The snake god. All sitting in pools of light. Bathed in luminescence. We walked in dark shadows, an eerie and unfamiliar darkness, surrounded by the gods of a lost people glowing with light. It was overwhelming. Quetzalcoatl was with us. Cuculcan. And a great stone coiled serpent. The ancient snake. Jim was home. These people had touched the same interior images that he had. Universal. Reptilian. Jungian.

> *Ride the snake, to the lake,*
> *The ancient lake.*
> *The snake is long, seven miles.*
> *He's old,*
> *And his skin is cold . . .*

Being with those stone effigies, those great stone deities, was one of the most memorable experiences of my life. Like Egypt. Ancient and lost civilizations that are the foundation of what we are. Who we are. And perhaps offer clues as to even *why* we are.

The bull ring concert never happened. The government pulled the plug. It would have been on the anniversary of the student riots of the year before. No way were the *jefes* going to allow fifty thousand young people to gather for gringo rock on that day of rebellion. It could happen again. So we wound up playing a sit-down supper club for the "Mustang" set. Rich kids. They liked the Ford Mustang. It was their symbol of swinging. Mod London and the Mustang . . . and the Oedipal Doors. "Father, I want to kill you. Mother, I want to fuck you." They loved it. They shouted it out in unison from their tables. From behind their fancy place settings. Their nappery. At the top of their lungs. Speaking in English. With Jim. "I want to *keeel* you!" *Machismo, eh? Muy macho!* What a trip.

⁂

Some gigs finally started to come in. We didn't know how many, or how long it would last, so we decided to record what we could for a live album. We wanted to get the Doors experience on tape. Live. One time. For the ages. We wanted to capture the distillate in the alembic. We wanted the shamanic, trance-inducing seance to exist on tape as a record of the healing. The palliation of the assembly.

> *I love the friends I have gathered together on this thin raft,*
> *We have constructed pyramids in honor of our escaping.*

We would record the construction of the pyramid. And in doing so, perhaps we could capture the moment of escape. Live.

Eventually we recorded performances at the Aquarius Theater in Los Angeles, the Felt Forum in Madison Square Garden, the Spectrum in Philadelphia, the Pittsburgh Civic Arena, and Cobo Hall in Detroit. The results are available on the album *Absolutely Live* and in the Doors' box set, the disc titled *Live from New York.*

These gigs, and all the rest, came with a new contractual proviso. We called it "the fuck clause." It was an obscenity clause that prevented Jim, or any other Door, from using profane language on the stage. If an obscenity were to be uttered, the entire concert would be halted and the Doors would forfeit *all* the proceeds. It was insane. And it lasted, sporadically, for the rest of our too-brief career.

We would take the stage in the less enlightened towns — meaning every city other than New York, San Francisco, and L.A. — and two representatives of the local vice squad would be waiting in the wings with warrants. Our names were on the warrants, the offense wasn't. They were waiting for the commission, for the utterance, for the display of public drunkenness, open profanity, indecent exposure, lewd and lascivious behavior . . . what have you. Any violation would do. And it was off to the slammer.

Sometimes the narcs were there, too. LSD was now illegal, and since the Doors were the "Kings of Acid Rock," let's see if we can bust 'em, went the thinking. And you could see *them* in the wings, too. They were dressed like plain, unmarked Plymouths. They'd be on the opposite side from the vice men. "Narcs to the left of us, vice to the right. Into the valley of death rode the four!" It was absurd. It was more Kafka. It was the dark, paranoid madness that had descended on our great country of the free and the brave. We had become afraid of each other. Americans, afraid of other Americans. It was not a good time. And it still isn't. Hallucinogens are still criminal. The "food of the gods" is illegal. The keys to the doors of perception are against the law. Their ingestion is an illegal act. The mere growing of a peyote plant is illegal. Using LSD therapy with convicts, drug addicts, and alcoholics is illegal. The great therapeutic tool of LSD that was proven so effective in case after case of psychological maladjustment has been taken away from the doctors of the mind by the fundamentalist, fascist guardians of our public morality. And that's the way it is to this very day. No medical research. And certainly no looking behind the veil. No breaking on through to the other side. Just booze and cigarettes and . . . guns. Yahoo! Yee haw!

***

Events started speeding up now. In a crazy, out-of-control vortex that was sucking us all toward the final curtain. But in our youthful hubris, our boyish naïveté, we thought we were immortal. Nothing could happen to the Doors. We could steamroll all the problems. Jim would grab hold of himself. He would conquer his drinking. He would be back to that young prince who lived with Dorothy and me in our little one-bedroom apartment on Fraser overlooking the "roofs and the palm trees of Venice." He would be back.

First, however, he turned himself in at the Dade County Public Sheriff's Department. He was officially arrested at 9:50 A.M. and made bail of fifty thousand dollars at 10:10. A formal not-guilty plea was entered by his attorney. Five days earlier, ironically, the Living Theatre had played in Coconut Grove without incident, without arrest. Miami! Shit.

***

A few days later, Jim was arrested at the airport in Phoenix, Arizona, on charges of "drunk and disorderly conduct" and "interference with a flight crew." It seems that Jim and Tom, A Baker, had had too many little bottles of Wild Turkey and Jack and Courvoisier on a flight to Phoenix to see the Stones concert and had taken to pinching the ass of a quite cute stewardess in the first-class section. The captain had to come back and tell the louts to cool it. They didn't. He called ahead for the police. They were busted. Bail was $5,000. The Doors paid for that, too.

Between Miami and Phoenix, Jim was facing a maximum of over thirteen years in prison. Three and a half in Raiford Penitentiary in the County of the Dead, and ten in a federal hoosegow because "interference with a flight crew" was an offense against the new skyjacking law. Even if it was only pinching the ass of a cute stewardess.

Cancel my subscription
to the resurrection.
Send my credentials
to the house of detention.
I got some friends inside.

He would probably get off. It was all minor shit. A good lawyer, with money, could get him off. But it weighed on Jim's psyche. His soul was heavy. It had lost the exquisite lightness it wore in the early years. It was as if fame had become a yoke placed upon the shoulders of Jim Morrison's spirit. Weighing him down. Making him do crazy things to shed the burden. Or forget the burden. But at the time I couldn't believe that Jim wanted to abandon his responsibilities. After all, what were they? To create? To write songs and make music with the Doors? That's too hard? For me, that was the *real* fun. Creating something out of nothing. Thinking up something and then bringing it to fruition. Manifesting a thought in reality. Conceiving a reality, a plan, a work of art in your mind . . . and then actually making it happen. It was incredible. We were actually doing it. Manifesting the dreams we had back in Venice. We were right up there with the Beatles and the Stones. I was loving it! And this was too hard for Jim? He wanted to get away from it all? I didn't believe it. Would you?

It was that rotter, Jimbo. The doppelganger.

the end times

W̶e went into the studio to begin the recording of *Morrison Hotel.* The enforced layoff caused by Miami resulted in a burst of creativity by Jim and Robby. We were loaded with hot new songs. The rehearsals were very productive. We were having fun again. Jimbo was nowhere to be seen. Jim was relaxed and as happy as a man facing possibly thirteen years in the slammer could be. He simply put it out of his mind, as we all did—we never spoke of it. Instead, he threw himself into creativity. And the songs were hot!

"Roadhouse Blues," "You Make Me Real," "Waiting for the Sun," "Peace Frog," "Blue Sunday," "Ship of Fools," "Land Ho!," "The Spy in the House of Love," "Queen of the Highway," "Indian Summer," and "Maggie M'Gill." All good stuff. And all to be played within our basic Doors format. No horns. No strings. Just Doors.

Pure Doors. Pure rock and blues and jazz and soul and love. Pure love. We were going to lay it down. Hard and fat. John Sebastian sat in on harp on "Roadhouse Blues," as did Lonnie Mack on bass. Ray Neapolitan played bass on all the other cuts.

It was a great album to record. The sessions were super. Mucho good times in the recording studio. Many friends and guests dropping in for moral and vibrational support. Hell, even Babe, Frank, and Paul Ferrara came by and were cool. Don't get me wrong, they were all good people but they, too, had been seduced by Jimbo. They would have followed him off a cliff. Like lemmings. They worshiped him. They were his puppy dogs. I'm sure they always said, "Yes, Jim." But they didn't know—hell, no one knew—they were saying yes to Jimbo. But Jimbo never made an appearance at the recording sessions. Everyone was cool. No mind games. Pure fun. Hence, the recording and creativity were at Nietzsche's "noon time." We were *Übermenschen*. At the upper extremity. We were on the etheric plane. And, man, it was fine.

We did a great improvisation, a jam called "Rock Is Dead." It came out toward the tail end of the sessions. It was Jim at his prescient best. Predicting the death of "rock and roll." The usurpation of rock by the corporate mind. The co-opting of the revolution by the power of the dollar. The loss of freedom to "the bottom line."

We could change it, you know. We could maneuver the world in whichever direction we wanted. We could shift the world. All we have to do is "do it!" It takes only an act of courage. An act of will. And we could create a new bottom line. The bottom line of the common good. "How does what I'm doing affect the planet . . . and my fellow man on this planet?" That's the question to ask. That's the new bottom line! We could take it to that place we tried to hit in those *Morrison Hotel* recording sessions. We did it then. We could *all* do it again. And *that* should be our goal for the twenty-first century. Enlightenment . . . and the planting of a new Garden of Eden. We can do it.

And we did our own crazy variation of it that long-ago night at Elektra's 10 percent–discount recording studio, across from the Doors' workshop on La Cienega Boulevard, after a dinner of riotous drinking, eating, and toasting at the Blue Boar Restaurant. A baronial setting. A manly-hunting-lodge Hollywood-theme restaurant.

Just down the street on "Restaurant Row." We were all there. The Doors, Botnick and Rothchild, Vince Treanor and Bill Siddons, Danny Sugerman and Leon Barnard, and the faux Doors.

We were ushered into one of the private, long-table rooms, complete with fireplace and banners of Germanic heraldry. We took our seats as beer and wine, mead and ale were brought to the table amid boisterous laughing and manly shouting. Great platters of beef and chops and sides of steaming vegetables and bowls of roasted, mashed, and baked potatoes were ordered for the table. More rounds of drinks came. And Ferrara, emboldened by the wine and the camaraderie, rose to his feet, toasted the Doors—"Here's to the Doors and their damn fine music!"—drained his wineglass, and hurled it into the fireplace. It shattered in the flames. An explosion! A moment of shock . . . and then we all roared our approval. "Hear, hear! Yes, Paul!"

"More wine," Jim cried out. "More wine for my men!" And more wine was brought by the serving girls in décolleté costume. And Babe rose for a toast. "Here's to the Doors . . . and my salary!" We drained our glasses. Ferrara hurled another glass into the flames. We roared again. Paul was in some Errol Flynn swashbuckler that was unreeling behind his eyes. He was zonked. And then Morrison toasted. "Here's to rock and roll!" And then we all toasted in our turn. Laughing and joking and shouting and reveling in the camaraderie of each other's company. Eating and drinking with boisterous abandon. With youthful joy and exuberance. It was friends, and life, and good to be alive.

But it was the last supper. It was the last time we would all eat together this way. Soon Jim would be leaving for Paris.

※

We went back to the studio, staggering and shouting along La Cienega Boulevard. And we captured "Rock Is Dead" out of the ether. We just snatched it out of the limbo state it was dwelling in and made it ours. We put it on tape. Jammed it into existence. And had one hell of a good time creating it.

On another night in the studio Jim brought along a pair of new acquaintances. He had just met them at dinner in a restaurant down the street and invited them to the session. They were the actor Laurence Harvey and, dig this, the chief of police of the city of Los

Angeles, Tom Reddin. They walked in just as Rothchild was rolling a joint from a small pile of freshly sifted marijuana resting seductively on the recording console. I don't think Jim knew who Tom Reddin was. But Rothchild did. He took one look, his eyes bugged out, and recognition hit! And fear! He quickly put his attaché case on his lap, opened it, and, hands trembling, began furiously scraping the stash, seeds and all, into the hiding place. Rolling papers and the half-rolled joint also were thrown in, and the case was quickly closed and even more quickly locked. Only then did Paul turn, sweat beading on his forehead, and introduce himself to the famous actor and the chief of police.

They stayed for quite a while. Enjoying the recording process and the erudite company of Rothchild and Morrison. When they finally left, Paul looked at Jim and could only laugh. "Jesus Christ," he said. "Only Jim Morrison would bring the fucking chief of police to a Doors recording session. I can see it in the *L.A. Times* gossip column now. 'The Kings of Acid Rock hang with Tom Reddin.' " We all laughed.

"And Paul Rothchild, noted producer, gets busted," I added.

Paul laughed hardest of all and then shoved Jim. "That was close, man."

Jim feigned innocence. "I didn't even know who he was!" We all roared our disbelief and Babe, right on time, arrived with two six-packs of very much needed ice-cold Tecates. What a night! What a session. What a great album to record. What fun. It was a good time for the Doors.

Jim and Tom, A Baker, flew off to Phoenix for their "hijacking" trial. The assaulted stewardess was confused as to who did what to her and which one of the bearded Irish manly drinking men was actually Jim Morrison. Jim and Tom were acquitted. It was a case of mistaken identity. He wouldn't be so lucky in Miami.

The Lords, and The New Creatures was published by Simon and Schuster. An actual hardcover book of Jim's poetry printed by a major publisher. The poems Michael McClure had first seen in London. The very poems Michael had helped Jim print in a private limited edition of 250 copies. Now for all the world to read. To be sold in bookstores. In the poetry section. Alongside Ginsberg, Rimbaud, McClure, and Kerouac. Jim was overjoyed. I'd never seen him so proud. It was a dream come true. Another one. First the Doors . . . then a book of his own verse. He was a happy man.

But Jimbo was waiting in the wings. Like the narcs and the vice squad boys at our gigs, he, too, was holding a warrant. But this warrant was a death certificate. And Jimbo was bent on serving it.

※

And the events kept spinning. In between recording, concerts, mixing sessions, album releases, book publishings, John and Julia's wedding, Lynn and Robby's wedding, interviews, photo sessions, songwriting, rehearsals, and drunken debauches with the faux Doors and Tom, A Baker, and whatever Hollywood harpy that would glom onto Jim . . . came the Miami trial!

The State of Florida vs. James Douglas Morrison, Metropolitan Dade County Justice Building, Miami, Florida, Case 69-2355.

It was a farce. It was absurd. It was Kafka, Beckett, and Ionesco all rolled into one. One hundred fifty photos were offered in evidence but there was not a single photo of Jim's schlong. There were photos of Jim with a skull-and-crossbones hat, Jim with a lamb, Jim kneeling in front of Robby, Jim leaping about, Jim being tossed offstage, Jim leading the snake line in the audience, the stage collapsing, the audience rioting. All of it. Photos of everything. But not a single photo of Jim's member. Nary a snapshot of the ivory shaft. Not *one* photo! Why? If he had whipped it out, why was there no photo? There were photos of everything else. One hundred fifty photos. It was Kafka again.

And yet they were convinced that he did it. The charge, as read in court, said: "He did lewdly and lasciviously expose his penis, place hands upon his penis, and shake it. And further, the said defendant did simulate masturbation upon himself and oral copulation upon another." That's a lot of hot sex. I missed all that shit. So did the photographers. Except for the simulation of oral copulation. That was Jim on his knees in front of Robby's guitar as Robby played a solo in "Five to One." Jim was feigning worshiping Robby's dexterous fingers as they flew over the fretboard. The powers that be—the police, the city fathers, the prosecutors—all thought Jim was feigning giving Robby a blow job! What nasty little minds. What a joke . . . on us.

And so it went. A farce. But with Jim's ass on the line. We were not allowed to use "community standards" as a defense. Our attorneys were going to take the jury to see *Hair* with full frontal nudity. They were going to see foulmouthed comics on the Miami hotel strip. *Woodstock*, the movie. Prostitutes working the streets. The argument was going to be . . . if you bust Jim for indecent exposure, public profanity, and lewd and lascivious behavior, then you must arrest these others. If you arrest one, you must arrest all. The judge, Murray Goodman—up for reelection—said, "Inadmissible evidence!" He was a hanging judge. He wanted to look tough. Every time we brought up a salient legal point concerning free speech, the rights of the artist in contemporary American society, or community standards, Judge Murray slammed his gavel and said, "Inadmissible evidence." We were fucked. We had no defense except for the lack of schlong shots and a lot of witnesses who would testify that *they* didn't see it, either.

It wasn't enough. We weren't able to change the obscenity laws of America as we had set out to do. We had seen it as a grand and noble cause for artistic freedom, for the rights of free speech; another battle against the encrusted, entrenched Establishment. But it wasn't enough. We lost. The judgment on the bench docket read: "It appearing unto this Court that you, James Morrison, have been regularly tried and convicted of Indecent Exposure and Open Profanity. It is therefore the judgment of the law that you are and stand convicted of the offenses as above set forth." The chilling sentence read: "It is further considered, ordered, and adjudged that you, James Morrison, be imprisoned by confinement at hard labor in the Dade County Jail for a term of six (6) months and that you pay a fine of Five Hundred Dollars ($500.00)." Six months in Raiford. Impossible. Brutal. Jim could never do it. An appeal was immediately filed. We would fight it all the way to the Supreme Court if we had to. It never came to that. Jim left for Paris before it even got to the state level. He carried that six months in Raiford with him for the rest of his life. And he began to drink more seriously. How he left the country with two charges against him I'll never know. He probably just bought a ticket and got on the plane for Paris. How could they check? He left from L.A. The case was in Florida. There were no computers handling that sort of criminal check in 1971.

⁂

Judge Murray did, however, let us take five days off in the middle of the trial to go to England to the play the last great hippie fest. The Isle of Wight Festival. It was an incredible lineup. Jimi Hendrix, who would be dead two weeks later; the Who, with the debut of *Tommy;* Miles Davis, with his new electronic funk aggregation; Joni Mitchell; Sly and the Family Stone; Jethro Tull; Ten Years After; Leonard Cohen; the Moody Blues; Donovan; Emerson, Lake and Palmer; John Sebastian; Kris Kristofferson; and the Doors. And half a million English hippies. A sea of soft garments and colors and nubile bodies. An ocean of humanity. An amazing two days. There was some absolutely brilliant music. Brilliant playing.

Our set was subdued but very intense. We played with a controlled fury and Jim was in fine vocal form. His voice was rich and powerful and throaty. He sang for all he was worth but moved nary a muscle. He remained rigid and fixed to the microphone for the entire concert. Dionysus had been shackled. They had killed his spirit. He would never be the same in concert again. They had won.

The satyr didn't even make an appearance. Five hundred thousand hippies and the satyr didn't show. He knew it was over. He knew Dionysus had been defeated by the forces of righteousness. By the Judeo-Christian-Muslim view of God as other. There would be no more feasting on young goat in a béchamel sauce, the ritual dish of Dionysian feast days. The "kid in mother's milk" of kosher dietary prohibition. They had won. There would be no more dancing with the maenads. No more hopping about on those silly little goat legs. No more humping. No more cackling. No more wine. Not for him. It was now time to retire. Into the trees of the forest. Into the ether. Where he waits with Pan to this day. Waiting to called again out of the green. The dark, fecund green of the earth.

⁂

The Isle of Wight was our last filmed and recorded concert. We would play only four more live performances after that. Bakersfield and San Diego on a weekend in California. And Houston and New

Orleans. That fateful last concert in New Orleans, where the bayou and the voodoo conjoined to snuff out Jim's spirit. It just left him. Halfway through the set his energy, his vital force, his chi, just left him. It became a vapor. An exhalation of the stomach that rose out through the top of his head. Off into the ether. Perhaps to join Pan and the satyr. Perhaps to dissipate into the universe.

I remember that concert like it was yesterday. A packed warehouse on the docks. Low, dark, and ancient. Slave vibes, juju vibes, Marie Laveau, and Dr. John walking on gilded splinters. It was musty with 150 years of cargoes coming and going on the Mississippi. I didn't like it. It was like Van Gogh's *Night Cafe*. It was not a place to make music. It was a place to plan a crime, buy drugs, or commit a murder. Halfway through a lackluster set, Jim suddenly left the stage. I could feel it. I usually played with my head down and my eyes closed. Concentrating on my left-hand bass, right-hand organ, John's beat, Robby's chords and fills, and Jim's words. I knew where everybody was at every moment. I could feel them. Their presence. Their essence. And at a most inappropriate place, in the middle of a song, in the middle of a short solo, Jim left the stage. Now in the middle of "Light My Fire" Jim would frequently leave the stage to get a beer as Robby and I soloed for upwards of ten minutes or more. But this was not "Light My Fire." And Jim was gone. I could feel him leave. And then I looked up and I was shocked. He was standing at the microphone! He hadn't left the stage. Only his essence had. And it was streaming up from his stomach and out through his crown chakra. Out into that voodoo night. Spreading itself over the assembled multitude. Disappearing into the sweat and heat and dust and rafters of that ancient edifice in the New World city of Orleans on the bayou. And then Jim began to sing again. But without any commitment to the words. Without passion. Without energy. He was spent. Exhausted. He badly needed to rest. He needed to rediscover himself. And he needed time away from his drinking buddies. He needed time away from those ne'er-do-wells on the Morrison dole. He needed to be a poet again. A quiet, contemplative poet.

John and Robby saw it, too. And they saw Jim lose it at the end of the set. They saw him pick up the mic stand with its heavy, weighted base and begin to smash the stand into the old plank flooring of the stage. Over and over and over. Smashing the stage to pieces. Smashing his life to pieces in a blind rage. A fury had overtaken him and he couldn't stop. He splintered the wood and shattered his soul. Vince finally came out from behind the amps and put his hand on Jim's shoulder. He immediately stopped. His rage dissipated with Vince's comforting touch. He put his arm around Vince's shoulder and just stood there, at the mic, looking out at the audience as we finished the final chorus of "The End." We would never play that song with Jim Morrison ever again.

※

When we got back to Los Angeles, Robby, John, and I had a short meeting and unanimously agreed to stop performing in public; Jim wasn't up to it anymore. It was too much of a strain on him. We couldn't risk his health, both physical and psychological.

We told him and he was happy with the decision.

"Listen, man. Why don't we not tour for a while and just concentrate on writing," I said. "What do ya say?"

"Sounds good to me," he responded. "I don't feel like touring, anyway."

"We thought we could just stay in L.A. and rehearse," Robby said. "You know, work on songs together."

"Cool," Jim said. "We gotta get ready for our last album, you know."

A silence hit the room. The dark green thing stuck its tentacles into my stomach and stirred my gastric juices in a nasty, evil way. Robby went pale. The air was sucked out of John's lungs. Last album? Robby finally spoke.

"What do you mean? . . . Aren't we . . . aren't we gonna *work* together anymore?"

Jim looked perplexed. "What are you talking about? Of course we're going to work together." He took a laconic pull off his Tecate. "I meant our contract with Elektra. It's over after this record."

The air rushed back into John's diaphragm. "We're free!" he jubilantly exclaimed.

The green thing released its stranglehold on my duodenum. "Seven records," I said, smiling. "And *this* one is the last. We can do anything we want after this." I was so relieved.

"I thought you meant you were gonna . . . work with . . . someone else," Robby said.

Jim laughed. "Like who?"

"I don't know, like anyone."

"Why would I want to work with someone else?" Jim asked. "Who can play better than you guys?"

"Well, *we* know that," said John laughingly. "We just wondered if you did."

"Shit, John, I'm not the 'little moron.' I know what I've got here," said Jim.

"You'd better, goddamn it," I said.

"I *do* wanna do a poetry album, though. But I'll get to that . . . when I get to that," said Jim. And he took another pull on his beer.

"Well, we got a lot of work to do right now," I said.

"Yeah . . . we got our 'last album' to make," Robby joked.

"You got a title, Jim?" John asked.

Jim pondered, bobbing his head laconically. "Yeah . . . I think so." He spoke slowly, thoughtfully. "I think . . . maybe . . . *L.A. Woman.*"

"Cool!" John said.

"I like it," I said.

"Kind of an ode to Los Angeles . . . and a woman, at the same time," Jim said.

"And Los Angeles *as* a woman," Robby added. "Wait till you hear it. We just started fooling around with it."

"Shit, let's try it now!" enthused John.

"Hey, anybody got someplace they have to be?" I asked.

Everybody shook their heads no.

"Well, let's get busy," I said.

"Yeah, we got an album to make!" said Jim, smiling. "Let's not be standing around and jawing idly. Hell, time's a-wastin'!"

We all laughed and mounted up. Climbed aboard our instruments and began the process that would create "Riders on the Storm," "The WASP (Texas Radio and the Big Beat)," "The Changeling," "Love Her Madly," "Been Down So Long," "Cars Hiss by My Window," "L'America," "Hyacinth House," and the title track, "L.A. Woman."

We worked and sweated and argued and laughed and agreed and disagreed. We put those songs through a shitload of permutations. We tickled them and cajoled them and pampered them, and whipped them into line. It was like the old days. We had no pressure on us. No tours. No "fuck clause." No narcs, no vice squad. No one to hassle us. All we had to do was make music. All Jim had to do was spin out his words from his internal *Webster's New World College Dictionary* and then sing them. And, man, he was on it. On the case. He was happening. And he was sober . . . at rehearsals. I don't know what he did away from the Doors' workshop. But at rehearsals he was a happy man. A few beers, that was all. Beers, pinball, Duke's food, and rock and roll. We were all happy. Deciding not to tour anymore was the best thing we could have done. It was all feeling good. And it was beginning to feel like *L.A. Woman* was going to be one of our best albums ever. Maybe even a "comeback" album. Certainly a comeback in terms of band communication, joy, and creativity. We were getting along the way we used to. Creating the way we used to. Laughing and joking the way we used to.

But Jimbo was lurking in the background. Jimbo was always clinging to the shadows; somewhere in the background. Carrying with him the negative influences of Felix, and Freddy and Wes, and Tom Baker, and who knows how many other reprobates, degenerate descendants of indentured servants, slimeballs, and general Hollywood trash.

Jim had always wanted the lifestyle of rock and roll. Except now it included a visit from the angel of death. That sweet little child that had visited Brian Jones, and Al Wilson, and Jimi Hendrix, and Janis Joplin.

Death, old friend,
Death and my cock are the world . . .

When Jim had asked for it, back in '65, in his inner imaginings, in the picture of the future we all create for ourselves, the rock and roll lifestyle did not include that final visit. And that final visit comes not from some spectral grim reaper but, instead, in the guise of a little child. A sweet and innocent little seven-year-old. A little mop-top who takes your hand and leads you over. Gently, without fear. As if you were going to a playground to play on the swings. Or as if you were going to the beach to lie in the sun. To play in the soft shore break, to build sand castles, dream castles with your little towheaded friend. Your sweet friend who has been waiting for you all your life. And it ultimately doesn't matter how long or short your life was . . .

because you're going to the beach. You're going to the park. And you're going to become like your little friend. Like a child again. Filled with a renewed sense of wonder and joy and adventure. Rid of the burden of obligations and responsibilities, rid of the weight of our too-weak flesh, rid of the laborious, incessant measure of time. Of gravitas. Of propriety. Of decorum. Of convention. Free again. Free to fly. Free to break the shackles that bind our hearts, the web of maya that ensnares us . . . and fly. Into the sun. Into that bright and golden orb of life eternal. Into our proper home. Into the spiritual warmth of radiant energy. To become one with the energy. To become the energy itself. The divine energy. All things. All life. All love. Free, at last.

And even though Jimbo won. Even though Jimbo finally took Jim to Paris, away from the magic circle of the Doors, and shattered the diamond. The diamond within the circle. The diamond that was Jim Morrison, Ray Manzarek, Robby Krieger, and John Densmore. Even though Jimbo destroyed everything in some kind of insane act of self-immolation. I know that Jim, in that bathtub in Paris, immersed in the baptismal waters of the unconscious, floating in the amniotic fluid of his mother once again; in the soft, warm, liquid womb of his divine mother, went out smiling. Into the light. Smiling into that bright midnight. Born again!

That day, which you fear as being
the end of all things, is the birthday
of your eternity.
—Seneca

epilogue

And so it ended in Paris. That journey into the creative impulse that started at the UCLA Film School. That joining that took us from the shore break of Venice Beach, with Jim singing in a haunted, almost whisper voice the words of a liquid love song—"Moonlight Drive"—a love song of desire and death; from the two of us having nothing but our dreams . . . to the top of the pyramid. The top of the charts. We stole the eye from the top of that pyramid of rock and roll. We climbed the mountain. We ascended Olympus. We drank the nectar of the gods and became one of the elite. We danced the shaman's dance together . . . and it was over. In the wink of an eye. In the flash of a thought. So brief, so quick; the snap of a finger and he was gone. Before he could even become a man. Twenty-seven years and six months; that's all the time he did on this planet, in this incarnation. He was still an apprentice at life, still on the hunt, still on the search, still the wild child, still the enfant terrible The dictionary says: "anyone constantly vexing, startling, or embarrassing others, as, in the arts, by outraging conventional opinion or expectations". . . . Is that Jim Morrison or what?

And he was taken so quickly. Too quickly. But then he was, according to Chinese numerology, only a one. In his first incarnation. Dorothy found a little book of Chinese parlor divination that explained how to calculate your incarnation of *this* lifetime. Ultimately you get nine. Once you jump back on the wheel from the void, back into the "red dust," back into life, you must ride the turning wheel of destiny nine times to get the point. Nine lifetimes—hence the nine lives of a cat—to realize the purpose of existence; the reason for your being. And then you're free to step off. Or come back again, as you so choose. Here's how you do the numbers: Add all the numbers of your birthday together and reduce them to a single digit. Jim's is December 8, 1943. 12/8/1943. $1 + 2 + 8 + 1 + 9 + 4 + 3 = 28$. Add $2 + 8$ to reduce to a single digit $= 10$. Reduce again $1 + 0 = 1$. Jim was a one. Fresh out of the void! Just beginning the journey, again. Just beginning the quest, again. No wonder he didn't know how far he could go before it would all be snatched out from under him. No wonder he was always trying to push things beyond the norm, beyond the pale. He was a one. An enfant terrible. A wild child.

And I was there to balance that. To bring a sense of order to his wildness. My birthday is February 12, 1939. $2/12/1939 = 27$. $2 + 7 = 9$. My incarnation is 9. This is my last time on the wheel. Jim Morrison, a one—Ray Manzarek, a nine—equals the Doors. The Dionysian and Apollonian balancing act. The synthesis of alpha and omega turning back on themselves. The snake biting its own tail. The Ouroboros. The wholeness.

So Jim came kicking and screaming and wild out of the void. Wild in the night. Filled with a desire for life and art. Filled with poetry.

Awake, shake dreams from your hair,
My pretty child, my sweet one.
Choose the day and choose the sign of your day,
The day's divinity,
First thing you see.

And the first thing he saw, when his eyes were opened by the ingestion of the psychedelic soma substance, was the divinity of the day. The purity, the holiness of this moment in time. The infinite holiness of this instant. This heartbeat. This tick of the clock. This clap of the hands. It's both infinite and time specific. It's divine. All things. And he tried to convey his visions through his poetry.

I tell you this . . .
No eternal reward will forgive us now
For wasting the dawn.

He tried to bring us some of his enthusiasm and excitement at just being alive! Being alive on this planet . . . in the holy now. In the infinite instant. He loved life. He loved being alive. It delighted him. He could see God in everything. Alive in everything!

A vast radiant beach in a cool jeweled moon.
Couples, naked, race down by its quiet side.
And we laugh like soft, mad children,
Smug in the woolly cotton brains of infancy.
The music and voices are all around us.

And he was alive in the music. And we were alive in him. The four of us, together. The Doors. Our music. Made in the infinite moment when we immersed ourselves in the waters of our deepest selves. Basking under the radiant sun of our father and drifting contentedly in the water of our mother. One with the universe, the rhythm, the energy. One with the great pulse of existence.

In the beginning was the rhythm

And Jim knew these things. That's what drew me to his words in the first place. That's what drew me to *him*. And his joy. And his delight. And his craziness.

But because his enthusiasm was so boundless, because his joy was so all-encompassing, death was also lurking nearby. Waiting to claim the wild child. The overexuberant first incarnation.

Death, old friend.

It was as if he were familiar with death. And he wasn't afraid of it. It was as if he knew what was coming. And it didn't bother him. He was a one. And he must have had vague remembrances of his pre-one existence, brief flashes of his time before time, intimations of his being in infinity before stepping back into the red dust. Back onto the wheel. And it comforted him. Supported him. For, after all, isn't it heaven? Pure potentiality. Pure energy. The I Am.

And he knew that was our final destination. He knew that was the point of our existence. But was he trouble? Oh, yes he was. That damned wild-child enfant terrible was a handful and a half. What a commotion! What chaos! What anarchy! Could that guy cause a ruckus? Wow!

> *I am interested in anything about*
> *revolt, disorder, chaos.*

Man, I'll say he was. But what fun. What a riot. What a crazed and wild existence. Damn, we had a good time. Big fun. Except for the aberration. The problem.

Shall we attempt to give it a name, this malady, this Jimbo? How about compensation for a perceived inadequacy (he could never live up to his father's expectations, hence he created a persona his father might like and understand)? Or emotional immaturity (he was a one)? Or perhaps emotional instability (his shamanic inclination)? Or societal maladjustment (Miami, for example)? Or antisocial hostility (arrested for inciting a riot in New Haven)? Or psychoneurotic Oedipal complex ("Father, I want to kill you, Mother, I want to fuck you")? Or obsessional moral deficiency ("There are no rules, no laws," as he said in Miami)? Or dementia praecox (multiple-personality disorder)? Or simply old-fashioned, Victoriana, *fin de siècle* "unsoundness of mind"? Or all of the above. Or none of the above. Why don't *you* pick one? If you really need that sort of summing up. That summing up that would put a neat bow around Jim Morrison and then allow us to file him away. To safely put him in a pigeonhole. To categorize him and then to be rid of him and his damnable charisma.

Well, it can't be done. He's been haunting me for some thirty years now. And I love it. He was wild and impetuous and overflowing with life. He was witty and charming, gracious and funny, elegant and sophisticated, but down in the trenches as well. He was literate and knowledgeable. He had an insatiable thirst for learning about the world. He wanted to know everything. The why of everything. The how of everything. The *connection* of everything. His brain was always in high gear, as were his emotions. It was always a rollercoaster ride, being with him. He created ecstatic highs for me. Joyous, transcendent moments. From Madison Square Garden, rocking in front of twenty thousand screaming Doors fans, to contemplative walks in the soft shore break of Venice Beach discussing Nietzsche's *Birth of Tragedy* and Sonny Rollins's tenor playing as compared with John Coltrane's. From the outsize spectacle to the microcosm. He was a joy to be with. And if not always a joy . . . he was certainly stimulating.

Was he obsessive? Of course. Was the obsessive behavior *necessary?* Of course. It's what made him Jim. You had to take the good with the bad, the bitter with the sweet, the genius with the rotter, the poet with the prole. But that was Jim. It was love it or leave it. And who, except a coward, would want to leave it? My mother said, "You're living life to the fullest, Raymond." And being with Jim was certainly a life fully lived. As was his. Overflowing. Filled to the top with wild emotions and then overflowing. Spilling out.

Effusive, exuberant, crazed, manic. What a time, my friends. Those sixties. And what a guy. God, I loved him. And I sorely miss him, and his slightly southern, goofy "heh, heh, heh." And his shy/sly grin when he was caught in a fantastical exaggeration. And the leaning of his head to one side as he listened intently to a new idea. And his laconic yet defensive "mmm" before answering a too-direct question. And his subtle modulation of weight from one hip to another as he shape-shifted before your very eyes. And his languid stretching of arms and body and tossing of his lion's mane of hair. And his leaping up out of a chair when adventure was proposed, for adventure was his *métier*. His reason for being. His main purpose for being here. And didn't he bring that sense of adventure to us? All of us. God, he was fun to be with.

There are times when I have this recurring dream about him. And he's back, and everything is cool. And we're all making music together. Inspired music. Doors' music. But every once in a while he tries to float away, carried off by the inspiration, into the blue canopy, off into the light. But I bring him back with a firm hand on his ankle and a cool blues line on the organ. And he's grounded again. Centered again. And Robby plays a snake slide line on his guitar and John does a rim shot whack on his skins and Jim is back where he's supposed to be. In the center of the maelstrom, in the eye of the sun, at the heart of the Doors. And, for me, everything is good again. All the parts are in place. Jim is young and vibrant and alive again. He is the poet again. He is the young god of the vine and he is leading us in an ecstatic dance around a bonfire, on a hillside, on a warm California night. And we are filled with potency. Filled with potential. The world is ours for the taking. For the loving. For the creating. The universe is ours. All things are ours, are *of* us, and we are all things. We are all one. In the energy.

And then I wake up, enveloped in warmth and contentment. And I wonder if the dream is my life . . . or if my life is a dream. Either way, Robby, John, and I are still together. Despite our minor differences of opinion and occasional aesthetic clashes. (Hell, that's par for the course in a rock band, isn't it?) We're still rabid supporters of the genius of Jim Morrison *and* each other. We all love the music and poetry we created together and, at bottom, we all love each other. We're still in love. With the Doors, with life, with existence. We *are* the Doors. For the rest of our lives.

And Jim is always with us. In the air, in the ether, in the electricity. In the sounds and rhythms of Doors' music. In the images of his poetry. In the joys and anguish of his soul, which he so publicly bared to us. In the hundreds of photos of the "young lion" that wink out at us from the collective media. In the radio's playing of "Riders on the Storm" on rainy days across America. In a blurb in a newspaper, or a book title, or a film title using one of his lines, one of his catchphrases. And his face on the T-shirts being sold from Venice Beach, California, to San Marco Square in Venice, Italy. I have seen them. And in each new generation's discovery of The Doors and Jim's plea of: "Please, please, listen to me, children. You are the ones who will rule the world." In each new generation's quest for its *own* freedom, Jim is there. The Doors are there.

※

He asked me once, as we walked along the beach to our monkey rings workout on a midsummer's California morning, through the light, filled with excitement at our newly conceived plan of destiny, filled with youth and joy and potency, "How long do you think you'll live, Ray?"

He snapped me out of my reverie. My mind raced back from the sea blue/sky blue horizon line, where it was doing a tightrope dance, and tried to lock itself into what it had just heard. It couldn't.

"What?!" was all I could say. Shocked.

"You know. How old will you be when . . . you . . . well, when you die?"

What a question! We were just pups. Just starting out. The future was infinite, and even then, at that fecund moment in time, at the just-realized conception of the Doors . . . even then he was aware of his own mortality.

"Ohh, God . . . probably . . . uhh," I stammered, trying to project myself from that golden day into a distant future. "Probably . . . uhh, like . . . eighty-seven."

"Whoa, not me, man. I'll never make it that far." And he spoke matter-of-factly, without any fear in his voice. "I see myself like a shooting star. You know, like when you're out at night, at the beach with a bunch of people, and somebody points up at the sky and says, 'Hey, look! A shooting star!' And everybody stops talking. And they see it, and say 'Ahh!' And it holds them for a brief moment . . . and then it goes out."

And he looked at me with his deep and trusting eyes. His wise and prescient eyes. . .

"That's how I see myself, Ray."

In that year, in our youth, we had an intense visitation of energy.

I shall always miss him.